CW00967573

Oral History
and Delinquency

Oral History and Delinquency

The Rhetoric of Criminology

James Bennett

The University of Chicago Press · Chicago & London

JAMES BENNETT is program coordinator for the social sciences, Office of Sponsored Research, University of Illinois at Chicago Circle.

THE UNIVERSITY OF CHICAGO PRESS, CHICAGO 60637
THE UNIVERSITY OF CHICAGO PRESS, LTD., LONDON
© 1981 by The University of Chicago
All rights reserved. Published 1981
Printed in the United States of America
85 84 83 82 81   5 4 3 2 1

Library of Congress Cataloging in Publication Data
Bennett, James, 1942–
  Oral history and delinquency.

  Bibliography: p.
  Includes index.
  1. Juvenile delinquents—Attitudes.   2. Oral
history.   I. Title.
HV9069.B55   364.3'6   81-7514
ISBN 0-226-04245-6   AACR2

For Bessie Cole Grammer and Katherine Gassaway

It is pleasurable likewise to observe that the higher classes are making themselves acquainted with the conditions of their degraded brethren; and that your eloquent advocacy is leading to a better understanding between the patrician and the plebian.

A "medical gentleman" writing to Henry Mayhew

Then the Queen said to Alice, "Have you seen the Mock Turtle yet?"
"No," said Alice. "I don't even know what a Mock Turtle is."
"It's the same thing Mock Turtle soup is made from," said the Queen.
"I never saw one, or heard of one," said Alice.
"Come on, then," said the Queen, "and he shall tell you his history."

Lewis Carroll, *Alice in Wonderland*

As absolute, or *sub specie eternitatis,* or *quatenus infinitus est,* the world repels our sympathy because it has no history. *As such,* the absolute neither acts nor suffers, nor loves nor hates; it has no needs, desires, or aspirations, no failures or successes, friends or enemies, victories or defeats.

William James

It is only through representation that a thing becomes plain. There is no easier way of understanding it than seeing it represented.

Novalis

Contents

Preface

Oral history has become a popular method of investigation and form of presentation, but it has been used and enjoyed more often than it has been understood. Similarly, life histories have appealed to sociologists, who nevertheless have not been able to bring them into conceptual focus. This book contributes to understanding oral history and life history by presenting a case study of their appearance in relation to juvenile delinquency. Under what conditions—social, personal, conceptual, and methodological—have oral histories of juvenile delinquents come into being? What characteristics have the histories had? What have they accomplished? Although I will draw no conclusions about oral history in general, studying a few examples in the little-known places that we shall look should be more suggestive about the possibilities of oral history than examining the mass of current projects.

In the process the reader should get an imaginative impression of some moments in the history of criminology, a field oddly neglected in a society where crime is spoken of as such an important problem. Indeed, this book may be read as a series of "adventures in criminology," since I shall run along the margins of sociology, political science, literature, philosophy, rhetoric, psychiatry, physical anthropology, religion, social work, and journalism. Precisely because oral history is of only peripheral professional interest in criminology today, this study is not bound by conventional categories but is free to cast light in several directions: on the lives and characters of criminologists, on various "feeling tones" (Studs Terkel's phrase) of young people's lives at various historical periods, on similar forms of expression (the anecdote, the mass interview, the sob story, and so forth), on the conceptual frameworks in which the stories appear, and on the institutions that use them and grow out of them.

I shall begin with Henry Mayhew, British journalist and co-founder of *Punch*, who used oral histories in his startling investigations around 1850 of London workers and street people, and end with a consideration of Saul Alinsky, the "professional radical" of the 1960s, and an autobiography of a girl drug addict. The book's most ambitious aim is to open up the rhetorical study of criminological and social science literature and to encourage the humanistic penetration of this area.

Acknowledgments

An earlier version of this book was written with the joint support of the Center for Research in Criminal Justice, University of Illinois at Chicago Circle, and the sociology department of the Institute for Juvenile Research, a division of the Department of Mental Health of the State of Illinois. Part of the institute's support came from a grant from the Illinois Law Enforcement Commission. My profound gratitude goes to the late Hans W. Mattick, whose interests transcending a narrowly defined criminology are reflected here, to Broderick E. Reischl, and to Joseph L. Peterson, all three of the Center for Research, and to Joseph E. Puntil, of the institute, for encouraging this project. For a brief period support also came from the Center for Studies in Criminal Justice at the University of Chicago Law School, through the assistance of Norval Morris and Franklin Zimring. I am also grateful to the typists who have labored so expertly over these pages: Centura J. Mullin, Mary Jane Lane, and Mary Pallen.

Chief among the sociologists who have helped this project is Helen MacGill Hughes, who has done everything from providing intellectual guidance and historical data to photocopying parts of her rare edition of one of Henry Mayhew's works. Howard S. Becker has also been very helpful over the years. Others are Henry D. McKay, Everett C. Hughes, Marvin E. Wolfgang, James F. Short, Jr., and William Simon. Without the approval and encouragement of these professionals, this work—which in many ways is marginal to sociological interests and styles today—would never have come into being.

A collective sign of recognition is all I am permitted toward the delinquents and former delinquents I interviewed as part of this project, since they were promised anonymity. The following people also helped this project in one way or another: Calvert Cottrell, Anthony Sorrentino, Florence Scala, Bruce Jackson, Solomon Kobrin, Gary Schwartz, Yale Levin, Nick Taccio, William Gilbert, Richard Buchanan, Allyn Sielaff, Carlos Aldana, Daniel Bertaux, Martin Bulmer, Ralph Grammer, David Schroder, Roy Farmer, Tony Ragona, William Stott, John C. Burnham, Michael Connolly, Lee Jenkins, Archie Motley, and Anne Humpherys. Special thanks to Terence Tanner and Paul Mackin. The interlibrary loan

ACKNOWLEDGMENTS

My ultimate intellectual debts are to Jim Corder, of Texas Christian University; to the late Jean Wahl, of the Sorbonne, and Christian Brunet, with both of whom I began studying philosophy; and to Richard McKeon, with whom I studied in the Committee on the Analysis of Ideas and Study of Methods at the University of Chicago. McKeon is the source of a schema that gives form to the essential part of this book. Whatever's the matter was my doing.

List of Abbreviations

The following abbreviations are used for works frequently cited in the text. Full references are given in the Bibliography. Citations are to page numbers or to volume and page, as, *CP* 28–29, *LL* 2:43.

ACT Jon Snodgrass, "The American Criminological Tradition: Portraits of the Men and Ideology in a Discipline" (1972).

BC Clifford R. Shaw, Henry D. McKay, and James F. McDonald, *Brothers in Crime* (1938).

CLH John Dollard, *Criteria for the Life History* (1935).

CP Henry Mayhew and John Binny, *The Criminal Prisons of London and Scenes of Prison Life* (1862).

DA Clifford R. Shaw et al., *Delinquency Areas: A Study of the Geographic Distribution of School Truants, Juvenile Delinquents, and Adult Offenders in Chicago* (1929).

DE William Stott, *Documentary Expression and Thirties America* (1973).

JD Clifford R. Shaw et al., *Juvenile Delinquency and Urban Areas: A Study of Rates of Delinquency in Relation to Differential Characteristics of Local Communities in American Cities* (1942; references are to 1972 edition).

JR Clifford R. Shaw, *The Jack-Roller: A Delinquent Boy's Own Story* (1930; references are to 1966 edition).

LL Henry Mayhew, *London Labour and the London Poor: The Condition and Earnings of Those That Will Work, Cannot Work, and Will Not Work* (1864 or 1865?).

NH Clifford R. Shaw, *The Natural History of a Delinquent Career* (1931).

PC Walter Lowe Clay, *The Prison Chaplain: A Memoir of the Rev. John Clay, B.D.* (1861).

SF Clifford R. Shaw et al., *Social Factors in Juvenile Delinquency: A Study of the Community, the Family, and the Gang in Relation to Delinquent Behavior* (Wickersham Report, 1933).

UM Eileen Yeo and E. P. Thompson. *The Unknown Mayhew* (1971).

VC Harold Finestone, *Victims of Change: Juvenile Delinquents in American Society* (1976).

Introduction

Probably the most significant concept of the study is the term *interstitial*—that is, pertaining to the spaces that intervene between one thing and another. In nature foreign matter tends to collect and cake in every crack, crevice, and cranny—interstices. There are also fissures and breaks in the structure of social organization.

F. M. Thrasher

It is, in fact, in this marginal region, where sciences meet and integrate, that productive ideas are most likely to arise.

W. I. Thomas

Raw documents have served as the sea upon which authentic scientific voyages of discovery have been launched.

Gordon Allport

Own Story

This book began as a project to evaluate a collection of life histories of juvenile delinquents that was on file at the Institute for Juvenile Research (IJR) in Chicago. When Clifford Shaw collected those documents in the 1920s and 1930s, life history was an important part of sociological method, but after World War II it almost entirely disappeared from the profession. Thus it was thought that a nonsociologist would be needed to revive the well-known IJR life history tradition. I was qualified for the job because in my doctoral dissertation I had used autobiographies to study ways individuals approach new beginnings in their lives and work. The project began in January 1973. In addition to reading more than ten thousand typewritten pages of delinquents' life histories, I had to search out the history of uses of life history in criminology to understand how and why the IJR collection had come into being. Ultimately, the historical inquiry expanded and became this book.

I also interviewed young persons on parole living on the South Side of Chicago and former juvenile delinquents then in an Illinois prison. At first my aim was to compare the experiences of delinquents in the 1930s and in the 1970s. I discovered, however, that life history interviews, in which a person is encouraged to speak at some length about his or her life, are difficult to compress into sound generalizations; and, when an apparently random stack of documents surviving after forty years is the source of one term in a historical comparison, the task becomes impossible to do well.

I was also unable to obtain new publishable life histories of delinquents. The one person I met whose account was extraordinarily vivid, detailed, and thoughtful was suspicious of my intentions, showed up only for every other planned meeting, and finally discontinued the project. I still believe that his narrative of his life at war in a Chicago street gang in the 1960s, his murder of a fifteen-year-old boy when he was himself fifteen, his mentally stalking the power structure at Saint Charles State School for Boys, and his eloquent ruminations about his parents and his world might have formed not only a classic of delinquency but also one of those books that somehow give us a voice for speaking to ourselves in reflection about our own lives. But "Andrew" said he would be killed if he told the truth—and by that he did not mean names and dates. I have concluded that most young people one might interview on such a project nowadays are probably no more politically conscious than their counterparts in the 1920s. But the most articulate speakers today take a more critical view than did earlier outstanding individuals—a more critical view of the motives of the researcher, among other things. To be a subject is to be subject. This is one of several elements of the current political paradigm that weighs against publication of oral histories of juvenile delinquents.

As for the remainder of the oral histories I collected, they did not differ, at least in those large aspects the genre is best at conveying, from the life histories published by Clifford Shaw and still in print, or from the stories that professionals hear every day firsthand from delinquents, or from the fragments of stories people hear from time to time on television news programs. Some of the main conditions for the genesis of delinquents' oral histories—the absence of *any* exposure to delinquents' lives, the widespread belief that "criminals" are by nature what they are—are missing at present, and I have ruefully come to realize that no life history project contrived for its own sake will revive this genre. Delinquents' oral histories will become fashionable when the main features of their social experiences need to be communicated in order to attract support for projects of social reform from professionals and members of the public. The routine means of soliciting support today in the "juvenile justice system" is the grant application, not the life or oral history. Political and legal reforms—to get people jobs or to give youths a fair trial in juvenile courts—are considered more critical than trying to change the slum or ghetto from within with the help of volunteers attracted partly by rhetorically effective literature.

In light of the criticism I will make of criminologists for not fully revealing their own experiences in acquiring oral histories from offenders, perhaps I should tell more of my own story on this project. However, since this book is not a collection of histories but a study of histories, perhaps I am justified in giving myself an exemption and letting the above suffice.

Variety of Varieties

One experience that helped shape my orientation in this book was my puzzlement over who was reading Tom Wicker's newly published *A Time to Die,* a partly autobiographical book about events at Attica prison, since made into a television movie. Did any of the principals in the drama read the book, such as Governor Rockefeller? Who did read it, what effect did it have on them, and what difference did it make that the book had been written? But these questions were only applications of a general rhetorical method I had cultivated for some time while studying with Richard McKeon.

It would be possible to do four quite different studies of oral history, using four different methods: rhetorical, logistic, generic, and dialectical. A *rhetorical* treatment would ask questions about the lives of the persons who collect oral histories, about the persuasive characteristics of the "speeches" they publish—the oral histories—and about the audiences that receive them. The aim of the study would be innovation. A *logistic* treatment would ask questions about causes and effects in the production of oral histories, about material elements such as grammatical forms, and about processes of editing, with the aim of proving a scientific hypothesis. A *generic* treatment would discriminate varieties of oral history and their potentialities, in order to determine the limits of the genres and develop them in appropriate directions. A *dialectical* treatment would assimilate opposing wholes with the aim of reaching a general "field equation" or encompassing principle.

This book applies a rhetorical method to oral history. Viewing oral history as a means of communication is innocuous enough and would be superfluous if an appropriate scheme of concepts were available. This book will not do the whole job either: it will not cover the whole of the rhetoric of criminology, not the rhetoric of oral history as a whole, not the immense virgin territory of rhetoric and the social sciences. But study of the rhetoric of oral histories of juvenile delinquents is a plausible place to begin, just as criminology itself began as inquiry into the bodies of convicts, an obvious and already-confined object, from which starting point criminology has advanced.

Within this dominant rhetorical orientation, the other three methods are also present. Logistic is present here in the extensive accumulation of relevant examples and material: the recovery of earlier commentary on life history, especially in the 1930s, will perhaps overcome amnesia in this area and prove useful in future work on oral history. (Hegel's remark about the Owl of Minerva spreading its wings only at dusk is exemplified by studies of life history done in the late 1930s and early 1940s, when the popularity of this material was ending, though the studies were intended to encourage life history inquiry.) Dialectic is present here in the form of neither an Idea that is never defined, as in Plato, nor a revolution that never occurs, as in Marx, but a principle that in this inquiry will only tantalize, never being analyzed directly—the principle of marginality, about which I will say more below.

The generic method is present here in a distinction among oral history, autobiography, and related forms of "personal document," such as letters. By "oral history" I mean a published account, usually two or three pages long, in the subject's own words, using the first person, about that person's life. An autobiography is longer and as a result poses problems of plot and character that typically do not arise in discussion of an oral history. Other varieties of personal documentation are usually shorter than an oral history or are not in the first person: newspaper stories, for instance, have been placed in this category. Though these genres are distinct, on occasion I will relate oral history to them.

An objection may be raised here over the correctness of this usage of "oral history," as well as of use of related terms such as "autobiography," "personal document," "life history," "life story," "documentary expression," "human documents," "first-person accounts," and "own story." Actual usage of these terms varies widely, especially across different disciplines and professions. What Norman Denzin calls an autobiography—Sutherland's *Professional Thief*—Karl Weintraub would classify as mere res gestae. And some things that Denzin includes under life history—"any record or document, including the case histories of social agencies, that throws light on the subjective behavior of individuals or groups"—Clifford Shaw would not accept as life history, since a case history of a social agency probably would not reveal an individual's viewpoint or career. It would show neither a life nor a history.[1] Even during the heyday of life histories, in the 1930s, psychologists and sociologists gave different definitions: Allport called a personal document "any self-revealing record that intentionally or unintentionally yields information regarding the structure, dynamics and functioning of the author's life," while Blumer said, "the human document is an account of individual experience which reveals the individual's actions as a human agent and as a participant in social life."[2] Even the general term varies: sociologists tend to use "life history" to designate all these phenomena, literary people use "autobiography," and historians use "documentary expression" or "oral history."

Currently, oral history[3] has evolved at least four varieties: the collection of accounts from historically important personages, which began at Columbia University in 1948; the capture by Studs Terkel of the lives of noncelebrities in order to provide a kind of anti-inferiority therapy to the ordinary people who read his books; the amassing of life stories by radical historians from workers and other oppressed people to promote communication and solidarity in the struggle for justice; and, finally, the accumulation by professional historians of testimony about historically important events from persons who were there.

Occasionally it is possible to point to an egregious violation of any plausible usage of a term, such as in David Dawley's *A Nation of Lords: The Autobiography of the Vice Lords,* which is by no stretch of the imagination an autobiography. But in the cases set out above and in many others, no one has the power or right to decree that a more consistent usage is definitive unless it can be proved more productive in many fields than the existing chaos. The meaning given in this book to "oral history" places less emphasis on *history,* the objective events or accounts of them, than it does on the *oral,* the qualities of speakers, speeches, and audiences (although in some cases the document was initially written out). Had I limited myself to the sociological tradition of life history, I would have risked failing to manifest implications for the almost untouched area of reflection on oral history. Nevertheless, while one will find in this book statements about oral history in general, for the most part I have kept a distance from the literature concerning oral history; in the absence of more evidence, my general statements can only be suggestions for further research.

I shall take a delinquent's oral history to be a statement about a life in which acts considered delinquent by the individual's surrounding society have a place, told by someone either under seventeen or usually not much older than that. (G. Stanley Hall would have called this a species of "ephebic literature.") I shall refer to the person who edits such a statement as a "criminologist," using a definition broader than professionals would prefer, but suitable here.[4] "Oral historian" would risk confusion between the criminologist and the delinquent, both of whom "speak." It is embarrassing to have to use the term "juvenile delinquent" at all. It has a monolithic appearance, when the truth is certainly otherwise. Indeed, one effect of oral histories is to cast doubt on such stereotypes in light of the continuities of experience between offenders and nonoffenders. In this sense oral history depends dialectically on that reification for one of its powers. However, the phenomenon under discussion is not so much *delinquency* as it is *oral history.* Though I shall describe the notions that writers have given out about juvenile delinquency, my main purpose is not to take those concepts apart. Criticism of political systems, proce-

dures, and policies that concern delinquency is being carried on in legis-
latures, in courts, and in society. This book has little to contribute directly
to that effort, except to reinforce "the humanistic tradition in criminology"—in which the offender is viewed not as a separate species but as a
member of the human race—or perhaps to develop an appreciation for the
variety of modes of communciation that might be used in the battle for
juvenile justice.

History of Histories

Is the selection of oral histories of delinquents given here exhaustive? I
have tried to make this book a comprehensive collection of examples and
ideas concerning the subject, but I would be foolish to think I have found
every example. Available scholarship here is not very helpful: for example, *A Bibliography of American Autobiography* lists only two of Clifford
Shaw's three published book-length life histories of delinquents. Having
poked around in bibliographies and bookstores for the past eight years, I
think I have discovered enough examples to arrive at a *form* of argument
that will withstand challenges, even if particular points require revision. I
have been especially eager to find instances in languages other than English, but without success.[5] Why would delinquents' oral histories be such
a peculiarly Anglo-American phenomenon?

Almost certainly no instance of a delinquent's oral history appeared
before A.D. 1800. This is not to say that no one ever sat down and listened
to a convicted young person discourse about his or her life, only that this
form of expression was not culturally valued until the first half of the
nineteenth century, though something similar has a long history.[6] The first
use of the word "autobiography" did not appear until 1796.[7] According to
Karl Weintraub:

> the autobiographic genre took on its full dimension and rich-
> ness when Western Man acquired a thoroughly historical
> understanding of his existence. Autobiography assumes a
> significant cultural function around A.D. 1800. The growing
> significance of autobiography is thus a part of that great in-
> tellectual revolution marked by the emergence of the particular
> modern form of historical mindedness we call historism or
> historicism.[8]

Life, according to Weintraub, "came to be seen as process; it was now to
be understood as development."[9] Even reason was historicized: Hegel's
translator has written about the "life-history of the human spirit," in a
preface to the *Phenomenology*.[10] Doubtless this is also connected to what
Richard Sennett has called the fall of public man, the intrusion of personality into public life with consequences detectable even in the area we
shall cover.

With regard to crime, historicism was manifest in a shift in attention from laws and punishments to the study of individual offenders, with their natural histories or life histories—what Foucault has called "the discovery of the man in the criminal."[11] Though there were many antecedents to this, the major landmark was the publication in 1876 of Lombroso's *L'uomo delinquente*. (The word "criminology" made its first appearance in 1885.) Nowhere was there greater stress on individualism than in the philosophy of the juvenile court, founded in 1899. Thus the shift in substantive principles from study of the *offense* to study of the *offender* and the methodological turn toward belief in the value of delinquents' oral histories were aspects of a single movement of historicism. But, though the individualism of the juvenile court has undergone searching criticism during the past decade and though oral history and autobiography have recently received new attention,[12] no major inquiry into the uses of oral history in criminology has been undertaken, and I shall leave to one side the area of life histories and autobiographies of adult offenders.

This book may be set beside a series of works on the history of thought and action concerning juvenile delinquency published during the past decade. Most have been written by historians—Hawes, Mennel, Schlossman, Rothman, Pickett, and Wiley—though occasionally a sociologist—Platt, Finestone—has taken a historical view. Another area of the ongoing history of ideas in which this book takes a place is the study of rhetoric, especially in the social sciences, exemplified by Joseph Gusfield's *The Culture of Public Problems* and by new interest in "stories" and "discourses." It is arguable that rhetoricians have been doing social science ever since Plato, in the *Phaedrus*, had Socrates point out the need for knowledge (which became *scientia* in Latin) of an audience in order to persuade it. Kenneth Burke has pointed out that the commonplaces that rhetoricians since Aristotle have used to invent persuasive arguments are actually statements of the values held by a particular audience or society. Studies of those commonplaces were then essentially sociology, long before its official birth in the nineteenth century. Under the onslaught of the natural sciences beginning in the seventeenth century, the term "rhetorical" became increasingly pejorative, but during the past two decades, small moves, such as the "New Rhetoric," have been initiated to determine the meaning and the vast current extent of rhetoric. It is worth noting that neither criminology nor rhetoric has a single subject matter (physical, psychological, social, or political): criminology has moved through several fields, and rhetoric is used on all subjects. The possibility of a deeper connection is worth pondering. Were the beginnings of the Oral History Association in 1967 and of the Law Enforcement Assistance Administration in 1969 results of a single cultural force?

Marginality of Marginality

If a *theme* is defined by analogy to a musical device that is given *variations* rather than a single form, then marginality is a theme of this book—ubiquitous yet, at least for me on this occasion, impossible to bring to a clear and consistent statement. As a sociological concept, marginality received its classic formulation in an essay by Robert E. Park that appeared in 1928: "The individual who through migration, education, marriage, or some other influence leaves one social group or culture without making a satisfactory adjustment to another finds himself on the margin of each but a member of neither. He is a 'marginal man.'"[13] The notion of marginality in this book relates not to the ethnic migrant but more broadly to the person who lives in at least two different contexts, with or without adjustment; works in a professional area without being a professional; or is both an academic and an activist, such as Clifford Shaw and his community workers, who tried to interpret the values of the slum and the larger society to each other.

This process of interpretation or communication is a clue to why oral histories should be used by a marginal figure. If the criminologist were politically or professionally powerful (and if the profession were in a powerful position), a "mainliner" in Horowitz's distinction,[14] he or she would not need to use a medium such as oral history to try to attract broad public attention. Instead such a person would announce propositions or promulgate laws to a more or less captive audience. Oral histories occupy a marginal area between two groups that need to communicate to each other, a need seen by a person who also occupies that area.

Even in studying the epistemological status of oral histories one runs across marginality when critics conclude that the histories fall between major analytic distinctions: for example, the subject matter of the oral history is neither the individual nor the environment but the interaction of self and society. Audiences may also be marginal: social workers dissatisfied with casework methods, or students on the verge of a career. The aim of the delinquent's oral history is to move readers toward a sociological, environmental, or community-based perception of the causes of delinquency. All this is in addition to the rampant social marginality of the criminal offender and of young people, who are on the margins of adult society.[15] The general conditions for the genesis of delinquents and of oral histories about them appear to be the same, a dialectical assimilation.

Hypotheses or new principles could emerge from this vision of marginality, but we should be careful to avoid the "lyricism of marginality" pointed out by Foucault: "the image of the 'outlaw,' the great social nomad, who prowls on the confines of a docile, frightened order."[16]

Because I am not an expert in any of the subjects this book enters, the discourse here will also be marginal to professional styles. But I am not after analysis of fact so much as *configurations of commonplaces,* those terms, experiences, or concepts that appear repeatedly in discussions of a subject: they are *topoi,* midway between the truism and the new principle, that are gathered into handbooks on persuasive argument because they have been found to be the rhetorically effective means to reach an audience on a subject. This is another sense in which my method is rhetorical. Every oral history I shall consider will be part of a criminologist's account of delinquency: an advantage of studying oral histories caught in such webs of meaning is that they will be easier to "place" in a conceptual configuration than they would be in the absence of such assumptions.[17] And assumptions are never absent; only more or less explicit.

Overview

An adequate book on delinquents' oral histories could have been written on Clifford Shaw's work alone: surely he used this material more than anyone else. But how much more illumination Shaw receives if we expand the scope of the inquiry. Of course, the expansion could have been made from other directions—from a study of childhood and adolescence, of literary form, of criminal autobiography, or even of economic forces. The selection made here is, inevitably, a reflection of my own interests.

The sequence of this book's ten chapters is mainly chronological, but the whole may also be divided into four parts. Chapters one and two, on Henry Mayhew, introduce the basic *images* of the entire study: the marginal worker, a variety of criminological theories with preference for environmental explanations, oral history pictures of delinquents' lives, in many respects the same today as more than a hundred years ago, and the ambiguous accomplishments of criminologists and their "humanistic" institutions.

The next three chapters trace the rather more dreary construction of *things* or programs. Chapter 3 is a study of chaplain John Clay's prison reforms by cellular arrangements.[18] Chapter 4 covers the prisonlike fortresses of the early American houses of refuge and the shipping of New York City young people out West. Chapter 5 presents the first juvenile courts and the first clinic to study delinquency and amass data on delinquents. In most of these cases oral histories did not appear, though similar material did: the reason for including them is to ask under what conditions and for what reasons delinquents' oral histories are not likely to appear, thus throwing into relief the conditions in which they do appear and contrasting oral histories with related forms of presentation.

Three more chapters discuss the classic period of Chicago sociology: the works of W. I. Thomas, Robert E. Park, Ernest Burgess, Frederic Thrasher, and Clifford Shaw. A chief preoccupation of these men was the use of life histories to illustrate *hypotheses* of scientific explanation. They moved attention back to the city, where Mayhew had been, but unlike Mayhew they advanced with an orderly scheme of concepts.

The final two chapters concern *principles*. Chapter 9 introduces political principles that conceptually or actually oppose the production of oral histories. Chapter 10 pulls together the system of significance generated by this book and is in that sense a presentation of rhetorical principles. Some aspects of technique relative to oral histories appear in the Appendix.

One

Eloquent Advocacy: Mayhew's Use of Oral History

The Importance of Henry Mayhew

Henry Mayhew (1812–87) is recognized today as a forerunner of the twentieth-century journalists, historians, and sociologists who have made use of oral or life histories: "Mayhew invented 'oral history' a century before the term was coined," according to John Rosenberg.[1] Studs Terkel has said, "If I have a model, it's Mayhew. He was a contemporary of Dickens who was great as a chronicler of the lives of the anonymous."[2] Terence Morris has written, "He was one of the first advocates and successful exponents of the technique of collecting first hand material by direct interviews and observations which would have delighted both Robert E. Park and Malinowski alike." "Probably only Clifford Shaw has brought home the poignant truths about the delinquent as a person with comparable skill."[3]

Later work with oral and life histories developed independent of Mayhew. Even his major works have not remained continuously in print, nor was he the founder of a profession that would have preserved his work and carved his name on the walls of its headquarters. Though Mayhew was a journalist, he founded no professional journal, as did his contemporary, Cesare Lombroso, the "father of criminology." Mayhew died poor and neglected, and though occasional articles have been written about him and a few prefaces to selections from his writings have been published for reasons historical (nostalgia or political interest in Victorian England) or literary (the tradition of "characters" going back to Theophrastus and La Bruyère), only one complete study of this founder of *Punch* has yet been published.[4] The rediscovery by Americans of Mayhew during the past two decades has occurred amid interest in "the other Americans" and in oral history. W. H. Auden wrote in 1965: "I am inclined to think that, if I had to write down the names of the ten greatest Victorian Englishmen, Henry Mayhew would head the list."[5]

Although there were earlier uses of oral history, which I shall examine in chapter 3, Mayhew himself had no doubts that he had invented what would later be called oral history. In the preface to his magnum opus, *London Labour and the London Poor: The Condition and Earnings of*

Those That Will Work, Cannot Work, and Will Not Work (hereafter referred to as *London Labour*), he says:

> The present volume is the first of an intended series, which is hoped will form, when complete, a cyclopaedia of the industry, the want, and the vice of the great Metropolis.
> It is believed that the book is curious for many reasons.
> It surely may be considered curious as being the first attempt to publish the history of a people, from the lips of the people themselves—giving a literal description of their labour, their earnings, their trials, and their sufferings in their own "unvarnished" language; and to portray the condition of their homes and their families by personal observation of the places, and direct communication with the individuals.

Investigators from government commissions and religious institutions had preceded Mayhew into the places of the poor, but they had studied mainly the lack of moral discipline, which, unlike Mayhew, thěy did not see as caused by economic conditions: for them poverty was the result, not the cause, of moral laxity. Mayhew's "personal observation" and "direct communication," less laden with prefabricated Victorian dogma, also make him a candidate for election as founder of participant observation. "For the omissions in the work," he goes on to say in the preface, not entirely overstating his case, "the author would merely remind the reader of the entire novelty of the task—there being no other similar work in the language by which to guide or check his inquiries."

Mayhew's inquiries were not equaled for many years, and his art of presenting "street-biography," as he once called it, has never been surpassed. As Eileen Yeo points out, though Charles Booth in 1904 wrote in *Life and Labour of the People of London* that to interpret the lives of people one must "lay open their memories and understand their hopes," it was Mayhew who did this, not Booth: "With the insides of the houses and their inmates," Booth wrote, "there was no attempt to meddle."[6] Indeed, although seventy-five years after Mayhew's acme the Chicago sociologists refined his encyclopedic methodological mixture of statistics, generalizations, descriptive prose, and oral histories, the Chicago work lacked Mayhew's drama as well as his political sensitivities. Chicago sociologist Clifford Shaw would have attacked neither a social policy nor a business establishment for its noxious effects on workers and their families, as Mayhew did.

In the study of crime, too, Mayhew was a pioneer. Years before Lombroso made the shift, Mayhew insisted that criminological classifications be made of offenders, not of offenses, as had been done since Beccaria in the eighteenth century (*LL* 4:30; cf. *CP* 87–88).[7] Mayhew's comprehensive view of the lives of the London poor and their children could not fail to put aspects of crime into broad social and even economic settings. But at the same time that Mayhew was viewing, with a roving eye, the worlds of criminal offenders, reformers and scientists with much narrower perspectives were establishing specialized areas of research and treatment that became paradigms in the field of crime and delinquency. These early social workers and physical anthropologists created professions that totally eclipsed Mayhew's criminological work until he was rediscovered by two Chicago sociologists in the 1930s.[8]

Our own discovery of Mayhew should give us a running start for understanding oral histories of delinquents, but it would be impossible to appreciate the overall pattern of Mayhew's accomplishment if I restricted my discussion to delinquency. Often my analysis will not use examples of delinquents' life expressions when some other example makes a point better about Mayhew's method, a method that is nevertheless the context in which young offenders' own stories appear.

Mayhew's Works

During the 1830s and 1840s, Henry Mayhew moved in London bohemian circles. He wrote light novels for middle-class audiences, composed farces and burlettas for the London stage, and edited and wrote for comic magazines, including *Punch,* which he helped found in 1841. John Bradley has discovered a serious interest in social affairs running through these entertainments.[9] Indeed, Mayhew exemplified that duality of character apparent in beatniks, hippies, or whatever they will be called in the future—irreverence for bourgeois values (even if he had to pretend to accept them to make a living) along with a deep concern about what he thought important, a concern that challenged the middle class. For a few years at the apex and precisely in the middle of his seventy-five years, Mayhew's energies were concentrated on a project to study the London poor, with special attention to their means of livelihood. After that vast integration of experience, Mayhew fell apart, desultorily lapsing into writing more light plays and books on various subjects: Germany, the London Exhibition of 1851, Benjamin Franklin, and so forth.

Mayhew's magnum opus began with an article published on 24 September 1849, in the London *Morning Chronicle,* entitled, "A Visit to the Cholera Districts of Bermondsley." During the previous summer, 13,000 deaths from cholera had been reported in London, and on 10 September alone 432 victims were recorded. While the debate continued about what could possibly be the cause of this, Mayhew paid a visit to an area with a high death rate. He saw people forced to bathe in and drink from a ditch into which human excrement was emptied, and he found that the owners of the dwellings refused to bring in a supply of fresh water. Mayhew wrote:

As we passed along the reeking banks of the sewer the sun
shone upon a narrow slip of water. In the bright light it appeared the colour of strong green tea, and positively looked as
solid as black marble in the shadow—indeed it was more like
watery mud than muddy water; and yet we were assured this
was the only water the wretched inhabitants had to drink. As
we gazed in horror at it, we saw drains and sewers emptying
their filthy contents into it . . . and the limbs of the vagrant boys
bathing in it seemed by pure force of contrast, white as Parian
marble.[10]

After this inquiry Mayhew persuaded the *Morning Chronicle* to run a
series of articles on the "moral, intellectual, material, and physical condition of the industrial poor throughout England," as the prospectus put
it.[11] Between 19 October 1849, and 12 December 1850, eighty-two "letters
from our Metropolitan Correspondent"—Mayhew—were published.
Other journalists reported from the agricultural and manufacturing districts of England and from Europe and Russia; these non-London articles
contain some quoted passages, but they tend to be factual testimony of
experts rather than expressions of ordinary people. Nothing of equal
scope had ever been seen in a newspaper before and perhaps has not been
seen since.[12]

Until the end of January 1850, Mayhew's articles appeared twice a
week, six long columns from three thousand to ten thousand words, then
once weekly to make room for parliamentary reports. The articles were
usually accompanied by letters from readers, which were often sent to the
paper with donations of money for the people whose sad stories had
appeared, or the letters contained suggestions about how to alleviate the
sufferings of one or another group of workers. In October 1850 Mayhew
either was fired or, according to him, resigned his position because of
editorial censorship imposed on an oral history having to do with free
trade (favored by the newspaper's owners) versus protectionism (favored
by the working man who had spoken to Mayhew). This followed several
controversies between Mayhew and the paper, one involving his attack on
a clothing establishment that was a heavy advertiser in the *Morning
Chronicle*.

In December 1850 Mayhew set up his own office and until March 1852
issued his articles in weekly and monthly installments, which included
new correspondence from readers and his replies. Perhaps people who
had not read the *Morning Chronicle* would come into contact with the
pamphlets or later with the books. Some of Mayhew's readers seem to
have become addicted to his "Answers to Correspondents" section in
these pamphlets, especially the endless learned disquisitions on the
etymologies of words, a favorite being *haberdasher*. Mayhew says he

used this marginal space to work out his "speculations" on economic issues, which he sharply distinguished from the "facts" in the work itself.[13] Some of the articles were reworked *Morning Chronicle* material. (Reading widely in Mayhew's various works, one frequently has the curious experience of coming across precisely the same text more than once.) In 1851–52 these pamphlets were bound under the title *London Labour and the London Poor: The Condition and Earnings of Those That Will Work, Cannot Work, and Will Not Work.* A dispute with his printer forced cancellation of further publication in 1852, and Mayhew seems to have lost interest in the project. Some new material was collected and published in pamphlet form in 1856 as part of another grand scheme to cover the whole of "The Great World of London," and a series of booklets on London prisons was issued by D. Bogue under that title in 1856. But of "Legal London," only *The Criminal Prisons of London and Scenes of Prison Life* was ever finished (published in 1862), "that wretched fragment of a well-meant scheme," as Mayhew later put it.[14]

In 1861–62, Griffin, Bohn and Company published four volumes of *London Labour,* the first two the same as the 1851–52 edition but without the correspondence with readers: the third contained some of the 1856 "Great World of London" material, and the fourth volume, most of it done by writers other than Mayhew, covered "those that will not work"—prostitutes, thieves, swindlers, and beggars. The text of *London Labour* I am using has no date but appears to be an 1864 or 1865 reprint of the definitive 1861–62 edition. This undated edition seems to be widely available in the United States, at least in libraries. (Clifford Shaw owned a copy of this edition.)[15] Much of the *Morning Chronicle* series was not included in *London Labour,* though recently some of the unused material was published in *The Unknown Mayhew.*[16]

While the patterns of oral history are the same in the newspaper articles as they are in the book, the emphasis in the newspaper was more on economic issues than was true in the later publications. The chief economic problem was as follows:

> How, then, are we to explain the fact that while the hands have decreased 33 per cent and work increased at a considerable rate, wages a few years ago were 300 per cent better than they are at present?
> The solution of the problem will be found in the extraordinary increase that has taken place within the last twenty years of what are called "garret masters" in the cabinet trade. [*UM* 381]

That is, rather than hire workers on a long-term basis, businessmen had instituted the "slop system," by which they would buy items piece by piece from individual laborers, such as cabinetmakers or seamstresses working in their own homes or shops, or from intermediaries. Since the businessman did not have to pay wages in periods of slack work, this system reduced his costs but increased competition, drudgery, and uncertainty of life for the worker. The consumer was delighted at the cheap goods in the stores but unaware, until Mayhew's revelations, of the human costs involved, including the increase in child labor (*UM* 395–96). Even then, of course, most buyers did not get the message or did not care. Mayhew supported legislation to put an end to that system.

The slop system also increased prostitution among seamstresses. Mayhew's best insights into social deviance and crime emerge from his presentations of social and economic conditions in various occupations. But Mayhew, ever ambivalent about Victorian middle-class values, includes a little bit of everything in his accounts, and he was not above moralizing. Just as *London Labour* begins Mayhew's decline from political analysis and protest (in the *Morning Chronicle* series) to character portrayal (of the colorful street people), so the fourth volume of *London Labour,* which specializes in prostitutes, imposter-beggars, thieves, and embezzlers, and all of *Criminal Prisons* do not view offenders' lives in broad social contexts and thus fail to build on the earlier economic observations.[17] Mayhew seems to have turned back to what would sell, to fill his ever-present need for money. And writing about crime pays much better when it focuses simply on the crime as an event than when it expands the context to the point that middle-class readers themselves might feel implicated, say, for buying cheap goods produced by a system that drove people to crime.

Mayhew's works contain oral histories of young offenders, though they are not so much part of a study of delinquency as they are a means of illustrating the futility of the then-popular alternative schools, the criminogenic features of cheap lodging houses, and the large number of youths who left intolerable or overly permissive homes. Many of these young runaways slept outdoors even in winter, in various crevices of great English cities.[18] I shall turn to a consideration of Mayhew's views on delinquency in the next chapter. This chapter aims at a general characterization of the rhetoric of oral history by studying a writer whose reasons for using oral histories stand out more prominently than in most other works. This is not because we can receive from Mayhew a direct answer to why he used oral histories. He did not write about his use of people's "statements," and he probably gave the subject very little attention. Writing on the subject might not have sold well. Who cared to understand it? There was no "it." Nevertheless, Mayhew left many clues in *London Labour* and elsewhere to a conception of oral history, and I shall arrange these to form a consistent method attributable to him.

Mayhew inserted oral history material at particular points in his writing to illustrate statements he had just made in more abstract terms and perhaps to create an aesthetic balance between human voices and the statistical data with which his texts are loaded. Of course, what he included always depended on the quantity and quality of material he had been able to collect on any particular topic. Apparently Mayhew included *so many* oral histories partly in order to show that he was not depending on only one individual, but that many witnesses agreed on basic points: in the preface to *London Labour* he refers to "the extraordinary agreement in the statements of all the vast number of individuals who have been seen at different times, and who cannot possibly have been supposed to have been acting in concert."[19] But why did Mayhew include oral histories at all?[20] I shall argue that Mayhew used oral history to:

1. express his own personality and interests
2. communicate between social classes
3. educate by entertaining
4. demonstrate authenticity of evidence
5. make a vivid impression on the reader
6. arouse emotion, and thus rouse readers to action.

Because these aims also apply to some writers since Mayhew who have used oral histories, the following study reveals continuing aspects of oral history in general, and one major dimension of oral histories of juvenile delinquents—the rhetorical.

Mayhew's most conspicuous aim is to persuade an audience. If we invoke the traditional rhetorical terms of speaker-speech-audience, the six "reasons" above (leaving unexamined whether these are really causes, motives, or intentions) may be reduced to three. Use of oral history is determined, first, by features of the writer or "speaker" (1), in this case Mayhew; second, by his goal—to let "the rich know something more about the poor," as he says (2); and third, by the means created to achieve this goal, a medium or "speech" that is attractive to the audience (3), convinces them that what they are reading is real (4), makes a lasting impression on them (5), and gives impetus to appropriate action (6). The second of these is the major factor: Mayhew's personality is background to his dominant intention, and he used oral histories because their several powers are effective to the end of cross-class communication.

The Character of Henry Mayhew

Henry Mayhew was born in 1812, one of seventeen children of a substantial London solicitor. Four of the boys became writers. At age ten Henry entered Westminster School, but he left five years later after he failed to complete a disciplinary chore imposed for his reading a Greek grammar during chapel and then refused to take the prescribed flogging. For the next year he served as a midshipman on the India run, "as if there were anything in a sailor's roving life, or its associations, to make a young man steady."[21] Then Mayhew took a minor position in his father's legal chambers. This, too, soon collapsed when Henry forgot to deliver some legal papers to the court; as a result his father was almost thrown into jail. Upon the bailiff's arrival Henry "rose and left the room. As soon as possible afterwards he left the house, and years passed before his father saw him again."[22]

Thompson views this breach with his father as underlying Mayhew's later rejection of respectable bourgeois property values and determining, in part, his use of oral histories: "The glorious irreverent statements of the patterers, street sellers, and Irish, which are his best known writings, are material which only a man at odds with the usual moralisms and hypocrisies could have gathered."[23] Andrews remarked in 1859 that

> perhaps a part of the old Bohemian tastes have clung to him, giving him that zest in inquiring into the habits and ways of the patterers, and waifs and strays of London, which always communicates itself to his reader, when he is telling those strange and captivating stories of the moneyless world.[24]

Presenting the truth about the lower classes in their own "unvarnished language" helped clear the air of Victorian social benevolence and piety, which had, not surprisingly, arisen at the very moment capitalist competition was getting started in cutthroat earnest.[25] In a review of *Jane Eyre* in 1848, a certain Miss M. A. Stodart wrote the following:

> Altogether the autobiography of Jane Eyre is pre-eminently an anti-Christian composition. There is throughout it a murmuring against the comforts of the rich and against the privations of the poor; which, as far as each individual is concerned, is a murmuring against God's appointment.[26]

Apparently what began as a strong distaste for a gap in communication between social classes grew to disgust at the active opposition he encountered from commercial London: "By the time Mayhew started publishing *London Labour* on his own, he was a very angry man. What was intended as an impartial and straightforward examination of poverty and industry had turned into a vicious dogfight with powerful ideological and vested interests."[27] Had he begun the whole enterprise at this point, one wonders whether he would have ignored oral histories and gone straight to economic analyses, such as he later presented in his treatise *Low Wages: Their Causes, Consequences, and Remedies* (1851), or manifestos, in the manner of his contemporary, Marx.

That Mayhew used oral histories may be seen as an indication not only of social irreverance but also of an independence of mind: both he and his father were self-taught, and in his books written for children the son recommends self-teaching as the best way to learn: "My object in such books as the present is to show boys that some of the greatest minds the world has seen have been self-taught."[28] Statements, often stark, from ordinary people, express their candor as well as Mayhew's. Oral histories may also have been expressions of Mayhew's compassion or, to use one of his favorite words, "kindness." As he wrote in the opening number of *Punch:* "How many generous and kindly beings are there pining within the walls of a prison, whose only crimes are poverty and misfortune!" Indeed, the phrase "the humanistic tradition in criminology" usually denotes a kind or sympathetic attitude toward the offender. Mayhew's kindness manifested itself in his judging ordinary people's statements to be worthy of publishing. He felt touched but kept his distance, expressing his own feelings in someone else's "touching words" (*UM* 149): "this has been done upon that Shakespearean rule of art, which often throws an internal moral principle into an external *dramatis persona;* and as the witches in *Macbeth* are merely the outward embodiment, in a weird and shadowy form, of Macbeth's own ambition."[29] Mayhew recorded the lives of the poor, to adapt a thought from Herodotus, in order to save them from oblivion. About an inmate of a cheap lodging house, he says: "I never beheld so gaunt a picture of famine. To this day the figure of the man haunts me" (*LL* 3:323). To translate their words into the statements of experts would be treason, exploitation. Transmitting their own words preserves and enhances their integrity and dignity.

For some years of his life we know nothing about Mayhew, but in the 1830s we find him the author of several light works for the London stage, some of them dripping with puns. Thus another piece of his background linked to oral histories is his appreciation of character portrayal in vivid language, often including dialects. Mayhew dramatized some of *London Labour* in 1856, and in 1881 a book of "characters" was made (not by Mayhew) from this material, just as in the 1960s Peter Quennell put together *Mayhew's Characters.* (This is an ever-present potentiality of oral history: another example is a musical that was made from Studs Terkel's book *Working.*) This explains a motive not only for presenting oral histories but also for reading them: they make a "lively text."[30] Like the farces, burlettas, and novels Mayhew wrote, they are more likely to reach a general audience than mere sociological commentary, and public attention surely stimulated Mayhew. Thackeray proclaimed that the metropolitan correspondent provided "a picture of human life so wonderful, so awful, so piteous and pathetic, so exciting and terrible, that readers of romances own they never read anything like to it."[31] Londoners were accustomed to the human interest story and the "lowlife" genre in literature: Mayhew was to the middle-class parlor what the "running patterers" were to the street people—reporters of "sensational" stories not about sensational events, but rather about the lives of ordinary people.

Perhaps the most intriguing features of Mayhew's character are its contradictions or dualities. He was a novelist, dramatist, and journalist, true enough, but he also saw himself as a scientist. According to Anne Humpherys, Mayhew conducted chemical experiments during the 1830s, and once nearly blew up his brother's house: "His tendency from the beginning was to be as objective as he could, to avoid emotional rhetoric and instead to describe what he saw as accurately and precisely as he would the results of a chemical experiment."[32] From time to time Mayhew begins a line of inquiry with an expansive classificatory scheme, but these have few consequences in the texts that follow. An elaborate outline of occupations appears in volume 4 of *London Labour,* along with a rebuttal of John Stuart Mill on a point of political economy, but none of this led anywhere: after the outline Mayhew did no further work on volume 4. In explaining his mission at the meeting of ticket-of-leave men (parolees), Mayhew says (echoing Socrates in Plato's *Phaedrus*):

> Some persons study the stars, others study the animal kingdom, others again direct their researches into the properties of stones, devoting their whole lives to these particular vocations. I am the first who has endeavoured to study a class of my fellow-creatures whom Providence has not placed in so fortunate a position as myself. [*LL* 3:440]

From this perspective Mayhew included oral histories not only because he was a dramatist but also because he was an anthropologist.[33] Oral history may be viewed as the "bisociation," to use Koestler's term, of drama and cultural anthropology.

A more subtle duality in Mayhew's character was his alternation between extreme concentration and extreme indolence, between seriousness of purpose and care only for entertaining, and the related ambivalence between rejection and acceptance of middle-class values. John L. Bradley has written:

> On the one hand, a critical investigator of man's institutions stamps his impression of them upon column after column of *Figaro;* on the other, a casual writer of farces, burlettas, and jest-books seems remote from all but entertaining at a miserably low level of intelligence. . . . He seems, from first to last, to have remained charming, amusing, consistently entertaining, intermittently enthusiastic and utterly irresponsible.[34]

Punch itself exemplified this ambivalence. Anne Humpherys attributes Mayhew's failure to finish anything to this conflict, which made it impossible for him to take a final position on any subject. However, this back-and-forth movement resulted in the perfect focus for his *Morning Chronicle* and *London Labour* work, even though this project also was never completed:

> Even though Mayhew's ambivalent responses to his society had negative effects on all his other works, in his great books on labor and the poor the result was almost entirely positive. On the one hand his rebelliousness and unconventionality permitted him to sympathize with his subjects and to encourage an unusual and productive relationship. At the same time the restraining influence of Victorian values provided a form of distancing and balance. Because the subjects of labor and the poor gave him an outlet for both sides of his personality, Mayhew's full energies were released in his social surveys.[35]

It is tempting to think of oral histories as expressions of Mayhew's passivity: to "let the people speak" is to let them do all the work. Accumulating "hard data" is hard, but collecting "soft data" requires nothing more than listening and perhaps taking stenographic notes, as Mayhew did. But this is a caricature. Applying one's own categories may be a form of mental laziness, in contrast to the difficult task of suspending judgment and generating new categories from as yet uncategorized reality. Publishing another person's account could be a form of disciplined selflessness for the scientist—a form of objectivity.

Even though Mayhew does not overtly assert himself in his oral histories, nevertheless they may be viewed as expressing aspects of his own experience, not merely his brief stint on a treadmill or the hour he spent in a jail cell. If he did not sell apples in the street—and he did not—he did appear in bankruptcy court two years before the *Morning Chronicle* series began, and he was constantly in debt. If he was not an intermittent, sweated laborer, he never had a steady job other than his year at the newspaper, when for once in his life he had the security to concentrate on a serious inquiry. Uncertainty of employment may have had the same unbalancing emotional effects on him as it had on the people he studied. If he was not a vagrant, never forced to spend the night in an asylum for the homeless, he did change residences frequently. Though he divided humanity into the civilized settlers and the uncivilized wanderers, he was himself an intellectual vagabond who abandoned some works unfinished—*Low Wages* in mid-sentence, *Criminal Prisons* on page 498. This man, "with an extraordinary mop of dark hair that sadly wanted trimming," according to his son Athol (*UM* 19), must have loved to roam the streets of London, an unconventional occupation for a middle-class Victorian gentleman, though he was not alone, since other writers explored and exploited the city to produce tourist guide books and other presentations of London street life. Yet none better than Mayhew assimilated the picturesque and the methodical into each other.

Mayhew occupies a middle position regarding autobiographical comment by an author in a work of criminological significance that is not simply an autobiography: John Howard is at one extreme (*The State of the Prisons* reveals a minimum of Howard's movements) and Tom Wicker is at the other (*A Time to Die* swings from Attica prison to Wicker's life, enormous outrage being held in check by gaining distance through autobiographical reflection). Since Mayhew's texts give clear indications of some of his actions and opinions, it is plausible to claim that he also included oral histories because they expressed so well his sense of his own life, just as his own character must have made it easy for people to open up to him.

Oral histories are also results of anthropologist Mayhew's interest in studying and recording languages. Though spoken in the streets of London, these speech patterns seemed exotic to the higher social classes, just as "ordinary language" was not a standard of poetic diction until Wordsworth and Whitman made it so. In writing about child street sellers, Mayhew gives part of a boy's own speech in the third person:

> Yes, he had heer'd of God, who made the world. Couldn't exactly recollec' when he'd heer'd on him, but he had most sartenly. Didn't know when the world was made or how anybody could do it. It must have taken a long time. It was afore his time, "or yourn either, sir." Knew there was a book called the Bible; didn't know what it was about; didn't mind to know; knew of such a book to a sartinty, because a young 'oman took one to pop [pawn] for an old 'oman that was on the spree—a bran new'un—but the cove wouldn't have it, and the old 'oman said he might be d—d. Never heer'd tell on the deluge; of the world having been drownded it couldn't, for there wasn't water enough to do it. He weren't a going to fret hisself for such things as that. [*LL* 1:530]

To justify including material in this way, Mayhew says in *London Labour:* "Wandering hordes have frequently a different language from the more civilized portion of the community, and that adopted with the intent of concealing their designs and exploits from them" (*LL* 1:4). He believed he had reduced the cryptic language of the costermongers to orthography for the first time (*LL* 1:25). He also planned to write a book entitled "Mr. Mayhew's Spelling-Book for the Working Classes."[36] Eileen Yeo has written: "Mayhew was a keen dabbler in the anthropology of his day. He

entered with great relish into learned discussions about the linguistic deri-
vation of coster slang with correspondents."[37] Mayhew also had a great
appreciation for speech in general: he was a voluble conversationalist at
various London watering holes. Opposing the "silent system" in prisons,
he called speech a "wonderous faculty" that prisoners should be allowed
to exercise so long as they spoke no evil (*CP* 107). Dialects also reveal a
speaker's present or past social class: an educated former member of the
middle-class who lives among the poor reveals more by how she speaks
than by what she says: "Here was a woman endowed with a fair amount
of education, speaking in a superior manner, making use of words that
very few in her position would know how to employ, reduced by a variety
of circumstances to the very bottom of a prostitute's career" (*LL* 4:244).

Communication between Social Classes

Mayhew used oral histories in the service of his dominant intention: to
communicate the plight of the poor to those who were better off and knew
little about the conditions under which the poor lived. His further goal
was to set in motion social forces and progress that would alleviate their
sufferings. In the preface to *London Labour* he announces that the book

> is curious, moreover, as supplying information concerning a
> large body of persons, of whom the public has less knowledge
> that the most distant tribes of the earth—the government
> population returns not even numbering them among the in-
> habitants of the kingdom; and as adducing facts so extra-
> ordinary, that the traveller in the undiscovered country of the
> poor must, like Bruce, until his stories are corroborated by
> after investigators, be content to lie under the imputation of
> telling such tales, as travellers are generally supposed to delight
> in.

Ending the preface, he says:

> My earnest hope is that the book may serve to give the rich a
> more intimate knowledge of the sufferings, and the frequent
> heroism under those sufferings, of the poor—that it may teach
> those who are beyond temptation to look with charity on the
> frailties of their less fortunate brethren—and cause those who
> are in "high places," and those of whom much is expected, to
> bestir themselves to improve the condition of a class of people
> whose misery, ignorance, and vice, amidst all the immense
> wealth and great knowledge of "the first city in the world," is,
> to say the very least, a national disgrace to us.

At the end of the three volumes of *London Labour* that he was responsible
for (volume 4 was written mostly by others), Mayhew gives three reasons
for holding a mass meeting of parolees:

> In the first place, I wish society to know more about you as a
> distinct class; secondly, I wish the world to understand the
> working of the ticket-of-leave system; and thirdly, I want to
> induce society to exert itself to assist you, and extricate you
> from your difficulties. [*LL* 3:440]

That oral histories in particular communicate across social classes
Mayhew does not say, but he might have. In a preface to one of Clifford
Shaw's life histories Ernest W. Burgess later wrote:

> No one will question the value of the life-history as a human
> document when written freely and frankly. It admits the reader
> into the inner experience of other men, men apparently widely
> different from himself: criminals, hobos, and other adventur-
> ers. Through the life-history he becomes acquainted with those
> far removed from the sheltered routine of his own existence in
> much the same way that he knows himself or a friend. As he
> lives, for the time being, their careers and participates in their
> memories and mistakes, aspirations and failures he comes to
> realize the basic likenesses of all human beings despite the
> differences, real as they are, of biological endowment and so-
> cial experience.[38]

Helen MacGill Hughes has related this to the newspaper:

> There remains always the fact that people do not easily pene-
> trate each other's minds. Artistic formulation, in poetry or
> fiction, supplies the entree through the author's intuition. But
> the newspaperman has no poetic license. Ultimately, then, the
> most revealing and readable communications a newspaper can
> print are autobiographical: interviews, diaries, letters, and
> confessions.[39]

Communication from lower to higher classes became necessary with
the growth of large cities in England by the middle of the nineteenth
century. London had tripled in population during the first half of that
century. Increases in the size of the urban lower class (where the deficiencies were located) and of the urban middle class (where most of the
newspaper readers were) had alienated these classes from each other.

> in small towns there must be a sort of natural police, of a very
> wholesome kind, operating upon the conduct of every individ-
> ual.... But in a large town, he lives, as it were, in absolute
> obscurity; and we know that large towns are sought by way of
> refuge...which...gives impunity....the gradual separation
> of classes which took place in towns by a custom which has
> gradually grown up, that every person who can afford it lives
> out of town, and at a spot distant from his place of business.

> Now this was not formerly so; it is a habit which has, practically speaking, grown up within the last half century. The result of the old habit was that rich and poor lived in proximity; and the superior classes exercised that species of silent but very efficient control over their neighbors.[40]

After the onset of the notorious alienation of big cities, with their rampant individualism, some artificial medium was needed to concretize abstractions such as "poverty" or "work." In general, then, some of the conditions for the use of oral histories were rapid social change, urbanization, confusion of values, alienation of classes, and the spread of individualism, precisely the same conditions alleged to account for the growth of crime.

In the same way, the invention of the prison and the asylum during the late eighteenth century increased the segregation of the deviant, who became the "outsider," from the conventional person, who thereupon required some means other than actual contact, such as a book or newspaper, to become acquainted with a criminal. The epigraph to John Howard's *Lazarettos* (1791) reads: "O let the sorrowful sighing of the PRISONERS come before thee." In Mayhew's day, however, prisoners were not so far outside the city as they later became: at least prison buildings, notably Newgate, were within London, even though the criminal had been exiled from city life.

"People in easy circumstances will hardly credit what I am about to relate" (*LL* 1:393), one of Mayhew's informants wrote him. Victorian ladies and gentlemen may have heard the street seller's cries through their curtained windows or may have quickly cast an eye on them, but they had not, God forbid, entered their homes. "'I was hard brought up, sir,' he said; 'ay, them as'll read your book—I mean them readers as is well to do—cannot fancy how hard'" (*LL* 2:428).[41]

Those in "high places"—often literally, living on a hill or today in a high-rise apartment building, need a raising of consciousness. This is akin to psychotherapy: when what one part of the psyche or society believes about the whole of it no longer fits with what is actually going on, autobiographical speaking, writing, or reading can bring together thought and action, adapting thought to reality and guiding intelligence to appropriate rather than futile action. According to Bracebridge Hemyng, one of the authors of volume 4 of *London Labour:*

> One only gets at the depravity of mankind by searching below the surface of society, and for certain purposes such knowledge and information are useful and beneficial to the community. Therefore the philanthropist must overcome his repugnance to the task, and draw back the veil that is thinly spread over the skeleton. [*LL* 4:246]

On occasion Mayhew himself compared his activity to that of a physician who studies "sores"—of society. Or the image of descent appears in this context: *Alice in Wonderland* is the mythological counterpart of Mayhew's histories, comparable to the fiction of Dickens, whose slumming expeditions with police during the 1850s were as novel as Mayhew's journalistic wanderings. In an uppity society, to dissent is to descend, though the aim may be to make the lower classes "upwardly mobile."

Mayhew never tried to encourage communication in the opposite direction: to take oral histories from members of the middle and upper classes and make them available to those socially beneath them. Many of the poor could not read or afford to purchase a newspaper, pamphlet, or book, and in any case the higher classes always have many opportunities to express themselves, one reason Studs Terkel does not do a book about "celebrities." What good would have been done by throwing in the face of the poor the pleasures or even the "miseries" of the rich? John Thompson, a photographer of London street life in the 1870s, made a similar move when he began taking pictures of London's elite about 1880; but the pictures were not meant to be seen by the street people.[42]

Precisely who is Mayhew addressing, and what does he expect them to do? Like Studs Terkel, Mayhew is far from precise on this. His typical statement along these lines is: "the facts which I have still to adduce in connexion with vagrancy are of so overpowering a character, that I hope and trust they may be the means of rousing every earnest man in the kingdom to a sense of the enormous evils that are daily going on around him" (*LL* 3:387). He reports that the boy thieves at an open meeting "were evidently sincerely grateful for the efforts being made to bring their misfortunes before the notice of those in whose power it may be to alleviate them."[43] What such alleviation consists in Mayhew does not say: if the low lodging houses were closed, where would the occupants stay but on the streets? Hardly an improvement. Surely Mayhew overstates the gratitude of these boys, who had only those places to live in! In the preface to volume 4 of *London Labour,* the publishers include among the series' readers the moralist, the philanthropist, the statist, and the general public. The English middle class was continuing its ascent to political power over the aristocracy, and a wave of philanthropy rippled through the society. Alan Thomas has said: "The largest part of Mayhew's readership appears to have been composed of philanthropic ladies and gentlemen."[44] Thompson has written:

> Mayhew's stance—and his audience—would seem to have
> been, firmly, with the metropolitan professional men and lower
> middle-class. The Chartists he seems to have seen as "fustian
> orators": their noise distracted men of good will from finding
> practical solutions to particular social evils.[45]

Some evidence, such as his desire to keep the price of the *London Labour* pamphlets low, suggests that Mayhew also wanted to reach the very laborers he discussed, but this does not seem to have been the major audience: they could best be reached and organized in meetings like those Mayhew held.

Apparently Mayhew hoped that informing these agents of social action, assuming their good motives to begin with, would be enough to increase private philanthropy—donations of both money and volunteers' time— and bring about appropriate legislation. In one place he proclaims:

> It is high time that some one took the bull by the horns, and since public opinion has made but little impression on the worthies above named [the proprietors of a sweat shop], it will be advisable to see whether fine or imprisonment will have any terrors for them.[46]

But Mayhew, thoroughly immersed in many-hued phenomena, gives hardly any details about what his proposals might be. On 8 February 1851, in a reply to a correspondent, he wrote that he hoped

> to induce some change in our social state (though at present he [Mayhew] hardly knows *what* change) by which the workman may ensure *his fair share of the produce*. There are many means proposed to obtain this end. Protection, Chartism, Cooperative Societies, Socialism, Communism, and many other social and political panacea; but with them, Mr. Mayhew has in his present vocation nothing to do, and he wishes it to be distinctly known and understood—without reservation or cavil—that he is in no way connected with any social or political party or sect whatever.[47]

The groups he did try to organize were made up of the laborers themselves, on the assumption that they had the talent to help themselves: "There is after all but one way to help the poor, that is to teach the poor to help themselves; and so long as committees of noblemen have the conduct of their household affairs, so long as my Lord this or that is left to say at what time they shall go to bed and when they shall get up, there can be no main improvement in their condition."[48] At least the public could help by not getting wrong ideas about workers (*LL* 3:232).

It is all very well to "enlist in behalf of the sufferers the sympathies at least of all those who desire to see justice prevail between man and man" (*UM* 474). But it may strike us as rather pale in the context of capitalist expansion (even "plethoric capitalists") added to the eternal inertia and self-interest of mankind. According to Eileen Yeo, Mayhew "was at work in London at a crucial time of transition between two phases of capitalism, when a more regulated and humane economy was giving way to a stage of intense and savage competition."[49] Scrooge was the symbol of this economic system. Why would anyone pay attention to the lives of the poor? Mayhew had one force working in his favor—fear.

After revolutionary outbreaks in France in 1789 and 1848, after political movements such as Chartism and communism in England in the 1840s, after the influx of impoverished Irish fleeing the potato famines, after the reform legislation of the 1830s with the resulting rise of expectations, after the London cholera epidemic with its aggravation of class tensions, the middle and upper classes in England were apprehensive about the masses beneath them. If they were not genuinely interested in improving the quality of life of the poor, at least they would pay enough attention to prevent revolutionary uprisings. Better to listen to the "perishing and dangerous classes" in the newspapers than to be confronted with their demands at the barricades. "The process may seem a slow one," Mayhew advised, "but there is no hastening it by force—conviction alone can work the change."[50]

Mayhew does not dwell on this, but fear is a specter that occasionally makes an explicit appearance in his writings. The epigraph to volume 4 of *London Labour* quotes Addison's warning: "Misery and Ignorance are always the cause of great evils. Misery is easily excited to anger, and Ignorance soon yields to perfidious counsels." When the *Economist,* a *Morning Chronicle* competitor, denounced Mayhew for encouraging people to go on relief and for propagating a communistic feeling against competition, he replied that it was just *that* pig-headed attitude that had encouraged communism in Europe already.[51] In *London Labour* Mayhew counsels his readers: "If our sense of duty will not rouse us to do this, at least our regard for our own interests should teach us, that it is not safe to allow this vast dungheap of ignorance and vice to seethe and fester, breeding a social pestilence in the very heart of our land" (*LL* 1:105). Again: "If we knew but the whole of the facts concerning them, and their sufferings and feelings, our very fears alone for the safety of the state would be sufficient to make us do something in their behalf" (*LL* 2:7). And again: "The public have but to read the following plain unvarnished account of the habits, amusements, dealings, education, politics, and religion of the London costermongers in the nineteenth century, and then to say whether they think it safe—even if it be thought fit—to allow men, women, and children to continue in such a state" (*LL* 1:8).

Although we are trying to account for Mayhew's use of oral histories, we might pause here and ask why he included so much statistical material, apart from its popularity after the founding of the Statistical Society of London in 1834.[52] Numbers have many functions in Mayhew's work, including casting doubt on fashionable theories, as more recent sociologists have done with statistics. In relation to his effort to get the upper class to act, he emphasized numbers to impress his readers with the extent of the problem and thus with the magnitude of the threat. If "the want, the ignorance, and the vice of a street-life [is] in direct ratio to the numbers, it becomes of capital importance that we should know how many are seeking to pick up a livelihood in the public thoroughfares" (*LL* 2:1). While the power of an impoverished individual is miniscule, the totals of people and of the things they sell are impressive, especially when official census returns greatly underestimate them. Unlike later sociologists, Mayhew does not seem to use oral histories to make qualitative interpretations of quantitative data: using more recent methodical categories, we can view sequences in the text this way, but that does not seem to be what Mayhew had in mind. Rather, Mayhew used numbers to magnify the qualities shown in personal statements in order to make an impression on his readers: each quality or thing presented is spread out over a large number of people or a large area, another reason for including so many oral histories. At the ticket-of-leave men's meeting, he says: "I wish to get bodies of men together in a mass, their influence by that means being more sensibly felt than if they remained isolated" (*LL* 3:440). In *The Criminal Prisons of London,* Mayhew remarks: "The ordinary citizen knows crime only as an exceptional thing—he hears or reads of merely *individual* instances, and has never been accustomed to think of it, much more look upon it *in the mass:* so that the first sight of a large concourse of thieves, and murderers, and cheats fills him with entirely new impressions" (*CP* 405–6).

Mayhew wants the reader to feel that he or she is at fault for the existence of deplorable social conditions: "I am anxious to make others feel, as I do myself, that *we* are the culpable parties in these matters" (*LL* 1:45). "It is *our* fault to allow them to be as they are and not theirs to remain so" (*LL* 1:44). For Mayhew, the press was a "Court of judicature, where the public acts of our leading men are daily tried."[53] But the fault lies not only in inaction by public officials but in a widespread hypocritical attitude. Mayhew could have demonstrated the guilt of the prosperous entirely in his own language, or he could have ornamented his claims with occasional insertions of the language of the street people. He went beyond that, presenting the lives and depicting the characters of the speakers in their own words. Why? He wanted the reader to *identify* with the speaker in the oral history and to feel responsible for—that is, willing to respond to—the class of people to which the speaker belonged. Mayhew's extensive correspondence indicates that many people did respond.

By "identify" I do not mean that someone reading the oral history of a pickpocket (see below) becomes in his mind a pickpocket, though he might feel a thrill of vicarious experience. I mean that he at least does not find the experience of a delinquent as unlike his own as he might have expected. This happens because an oral history, in addition to presenting a unique state of affairs, reveals in the speaker common human qualities and experiences—"basic likenesses of all human beings," according to Burgess. This is what enables oral history, perhaps better than any other medium of communication, to generate understanding between people of quite different backgrounds. No matter how alien they may be in some respects, all human beings can understand laughter and suffering, travel and food: "The 'strong' flavour of these preparations [cakes and pastries] is in all probability as grateful to the palate of an itinerant youth, as is the high *gout* of the grouse or the woodcock to the fashionable epicure. In this respect, as in others which I have pointed out, the 'extremes' of society 'meet' " (*LL* 1:531–32). "Many a street-seller becomes as weary of town after the winter as a member of parliament who sits out a very long session" (*LL* 1:541). Extremes of society meet: the analogical content of Mayhew's descriptions supports their rhetorical aim.

Oral history both makes use of and fortifies the concept of an essential human condition individualized by various turns of good or bad fortune: "We have seen the brutified state in which the costermonger is allowed to remain, though possessing the same faculties and susceptibilities as ourselves—the same power to perceive and admire the forms of truth, beauty, and goodness, as even the highest in the state" (*LL* 1:27). This attitude is more likely to result in action to change people's environments than the attitude that people are born into certain states and that their "natures" cannot change. Oral histories tend to dissipate snobbery by suggesting that everyone's life might have been different but for one or another event over which he had no control. Mayhew includes oral histories less to present "social processes," to mention a later category, than to set out a typical plot of misfortune striking down a basically good person. Might someone as a result of reading Mayhew's histories increase his self-discipline to overcome the threat of misfortune? Mayhew was not blind to moral failings: "all, dragged down by a series of misfortunes, sometimes beyond their control, and sometimes brought about by their own imprudence or sluggishness" (*LL* 1:351).

Indeed, Mayhew equivocates on this crucial point, evidence of his own attitudinal marginality. In one place he proclaims: "Ordinary people are ordinary, simply because they lack energy—principle—will (call it what you please) to overcome the material elements of their nature with the spiritual" (*LL* 1:348). But in another place he says that the doctrine he had "endeavoured to enforce throughout this publication [was] the degrading influence of circumstances upon the poor" (*LL* 2:175). Similarly, the first volume of *London Labour* begins by dividing all human beings into two classes—wanderers and settlers. This merely expresses Mayhew's own itinerancy and his desire to play anthropologist, since this classification, like others he made, does not organize the subsequent text. There is no evidence that Mayhew ever met in person a member of a "barbarian race," a stunning contradiction to his usual procedure of avoiding rhapsodies in favor of reporting from notes taken on the scene. Among settlers (the civilized peoples), there exist wanderers: the London street folk are wanderers among the settled. These tribes are as diverse in species as different races, according to Mayhew: this notion both leads him toward the concept of a subculture[54] (they have their own values) and prevents him from fully grasping the concept (his attitude is too brimming with how alien it all is). But his oral histories almost inadvertently give an impression that life is familiar everywhere, and to that extent they undercut moves toward reforming what is after all normal.

Once the reader has identified with the speaker of an oral history, once he is reassured that the terrain is not entirely foreign, he can begin to notice unfamiliar values. Mayhew says he "was anxious to see the room in which the gang of boy crossing-sweepers lived, so that I might judge of their peculiar style of housekeeping, and form some notion of their principles of domestic economy" (*LL* 2:569). Even the dietary needs of the industrious poor differ from those of the nonworking rich (*LL* 1:124). This effort to understand people on their own terms is necessary for effective reform action: "If you really wish to do these poor creatures good, you must remember that your instructions are not intended for so-called fashionable society, but for those who have a fashion of their own" (*LL* 1:346). Oral histories communicate mores, customs, and values in their own often ambiguous contexts: in contrast, the more atomistic, unambiguous description of the researcher may be more or less off target. On the other hand, when these alien customs are the modes of operation of one sort of criminal or another, oral history material on the "tricks of the trade" may be presented to put a gullible public on guard: this appears in volume 4 of *London Labour* in John Binny's treatment of embezzlers and thieves and in Andrew Halliday's exposure of deceptive beggars. The public's mental distance from the criminal is reduced in order to increase their physical distance.

One wonders whether Mayhew included some material in *London Labour* to ease the reader's transition from higher-class beliefs to lower-class realities. For example, why does the division of humanity into civilized settlers and uncivilized wanderers open volume 1? Is it because Mayhew wanted to begin, in standard rhetorical fashion, with what his audience believed, then move into phenomena that gradually induced them to change those beliefs, to realize that costermongers are not uncivilized but have a highly developed civilization of their own? Probably not. These occasional sallies into anthropology and morality seem to be authentic expressions of Mayhew's own often contradictory beliefs.

When he says, "It is strange how all castes of criminals would make out their lot in life to be a matter of ill luck" (*CP* 381), he is contradicting his own oral histories, which reveal that everyone, including criminals, suffers misfortune. Mayhew is also reflecting the coexistence in contemporary English society of two strains: traditional moral censure and the more modern causal explanation of deviance and deprivation.[55]

However, all this is only to say that Mayhew was a "marginal worker," to use a later term, who did not belong fully to either region but had one foot in each social class. Thus the middle-class reader could identify first with Mayhew, who remains present (by commentary and parenthetical remarks) throughout, then gradually with the outcast.

Oral histories used in this way equalize the classes: they demonstrate the hidden virtues of the lower classes and humble the upper classes.[56] In his preface to *London Labour* Mayhew says: "It is but right that the truthfulness of the poor generally should be made known. . . . Those persons who, from an ignorance of the simplicity of the honest poor, might be inclined to think otherwise, have . . . only to consult the details given in the present volume." The secretary of the Ragged School Union and others of his ilk did not believe that the poor or the delinquent possessed any virtues at all: these latter certainly could not be counted on to give truthful testimony about anything. (See the Appendix.) Mayhew denied that the skilled masses and others "are the unenlightened and unthinking body of people that they are generally considered by those who never go among them, and who see them only as 'the dangerous classes'" (*LL* 3:243). But he had to do more than merely *state* their honesty: he had to *show* it in some appropriate way. Conveying their own statements, when checked *against each other* (without giving any upper-class gentleman the, right to veto) and guaranteed by Mayhew, conveys their honesty not only in the *content* of the stories—which, after all, could have been attested by Mayhew—but in their very *act* of their telling the story. Transmitting their story in their own words conveys "the slang beauty and inventiveness of the spoken voices."[57] For Mayhew oral history demonstrates the creativity of the common man; if he has nothing else, at least he has language. Nothing better than Mayhew's work so utterly refutes the following statement that issued from William Gass in 1975: "I am firmly of the opinion that people who can't speak have nothing to say. It's one more thing we do to the poor, the deprived: cut out their tongues . . . allow them a language as lousy as their lives"[58]

From time to time Mayhew will remark that if, for example, all street sellers are not honest, neither are all shopkeepers, or if they are ignorant "it is no demerit to them, even as it is no demerit to us to know the little we do" (*LL* 2:4). But after his description of the Asylum for the Houseless Poor, an utterly ghastly scene, Mayhew explodes:

If you in your arrogance, ignoring all the accidents that have
helped to build up your wordly [sic] prosperity, assert that you
have been the "architect of your own fortune," who, let us
ask, gave you the genius or energy for the work?

Then get down from your moral stilts, and confess it honestly to yourself, that you are what you are by that inscrutable
grace which decreed your birthplace to be a mansion or a
cottage rather than a "padding-ken," or which granted you
brains and strength, instead of sending you into the world, like
many of these, a cripple or an idiot.

It is hard for smug-faced respectability to acknowledge these
dirt-caked, erring wretches as brothers, and yet, if from those
to whom little is given little is expected, surely, after the
atonement of their long suffering, they will make as good
angels as the best of us. [LL 3:439]

One of my claims in this book is that delinquents' oral histories do not
appear in a political paradigm because the "boy's own story" about his
immediate circumstances does not explicitly represent systems of power
that transcend his experience. However, it should be obvious from the
discussion above that in another sense such documents do have political
significance. M. K. Blasing has put this admirably:

The autobiographical mode commands so much power that
it can become a political weapon. In autobiography the very
means of telling one's story—in the first person and from the
inside, so to speak—are an assertion of the power of the teller
and establish the credibility of one's story. It is for this reason
that autobiographical writing has proved so useful to oppressed peoples. For example, autobiography has become the
predominant form of Black literature in America because it
commands the potentially political power to change minds.[59]

This power is "potentially" political, not actually. Oral histories do not of
themselves affect *structures* of power. But studies by the group of their
own histories may develop their identity and unity. Extragroup communication of those experiences may change public attitudes so as to promote
eventual overt political action. Or, like Foucault, one can discover evidence of power in the texts of everyday life.

The Pleasures of Oral History

Why would anyone buy a book or newspaper containing Mayhew's writing, with its catalog of human misery? That people did so is attested by the
increase in circulation of the *Morning Chronicle* during the poverty-labor
series (which provoked claims by a competing newspaper that it was only
a stunt in the first place).[60] Massive social conflict may account for the

need for cross-class communication, but the need might have remained
unmet or not been met in Mayhew's way. Social classes do not buy
newspapers; individuals do. How do you get an individual to lay out a few
pennies for something to read?

One reason people were attracted to the *Morning Chronicle* series and
the subsequent book was that, in addition to including serious points, they
were a cornucopia of human qualities, and thus were entertaining. The
publisher of "The Great World of London" announced on the cover of one
of the booklets that Mayhew's aspiration had been

> to present to the public such a word-picture of the Great
> Metropolis as it exists at the present time, that those who are
> familiar with the scenes and characters described, may be
> pleased with the book for its mere truth, while those who have
> never visited the places and people may yet have some ideal
> sense of them, and so find a picturesque charm in the very
> peculiarities of the subjects themselves.

Not all the oral histories stressed suffering, and those that did included
ways individuals adapted to circumstances to achieve satisfactions, even
minimal satisfactions: that a person is able to speak at all implies that he
still has life in him. Oral histories will most likely not be acquired from the
most destitute cases—someone dying from neglect in prison, for
example—though the existence of such extremes could be *stated* by the
likes of a John Howard, stated to the influential persons who sought
Howard's company. Mayhew remarks that the reader "will marvel like
me, not only at the fortitude which could sustain him under all his heavy
afflictions, but at the resignation (not to say philosophy) with which he
bears them every one" (*LL* 1:364). Auden's final impression of the London poor was "not of their misery but of their gaiety in conditions under
which it seems incredible that such virtues would survive."[61]

Many of the oral histories are not so much about lives as about what we
might call consumer information or techniques of producing goods, or
street arts. All of these have some degree of delight—evoke a "feeling
tone," to use Studs Terkel's term—and some are rather humorous. A
street performer of "Chinese shades," where puppets in front of a light
cast shadows on a sheet, speaks here:

> Then the wife calls the daughter Kitty, and tells her to see that
> the pot don't boil over; and above all to see that the cat don't
> steal the mutton out of the pot. Kitty says, "Yes, mother, I'll
> take particular care to see that the mutton don't steal the cat
> out of the pot." Cross-questions, you see—comic business.
> Then mother says, "Kitty, bring up the broom to sweep up the
> room," and Kitty replies, "Yes, mummy, I'll bring up the

room to sweep up the broom." Exaunt again. It's regular stage
business and cross-questions. [*LL* 3:82]

Mayhew the scientist labels most of his oral histories "statements."
This suggests that he is constructing a wall of data, as opposed to creating
a mosaic, to use Howard S. Becker's analogy,[62] but Mayhew clearly is
creating a picture. Even more fitting metaphors for Mayhew's work are a
"happy family"—an "assemblage of animals of diverse habits and propensities living amicably, or at least quietly, in one cage" (*LL* 3:224)—
such as was shown on London streets; or, not so quietly, a "charivari,"
as in *Punch; or, The London Charivari* (which *Webster's* defines as "a
mock serenade of discordant noises, made with kettles, tin horns, etc.");
or a "huge human *vivarium,* wherein one learns the habits of the many
'odd-fish' collected within it."[63] Without oral histories, Henry Mayhew's
work would not have such a diversity of "propensities" and voices.

Mayhew was a sociological Dickens or a politically minded P. T. Bar-
num. He says in the preface to *London Labour* that he will "adduce facts
so extraordinary" and novel that no one will believe him, and he occasionally stops to reassure his readers that some story so "curious and
extravagant" is nevertheless true (*LL* 1:48). One wonders to what extent
Mayhew and his readers were motivated by the believe-it-or-not aspects
of the oral histories, more apparent in the book than in the newspaper
series. Doubtless these stories of prostitutes and thieves appealed to the
voyeurism of the public. How nice to find the material in a socially
redeeming context.[64]

Mayhew expressed his reason for using oral histories, from this point of
view, in his prefaces to children's books he wrote in the 1850s about
exemplary figures in science. You cannot force people to learn, Mayhew
asserts; they must enjoy it: "This consists in exciting the *taste* of the
youth towards the subject to which the attention is required to be
given.... To create a taste for a certain pursuit, it seems to be essential
that the individual should be made to experience a vivid sense of pleasure
in connection with it."[65] In *Criminal Prisons,* Mayhew criticizes prison
officials for not arousing convicts to an interest in higher things: "to
discourse pleasantly—to clothe interesting subjects in an interesting
form... even as the dramatist is hissed as incapable from the stage, when
he is found to lack the power to rivet the attention of his audience" (*CP*
107–8). The feelings most often mentioned in these prefaces are wonder,
curiosity, and surprise. (Mayhew even wrote an essay entitled "What Is
the Cause of Surprise?") The oral histories in *London Labour* must have
aroused these feelings in Mayhew's day as they do today, providing some
relief from the more obdurate features of the text, lining the wormword
cup of science or truth with the honey of poetry, to use Lucretius's
phrase.

However, a question arises whether this means of attracting and holding the interest of an audience does not somehow dilute the speaker's message: might it even be a form of the very hypocrisy one seems to be opposing? If viewing lives at a distance is used as a kind of entertainment, may the reader not conclude that the lives themselves have a light side and thus ask why he should bother about people who are basically happy with their lot? Or why do anything more with a criminal offender than lock him up where he can no longer have any fun?[66]

The Authenticity of Oral Histories

Just as Henry Mayhew was both dramatist and scientist, his oral histories have the dual function of giving readers both the delights of fiction and the assurances of authenticity they would have gotten had they been present at the interview. (Though had they been present they might have felt more threatened than delighted.) Mayhew, unlike many of his contemporaries, approached the poor themselves for information. He complained that conventional economists had the same aversion for facts as dogs had for water.[67] Some people "are *afraid* of ascertaining the sentiments, feelings, and habits of the more wretched part of the population" (*LL* 1:343). Mayhew, after making appropriate checks for representativeness and accuracy, gives an account of a gentleman's history "from the only authentic source. It is, indeed, given in the words of the writer from whom it was received" (*LL* 1:283). (For Mayhew's techniques of acquiring and presenting oral histories, see the Appendix.)

Mayhew presented some of his data as acquired partly to reinforce the belief that, since it retained the "freshness of the impression" (*LL* 3:332), the material was indeed an *authentic* representation of what someone actually had said. If nothing else, his oral histories strongly suggest that Mayhew himself was on the scene. In his preface to *London Labour*, he claims that his work was "the first commission of inquiry into the state of the people taken by a private individual." A government commission of inquiry would have had the reputation of the government behind its report: as a private citizen, Mayhew had to give weight to his evidence by conveying some of the actuality of his original experience.

Of course, someone could claim that Mayhew made up all these characters and speech patterns without ever leaving his office. But the number and variety of oral histories, and for that matter their extraordinary and unique qualities (fact being harder to imagine than fiction), give the impression that Mayhew was indeed out on the streets. The oral histories, as well as descriptions of his own movements, support his assurances to a skeptical reader that not a line was written unless a note had been taken on the spot (*UM* 116). If a reader's experience differed from Mayhew's, the reader's experience was deficient, because Mayhew had been there (*UM* 105) and the reader probably had not.

Another reason for leaving a person's statement in its own "un-varnished language" was to render a truthful version of reality. In their book *The Magic of Kindness,* the Mayhew brothers declare that they "believe they have been truthful—and indeed, with this view, they have often preferred the language of those from whom they have gleaned their facts to their own."[68] However, when a speaker waxes especially eloquent, truthfulness is questioned rather than reinforced, and Mayhew has to guarantee that the words are the speaker's own: "with forty people's breaths perhaps mingling together in one foul choking steam of stench [the man's own words]" (*LL* 1:455).

The "Presence" of Oral Histories

Neither pleasure nor information is enough to place a reader, through words, inside a scene or a person's life. Discursive devices are needed that seem to bring him into the very *presence* of the speaker. This requires *showing,* not merely *telling.* According to Aristotle, the inventor of rhetoric as the technique of persuasion, presenting the facts should be enough, as in teaching geometry; but in every system of instruction some attention must be paid to style, delivery, or acting—"for the purpose of making a thing clear," but also "because of the corruption of the hearer."[69] That is, if human beings were computers, oral histories would be superfluous.

"Demonstration" (showing) is usually required in addition to "demonstration" (proving). How are matters put "before the eyes," to use Aristotle's phrase *(prosommaton poiein)?* As Mayhew says, "It struck my mind very forcibly." How to convey that in words? The massive features of the London poor can be projected in charts. The actualities of the individual person or place emerge most sharply in Mayhew's descriptions and oral histories. His introductions of speakers are probably the most vivid spots in his writing. He had to supply these, since a speaker most likely would not spontaneously give a physical description of himself, at least not from the viewpoint of the outsider; nor could the speaker depict his surroundings from that perspective. The observer begins the process of reading character by noting external marks, to apply Richard Sennett's notion, and the oral history completes the process by moving inward.

Aristotle advises that the best verbal device to achieve perspicuity is metaphor. Just as Mayhew the "marginal worker" crosses over from one perspective and value system to another, so metaphors and similes can bring a reader into a foreign setting by comparison with something he knows. Mayhew describes the street where the boy crossing sweepers live:

> before entering one of the narrow streets which branch off like
> a fish's spine from that long thoroughfare, they thought fit to

caution me that I was not to be frightened .... Seated on the
pavement at each side of the entrance was a costerwoman with
her basket before her, and her legs tucked up mysteriously
under her gown into a round ball, so that her figure resembled
in shape the plaster tumblers sold by the Italians .... The
parlour-windows of the houses had all of them wooden shut-
ters, as thick and clumsy-looking as a kitchen flap-table, the
paint of which had turned to the dull dirt-colour of an old
slate .... From the windows poles stretched out, on which
blankets, petticoats, and linen were drying; and so numerous
were they, that they reminded me of the flags hung out at a
Paris fete .... As I entered the court, a "row" was going
on ... and in her excitement thrusting her body half out of her
temporary rostrum as energetically as I have seen Punch lean
over his theatre .... whilst the sweep's wife rushed about,
clapping her hands together as quickly as if she were applaud-
ing at a theatre .... This "row" had the effect of drawing all
the lodgers to the windows—their heads popping out as suddenly as dogs from their kennels in a fancier's yard. [*LL* 2:570]

Odors are notoriously difficult to communicate: "I was no longer sick-
ened with that overpowering smell that always hangs about the dwellings
of the very poor" (*UM* 154). But what *was* the odor? No way of telling. In
his own descriptions, Mayhew exercises sight most often, and in *London
Labour,* though not in the *Morning Chronicle* series, illustrations made
from photographs accompany the text. They also appear in *Criminal Prisons,* though prison officials objected to further photographs when earlier
ones had looked too pleasant, not deterrent enough (*CP* 408). Photography was then in its infancy and became increasingly popular. However,
Mayhew denies that even the best possible work of this medium can
render "what only human genius can seize and paint—the expression, the
feelings, the soul."[70] Susan Sontag has compared a photograph to a quotation;[71] in a larger sense of the visual, Mayhew's quotations are "pictures of life,"[72] as Thackeray called Mayhew's work. Mayhew's oral
histories still retain their human power, while the illustrations in his books
have fallen victim to changing fashions in clothing.[73]
    Mayhew's oral histories make use not so much of sight as of sound.
Transmitting as well as possible how a person or a place sounds helps
bring the reader closer to the original, though transcriptions of dialect can
be difficult to follow at first and therefore may act as a deterrent to reading. One imagines a voice and wishes he could hear the original. One of
the overall impressions that *London Labour* makes is of the "tumult of a
thousand different cries of the eager dealers, all shouting at the top of their
voices, at one and the same time" (*LL* 1:11).
    A related motive for Mayhew's use of oral histories is his tendency
toward comprehensiveness of *intellectual* vision. One reason to devise

classificatory schemes is so that "the mind can grasp the whole at one effort" (*LL* 4:4). The most remarkable symbol of this expansionary tendency is Mayhew's ascent to the top of the dome of Saint Paul's Cathedral for a panoramic view of London, an experience he describes at the beginning of *The Criminal Prisons of London,* which was to be the first installment of "The Great World of London":

> London is a strange, incongruous chaos of the most astounding riches and prodigious poverty—of feverish ambition and apathetic despair—of the brightest charity and the darkest crime; the great focus of human emotion—the scene of countless daily struggles, failures, and successes; where the very best and the very worst types of civilized society are found to prevail—where there are more houses and more houseless— more feasting and more starvation—more philanthropy and more bitter stony-heartedness, than any other spot in the world. [*CP* 18–19]

A traditional method of achieving comprehensiveness is to assimilate contraries into a large, transcendent whole, and this has often been symbolized by the view from a high place: attempting to describe London from all perspectives, Mayhew also flew over the city in a balloon. Thus he used oral histories to embrace both stylistically and substantively the antipodes of his verbal continent, to capture "a more enlarged series of facts" (*LL* 4:2) or an "enlarged vision of experience" (*CP* 381). In his *London Labour* preface Mayhew refers to "that comprehensive manner in which I am desirous of executing the modern history of this and every other portion of the people." Mayhew aimed at nothing less than an encyclopedia of the human condition: on one occasion he admitted that "the subject he has undertaken is so vast that it becomes almost fearful to contemplate."[74]

Emotions and Motions of Oral Histories

Mayhew's intention was not merely to change the attitudes of the rich and the middle class. The poor as a class should not be thought of as naturally depraved, since their condition was due to the insatiable greed of those more well-to-do (*UM* 258), but arguments alone would not motivate people to counteract greed. Motivations were generated when emotions were aroused: "the sympathies stir the mind to action without any sense of effort" (*LL* 1:44). If the ends of persuasive speech are to please, to teach, and to move to action, then oral histories, alongside Mayhew's own similarly oriented descriptions, are effective insofar as they are delightful, informative, and "moving." "To hear the cries of the hungry, shivering children, and the wrangling of the greedy men, scrambling for a bed and a pound of dry bread, is a thing to haunt one for life" (*LL* 3:427).

Ideally, the impact of the situation stays with the reader until he acts to change the situation (rather than trying to change his feeling).

About the street children, Mayhew wrote: "An ample field is presented, alike for wonder, disgust, pity, hope and regret" (*LL* 1:535). Disgust arises even at ourselves: "The facts detailed . . . are gross enough to make us all blush" (*LL* 1:458). Mayhew must have known that overstating these emotional qualities would have been as ineffective as omitting them entirely. In his preface to *London Labour* he says: "Be the faults of the present volume what they may, assuredly they are rather short-comings than exaggerations, for in every instance the author and his coadjutors have sought to understate, and most assuredly never to exceed the truth." He refused to "varnish matters over with a sickly sentimentality."[75] Thus, another reason to let the people speak in their own language was to promote social action as forthright as the oral histories. But concerning just what that action should be, Mayhew was hardly forthcoming.

Two

Mayhew on Delinquency and "Street Biography"

Mayhew interviewed juvenile offenders both on the streets and in detention. His approach to young people outside prison does not seem to have differed from the ways he made contact with adults, described in the Appendix. Inside a prison he had to work through the director. Usually he would spend a full day there, beginning in the morning by talking with officials. Apparently a prison official was always present when he interviewed young inmates, and one suspects this is why he acquired so few oral histories there. I know of only two published histories obtained from incarcerated youths, both concerning the Ragged Schools.[1] Perhaps the prison officials agreed with Mayhew that those schools increased juvenile crime and thus added to the prison population, and so were eager to put as much damning testimony as possible before the public. As might be expected, there is no talk about the evils of incarceration from incarcerated boys: evidence for that comes from former inmates and from Mayhew's own observations and conclusions (cf. *LL* 3:391).

It appears that Mayhew typically interrogated young prisoners in a large workroom. He would ask about each person's age, number of times in jail, and offenses (*CP* 415); in some cases excerpts from these interviews were published as very brief quotations, in the manner of reports by government commissions. The boys probably enjoyed even this limited opportunity to speak, since under the "silent system" they were forbidden to talk during most of the day. (At night they were unsupervised—a glaring breach of moral discipline, Mayhew declared.) Despite the inhibitions of the place, they seem to have spoken frankly: several admitted that on being released they would return to stealing.

Following is an oral history of a juvenile offender, which Mayhew probably wrote down in the street. It originally appeared in the *Morning Chronicle* on 29 January 1850, and later it was used in *London Labour* (1:456–58) as part of Mayhew's discussion of vagrancy and the low lodging houses.

A YOUNG PICKPOCKET

To show the class of characters usually frequenting these lodging-houses I will now give the statement of a boy—a young pickpocket—without shoes or stockings. He wore a ragged, dirty, and very thin great coat, of some dark jean or linen, under which was another thin coat, so arranged that what appeared rents—and, indeed, were rents, but designedly made—in the outer garment, were slits through which the hand readily reached the pockets of the inner garment, and could there deposit any booty. He was a slim, agile lad, with a sharp but not vulgar expression, and small features. His hands were of singular delicacy and beauty. His fingers were very long, and no lady's could have been more taper. A burglar told me that with such a hand he ought to have made his fortune. He was worth 20*l*. a week, he said, as a *"wire,"* that is, a picker of ladies' pockets. When engaged "for a turn," as he told me he once was by an old pickpocket, the man looked minutely at his fingers, and approved of them highly. His hands, the boy said, were hardly serviceable to him when very cold. His feet were formed in the same symmetrical and beautiful mould as his hands.

"I am 15," he said. "My father was a potter, and I can't recollect my mother" (many of the thieves are orphans or motherless). "My father has been dead about five years. I was then working at the pottery in High-street, Lambeth, earning about 4*s*. a week; in good weeks, 4*s*. 6*d*. I was in work eight months after my father died; but one day I broke three bottles by accident, and the foreman said 'I shan't want you anymore'; and I took that as meant for a discharge; but I found afterwards that he didn't so mean it. I had 2*s*. and a suit of clothes then, and tried for work at all the potteries; but I couldn't get any. It was about the time Smithfield fair was on. I went, but it was a very poor concern. I fell asleep in a pen in the afternoon, and had my shoes stolen off my feet. When I woke up, I began crying. A fellow named Gyp then came along (I knew his name afterwards), and he said, 'What are you crying for?' and I told him, and he said, 'Pull off your stockings, and come with me, and I'll show you where to sleep.' So I did, and he took me to St. Olave's workhouse, having first sold my stockings. I had never stolen anything until then. There I slept in the casual ward, and Gyp slept there too. In the morning we started together for Smithfield, where he said he had a job to sweep the pens, but he couldn't sweep them without pulling off his coat, and it would look so queer if he hadn't a shirt—and he hadn't one. He promised to teach me how to make a living in the country if I would lend him mine, and I was persuaded—for I was an innocent lad then—and went up a gateway and stripped off my shirt and gave it to him, and soon after he went into a public-house to get half a pint of beer; he went in at one door and out at another, and I didn't see him for six months afterwards. That afternoon I went into Billingsgate

market and met some boys, and one said, 'Mate, how long
have you been knocking about; where did you doss?' I didn't
know what they meant, and when they'd told me they meant
where did I sleep? I told them how I'd been served. And they
said, 'Oh! you must expect that, until you learn something,'
and they laughed. They all know'd Gyp; he was like the head
of a Billingsgate gang once. I became a pal with these boys at
Billingsgate, and we went about stealing fish and meat. Some
boys have made 2*s*. in a morning when fish is dear—those that
had pluck and luck; they sold it at half-price. Billingsgate market is a good place to sell it; plenty of costermongers are there
who will buy it, rather than of the salesmen. I soon grew as
bad as the rest at this work. At first I sold it to other boys, who
would get 3*d*. for what they bought at 1*d*. Now they can't do
me. If I can get a thing cheap where I lodge, and have the
money, and can sell it dear, that's the chance. I carried on this
fish rig for about two years, and went begging a little, too. I
used to try a little thieving sometimes—that's the artfullest; but
I could do no good there. At these two years' end, I was often
as happy as could be; that is, when I had made money. Then I
met B——, whom I had often heard of as an uncommon clever
pickpocket; he could do it about as well as I can now, so as
people won't feel it. Three of his mates were transported for
stealing silver plate. He and I became pals, and started for the
country with 1*d*. We went through Foot's Cray, and passed a
farm where a man's buried at the top of a house; there's
something about money while a man's above ground; I don't
understand it, but it's something like that. A baker, about
thirty miles from London, offended us about some bread; and
B—— said 'I'll show you how to do a handkerchief;' but the
baker looked round, and B—— stopped; and just after that I
flared it [whisked the handkerchief out]; and that's the first I
did. It brought 1*s*. 3*d*. We travelled across country, and got
to Maidstone, and did two handkerchiefs. One I wore round
my neck, and the other the lodging-housekeeper pawned for
us for 1*s*. 6*d*. In Maidstone, next morning, I was nailed, and
had three months of it. I didn't mind it so much then, but
Maidstone's far worse now, I've heard. I have been in prison
three times in Brixton, three times in the Old Horse [Bride-
well], three times in the Compter, once in the Steel, and once
in Maidstone—thirteen times in all, including twice I was re-
manded, and got off; but don't reckon that prison. Every time I
came out harder then I went in. I've had four floggings; it was
bad enough—a flogging was—while it lasted; but when I got
out I soon forgot it. At a week's end I never thought again
about it. If I had been better treated I should have been a better
lad. I could leave off thieving now as if I had never thieved, if I

could live without.'' [I am inclined to doubt this part of the statement.] "I have carried on this sort of life until now. I didn't often make a very good thing of it. I saw Manning and his wife hung. Mrs. Manning was dressed beautiful when she came up. She screeched when Jack Ketch pulled the bolt away. She was harder than Manning, they all said; without her there would have been no murder. It was a great deal talked about, and Manning was pitied. It was a punishment to her to come on the scaffold and see Manning with the rope about his neck, if people takes it in the right light. I did 4s. 6d. at the hanging—two handkerchiefs, and a purse with 2s. in it—the best purse I ever had; but I've only done three or four purses. The reason is, because I've never been well dressed. If I went near a lady, she would say, 'Tush, tush, you ragged fellow!' and would shrink away. But I would rather rob the rich than the poor; they miss it less. But 1s. honest goes further than 5s. stolen. Some call that only a saying, but it's true. All the money I got soon went—most of it a-gambling. Picking pockets, when any one comes to think on it, is the daringest thing that a boy can do. It didn't in the least frighten me to see Manning and Mrs. Manning hanged. I never thought I should come to the gallows, and I never shall—I'm not high-tempered enough for that. The only thing that frightens me when I'm in prison is sleeping in a cell by myself—you do in the Old Horse and the Steel—because I think things may appear. You can't imagine how one dreams when in trouble. I've heard people talk about ghosts and that. Once, in the County, a tin had been left under a tap that went drip—drip—drip. And all in the ward were shocking frightened; and weren't we glad when we found out what it was! Boys tell stories about haunted castles, and cats that are devils; and that frightens one. At the fire in Monument-yard I did 5s. 7d.—3s. in silver and 2s. 3d. in handkerchiefs, and 4d. for three pairs of gloves. I sell my handkerchiefs in the Lane (Petticoat-lane). I carry on this trade still. Most times I've got in prison is when I've been desperate from hunger, and have said to B—— 'Now I'll have money, nailed or not nailed.' I can pick a woman's pocket as easy as a man's, though you wouldn't think it. If one's in prison for begging, one's laughed at. The others say, 'Begging! Oh, you cadger!' So a boy is partly forced to steal for his character. [That is, for his reputation—J. B.] I've lived a good deal in lodging-houses, and know the ways of them. They are very bad places for a boy to be in. Where I am now, when the place is full, there's upwards of 100 can be accommodated. I won't be there long. I'll do something to get out of it. There's people there will rob their own brother. There's people there talk

backward—for one they say eno, for two owt, for three eerht,
for four rouf, and five evif, for six exis. I don't know any
higher. I can neither read nor write. In this lodging-house there
are no women. They talk there chiefly about what they've
done, or are going to do, or have set their minds upon, just as
you or any other gentlemen might do. I have been in lodging-
houses in Mint-street and Kent-street, where men and women
and children all slept in one room. I think the men and women
who slept together were generally married, or lived together;
but it's not right for a big boy to sleep in the same room. Young
men have had beds to themselves, and so have young women
there; but there's nothing wrong. There's little said in these
places, the people are generally so tired. Where I am there's
horrid language—swearing, and everything that's bad. They
are to be pitied, because there's not work for honest people, let
alone thieves. In the lodging-houses the air is very bad, enough
to stifle one in bed—so many breaths together. Without such
places my trade couldn't be carried on; I couldn't live. Some
though would find another way out. Three or four would take a
room among them. Anybody's money's good—you can always
get a room. I would be glad to leave this life, and work at a
pottery. As to the sea, a bad captain would make me run
away—sure. He can do what he likes with you when you're out
at sea. I don't get more than 2s. a week, one week with the
other, by thieving; some days you do nothing until hunger
makes your spirits rise. I can't thieve on a full belly. I live on
2s. a week from thieving, because I understand fiddling—that
means, buying a thing for a mere trifle, and selling it for double,
or more, if you're not taken in yourself. I've been put up to a
few tricks in lodging-houses and now I can put others up to it.
Everybody must look after themselves, and I can't say I was
very sorry when I stole that 2s. from a poor woman, but I'd
rather have had 1s. 6d. from a rich one. I never drink—eating's
my part. I spend chief part of my money in pudding. I don't
like living in lodging-houses, but I must like it as I'm placed
now—that sort of living, and those lodging-houses, or starving.
They bring tracts to the lodging-houses—pipes are lighted with
them; tracts won't fill your belly. Tracts is no good, except to a
person that has a home; at the lodging-houses they're laughed
at. They seldom are mentioned. I've heard some of them read
by missionaries, but can't catch anything from them. If it had
been anything bad, I should have caught it readily. If an innocent boy gets into a lodging-house, he'll not be innocent
long—he can't. I know three boys who have run away, and are
in the lodging-houses still, but I hope their father has caught
them. Last night a little boy came to the lodging-house where I

was. We all thought he had run away, by the way he spoke. He stayed all night, but was found out in two or three falsehoods. I wanted to get him back home, or he'll be as bad as I am in time, though he's nothing to me; but I couldn't find him this morning; but I'll get him home yet, perhaps. The Jews in Petticoat-lane are terrible rogues. They'll buy anything of you—they'll buy what you've stolen from their next-door neighbours—that they would, if they knew it. But they'll give you very little for it, and they threaten to give you up if you won't take a quarter of the value of it. 'Oh! I shee you do it', they say, 'and I like to shee him robbed, but you musht take vot I give.' I wouldn't mind what harm came to those Petticoat-laners. Many of them are worth thousands, though you wouldn't think it." After this I asked him what he, as a sharp lad, thought was the cause of so many boys becoming vagrant pickpockets? He answered, "Why, sir, if boys runs away, and has to shelter in low lodging-houses—and many runs away from cruel treatment at home—they meet there with boys such as me, or as bad, and the devil soon lays his hand on them. If there wasn't so many lodging-houses there wouldn't be so many bad boys—there couldn't. Lately a boy came down to Billingsgate, and said he wouldn't stay at home to be knocked about any longer. He said it to some boys like me; and he was asked if he could get anything from his mother, and he said 'yes, he could.' So he went back, and brought a brooch and some other things with him to a place fixed on, and then he and some of the boys set off for the country; and that's the way boys is trapped. I think the fathers of such boys either ill-treat them, or neglect them; and so they run away. My father used to beat me shocking; so I hated home. I stood hard licking well, and was called 'the plucked one.'" This boy first stole flowers, currants, and gooseberries out of the clergyman's garden, more by way of bravado, and to ensure the approbation of his comrades, than for anything else. He answered readily to my inquiry, as to what he thought would become of him?—"Transportation. If a boy has great luck—he may carry on for eight years. Three or four years is the common run, but transportation is what he's sure to come to in the end." This lad picked my pocket at my request, and so dexterously did he do his "work," that though I was alive to what he was trying to do, it was impossible for me to detect the least movement of my coat. To see him pick the pockets, as he did, of some of the gentlemen who were present on the occasion, was a curious sight. He crept behind much like a cat with his claws out, and while in the act held his breath with suspense; but immediately the handkerchief was safe in his hand, the change in the expression of his countenance was most marked. He then seemed almost to be convulsed with delight at the success of his perilous adventure, and, turning his back, held up the handkerchief to discover the value of his prize with intense glee evident in every feature.

Mayhew's Definitions of Juvenile Crime

Juvenile crime was an important subject for Mayhew. It had been increasing in England since the turn of the century, the greatest proportion of all criminals were in the age group fifteen to twenty-five (*CP* 91), and repeat juvenile offenders often became professional adult criminals (*CP* 395). According to J. J. Tobias: "For much of the time between 1815 and the mid-1850s the nation was, just as it is today, anxiously talking about an upsurge of crime, especially among juveniles, and was wondering what to do about it." Tobias attributes the rise in juvenile delinquency to the rapid growth of the towns and the "violent economic and social transitions" of early industrial England.[2] In their survey of British social work, Young and Ashton write: "Conditions were altering very quickly in the first half of the nineteenth century. It is arguable that neither before nor after did change reach the alarming momentum of 1800–50."[3]

Mayhew was much less original in his study of crime than in his use of oral history, since observations on the social contexts that generate lawless behavior were commonplace during this period, both used and reinforced by Charles Dickens's *Oliver Twist*, published in 1839.[4] Also in that year some separate detention facilities for juvenile offenders had been established. In many prisons young and older people were thrown together, a state of affairs hotly opposed by penal reformers of the day, such as John Clay and Mary Carpenter, whom I shall discuss in the next chapter. Government commissions had looked into "juvenile depredation," but little action had been taken. No juvenile court existed until 1899, in Chicago; this was to become an official organ for declaring a child "delinquent." In writing contemporary with Mayhew the term "juvenile delinquent" does not seem so reified as it does today: Mayhew usually refers to "juvenile crime," avoiding the appearance of labeling anyone "a delinquent" once and for all.

In the 1840s, however, the social industry was being established that would give nominal unity to a concept of delinquency that the variety of juvenile offenders and offenses would never itself require, an industry that would burgeon into our own "juvenile justice system." According to Eileen Yeo:

> New fields for diagnosis and treatment of social problems had emerged during the "hungry forties"—most important among

them were public health or sanitary science and juvenile delinquency or reformatory science—which dealt with partial aspects of poverty and the poor. The development of these fields
was related to the professionalization of certain groups, especially doctors and lawyers, who saw a public service image as
one way to establish their legitimacy.[5]

Mayhew, the roving journalist, was not a part of the delinquency profession, and in one notable case—the controversy over the Ragged
Schools—he did verbal combat with a leading representative of that
movement, Mary Carpenter.

Juvenile crime appears in its most extended social setting in Mayhew's
treatments of low lodging houses, vagrancy, and child street sellers, all in
London Labour, and in his critique of the Ragged Schools in the *Morning
Chronicle*, which was not reprinted in *London Labour*. In volume 4 of
London Labour John Binny exposed the modes of operation of criminals,
mostly adults: following Mayhew's lead, Binny included some oral histories that mention delinquency. But the book that contains Mayhew's
most direct observations about delinquency, *The Criminal Prisons of
London*, has no oral histories at all—at best only notes on very brief
interviews with inmates in the presence of prison authorities. Thus the
richest presentation of phenomena and the fullest theoretical analysis
appear in separate places in Mayhew's works, which may somehow account for the diremption between evidence and thought in his account of
delinquency. (On the other hand, this gap may be inevitable: even a book
with so deliberate a plan of relating theory to experience as *Manny: A
Criminal Addict's Story* (1977), by Rettig, Torres, and Garrett, does not
succeed in making a close fit.)

Mayhew's procedure in *The Criminal Prisons of London* partly
determined—or perhaps merely reflected—his general criminological position. He says he would have begun his examination of "The Great
World of London" with "Legal London," which would have been in his
view to start from the top and work down. But the courts were not always
in session, and apparently he did not have time or patience to wait on their
"periodical" character. Instead, he started at the bottom, with the criminal prisons of London, and worked up (*CP* 79): prisons certainly are
always in session! Had he begun with legal procedures, including ways of
acting on juvenile cases, he might have developed some notion of youth
rights. If he had studied "Professional London" (*CP* 64), he might have
run into white-collar crime. As it was, what Mayhew includes under
juvenile crime is manifest in what he accepts as having legitimately led to
the incarceration of a boy under seventeen in the Tothill Fields House of
Correction (for anywhere from seven days to two years).[6]

Having asked 194 boys in Tothill Fields why they were there, Mayhew
concludes that the majority had been arrested for picking pockets; steal-

ing metal was the next most prevalent offense; few were there for serious crimes such as burglary, housebreaking, or highway robbery; there were some "sneaks" who pilfered items from shops; a small group was present who had robbed their employers—these were "casual" as opposed to "habitual" offenders—and finally:

> there is a considerable number who are confined for offenses that not even the sternest-minded can rank as crime, but for which the committal to a felon's prison can but be regarded by every righteous mind, not only as an infamy to the magistrate concerned, but even as a scandal to the nation which permits the law-officers of the country so far to outrage justice and decency. To this class of offenses belong the spinning of tops, the breaking of windows, the heaving of stones, the sleeping in Kensington Gardens, getting over walls, and such like misdemeanors, for many of which . . . the lads were suffering their first imprisonment. [CP 420]

We have come to call these "status offenses," acts not considered criminal if done by an adult. Their allegedly offensive quality arises from the fact that the agent is a juvenile. Mayhew revealed that between 1850 and 1855 three thousand boys had been sent to prison for "throwing stones, obstructing highways, unlawful ringing and knocking at doors, etc.; matters surely for which it is unwise, if not unjust, to subject a child to the lasting disgrace, if not contamination, of a jail" (CP 396). Theft is the crime by male juveniles that Mayhew attends to most often and most seriously, since it was apparently the most widespread juvenile offense at the time. In terms of a more recent distinction, youth did not seem to have entered in conspicuous numbers into "retreatist" (abuse of drugs and alcohol) or "conflict" (fighting) groups.[7]

Mayhew's view was that delinquency among girls consisted mostly in prostitution, but this subject is exceedingly confused in his writings.[8] Although he discriminates religious sin, moral evil, and legal criminality (CP 383), although he does not include prostitution in his classification of crimes (CP 88–90), although London Labour states that the British legislature does not interfere with prostitution (LL 4:212), and although his reporting on the slop-working needlewomen showed that they were forced into prostitution by a new economic system, Mayhew nevertheless clearly places prostitutes in the class of the "voluntary non-workers, or professionally criminal class," along with vagrants, swindlers, cardsharps, embezzlers, beggars, cheats, and thieves. Some of these forcibly take property from others; others, such as prostitutes, "seduce the industrious to part with a portion of their gain" (LL 4:31–32) but may steal to support a pimp or to get caught and sent to prison so as to receive medical care or escape from an intolerable life, according to Mayhew.[9]

Prostitution consists in "putting a woman's charms to vile uses" (LL

4:36), Mayhew proclaims in his introduction to a long study of the field, which he said was made to determine whether moral disgust at this practice is a matter of taste or "a part of the inherent constitution of things." We are never offered an answer to this question; he published no further work on the subject. One wonders if the 183-page report on prostitution in forty-eight cultures, prepared by one Horace St. John and accompanied by illustrations of bare-breasted women, is really a necessary preamble to a presentation of prostitution in London in a volume on *London Labour and the London Poor* or whether, with or without Mayhew's approval, the publishers were piously exploiting the subject for increased sales. The first three volumes of the 1860s *London Labour* are remarkably free of sermonizing, but this fourth volume begins with a catalog of private agencies in London combating this vice, "to inspire hope and confidence in those who would shudder and lose heart in the perusal of such a record of crime and misery," as the publishers put it in their preface. Odd that the loftiest moralizing and the most definite suspicion of prurience arise in the same place. It is also interesting that when some of the material on prostitution first appeared in the 1851 issue of *London Labour,* the prostitution issues were priced at three pence but issues having to do with labor questions sold for only a penny "so that, appealing to a large body of operatives, the cost of the work may be suited to their means."[10] One of Mayhew's readers complained that publicizing prostitution might promote it; Mayhew disagreed, saying young girls needed to have put constantly before them the inevitable catastrophes that follow unchastity— the invariable "sequences of moral events"—in order to prevent vice. Thus the stories should be read by everyone, even though they cost more; at least they were cheaper when purchased in the "fascicular" form of booklets rather than as bound books, enabling the poor "to obtain expensive treaties by small installments."[11]

Other than discussing prostitution, Mayhew has little to say about female delinquents. There are fewer female than male offenders at all ages, though the proportion was changing toward more females, he said, as is also said today in the United States.

Causes of Juvenile Crime

In the development of theory and policy concerning delinquency, Mayhew occupies the sort of place the pre-Socratic philosophers hold in the history of Western thought: before academic institutions and elaborate theories were established, they took a crack at the problem. Almost every basic position ever proposed on the causes of crime appears somewhere in Mayhew's works, either as an explicit assertion or as a casual observation. Undoubtedly this is partly the result of his contact, as a reporter, with a multiplicity of cases calling for a variety of explanations.

Perhaps Mayhew's best observations about crime are the multitude of causal insights he tosses out, such as his remarks that apprentice chimney sweeps get into trouble because their work is over early in the day and that they make good burglars because they climb well (LL 2:398–99).

Mayhew's grasp extends from innate and physical dispositions, through absence of parental control, to transmission of delinquent values from one person to another, and finally to the criminogenic effects of legal institutions. He furnishes a spectrum (or hierarchy) of places for locating causes of crime that later criminologists would cover in more detail: Lombroso writing on the born criminal, Healy on the psychological effects of early family life, Shaw and Sutherland on "differential association," and, in our own day, authors pointing out the nefarious consequences of labeling people delinquent and the injustices of state agencies of justice. During the past one hundred years each of these specializations has left its mark on theory and practice about delinquents, giving the scene today something of that piled up, disordered appearance it had in Mayhew's works—a triumph for a cyclical, if not a cynical, view of history.

After beginning his analysis of juvenile crime in *The Criminal Prisons of London* with the numbers of juvenile offenders, Mayhew examines popular theories about the causes of juvenile delinquency by seeing if any of the alleged causes are in greatest evidence in the areas where delinquency rates are highest. He concludes that neither ignorance, nor density of population, nor poverty, nor vagrancy, nor the temptation of large masses of property, nor drunkenness, nor breach of the Sabbath, all measured in appropriate ways, can be the cause of juvenile crime (*CP* 381–83). He also refutes the notion that crime rates vary inversely with economic prosperity (*CP* 440). At this point one might expect Mayhew to rise above these errors toward a more enlightened view. Unfortunately, he slips back down.

Crime, he says, is due "simply to that innate love of a life of ease, and aversion to hard work, which is common to *all* natures, and which, when accompanied with lawlessness of disposition as well as a disregard for the rights of our fellow-creatures, and a want of self-dignity, can but end either in begging or stealing the earnings and possessions of others" (*CP* 386). Mayhew was much taken with the Report of the Constabulary Commissioners, published in 1839, declaring crime to "proceed from a disposition to acquire property with a less degree of labour than ordinary industry" (*CP* 84). Some men, he says, "are naturally of more erratic natures than others" (*CP* 384), a condition endemic in youth—"when human beings begin to assert themselves"—and some youths are of especially "indomitable natures who cannot or will not brook ruling, then become heedless of all authority, and respect no law but their own" (*CP*

384). These juveniles will probably commit crimes. "Their errors seem to have rather a physical than an intellectual or a moral cause. They seem to be naturally of an erratic and self-willed temperament, objecting to the restraints of home, and incapable of continuous application to any one occupation whatsoever" (LL 3:327).

This is like saying that opium has a dormitive virtue, or rather that opium has an awakening virtue, since Mayhew goes on to point out that criminal activity can imply discipline: "The great mass of crime is a trade and profession among us...practiced...regularly as honesty is pursued for the same purpose by others" (CP 413; cf. CP 452). (Cf. Peter Letkemann's Crime as Work, which includes first-person accounts of techniques of safecracking, victim confrontation, etc.)

Mayhew seems to take the word physical both in the sense of natural and in the sense of bodily: "the physical causes of crime...must be in some measure due to the bodily conformation of the individuals."[12] This could imply that a criminal nature, temperament, or disposition could be manifest in the offender's physical appearance. Of the costermongers, Mayhew says: "instinct with all the elements of manhood and beasthood, the qualities of the beast are principally developed in him" (LL 1:27). These "street-nomads," according to Mayhew, show a greater development of the jaw than of the head, which makes them similar to members of "primitive tribes" (LL 1:1). Looking around him in a juvenile prison, he is tempted to discover the infamous criminal look, since some of the boys "had such shamelessness and cunning printed on their features, that the mind was led insensibly towards fatalism, and to believe in criminal races as thoroughly as in cretin ones" (CP 402). But he also saw "frank and innocent-looking faces, that we could not help fancying had no business there" (CP 402). People tend to believe that moral and physical beauty are connected, but Mayhew goes on to deny this emphatically: "Crime is an effect with which the shape of the head and the form of the features appear (so far as our observation goes) to have no connection whatever—indeed it seems to us, in the majority of instances, to be the accident of parentage and organization" (CP 413). By "organization" he appears to mean the character the person is born with (cf. LL 1:348), certainly not community organization. Since Lombroso's theories, which took the position Mayhew here opposes, had not yet been published, Mayhew must have been rejecting a common belief that Lombroso later used to support his allegedly scientific theory. (See below, chap. 5.)

Mayhew most frequently invokes lack of parental control as the chief cause of delinquency: "Juvenile crime will be found to be due, like prostitution, mainly to a want of proper parental control" (CP 386–87). Tobias calls this a common theme throughout the century.[13] This arises, Mayhew proclaims, from the absence of either especially the father (CP

452) or especially the mother (*CP* 387): Mayhew seems not to understand the logic of the word *especially*. He comes closest to explicitly linking delinquency to economic conditions when he complains about the "artificial state of society" (the high prices of food and shelter) that forces a mother to leave home to work (*CP* 387). Or the child may be an orphan and wander about the streets. *Proper* control is lacking when the parents are either too strict or mean, or too indulgent or negligent. In Mayhew's day a large number of young people ran away from home, often from solid middle-class or even upper-class homes, to escape oppression or to find excitement. Other children were born into families of thieves and kept up the family tradition, or were forced into the streets to support their families and there turned to crime (*LL* 1:39).

> Parental instruction; the comforts of a home, however
> humble—the great moral truths upon which society itself
> rests;—the influence of proper example; the power of educa-
> tion; the effect of useful amusement; are all denied to them, or
> come to them so greatly vitiated, that they rather tend to in-
> crease, than to repress, the very evils they were intended to
> remedy. [*LL* 1:537]

Despite Mayhew's rejecting poverty as the cause of crime "in the abstract," he uses it to explain why so great a proportion of Irish youths are delinquent, noting that because of their families' poverty they are sent into the streets and lack parental supervision (*CP* 387–403).

Though Mayhew often declares that the family is the cause of juvenile delinquency, his studies of broader social phenomena are filled with observations connecting them with delinquency. Chief among these is vagrancy: "That vagrancy is the nursery of crime, and that the habitual tramps are first beggars then thieves, and finally convicts of the county, the evidence of all parties goes to prove" (*CP* 43). In other places Mayhew labels vagrancy *itself* a crime, like prostitution, that consists in getting the more industrious members of society (through charity agencies) to support the more indolent (*CP* 90).[14] The dull vagrant boy, in Mayhew's scenario, "sinks into a mere beggar," while "the acuter and more daring lad, step by step, becomes the expert thief."[15] Mayhew devoted more space to vagrancy than to any other subject in the *Morning Chronicle* series, since he believed it to be "the source of the principal part of crime of the country."[16] And vagrancy "*is largely due* to, and indeed, chiefly maintained by the low lodging-houses," cheap hostels where delinquents initiate newcomers into their evil ways (*LL* 3:388).

Mayhew also pointed to two other places where delinquency developed: the Ragged Schools and the houses of correction themselves. The Ragged Schools had been started in London in the 1840s by private philanthropists on the assumption that teaching street children to read and write would make them less likely to become or remain delinquent. Apparently this was not viewed, as today, as a "survival skill" necessary to apply for and hold a job; ignorance itself was thought to somehow cause crime. In his articles in the March 1850 issues of the *Morning Chronicle,* Mayhew revealed that delinquency rates did not decrease in the area of the Ragged Schools; they increased. However, more delinquents could read and write (barely) than ever before! Mayhew accounted for some of the increase in juvenile crime by what he heard from outside observers of the schools as well as from the students themselves. They were generally rowdy places, and "about half the boys at the school were thieves" (*LL* 2:176). The Ragged Schools provided habitual thieves a warm place to meet, convenient to their haunts, and gave them the opportunity to attract new boys to their depredations. The same people attended these schools that inhabited the cheap lodging houses.[17]

Mayhew vigorously condemned prisons as nurseries of crime, where children were sent for "offenses" much less serious than the ones they learned while imprisoned. Work in prison was presented so much as a punishment and disgrace, he felt, that young people might never develop the attitude toward working necessary for social adaptation. They might even find prison less hazardous than the street and prefer to stay there (*LL* 1:174).

> True, the place is called a house of correction; but, rightly viewed, it is simply a criminal preparatory school, where students are qualified for matriculating at Millbank or Pentonville. Here we find little creatures of six years of age branded with a felon's badge—boys, not even in their teens, clad in the prison dress, for the heinous offense of throwing stones, or obstructing highways, or unlawfully knocking at doors—crimes which the very magistrates themselves, who committed the youths, must have assuredly perpetrated in their boyhood, and which, if equally visited, would consign almost every child in the kingdom to a jail. [*CP* 406; cf. *CP* 408]

Today we speak of "labeling" rather than "branding," but we make the same point. What this shows, Mayhew says, is "that juvenile crime is not *always* begotten by bad or no parental care, but springs frequently from a savage love of consigning people to prison for faults that cannot even be classed as immoral, much less criminal" (*CP* 420). Of course this was not a new observation. John Howard had proclaimed in 1777:

> If it were the wish and aim of magistrates to effect the destruction present and future of young delinquents, they could not devise a more effectual method, than to confine them so long in

our prisons, those seats and seminaries . . . of idleness and
every vice.[18]

This quotation was used by Edwin Sutherland in 1934 to make the same
point once again.

What Mayhew's Oral Histories Show

Mayhew claimed he "had no theory to advocate" concerning juvenile
crime.[19] In the sense of a monolithic system, he had none; in the sense of
an emphatic pluralism, his claim is inaccurate, and it is inaccurate too in
that he gave one alleged cause of delinquency more weight than
others—lack of parental control. Although Mayhew used statistics to re-
fute several popular notions about the causes of crime, he did nothing to
prove his assertions about the family background of delinquents, and in
any event words like "proper" as applied to "parental control" make the
explanation circular. His position seems to be based on his observation of
the great numbers of young people who ran away from their homes and
drifted into petty theft. It was also a popular notion at the time—and has
been ever since. But it was clear that not all runaways became thieves.
The evidence Mayhew does provide, and the evidence anyone else has
ever provided, yields no one certain cause. But what do the oral histories
make evident?

A greater cause of delinquency seems to be a youth's living in a
place—a cheap lodging house, a Ragged School, or a prison—where he or
she meets delinquents who encourage or bully him or her into joining
them. In this context Mayhew invokes the notion that crime is a "contagion," another commonplace of his day. Nor was the view that criminality passes from one person to another a new hypothesis: Democritus
said in the fifth century B.C.: "Continuous association with base men
increases a disposition to crime."[20] In the twentieth century this has been
elaborated as the theory of "differential association." Is this a bias in
delinquents' oral histories?

After all, it would be impossible for a speaker to give direct evidence in
an oral history of a vicious *nature,* since only manifestations—
appearances—of that nature, even if it exists, can possibly come out in
personality and action. Nor could we expect anyone but a Jerome Cardan
to lay bare his own hereditary or bodily peculiarities. Further, there
seems to be little predilection on the part of the youths Mayhew interviewed to speak at any length about their family experiences, which may
have been too painful to recall or may have seemed irrelevant to their
efforts at personal independence. What was more current, fresher in their
minds, more exciting to recall were those *friendships* or peer associations

they first made when they went out into the world on their own. And this is what delinquents tended to emphasize in Mayhew's oral histories.

There is also a bias against explicit political meaning in Mayhew's oral histories of juvenile offenders, for most youths, even the more sophisticated ones in so politically aware a period as today, cannot link their experiences with systems of power that transcend them; even professional sociologists can barely do this. Mayhew observed that the eight-year-old girl who sold watercress in the streets of London "knew no more of London than that part she had seen on her rounds" (*LL* 1:157). "As to the opinions of the street-children I can say little. For the most part they have formed no opinions of anything beyond what affects their daily struggle for bread. Of politics such children can know nothing. [They are] in general honest haters of the police and of most constituted authorities" (*LL* 1:531).

But the collector and interpreter of oral histories neglects this dimension, too. If the cheap lodging houses were places where juvenile crime was generated, then a way to reduce such crime would be to eliminate or change those places. They were not charitable institutions: people paid to stay there, and they made considerable profits for their owners, according to one of Mayhew's informants (*LL* 1:455). *Who owned them?* Mayhew, the reporter who exposed clothing establishments that contributed to the misery of workers by the slop system, failed to find out the identities of the reputable gentlemen on their country estates living off the profits from these dens of iniquity. (We shall also find neglect of political factors in the early Chicago sociologists. In more recent sociology, which is brimming with analysis of power systems, we shall find few oral histories in criminology.)

Indeed, Mayhew missed an opportunity to connect his article on vagrancy and juvenile crime to the economic analyses he had made of sweated labor during the previous two months in the *Morning Chronicle* or, for that matter, to any broader political or economic context at all: he does not relate delinquents' lives to the economic conditions of their parents.[21] In fact, as in comic strips with child characters, grown-ups seldom have a major role in these oral histories. Even the possibility of such a connection, suggested by the juxtaposition of topics in the newspaper series, vanished in *London Labour,* overwhelmed by the colorful street people. A view of delinquency as a result of the gap between desires for legitimate satisfactions and limited economic opportunities, a gap that might be closed by illegitimate activity, is also missing from Mayhew. Apparently it was missing from the experience of the youths themselves, who seem to have had no doubts about their place in the British class system, and no desire to rise. (In Mayhew's texts "rising" is most often mentioned in a theological context.) The life of a costerboy is hard, Mayhew says: he is concerned exclusively about his girl, his eating, and his gambling (*LL* 1:40). People steal because they are hungry or need a place to stay for the night. Once they learn to steal it becomes a habit. And that's that. Nor is there any sign that Mayhew foresaw the later explanation of delinquency using a concept of social disorganization, though a century later a commentator would find that the concept fit the contemporary scene well: "Those who came into the large towns [in the late 1840s] found themselves in a bewildering place, in which many of their former standards did not apply and in which they lacked the support of a small, cohesive community to which they were accustomed."[22]

Another of the delinquency topics that Mayhew omits although it later became fashionable among sociologists is juvenile gangs. That there were contemporary gangs is revealed by at least one passage in a *Morning Chronicle* oral history. (Oral history has the rather perverse potentiality of allowing a reader to give central attention to what the editor of a document may have thought peripheral, though interesting enough to include.) Mayhew's informant speaks of young vagrants who

> often come down to the casual wards in large bodies of twenty or thirty, with sticks hidden down the legs of the trousers, and with these they rob and beat those who do not belong to their own gang. The gang will often consist of 100 lads, all under twenty, one-fourth of whom regularly come together in a body; and in the casual ward they generally arrange where to meet again on the following night.[23]

According to Tobias: "Often enough, of course, the references to 'gangs' which are frequent in the literature are to casual partnerships of a few youngsters without any element of permanence or subordination. However, there were some gangs that can be properly so called."[24] After all, pickpockets had to work in at least a small gang because of the necessary division of labor: someone to distract the victim, someone to pick the pocket, and someone to act as decoy during the pursuit by police. But the extent and characteristics of gang wars are not shown: Mayhew covers neither that subject nor rape, despite the likelihood that rape took place amid the sexual goings-on in the lodging houses as reported in the oral histories.

One might reply that it is not fair to select a particular aspect of Mayhew's studies and find fault with it for not being comprehensive or coherent. Mayhew never considered delinquency his main subject. I have "criticized" Mayhew's oral histories only in the sense of determining their limits. It will become clear that his lack of conceptual cogency is not so very different from that of other writers who have used oral histories of delinquents but have made delinquency a more central concern.

Mayhew's Accomplishments

Activating all the powers of oral history set forth in chapter 1, Mayhew accomplished what? Thompson says that at its peak, which it reached shortly after starting and held for three months, the *Morning Chronicle* series "seized public interest in a way which has scarcely ever been equalled in British journalism."[25] Other writers quoted the series and undertook their own investigations. "Editors and M.P.s, economists and Christian Socialists, Philanthropists and Chartists, argued about his findings."[26] According to Humpherys, the interviews themselves captured the attention of the public who read the series.[27] How many people read it? At the end of 1854 the circulation of the newspaper was only about 2,500,[28] and it was probably no more than 5,000 at the height of its popularity while Mayhew was publishing.

Bradley reports that the *London Labour* project "gave impetus to the social amelioration which slowly advanced as the age itself moved forward."[29] But the immediate effect of Mayhew's exposures was predictable: the establishment moved to protect itself against blame or the prospect of change. Mayhew says that "denouncing institutions that were admitted by all to have been designed and sustained by the purest and most benevolent feelings caused [him] no little pain."[30] More painful still to him must have been the response: after the articles on the Ragged Schools appeared, "we·were pelted with dirt from every evangelical assembly throughout the Metropolis" (*CP* 390). At the conclusion of these articles, even before a complaint had been received from the secretary of the Ragged Schools Union, the newspaper itself added a note crowning the schools as "the beginning of the greatest of all social reforms," with any failures attributable neither to principle nor to personnel but to "external conditions" (the very conditions the schools were supposed to be changing).[31] The newspaper editor suggests that the schools need to be supplemented with a plan for emigration of the excess population. He made this proposal because it was the hobbyhorse of the newspaper's owners; they had also recommended it as the way to alleviate the plight of the needlewomen, opposing Mayhew's proposal to enact protectionist legislation against unregulated competition. One of the difficulties that arise in publishing Mayhew's sort of material is that publishers generally belong to the very social classes one may be calling to task.

While donations sent to Mayhew for distribution might relieve an individual briefly, Mayhew did not believe in charity, because it gives people the notion that they can obtain money without working for it and in any case is not a "systematic" remedy. It is likely that one who has been personally involved in collecting personal histories that have implications for action will initiate some sort of action himself. Mayhew tried to start a group of parolees and to organize workingmen into trade unions: one source of his oral history material was the meetings called for this purpose. (Compare this with Clifford Shaw's obtaining life histories through his community organizations.) Mayhew founded the Friendly Association of London Costermongers for the following purposes: to establish a fund for sickness and old age, a savings bank, and a loan fund; to promote the use of accurate scales; to acquire legal counsel; to provide harmless rather than pernicious amusements, especially for the children; and to provide free education (*LL* 1:105–6). He also helped establish a Mutual Pension Society and a Mutual Investment Society along self-help lines. He proposed that the rich devise ways the poor could use their own talents to help themselves (*LL* 2:264), but he did not go so far as Clifford Shaw to organize a program along these lines. According to Mayhew, "The political character and sentiments of the working class appear to me to be a distinctive feature of the age, and they are a necessary consequence of the dawning intelligence of the mass" (*LL* 3:243). Mayhew doubtless raised the consciousness of some of the workers he associated with, adding to the progressive trend of the times. But he had no more definite or striking effect: there is no evidence that his "friendly association" or the parolees association came to anything.

One of Mayhew's most definite influences was on other writing. Bradley and Humpherys mention several novelists and social investigators who followed Mayhew's example.[32] We can add to that list Studs Terkel, for whom Mayhew has been a model, as I noted at the outset. Thompson says that one effect of Mayhew's work was to whet the appetite of the rich for further acquaintance with the poor, preferably for entertaining information "using the poor as grist for the literary mill."[33] That is to say, talk produces more talk. Oral histories *purge* pity and fear, but they do not necessarily lead to the action they seem to cry out for, as might a simple pamphlet or broadside announcing a mass meeting. Mayhew tried to be a statistical atomist, an oratorical oral historian, and a social system-builder, but the *writer* won out over all of these. As for Mayhew's use of oral history after *London Labour*, there was none.

Did Mayhew accomplish anything regarding delinquency? He said he hoped that "more earnest and philosophical experiments [would] be tried in connection with the reformation of our young convicts" (*CP* 396). But he did not say what they would be. Like Studs Terkel, he held that work should be made pleasurable, perhaps as enjoyable as it was for him. He recommended industrial training for delinquents and often called for the state or "society" to take responsibility for reforming "young outcasts" (*LL* 1:524; cf. 414–15). Perhaps Mayhew's calling attention to these problems was part of a movement to increase social services: of the thirty-eight organizations in London in 1860 for the benefit of delinquents, sixteen were founded in 1800–1850, eighteen in 1850–60.[34] As for the Ragged Schools, Tobias says:

> Though Mayhew has some justification for what he wrote, the Ragged Schools probably did good on balance. They provided education for those who would otherwise have received it only in jail. The teachers took an interest in those in whom no one else was interested. They had kind words for those for whom most other people had only harsh words or blows. It was probably from this social side of their work that the main benefits came.[35]

After all, Mayhew had not studied a cross section of the hundred or so Ragged Schools in England, and it has been suggested that he overstated his case because of an earlier controversy with one of the schools' patrons.

By the late 1850s the crime rate in England had begun to drop: "The criminal youngsters whom Henry Mayhew saw in the 1850s were virtually the last of the long line. There continued to be small pockets in the towns where such children lived, but Charles Booth and his associates in the 1880s and 90s did not find rookeries of the type Mayhew saw."[36] Tobias reports that many saw this drop in delinquency as a result of the reformatories, industrial schools, and Ragged Schools that had been set up in the 1840s and 1850s, "and this seems an inescapable conclusion."[37] However, Tobias apparently escapes this conclusion, since he elsewhere states: "Though the reformatory schools helped to inaugurate the change, the real explanation is to be found in the improvement of conditions of life in the country as a whole."[38] In fact, Tobias finds most appropriate the explanation that W. I. Thomas and Clifford Shaw would later give:

> To some extent the pace of change had slowed down, and the children of the towns were to a much greater extent living in the sort of world in which their parents had lived and were to a much greater extent prepared for the sort of life they had to lead.[39]

Mayhew's accomplishment might have been a generalized critique of institutions dealing with juvenile delinquents: he had the spirit and experience to have realized how shot through with contradictions are private and public social programs. His own study of the juvenile prisons should have made him wary of any government move, just as the counter-productiveness of some of the Ragged Schools might have raised caution flags on any private, voluntary effort. He could have provided an invaluable service by casting a skeptical eye on the rush toward reform and institutionalization. But his virtue was in presenting actualities, and the defects in "doing good" in those early days had not yet come fully to light.

Reforms concerning delinquency that Mayhew urged are remarkably like those that reformers are still urging: alternatives to detention, respect for parolees,[40] job training, and so forth. Thus Mayhew had no permanent revolutionary effect. He lived by the image and died by the image. He did not even have literary historians to keep his works alive as they have preserved the fiction of Dickens. Concerning economic issues of his day, Eileen Yeo has written: "He did not have the colossal intellectual equipment of a Marx, necessary to mount a successful attack. He had to make his forays sporadically in weekly installments and this could not lead to thoroughness, profundity, or even consistency."[41] Marx, of course, did not employ oral histories: for one thing, he was not trying to communicate to the upper classes, who are in the grip of underlying forces not subject to persuasion. For another, the conditions of the lives of laborers in a capitalistic system were obvious enough to members of the Party so that oral histories were irrelevant, as they later were for Saul Alinsky after he had begun a career as a "professional radical" (see below, chap. 9). Training converts seemed to require techniques more laden with ideology than oral histories usually are. To borrow a metaphor from classical rhetoric, Marx's analysis was the closed fist of dialectic, while Mayhew's writing was the open hand of rhetoric.

In Mayhew's "Great World of London," no assimilation of contraries (rich and poor, unconcerned and concerned) takes place, no new place, no alternate system is worked out; instead, *communication* is intended to occur between the contraries, a comprehensive *view* is presented, not a comprehensive set of concepts that revolutionaries could use as a goal and guide. For lasting effect a *bible* is needed, not an ephemeral journal, even if articles are later bound into a book. For Mayhew, "system" meant an arrangement of procedures, not an overarching network of political powers; he pointed to ultimate sources of power, but he did not explore them directly. He detested "theoreticians,"[42] but he was stuck in happenings, in oral histories, in the particular Victorian audience he was addressing. E. P. Thompson has said: "It was forty years after 1849 before the middle class consciousness of poverty was discovered again."[43] The force of the images he set out vanished as soon as those images passed from the sight of his audience, until other writers, confronting new audiences, revived much the same set of images and, like Sisyphus, again pushed the boulder up the hill only to see it roll back again. Ironically, Mayhew might have accomplished more for human life if he had not communicated and preserved the lives of individuals but transcended them by working with more abstract, impersonal, and systematic ideas, or at least with concrete proposals. However, having seen the futile or counterproductive results of one proposal after another concerning juvenile delinquency during the past hundred years, perhaps I should end this appropriately ambivalent judgment on Mayhew with praise for his wisdom in keeping hands off.

Delinquency and the Journalist

Juvenile delinquency has been a recurring topic of journalists since Mayhew, but oral histories have been used in only one other case I know of: Benjamin Fine's *1,000,000 Delinquents,* published in 1955, when Fine was education editor of the *New York Times.*[44] A farmer's son, Fine began his training in agriculture and animal husbandry in the 1920s, and later, at Cornell, he developed an interest in journalism. In 1941 he received a Ph.D. from Columbia University with a dissertation "College Publicity in the United States," and his main field of interest was American schools. Thus he was marginal to professional criminology, which by the 1950s was no longer using "life histories" as it had done so often during the 1920s and 1930s (see below, chaps. 6–8).[45] (One motive for using oral histories could be for a "nonexpert" to let the "expert"—the offender—present the facts.) In ways other than his marginality, Fine's outlook is remarkably similar to Mayhew's writing about delinquency.

Fine wrote amid a "tragic upswing" in juvenile crime, and his title dramatized the extent of the problem. (Cf. the Gluecks' *500 Delinquent Women* and *One Thousand Juvenile Delinquents,* titles that indicate the numbers of persons directly studied.) Although Fine was a newspaper reporter, his first chapter, "Headlines and Facts," states: "We must look beyond the front-page news, now shouting daily from every state in the nation, and ask ourselves one all-embracing question: *Why did they do it?*" (p. 29). Fine got inside the problem by interviewing fifteen hundred delinquents "in public and private training schools, in the courtrooms, and in their own backyards" (foreword). He asked delinquent boys and girls to write down their stories, to tell him why they thought they had gotten into trouble. "The most vivid picture of delinquency is presented by the children themselves; their stories define delinquency in a way that is frightening and clarifying at the same time—and, moreover, in a way that is very, very real" (p. 32). Spelling and punctuation are preserved from the originals: "The way these children express themselves, the way they write and spell, is peculiarly their own" (p. 39). Only names and places were changed to protect individuals' privacy.

Though Fine's oral histories remain for the most part in the region of external events, occasionally infused with expressions of anguish, they do accomplish one task he clearly wanted them to accomplish—they give the impression that those one million delinquents are human beings: "The normal and the delinquent child possess the same basic drives and feelings . . . the only difference between the two is that, while the normal individual has gained control over his impulses, the delinquent child expresses his aggression in overt acts" (pp. 52–53). "A juvenile delinquent is not simply a thief, or a murderer, or a vandal; he is a troubled human being who steals or destroys as a result of pressures both within and without" (p. 51).

Fine recommends taking a "holistic attitude" toward delinquents, considering them from the viewpoints of medicine, psychiatry, anthropology, sociology, economics, and so forth (p. 339), in order to capture that "complex combination of traits that make each child unique" (p. 127). However, Fine himself leans rather more heavily on two viewpoints than on the others—the psychological and the social reformist. "The lasting answer is more psychiatric help and less switch and slipper" (p. 142), and less talk about cutting out a part of someone's brain (p. 154). He emphasizes the importance of "that bit of kindness and sympathy that is so badly needed when one is in trouble" (p. 293). "There is no delinquent boy—only an emotionally disturbed child . . . there is no 'bad' girl—only an unhappy one" (foreword). Thus the family comes in for a good deal of attention. But the real culprit, according to Fine, is "society": "If Billy 'goes wrong,' the finger of blame can be pointed in just one direction: at society—at you and me—for having given him no chance to 'go right' " (p. 105). At the end of one oral history Fine asks rhetorically: "Will society help him? He cannot help himself alone" (p. 45). (Of course, *society* here means simply the *audience* the journalist is addressing.)

Through much of his text it is not clear what particular action Fine is recommending. He makes statements such as: "There is no finer crusade for us to follow" (p. 354). Or, more definitely but even more sweepingly, he says: "In spite of the complexities, it is clear that the slum must go, that gangs must be deflected from their devastating activities" (p. 99). But, when he gets around to giving examples of specific programs, these are community-based, often "spearheaded by the public school system" (p. 179), his own field of expertise. The local community organizations should include "all adult members of every community" (p. 130)— unfortunately, an unlikely prospect. "The control must come from the local community, although the support and the guidance should, in most cases, come from state and federal governments" (p. 349). We have already seen this commonplace of local autonomy in Mayhew, and it will also be found in other criminologists who have used oral histories of delinquents. Fine gives the standard arguments about the need to divert most delinquents away from formal institutions, such as that community-based alternatives are cheaper. He even shows some appreciation for the fact of interagency rivalry (p. 227). When he writes about these programs, he does not quote youths but rather reports the opinions of experts.

Lest we forget what Fine's book and humanistic criminology are up against, consider another book on delinquency that was written four years later by another journalist, Len O'Connor: *They Talked to a Stranger*. O'Connor later became a well-known Chicago author and television news commentator. He is, of course, the "stranger" of the title, and "they" are ten boys, referred to as "the First Boy," "the Second Boy," and so forth, as well as by snappy nicknames such as "Mustache," "Mr. Slick," "Joy Ride," "One-Arm," "the Champ," and so forth. No oral histories are included. Interviews are reported in dialogue form, expressing the boys' contempt, insolence, and cynicism. The interviews took place in tense, pressured situations: the first occurred soon after a boy who had killed a policeman was apprehended and brought back to the police station. The dramatic tensions there may well be imagined!

In the introduction Senator Paul H. Douglas compliments O'Connor for getting at "the deeper realities of environment, motives, and aims" (p. ix), but O'Connor does no such thing. The interviews never transcend a sense of the boy being grilled, a mild form of the third degree, or at best a jousting match between two wise guys. O'Connor is preoccupied with scenes in jails, police stations, and prisons; he has much more admiration for detectives than sympathy for "young punks"; he agrees with a United States Senate committee report that "pornography is a constant concomitant of delinquency" (p. 246); and he complains that delinquents have "almost total non-rapport with the good and a corresponding rapport with evil" (p. 70). This latter "paradox" is to him, he says, "the question penologists and psychiatrists must resolve." Thus O'Connor gives almost no support for community-based programs or for forms of social change, though in routine journalistic fashion a few authorities are briefly quoted recommending neighborhood clubs and warning against stigmatizing young people. O'Connor's own opinion about delinquents is that they "have a twisted, distorted view of life, certainly" (p. 249). "You may have felt a kind of horror as you read the cold, brittle comments of young criminals" (p. 248). For what purpose did O'Connor send all this out to the public? Even if one agreed with these attitudes, surely one would have to admit that these stereotypes are widespread enough among the American public without authors' exploiting and reinforcing them.

Three

John Clay and the "Cell Confessional"

Prison Reports

During the eighteenth century an English convict was more likely to be put to death, even for a minor offense, or to be shipped off to a British colony than he was to be imprisoned for any length of time.[1] The first two might have been preferable to confinement in one of the hellholes visited by John Howard in the 1770s and Elizabeth Fry in the early 1800s. These two reformers, among others, had little effect on the system. But as the death penalty was curtailed, as colonies began to refuse British felons, and as the crime rate in England rose amid increasing urbanization and population growth, old prisons were filled and new ones constructed. In this context agitation for systematic prison reform increased. One of the leaders was John Clay (1796–1858), chaplain of the jail at Preston in northern England, one of the little towns surrounding Manchester that Engels described in his study of the English worker in the 1840s.

Under the assumption that religion would convert convicts, pastors had been admitted to English jails, but they had not spent much time there. John Clay's son Walter Lowe Clay, in his biography of his father, wrote that in the last quarter of the eighteenth century "any needy priest of damaged character was thought good enough to minister among rogues" (*PC* 107). "To perform a single service on the Sunday, and to attend condemned criminals in their cells and at the gallows, constituted the whole duty of the spiritual power of a prison" (*PC* 102). In the late eighteenth century, legislation had begun slowly to improve the status of the prison chaplain, but it was not until the Gaol Act of 1823 that prisons were authorized to hire and pay a full-time person for this position. In *Religion in Prison*, J. Arthur Hoyles states: "The man who was responsible more than anyone else for defining the chaplain's position in a prison was the Rev. John Clay . . . . It would almost be true to call him the patron saint of prison chaplains."[2]

Unfortunately, almost no scholarly attention has been devoted to Clay. The most ample source of information is the biography his son wrote as a memorial. W. L. Clay is not given to idolatry; this book is often quoted as an authority on early nineteenth-century penology. But neither is he given to criticizing his father. In the absence of more independent research, one should be wary of accepting any of the following as a final judgment on John Clay, yet the available material is adequate to sketch one more variety of context in which delinquents' oral histories have come into being.

The 1823 Gaol Act stipulated that the chaplain should submit an annual report to the local magistrates in charge of the institution—"a statement of the conditions of the prisoners, and his observations thereupon," to quote the act (PC 123). Clay filed his first report in 1824, apparently the kind of perfunctory statement that other prison chaplains continued to write years later; Clay did not even keep a copy of it. But he soon hit his own stride. His son writes that the report for the following year "contained not only some wholesome criticism on the discipline of the prison, but also a careful condensation of a year's diligent observation on the nature of crime" (PC 123). Clay's writing soon began to be reprinted in newspapers, in government reports, and in pamphlets and books. Until he resigned in 1858 owing to ill health, Clay used these publications to make the public aware of the causes of crime and to attract support for his scheme of prison reform—the "separate system," whereby inmates were confined to individual cells to prevent moral contagion. This was partly justified as a way of keeping younger offenders (or worse, juvenile defendants before trial) separated from older convicts, since every sort of detainee from the area was sent to this provincial jail. When it became clear that solitary confinement was less beneficial for young people than it appeared to be for adults, Clay threw his reformist energies into support of reformatory schools for juvenile offenders.

From 1825 on, Clay "set himself to study, through the prisoners, the habits, characters, wants, temptations, and vices of the masses from which they were drawn. Many years passed before he learnt how to work this mine in the easiest way; but in 1839 he caught at a hint thrown out by the Constabulary Force Commissioners, and began the practice of inviting specimen prisoners to write or dictate the stories of their lives" (PC 128). The hint Clay caught at was on page 26 of the "Report of the Commissioners on the Best Means of Establishing an Effective Constabulary Force in the Counties of England and Wales," presented in March 1839:

> We submit the following extracts from the confession obtained by the Rev. Mr. Bagshaw from a delinquent aged nineteen, recently removed as a convict from the gaol at Salford. Though the delinquent's character and adventures were peculiar, his career of depredation may be adduced as an instance characteristic of a career common to many others. The answers were given to a set of fixed interrogatories which we had prepared for guiding the course of similar inquiries, in cases

where we had no means of attending and conducting them personally. (See appendix No. 5.) From our partial experience under this Commission we are satisfied that similar inquiries, instituted after conviction, would serve as a means of obtaining highly valuable information for the prevention of crime and the advancement of the general objects of penal justice: and we are prepared to recommend that express arrangements be made for the purpose.

The report quotes the testimony of magistrates and public authorities; accounts by offenders themselves are included as if they were testifying to the commissioners, but the commissioners themselves apparently did not want to hold meetings in prison and thus used material collected by prison chaplains. The report "comprehends the examinations of numerous witnesses of every rank and class in society down to the confessions of criminals."[3] Most of these "confessions" are rendered in the words of the original speaker, some of them are rather long, and a few of the speakers are youths. But these documents contain only reports of crimes and other external or quantified items, obtained by what we would call an "interview schedule" of seventy-one questions and put together to form a continuous narrative. Nothing of an offender's early life, personality, or social circumstances is explored other than the immediate setting of a criminal offense. Like Edwin Sutherland's *The Professional Thief, by a Professional Thief* one hundred and two years later, these documents emphasize the "career of depredation, and the descriptions of their associates."[4]

The purpose of this parliamentary report was to recommend the establishment of a professional police force supported by public funds, to replace the private watch services then still widely in existence. Oral history material from criminals was included to inform the public what it was up against and thus show the need for police departments. From this perspective it was most gratifying to hear migratory thieves say they stayed away from cities that had such police forces. One of the curious features of this report is the commissioners' apprehension that their disclosure of inadequate police protection might incite people to commit crimes, since they held that a main element in the cause of crime is the criminal's belief that he will not be caught. (Clearly this concern that oral histories will reveal secret information appropriately arises only to the extent that they contain information about criminal techniques, rather than expressions of particular lives, which can hardly be learned.) The commissioners' answer to this objection was that the criminal as well as a "far larger proportion of the lower classes" knew very well "the absence of proper preventive means," knew it far better than a two-hundred-page report purchased at Her Majesty's Stationery Office would ever tell them.

"It is the honest portion of the community only who are in ignorance, who require to be put on guard and convinced of the necessity of taking effective measures for the abatement of the evil." What was needed was a "better knowledge of the habits and practices of the classes to be guarded against."[5] To that end, the commissioners "received the most complete and explicit statements of their own habits from the depredators themselves, made to clergymen who have obtained their confidence and carefully interrogated them."[6]

The role of the clergyman in obtaining this material and the concept of crime as sin determined the application of the category of *confession* to these autobiographical acts, a term Mayhew rarely used. (If in Mayhew oral history is burlesque gone straight, in Clay it is a religious act used for secular reform.) It appears that John Clay was not the only prison chaplain taking statements from inmates. A contemporary of Clay's, Mary Carpenter, quotes a Sheriff Barclay as saying, "Let a boy tell his own story, taken at random from many similar ones to be found in the prison reports."[7] Brief quotations from criminals were commonplace in government reports in England during the nineteenth century.[8] But there is reason to believe that only Clay explored the individual's life beyond the event of his crime, or at least only Clay published such material. If others heard, they did not write down, or if they wrote down they did not think significant those expressions that gave a larger picture of an offender's life than the offense alone. If anyone but Clay had done this, at least before the 1850s, it is likely that Mary Carpenter would have quoted him in her books about juvenile delinquency, but she used only Clay's histories. Carpenter was perhaps the most influential nongovernment individual working to set up schools for the lower classes in England, including reformatory schools, and it is mainly through her work that Clay's oral histories had an impact in the field of juvenile delinquency.

The Prison Chaplain

As a youth John Clay received a commercial education to prepare him to be a clerk in a mercantile office, which he entered at age fifteen. After a few years this business failed, as did the next mercantile house he worked in, leaving him "at the age of twenty-one without employment, and under the necessity of beginning life over again" (*PC* 3). A friend recommended that he take holy orders, and he began reading privately with the headmaster of the Preston Grammar School. Throughout his life Clay was self-taught, like Mayhew. In August 1821 the post of assistant chaplain at the Preston House of Correction was unexpectedly offered to him. Although "there was no precedent for accepting a prison chaplaincy as a title to orders" (*PC* 8), he was ordained a priest in 1822. A month after passage of the Gaol Act in 1823, Clay was appointed full-time chaplain, a post he would not have accepted had there been an alternative (*PC* 101). His son says: "The Gaol Act, under which he was appointed to the sole chaplaincy, virtually called into existence a new office.... He had no exemplar to follow; no traditions of Gaol chaplaincies to guide him; he had not only to perform, but also to find his work" (*PC* 109).

John Clay was a pioneer, and he was also another instance of the "marginal worker," someone who does not fit into a conventional social slot: in both background and character he differed from the prison chaplains of his day. He had not been given the classical education that was normal for a clergyman, and his situation in a provincial jail enabled him to prolong his separation from institutionalized religion: "I am thankful that my isolated position as a gaol-chaplain, saves me from the danger of religious partisanship" (*PC* 577). On the contrary, Clay kept up with the latest scientific discoveries and evinced an experimental frame of mind: "At the time when there was so much talk about demonstrating the rotation of the earth by the motion of a pendulum, he hung an enormous pendulum in one of the prison corridors to test the assertions of the newspapers himself" (*PC* 584). He was interested in languages, elocution, and speech, and he spent his leisure time learning modern languages. He founded and lectured at the Preston Literary Institute and was an amateur actor.

Clay's chief character trait seems to have been "his almost womanly kindness," as his son put it (*PC* 116). "In every case that came before him, he searched with eagerness for some means of doing a judicious kindness. He would bring news from home to the prisoners, and write, or take in person, their messages back" (*PC* 116). Though this may not sound impressive today, not many years before this time men's backs had been broken on the wheel and people were locked away to rot rather than allowing them an appeal that would send them back to court, where they might give the judges "jail fever."

All this being the case, it may come as a surprise to hear that the gentle Clay's radical reform scheme was to put all prison inmates in solitary confinement. But three points should be made to put this in context. First, this system was proposed as an alternative to the notorious prison yard, where young and old, male and female, the convicted and those as yet untried were thrown together. Clay said: "The child of 14, or 10, or even 8 years old, is now turned into a yard or 'day-room' tenanted by forty or fifty older criminals" (*PC* 143). Rehabilitation or "reformation" could get no foothold where experienced convicts would not only bully anyone who showed an interest in reforming but also instruct the less experienced in criminal techniques and make plans for crimes to commit upon release. Hoyles has pointed out that separate cells also gave the individual privacy.[9] Before Clay's time, severe discipline, including gruesome torture, was often accompanied by a total lack of order inside a prison, especially when a jailer made his living by payments from inmates for his services, such as providing prostitutes. (Before the full-time chaplaincy was established, jailers had begun to be paid by the state.)

Second, Clay did not invent this prison system, though he was a chief spokesman for its adoption in England. Although cellular confinement had antecedents in the monasteries, the separate system is usually traced back to the Pennsylvania Quakers in the 1770s, who recommended it as a way of making prisons an acceptable alternative to the death penalty, which they opposed. The "silent system," where prisoners worked or ate in groups but were not allowed to talk (at one English prison inmates even wore masks so they would not be able to recognize each other—the extreme of depersonalization), and the "separate system," where people were locked in separate cells, usually with a Bible, and never saw anyone, the better to meditate on their sins (hence "penitentiary"), were widely debated in England and America during the first half of the nineteenth century.

Third, while accepting the separate system as the only promising "experiment" (*PC* 275) for rehabilitation efforts—or at least for the prevention of further crime caused by the prison itself—Clay modified this scheme in the direction of greater humaneness. Some people (though apparently none at Preston), isolated from all human contact over long periods had gone insane or killed themselves: the mind would become "languid and listless with the dreary monotony of the cell" (*PC* 197). In Clay's modified separate system, "prisoners were permitted to see each other at exercise, at divine service, and, after a little consideration, at school" (*PC* 332). "In the school, the men met in open classes, and were not locked up in boxes, as in other cellular prisons.... Great care was taken to make the lessons so interesting, short, and infrequent, as to ensure their being enjoyed and prized" (*PC* 198). Eventually other prisons also made these modifications, but whatever therapeutic power the system had must have depended on the character of those who operated it: when the staff were not humane the separate system was nothing but a form of mental torture.

Like other critics of penal policy in his day, Clay recommended that if the only alternative were to send youths to a prison where they would mix with other offenders, it would be better to give them a flogging behind the police station and set them free (*PC* 136 n). "Community corrrections" with a vengeance! Once a young person has entered a prison, as juvenile officers claim even today, the deterrent fear of the place is diminished for that person (*PC* 138). For repeat juvenile offenders Clay came to realize that solitary confinement for more than a month was not effective; the cell did not have "those bracing methods for fostering self-control" that a reformatory school might provide (*PC* 370). Margaret May has claimed that the call for reform schools as alternatives to prison was stimulated by the "contrast between a small vulnerable child and the fortress-like condition of the prisons" and by "a new awareness among prison officials of children's reactions to confinement": "The all-embracing separate system proved particularly unsuitable for children, endangering their health and providing no outlet for their 'restless minds.'"[10] Nevertheless, Clay held that "the cell is invaluable as a preparation for the school" (*PC* 371). The Reformatory School legislation of 1854 required that the youth spend a short period in prison before being sent to a residential school.

Clay alleged that separate confinement was beneficial to young people *even before their court appearance:* perhaps this was an "unconstitutional severity," Clay admitted, but it was "ordained by a higher law" to preserve them from the corruption of the yard (*PC* 144). However, those children whose parents' cruelty or neglect drove them to stealing, or whom older thieves had lured into villainy, should be sent directly to the reform school as if to the home they never had. Clay claimed that from the moment "all boys committed for trial were placed in separate confinement... youthful criminality, as a system, carried on by habitual and associated thieves, ceased to exist" in the Preston area (*PC* 328). But Preston had never had as much juvenile delinquency as the larger English cities: "Some more radical remedy would have been required to extirpate the Arabs of our great cities" (*PC* 371).

Prison Voices

Clay began calling for the introduction of the separate system in his 1827 report. Until then, he had urged that the discipline of the prison should be made "sharp and stringent" so as to make the institution an "object of terror" (*PC* 120). Doubtless he urged this simply in hopes of keeping people away from the place, but it did express the same naive hope as developing more horrible weapons of war in order to prevent wars. At first Clay even supported use of the treadmill, where men walked on a revolving cylinder, accomplishing nothing whatever. Tentative efforts at *encellulement* were made at Preston in 1834 and 1835, but money was lacking to build new cells. The experiment was finally put into effect for some inmates, at first only boys, in 1839, the same year Clay began deliberately to acquire oral history material from the inmates. The activity of doing an oral history relieved the pressures of this separate confinement: it does seem fitting that Clay, who doubtless was more humane in

the context of his times than his proposals make him appear to us, would
devise a way of exercising the human qualities of the spoken or written
voice in the midst of an inhuman silence.

But Clay was creating a profession, too. Walter Lowe Clay says his
father "never considered he had a fair field for his ministry until the
introduction of the separate system" (*PC* 109). Clay's aims in having
people write or speak at length about their lives were not only to fill their
time and prevent casualties that could be blamed on the system, but to
cure them of their "disease" or convert them to Christianity and to provide Clay with material to use in his agitation for penal and social reform.
Clay wrote in his 1846 report:

> I have yet further evidence in support of the views I advocate,
> which if not more convincing than what I have already brought
> forward, is perhaps more interesting,—that of the prisoners
> themselves. During the process of self-examination which a
> prisoner, capable of exercising it, must undergo in his cell, he
> is encouraged to review his past life, and to trace to their
> source his faults and sufferings. Many of the prisoners have
> availed themselves of this encouragement in a way which,
> while useful to themselves, will be, I think, also useful to those
> who inquire into the mental and moral state of the labouring
> classes. They have written, and sometimes dictated to me or to
> the schoolmaster, short narratives of their lives, their de-
> linquencies, their self-convictions, and their penitence. Of
> these narratives I possess a volume consisting of more than 300
> folio (MS.) pages; and it is scarcely too much to say that while
> evincing the beneficial process going on in the writers' minds,
> every page illustrates a history of which we are yet too
> ignorant,—the actual social and moral state of our poor
> fellow-subjects. [*PC* 274]

Clay interviewed every prisoner committed to the Preston jail for trial
and entered in his "character book" the person's age, occupation, earnings, birthplace, ability to read and write, and knowledge of religion (*PC*
258). "Do you know the meaning of vice?" he would ask, and the reply
might be, "Yes, I've often heard of good 'vice [advice]." "Do you know
what righteousness means?" "No, except it means naughtiness" (*PC*
259). At this initial interview he at least tried to speak to newcomers in a
kindly manner and prepare them "for the fearful ordeal" before them (*PC*
117). Before the introduction of the separate system, Clay mixed with
prisoners and tried to draw them into conversation, "but he soon found
that this was a labour lost, for no prisoner in the presence of his companions would ever speak frankly and truly. He was therefore obliged to rest
content with making himself as accessible as possible to all who wished
for private interviews" (*PC* 116). Once inmates were confined in separate

quarters, Clay could meet with them individually. Clay's son says that all he asked from this arrangement was "that it should guarantee the prisoners from mutual corruption, and make them think" (*PC* 196). It also made his ministry more feasible. During a three-year period he conversed with 1,234 males and 199 females,[11] though he did not take verbatim notes from all of these. Some inmates went on to write down their own stories, and others dictated to the jail schoolmaster.

Clay "discovered the curious autobiographical tendency of convicts, a tendency which solitary confinement was found to stimulate greatly" (*PC* 128). "Where tears, or mental uneasiness, or the desire to relieve the conscience by speaking was manifest, he would stay at once to offer help and sympathy, and to encourage the outpourings of confessions. These outbursts of confession were very frequent. As soon as the new system was introduced into the Gaol, he began to spend from five to six hours daily there, the greater part of which time was devoted to ministrations in the cells" (*PC* 207). The separate system was seen as a way of removing external inhibitions to "memory, conscience, and reflection . . . working their joint and several benefits" (*PC* 312). W. L. Clay aptly dubs this oral history site the "cell confessional" (*PC* 207), since a chief purpose of the *activity* was to enable prisoners "to see more clearly the certain connexion between sin and suffering." A purpose of the *statements* was to give society "an insight into the (preventable) causes of crime" (*PC* 319). Thus both the speaker and the audience were to undergo therapy. Lest "confession" be used against them, no attempt was made to solicit oral or written histories from people before their trials (*PC* 522); this was also because Clay wanted to avoid being solicited by defendants to influence the court on their behalf (*PC* 118), though this might have motivated inmates to participate.

Probably the most crucial factor in Clay's success at getting oral histories from his captive speakers was his kindness. Writing to M. D. Hill in 1851, Clay said: "I am very sure that most of my juvenile offenders *never had been spoken to in a kind tone till them came into our Gaol*" (*PC* 451). Clay's kindness was more effective in being exercised in a setting of threatened or actual cruelty. According to the younger Clay, since "the illiterate working classes have an indistinct idea that the people who make the laws are their natural enemies" (*PC* 201 n), this prison chaplain tried to distinguish himself from other jail personnel: "The cause of religion must—does—suffer greatly when the preacher is identified with the persecutor" (*PC* 568). To that end Clay performed as an advocate: "He often sharply rescued poor creatures from the rapacity and brutality of constables, and not seldom forced his remonstrances and complaints on the notice of heedless or tyrannical justices. By such means he gradually acquired great influence, both among the prisoners and the classes from which they were drawn" (*PC* 117). Clay said he had been insulted only twice in his entire career, once by a Chartist, a political revolutionary of the day (*PC* 118).

Clay promised his confessants that their statements would be privileged communications, and his son says that he published only two or three accounts, which had been entrusted to him "with the express hope that 'they'd p'haps do somebody else good to hear tell on'" (*PC* 231). However, many more than three histories appear in the annual reports. Most are presented with initials for names, though the names might have been recognized if the initials were the same as the speaker's. Some names used appear to be those of the actual speakers.

An indication that Clay identified with his flock is his frequent reference to his own "imprisonment." About midway in his chaplaincy he stopped calling his congregation "prisoners" and began referring to them as "fellow-sinners" (*PC* 205). He said: "Had our opportunities been otherwise distributed, which might have been the Chaplain, and which the prisoner?" (*PC* 541). His acquaintance with the "language, habits, and feelings of the working and criminal classes was of great use to him. He could at once draw up even a thought unfamiliar to them in their own words" (*PC* 201–2). He avoided "evangelical phraseology" (*PC* 206). At the same time as he began addressing the audience as fellow-sinners, he began speaking ex tempore rather than reading a sermon: "His old studies in elocution now served him in good stead" (*PC* 199). With all these special efforts, however, he discovered that not one-third of his congregation understood what he was saying (*PC* 559).

Clay was accused of credulity in accepting the words of criminals, but the problem did not escape him. "The histories necessarily abounded with references to recent occurrences; a dozen short letters, therefore, to the parties concerned would produce superabundant testimony of their truth or falsehood. When he selected a sample narrative for publication, he proved it in this way to the utmost, and only if its accuracy was demonstrated in every tested detail did he venture to infer the credibility of the remainder" (*PC* 128). At one time several prisoners were at the Preston jail who had all served time on the hulks (prison ships) at Bermuda. From the testimony of these men, Clay learned about the scandalous conditions there. He emphasized that each convict had told his story separately (another advantage of the separate system), yet that each confirmed the other, to support the validity of his appeal to the Colonial Office (*PC* 318). He used the same procedure in acquiring histories from a gang of pickpockets (*PC* 523).

John Clay collected hundreds of pages of "autobiographies"[12] from delinquents and older offenders and, beginning in 1846,[13] he used this material in his reports, extracting very brief quotations or reproducing the person's own words at somewhat greater length. Unfortunately, I have been able to examine only three of the post-1846 reports—1848, 1849, and 1852—in addition to the 1841 report. W. L. Clay includes rather long excerpts from the reports in his biography, but he quotes no long oral history. One of Mary Carpenter's works does contain such material, which she read in the annual reports as well as in manuscript form.[14] The following are selections from her use of Clay's oral histories in her book *Juvenile Delinquents,* published in 1853 and probably more influential concerning delinquency than any of Clay's reports. The first selection is typical, insofar as it demonstrates the evils of alcohol, of the oral histories in the *Chaplain's Reports* I have examined. The second, which Carpenter acquired in manuscript form, is not typical of Clay's reports, and the contrast between what Clay published and what he chose not to publish is revealing. Carpenter says this first story was taken down by the school-master at Preston, at the dictation of W. M., aged eleven years, then serving a sentence of eighteen months for stealing money from a shop drawer. He had been committed for theft twice before.

I was born in Lancaster, and when we came to Preston I was very young; my father kept a jerry-shop in Heatly-street, till my mother died, about three years ago; my father was drunk every night, *very near;* my mother died through father beating her. She used to *sauce* him for going to other beer-houses to drink, when we had plenty of our own; and then he punched her up and down the house, and she was crying with him punching her, and when he was *agate* ["well under way"; here, "on the rampage"—J. B.] she many a time shouted "murder!" She did not die all at once; she was badly two or three weeks. We were getting our breakfast one Monday morning when father fetched us upstairs, mother was dying; my father was crying, and *Hanny* (the youngest child) was laughing; father tried to make it give over; (there was four children, James, William, John, and Hannah.) It was not long before father got wed again, it might be two, three, four, or five months, the woman's name was *Aggy S.,* she had a child when they were wed; father give o'er drinking a bit, but soon began again, and when he got his wage he came home drunk at twelve o'clock on Friday night. One night he came home very drunk, and James and I were in bed; he made us get up, and said he would take us to the canal and drown us; he asked my step-mother for our shoes, but she said, 'If you are going to drown them, you might as well leave the shoes for Johnny.' He threw me in the canal *a good way,* but a boatman jumped in with his clothes on, and got me out, or I should have been drowned; then the boatman took out his knife, and said to father, 'If you don't let them alone, I will stick you:' there was two policemen

on the bridge with their lamps, but they did not come to us; we
ran away and got home before father; and when the policemen
came to our house and wanted to know what father was doing
on the bridge with the two children at two o'clock in the
morning, which was not a proper hour; father threatened to
punch them, and did push them out, and locked the door; he
was as drunk as he could be, and had been knocked off his
work. He drinks yet, but not so oft as he did; stepmother never
got drunk. I have been to three schools—I first went to Trinity
Day and Sunday School for six months, Croft Street Day and
Sunday for three months, and Bow Lane for a short time.
When I was near nine years old, I went to the factory for three
weeks. Johnny and me ran away once, when stepmother was
talking to some folk, and we was afraid of going home again for
fear of being licked. We had no caps, and we stole two Scotch
caps, and got a month each for it, and that was the way we got
into prison at first. My stepmother often locked us up in the
house; and one day she tied Johnny to the bed and locked him
up, but he got a table and the cradle, and got through the
skylight, and a boy helped him down at the bottom of the yard.
The second time I was in prison was with Francis and Peter
Forrester—these lads took me to a shop and lifted me up to
the window, and showed me the money-drawer with the keys
in it; we then went to the back to see who was in the kitchen,
and we came again to the front, when I went in and fetched £2
11s. from the drawer. I got six months, Francis eight months'
imprisonment, and Peter seven years' transportation. About a
fortnight after Francis came out, I met him in Bridge Street, I
had been for coals, he had just stole twopence and was going to
hide his clogs, to go to another shop in Walker Street; he did
not like to go in himself, so he asked me, and I went in and
brought out a cup with 8 1/2d, that is what I am now in for, and
Francis got seven years' transportation.[15]

Carpenter adds: "Investigations have been made by a reliable official
respecting the truth of these statements, and the result most fully corrobo-
rated the poor child's narrative, which has also been confirmed by the
evidence of the police force."[16] After some trumpeting about the need to
punish parents for neglecting their children, Carpenter gives one of Clay's
histories from the original manuscript, abridged "but otherwise unaltered,
except occasionally in spelling and grammar," and broken in the middle
by more oration about "justice to the child" and "justice to society."
But the "expressions of deep penitence" that are interspersed in the
original, she has, she says, omitted. Following is the "narrative of X, aged
about 20, then under sentence of transportation."

When I was a child of about eighteen months' old, my mother got married to a man who had been under the same circumstances as I am now in, but with having bad health he got his liberty after serving three years and a half. It seems that for some time after my mother had got married, her husband went on tolerably well as a moral man, but after a time he began to frequent the alehouse; till this time he seems to have had middling good health, and *to be in easy circumstances as a labouring man;* but this soon began to fail, for he began to get into debt, but still loved pleasure and drink. The first kind of wickedness which I learned to commit, was carrying things of small value out of our house; you may perhaps ask me how this originated in me, which, no doubt, was in this way. My stepfather used to ramble in the fields on the Sabbath day, and we came across any places where there were apples, turnips, or anything of that description, he would not mind taking a few, *although he often told me it was wrong to do the same.* I also learnt to curse and swear, for both father and mother were swearers, especially the latter; if she was offended by any one of us, the first word would be a curse, and perhaps a blow, with a demand why we had done so and so; we even heard my little brothers curse before they reached the age of five years; this all originated from the bad example of my parents. When I was about the age of eight years, my father and mother worked in the factory, and left me to take care of the house and four children; when I had arrived at the age of 10, after being left to do as I chose for two years, I was ready for anything, and from this age may be dated my course of wickedness.

About the age of six I was sent to a National School, where I continued to go, or rather should have gone, for the space of two years; but *four-fifths of the time I ran away,* for which perhaps my father might beat me, but never told me the value of an education, or how to obey my parents, and I never knew either father or mother to go to a place of worship, except to bury one of their children, of whom they have buried three. Very seldom did my parents request me to go to the Sabbath School, and never went to such a place themselves. Having a good deal of spare time, and all the Sabbath to myself, I formed company with some lads of about my own age, by whom I was very well liked, for my father having taken me with him in the fields to places where were plenty of nuts and other wild fruit, I could of course show these boys where we could get plenty of such like things. But we did not stop here; from rambling in the fields we commenced robbing gardens, *which we did for a long time in the most crafty manner, without being in any way found out.* My conscience was so hard by this time that it never smote me; but my advice now is, not to know sin in any way, and by God's blessing resting upon your own endeavours, you will never practise it, *for the best preservative from sin is not to know it.*

At the age of about 13, I commenced learning to work in the factory with my stepfather, who used me more like a brute beast than a child to whom he had promised to give support, protection, example and encouragement. The factory was a thing for which I had no great liking, and my father did not explain its utility to me; steam-loom weaving was not a thing in which I took any liking, which no doubt made me very careless; my father had a term to check this carelessness in me, which he termed 'a pair of spectacles,' which consisted in a blow with some unlawful weapon, or a kick, which he said made me see better.

By and bye my father was thrown out of work, and so remained for a long time. I played me for the space of two years; during this time I learned and made more progress in wickedness than ever I had before. I began to stop out late at night with bad company, committing all sorts of outrage, such as robbing gardens, playing tricks with gunpowder upon people while they sat in their quiet habitations, opening their doors, and throwing an old mop up the house all daubed with soil, and some such thing. I also learned to swear in the most horrid manner, to fight and quarrel with my fellow-creatures, and if any one offended me the most brutal oath would come out of my mouth (which, no doubt, originated in my parents). At last, many of my companions, who were better disposed, would not have anything to do with me or say to me; in short, I was that debased, I, and more of my companions with me, could not even let the brute creatures alone; we had used to get cats, and other small animals, to torture them, setting them to fight, tying their tails together, and throwing them over a clothesline, to tear each other to pieces. Thus was my time spent from 13 to 15 years of age . . . . I had now made such vast progress in that which was bad, that there was nothing but what I was ready for and equal to; I commenced making marauding expeditions in the night—sometimes not seeing a bed for weeks together, but ready for plunder night and day; robbing gardens, selling the fruit, taking the tools that might be in them, and selling them to the pawnbrokers and others who would buy them. I did not carry on these games long before I was, in a certain measure, stopped, for me and two more one night went to sleep in a boiler-house belonging to a factory; but we did not sleep the night out there, for about eleven o'clock at night the master and a police-officer came and took us all three prisoners, for which two of us got one month, and the other, being an old offender, got three months; this was the first time I ever saw a prison, either inside or out.

The first shock which struck me was the mass of bars and impenetrable walls; it seemed to me to wear more the aspect of death, than a place of correction; this I felt at first, but it made no abiding impression, and the reason it did so is, perhaps, as follows: —We mingled together, and my companions, seeing that I was much cast down, would now and then comfort me—if I may use the phrase—by telling me to cheer up, and that it would be better in a day or two. I tried to do so, and succeeded very well in stifling the still, small voice of God. While here I made as much progress for further imprisonment as possibly could be, by hearing men, of all ages, tell of their grand exploits, how they got their money by robbing, and that they knew plenty of places that could be easily plundered. All these, and many other things equally as bad, I saw and heard; before I left it I got pretty hard, for I got once or twice in punishment. The time drew nigh when I was to be discharged, but some misconduct on the Saturday kept me from leaving the prison on the Tuesday morning, and I was kept in the black hole till about half-past three in the afternoon. I was about fifteen miles from home, without knowing a single yard of the way; however, I got to —— that night, though I did not go home until the next morning. My father told me to get work, and mind and not get into prison any more; my mother told me I was not the only one that had been in prison. I believe that this forms the whole of the reproof that I got from my parents, whereas, I firmly believe, that had my parents set the thing in its true colours before my eyes, I should never have seen the inside of a prison again. I did as I was directed, got work, and there remained till the ensuing spring, when I again broke out in my mad career. As soon as summer came, I commenced my old games with tenfold fury, stealing all that I could lay my hands on, robbing gardens in the most shameful manner, selling the fruit for a mere nothing, cursing and swearing, calling God's vengeance down on my head and the head of my companions in the most brutal manner, a profound Sabbath breaker, hating and hated of the better of my former associates. I did not continue long before I was taken up for stealing apples, for which I got three months in prison, and a most horrid three months it was to me, for I commenced my old rigs of disobedience, until I assaulted the governor and one of the officers, for which I was taken before the magistrate and ordered to be whipped; this took no effect on me, for I had now got so hard that I laughed at it, although I should at one time have trembled to have thought of it. I kept growing harder, thinking nothing of what would become of body or soul; no sermons made any impression on me, nor advices from the minister or schoolmaster, but rather laughed at all who tried to do me any good; the four dozen lashes took not the slightest effect, but rather hardened my impenetrable heart, and ripened me for the fate that awaited me. The time came that I was to be released, with this promise from the governor for my bad conduct, that if ever I came for trial he would have me transported.[17]

This Mr. X did indeed come up for trial again, for poaching, and at the time of writing this he was on his way abroad, probably to Australia.

Good Works

Like Mayhew, Clay filled his annual reports with tables, reflecting his "natural faculty and fondness for statistics, which his commercial training had considerably developed" (*PC* 130). Clay became well known for his statistics on crime, which were apparently the object of Dickens's ridicule in *Hard Times*.[18] Also like Mayhew, Clay showed an interest in the geographical distribution of crime and used maps to show relative amounts of criminality in various areas.[19] (However, one detects chauvinism in this part of Clay's work, some spirit of "our county has less crime than your county.") The oral histories—or "narratives"—themselves appear in the appendixes to the reports. This "confinement" of prisoners' testimony to the back pages was also practiced in institutional annual reports in the United States during the nineteenth century, as we shall see in the next chapter. A few of these "statements" are only a sentence in length, but many are two or three pages of the inmate's own words. In rare cases evidence is given in this place by experts about criminological topics. All the oral histories in the 1852 appendix concern counterfeiters and other professional criminals, though even in these some features of the individual's nonprofessional life show through.

Clay's primary purpose in using offenders' oral histories, including those from young people (whose stories appear alongside those from adults), was to show that drunkenness and ignorance of religion were the two chief causes of crime: "Religious ignorance is the chief ingredient in the character of the criminal. This combines with the passion for liquor.... As directly connected with this subject, I again crave attention to the Narratives and Statements written or dictated, by prisoners themselves, and given in the Appendix."[20] The cause of crime that stands out most clearly in these texts is alcohol abuse: religious ignorance appears mostly in the form of repentance, a kind of religious knowledge, whereby the criminal is reformed. One wonders to what extent inmates were merely pretending to be reformed, but the histories are often accompanied by a letter from a clergyman confirming that the former inmate was still on the straight and narrow.

The two most prominent motives of the prisoners in relating their life stories were to confess their sins and to warn others not to go astray: that is, not to succumb to alcohol. Almost every one of Clay's oral histories pounds away at the disasters wrought by drunkenness: either the parent of the delinquent was an alcoholic or the young person became involved in crime through overindulgence.[21] If this is not clear enough in the longer accounts, even with the often copious italics emphasizing the point at every opportunity, brief quotes are inserted here and there:

NO. 4.
J. M., aged 17, sentenced to 12 months' imprisonment for felony:—

> My mother did her best to send me to a Sunday School, and I
> believe, I should have taken her advice, but for seeing my
> father's bad example. There is one lesson it has learnt me, that
> is never to be a drunkard, as bad as I am. If my father had been
> as my mother, instead of being in prison I should have been in
> an honourable situation.[22]

Since Clay did not start collecting oral histories until the separate system had begun at Preston, many of the documents he published show alleged successes of the system in order to promote its adoption elsewhere. On the other hand, Clay thought he saw a situation outside the prison walls that was sending him criminals in the first place, and he included longer, fuller narratives of people's lives to show the disasters of drink. Even in these one can see beyond parental alcoholism to the youth's association with others in delinquent activities. In the longest narratives, those that go well beyond the brief success-story genre, such as the one Clay acquired and Mary Carpenter published, an even fuller picture of extrafamilial environment is shown. Carpenter used this document as part of her effort to establish a new kind of institution, not to show successes of a place already in existence: if an individual comes from a corrupt environment, he or she needs a better, artificial environment—a reformatory school. Had Carpenter been the type of person who so values internal principles of expression and action that she herself would have initiated the collection of delinquents' oral histories, she might have gone further and even advocated that the new environment be the community where the child grows up, with its own internal resources for self-improvement. As it was, the second history reproduced above only shows that associations with evil chums the boy made in the street will be made more easily in an institution, even an institution of the sort Carpenter was proposing.[23]

Clay's histories are a mean between the extremes of Mayhew's lively texts (after all, the cell confessional is more tedious than the street corner) and the success stories promulgated by the American Houses of Refuge during the nineteenth century (see chap. 4). Nevertheless, they were meant to perform some of the same functions as Mayhew's narratives. One aim of Clay's publications was to put the public on guard by exposing criminal practices:

> It consists with the objects of a Report like this, to give any information which may throw light on the habits and practices of men who, living almost entirely by crime in one shape or another, have, nevertheless, been tolerated to a degree altogether at variance with what is due to the rights of property, and of personal safety.[24]

Elsewhere he says: "I believe it to be a momentous necessity that the public, especially the Christian public, should be kept fully informed of the progress made by the malign powers."[25] Firsthand testimony is also useful in informing higher authorities of conditions among the lower classes: of the Bermuda hulks Clay said: "The evidence . . . *could only be given by convicts*. The higher the rank of the official, the more ignorant he is *kept* of the true nature and extent of such evils as these papers describe" (*PC* 324).

Clay's presentation of the very words of convicts was an indication of his belief in the delinquent's essential humanity, though this was typically bound up with more pious Christianity than Mayhew showed: "This poor child possesses natural qualities which, by God's blessing, would amply repay the labour of cultivation" (*PC* 525). The epigram to Clay's 1852 report was a quotation from the gateway to a Madrid prison: *Odia el delito y compadece el delincuente*—Abhor the crime and pity the criminal. Delinquents may be as ambitious as anyone else though in the wrong direction (*PC* 138), and they should never be abandoned: "No cases whatever must be considered as precluding hope" (*PC* 208 n). Showing the circumstances of their lives, even if mainly the one circumstance of parental alcoholism, implies and conveys that something other than a criminal nature is at work here. But Clay opposed the notion that youths were not responsible for their actions while adults were; in fact the opposite may be true, he held, since men were probably under the influence of liquor when committing a crime, while boys' crimes are usually premeditated (*PC* 338–39), a distinction that neglects responsibility for alcoholism, among other things.

Clay himself had no power to alter prison rules; his only power lay in his ability to generate support from local authorities in charge of the jail or to put pressure on them by appealing to the broader public. For many years, Clay was saddled with pigheaded prison governors and unsympathetic justices, so he went over their heads: "His hopes for the future rested almost entirely upon the possibility of rousing, not merely a few here and there, but the general public" (PC 492). Like Mayhew, he drew considerable opposition from the establishment: "Among justices he acquired the character of being restless and meddlesome, and of course he earned abundant ill-will among the officers of the prison" (PC 111). As Manton says of Mary Carpenter: "Every humane consideration seemed to offend someone."[26]

Clay's major enemy was "selfish cowardice crying for indiscriminate vengeance on all sorts and conditions of criminals" (PC 212). In this regard, the cause célèbre was Carlyle's outburst in his pamphlet Model Prisons against the "luxuries" of prisons. In fact, some people did commit crimes in order to be sent to prison, as an improvement over their even worse situation outside (PC 115–16), and some parents complained that delinquents were being treated better in institutions than their own good children (PC 447). But "poor Feeblewit," as W. L. Clay calls Carlyle, had based his conclusions on one visit to one prison, not the one at Preston. John Clay replied in his 1850 report by printing two oral histories "to illustrate the manner in which unfortunate boys are often forced into their first crimes." He added: "I submit that the process of correction for faults traceable to such causes as are laid open in these short histories, and in hundreds of similar ones which have been made known to me, does not so much require severity and punishment as the application of means to arouse into conscious existence the hitherto dormant qualities proper to humanity" (PC 214–15).

On occasion Clay even made remarks that connected the conditions he typically alleged to be criminogenic to broader social factors. His son says:

> In common with most practical philanthropists, he considered
> that almost all crime was traceable to three closely linked
> causes, drunkness, ignorance, and the habit of living in filthy,
> over-crowded dwellings. But he maintained that these, in their
> turn, were due, in a great measure, to the want of sympathy
> and intercourse between the upper and lower classes. [PC 492]

The upper classes showed "heartless selfishness . . . disgraceful ignorance of, and indifference to, the brutal degradation in which they suffer the poor to lie," and this was "the primary cause of almost all the crime in the country" (PC 211–12). For example, "It is well known," Clay wrote in his last report, "that liquor dealers in any borough could turn an election.

Legislators, therefore, chosen under such influence, will not do much to counteract it: and consequently the question as to the means of repressing drunkness is legislatively brought to a standstill" (*PC* 582; cf. 498). Clay was "angrily intolerant of the vices of the wealthy and the educated" and in no way favored the few of that class who showed up as prisoners (*PC* 215), according to his son.

Like Mayhew, he viewed the solution to the split between classes in terms of communication:

> The wealthy and instructed have a great task before them, which must be accomplished,—in promoting education and religious knowledge among their inferiors, and also winning and deserving their confidence and good opinion. The ties which should bind all classes together have been fearfully loosened; there is mutual distrust, and, it must be said, too much of mutual antipathy, where, if each party only understood the other more fully, there would be mutual reliance and regard. [*PC* 505]

Clay pointed out that if a group of ignorant and demoralized people such as he encountered daily at the Preston House of Correction had been brought to the attention of British Christians, "missionaries would be poured upon their shores." Why, then, he asked, "are our own *home heathens* so long overlooked?" (*PC* 493). Though Clay writes in places as if he thinks he is deterring people from crime by showing that drunkenness and crime do not pay, surely the majority of his readers were good Christians who would not have erred anyway. Like Mayhew, Clay says he is addressing "those who may possess, in any degree, the power or the inclination to render those features [in the mental and spiritual constitution of criminals] less painful."[27] "It *is* palling to the attention to have it dragged through successive stories of neglected infancy, idle and godless youth, drunken and profligate manhood: but nevertheless, these stories should be read—let me say studied—by every one to whom the real state of society is a matter of either temporal or spiritual solicitude."[28]

It is impossible to know who actually did read Clay's reports and what effect the oral histories themselves had. At first the reports appeared in local newspapers. From 1837 to 1844, before oral histories were included, they appeared not only in newspapers but also in an edition of a few hundred pamphlets. After that they were bound: five hundred copies were sent to justices throughout England and three hundred to five hundred copies were printed for general use. W. L. Clay says: "Never more than a thousand copies were printed of any report, but such lengthy extracts were reproduced in official Blue-books, temperance papers, educational periodicals, &c. and they were so frequently retailed in all reviews, books, sermons, &c. . . . that many persons became quite familiar with his opinions, assertions, and arguments, who had never seen the original pamphlets" (*PC* 126–27). Some people grumbled about the "chaplain's annual fairy tales" (*PC* 124) and "the simplicity of the worthy chaplain in swallowing such thieves' frummery" (*PC* 128). But according to Hoyles: "His annual reports became noteworthy documents and contributed much to the development of prison discipline throughout the country."[29]

Clay succeeded in making some improvements at the Preston jail. He stopped the bribing of guards. He got the treadmill removed and the prison yard abolished. He set up a school and brought in a matron for the female inmates. He finally got seventy-five "separate" cells built, though the institution contained up to three hundred inmates. Did the system work? Few were converted to religion under the separate system, but most seemed to resolve, "more or less strongly, to make a vigorous effort for their own restoration" (*PC* 395). About six or eight months after the release of a prisoner who had been on the separate system, Clay would write letters to the local minister and police chief, and he would accept the less favorable of the two replies: "Year after year . . . about half the men were reported as more or less reformed" (*PC* 229). Clay must have been delighted when the man about whose copious oral history Dickens expressed great skepticism (*PC* 325) did indeed reform as he had promised (*PC* 459). At least Clay's prison reforms may have broken up juvenile gangs in the Preston area (*PC* 328): earlier, each gang had been led by a youth "duly qualified for his post by a previous training in Gaol" (*PC* 273).

But Clay recognized the difficulty of "reforming a child who has been born and reared amidst poverty, neglect, and ill example" (*PC* 144).[30] Having so often heard about the difficulties faced by an ex-convict in leading a normal life, in 1846 (the same year he began publishing oral histories) Clay started a small association "with the object of obtaining employment for such discharged prisoners as manifested a wish to reform" (*PC* 234 n). Apparently this included young people, who might be placed as apprentices. Like Clifford Shaw a century later, Clay tried to attract volunteers from the community: "I applied to several benevolent and judicious men belonging to the superior class of operatives, and one or two shopkeepers of the same humane character, and stated to them my views" (*PC* 234). Clay's son says, "He would sometimes guarantee the good conduct of a libertine to overcome the caution of an employer; and he was hardly ever a loser by his suretyship" (*PC* 234).

Clay's reports, as well as the books by Mary Carpenter that used Clay's oral histories, were read by growing numbers of professional providers of social services to the poor. In addition, in the period before textbooks had been assembled these publications could be used as training materials. Appeals were made to "the public," but surely the public en masse then, as today, cared very little about all this except insofar as it would make troublesome juveniles disappear. Carpenter's special audience seems to have been actual or potential volunteers; this was and is a mean between the extremes of the professional audience and the general public. Oral histories were a way to recruit people as volunteers and to give them a preliminary contact with the lives of the people they would meet and help. Carpenter put her finger on a central point of these oral histories when she wrote:

> The treatment of our Convicts is entirely in the hands of the Government, and society has no power of changing it, except through the influence of public opinion, which it is the object of this work to awaken.
> The prevention of crime rests, to a great extent, with the community; in this a Government cannot do more than make such enactments as may be necessary to promote the welfare of society, and to second individual effort; —it is the duty of every individual man and woman to do something, either by direct exertion or by example and influence, to weaken the power of evil, and to prevent the enormous criminality which exists in our land.[31]

The causes volunteers might join she lists as: temperance, antiprostitution, pure literature, housing improvements for the poor, reformatories, pauper schools, industrial schools, Ragged Schools, and aid to ex-prisoners. Carpenter makes an interesting statement about the social conditions of volunteer effort: "Probably in no country does there exist so large an amount of voluntary action as in our own, because in none is there so great a degree of freedom combined with a reverence for law."[32] But voluntary effort must be united with knowledge, power, and money, she adds. Perhaps such needs aroused doubts in her about the effectiveness of mere oratory: "I perceive that no writing, or printing, or talking, can induce people to take up the subject; it is only determined action."[33] That is, action by organized groups, inspired in those days primarily by religious motives. Hoyles has written: "Neither the philosophy of Rousseau and Bentham, nor the politics of Romilly and Peel, could have achieved large scale reforms had not they received the backing of a powerful religious movement. The mainspring of reform was the evangelical movement."[34]

Institutionalizing Humaneness
Juvenile crime seems to have declined after the middle of the nineteenth century in England. Insofar as the institutions Clay and Carpenter helped to set up were responsible for this, the oral histories they used to propagate their proposals should be given credit. However, declining crime

rates could also be attributed to declining Irish immigration and to increased social stabilization in the cities after the century's very turbulent first half. Doubtless the friendlier atmosphere in which these humanitarians sought to place children was an improvement in the lives of many individuals. But from our own perspective of massive criticism of custodial institutions, the faith of these pioneers in institutionalization is alien indeed.[35] Clay and Carpenter seen to have had no doubts that the ideals they espoused could be applied without arousing manifold shifting ambiguities and contradictions in human situations. Dickens pointed out that the advocates of the separate system did not know what they were doing, that they did not see the unintended consequences of their reforms, such as suicides and mental aberrations, and the separate system was gradually abandoned. The cells, however, remained. What Foucault has called the "carceral archipelago" had begun to evolve—"a whole series of institutions which [went] beyond the frontiers of criminal law."[36]

The humaneness of all these reforms depended on the presence of the very sort of individual who would be capable of understanding a person's life as shown in the oral history documents they acquired or appreciated enough to publish. But these workers proposed institutional arrangements, "systems," that would survive their departure. Although their intentions were good, in their enthusiasm for solutions to existing evils they overlooked possible evils in the alternatives they proposed. The exclusive categories of good versus evil served them ill. What would happen when the charismatic pioneer, whose innovative principles of kindness were kept alive in daily application, departed the scene, to be replaced by a herd of institutional personnel who would make crucial shifts in interpreting those principles? In the hands of a less humane person, a less reflective person than the innovator must be ("thoughtful" in both senses), the principle of individual treatment in a familylike setting could easily become an arbitrary violation of individual rights.

Insofar as oral history contributed to (and was a reflection of) this movement for the establishment of personal, domestic institutions, the spirit of which survived only so long as the institution was led by the sort of person who found oral histories significant, we can, in the superior wisdom made possible by hindsight, judge these documents to have contributed to a deception.

Religion, Delinquency, and Oral History
The oral histories gathered by John Clay and Henry Mayhew have many features in common; a major difference is that Mayhew surrounded his with much less preaching than Clay put in his commentaries and even encouraged in the narratives themselves. The use of oral histories to predispose an audience in favor of a social reform can make use of almost

any delinquent's story, because some need will emerge from any life. The religious use of such histories is much more likely to broadcast a special message—the importance of religion in the successful reformation of a delinquent. As "confessions" have always been, religious uses of delinquents' oral histories are more blatantly promotional than oral histories used by social reformers; these latter have messages, but they point more to a need, an open place, than to a seemingly sure means of success—a kind of closure. (Success-story autobiographies, such as Joseph Sorrentino's *Up from Never*, resemble religious literature in their spirit of "you can do it, too.")

Even a book-length autobiography of a former delinquent such as *Run Baby Run*, by Nicky Cruz (written with Jamie Buckingham) could be reduced to a much briefer story were it not that the length of the text gives an appropriately disposed reader a longer glow, and a full-sized paperback book is easier to distribute to supermarket shelves than a pamphlet would be. As if the text did not hammer home the point of salvation through Christ in stereotyped episode and unctuous tone throughout, the book begins with a preface by Buckingham, an introduction by Billy Graham, and a foreword by a University of Notre Dame professor. It ends with an address to write "if you wish to share in Nicky Cruz's work or need counseling." This is a typical intention of such writing—to attract resources. But this book also intends to attract young people themselves. Surely a book of this sort appeals only to those who are already convinced of its message or want to be; yet who knows exactly what such books have accomplished? This book's cover declares that nearly two million copies have been sold, more than any other delinquent's oral history ever.

Four

Boosterism: The Art of the Appendix in Nineteenth-Century America

The first major use of oral histories of juvenile offenders in the United States was by Clifford Shaw, initially in a 1926 article and most notably in *The Jack-Roller: A Delinquent Boy's Own Story,* published in 1930. But this was not the first use made of juvenile delinquents in America. A century before Shaw, the transformation of a colonial into an urban society was accompanied by apparently rising rates of delinquency, with the result that houses of refuge were opened for delinquent, dependent, and vagrant children in New York (1825), Boston (1826), and Philadelphia (1828), and other American cities. At midcentury an alternative to these institutions, which were in reality mock penetentiaries for youths perceived as mock adults, was launched in New York City under the leadership of Charles Loring Brace: this program consisted of lodging houses and schools in the city and a system of "placing out" slum children to farm families on the American frontier. After the establishment of the first juvenile court, in Chicago in 1899 (before this, young people had appeared in the same courts as adults), a child study institute was set up to make physical and psychological examinations of the individuals who appeared before the court. William Healy, the director of this clinic, could find in his cases none of the bodily marks that Cesare Lombroso, in the late nineteenth century, had alleged to be stigmata of criminality. In Denver, Ben Lindsey developed a juvenile court in 1901 and became embroiled in a series of conflicts over related reforms. I shall take up Lindsey, Healy, and Lombroso in chapter 5.

All of these were prominent initiatives in dealing with juvenile delinquents, but these individuals and institutions almost never published a delinquent's oral history. Why then should we consider them? First, in the annual reports of the institutions, the monographs of the scientists, and the speeches of Lindsey the politician, young people were not mute,[1] and our subject may be illuminated by contrast with those distinct but related forms of expression: for example, the most blatant promotional uses of personal documents will highlight promotional uses of oral histories. Second, if we are to determine the conditions under which delinquents' oral histories appear, a work of imagination at best, we should study situations in which they have *not* appeared, as a way of controlling our imaginations, if not of setting up a control group. And third, briefly reviewing the history of delinquency theory and practice in nineteenth- and early twentieth-century America will provide background for the work of Clifford Shaw.

Letters "Home"

The association of juvenile and adult offenders in penitentiaries, along with the vagrancy and noxious parental backgrounds of multitudes of children in the city streets—problems John Clay began to confront in the late 1820s—also distressed the members of the New York Society for the Prevention of Pauperism. In 1823 a committee of this society produced a report entitled "Expediency of Erecting an Institution for the Reformation of Juvenile Delinquents," and in Appendix A of this report were printed "specimens of the four hundred and fifty cases of Juvenile Offenses, furnished by the District Attorney, from the Records of the Police Office, for 1822," for example: "William S. aged 11, his father turned him out of the house, was found sleeping in a boat at night; 6 months Penitentiary." "Sophia H. aged 14, was charged with stealing, goes about begging, has been in Bridewell six times, no means; 6 months Penitentiary."[2]

As soon as the New York House of Refuge opened on 1 January 1825 and commenced issuing annual reports, the practice began of including in the appendixes brief sample case histories of the juveniles processed by the institution. In subsequent reports, the record expands somewhat beyond a simple statement of name, age, and offense. The appendix to the society's 1835 report begins:

CASES OF GIRLS

The case of A. B. is a rather remarkable one. Her widowed Mother died on the 15th of March, 1834, at which time we had her elder sister in the Refuge about 16 years of age, who had been broadly astray, but whose deportment and manners had become womanly and satisfactory. She very ardently desired to see her Mother's remains and to attend the funeral, which we were pleased to have it in our power to indulge her in. She became very much affected at parting with her two youngest sisters, saying that all the rest were bad, and if these were left, she had no doubt but that they would soon become ruined; they would have no home but with these sisters, and begged me to try and get them to the Refuge, it was a delicate thing for me to undertake, but I allowed her to go to the Police Magistrates and tell her story to them, which she did with much effect for they immediately sent for them, and had them committed here as vagrants. A. B. proved to be a charming dispositioned active child, and we all loved her much. One of the

Ladies' Committee was delighted with the child, and requested
her to be reserved for a friend of hers, and in about 8 Months
she was indentured to Mr. J. P. some 200 miles from this city,
where she will doubtless be trained up in the way "she should
go," and be saved from ruin and disgrace—we often hear very
favorable accounts of her verbally.[3]

These "Histories and Accounts" of children received and bound out as
apprentices or servants by the houses of refuge usually followed an
opening text expounding the institution's accomplishments. Also included
in appendixes (in smaller type than the opening salvo) were reports by the
physician, teachers, and the treasurer, plus statistics on the numbers of
boys and girls involved, and extracts from the official daily journal.
Nothing exposes the conspicuous boosterism of these annual reports
more than the letters from masters who had taken in former inmates, as
well as the letters from the children themselves, separated into "cases of
girls" and "cases of boys," and in the Philadelphia reports into "white"
and "colored" cases. In the twentieth annual report (1845) of the New
York Society for the Reformation of Juvenile Delinquents, as their name
had become, a letter from "a colored boy, indentured from the refuge
during the past summer" is "given very nearly in his own words":

Mr. De Voe,
Dear friend, I take this opportunity to write to you, and I
hope to find you well. I suppose you would like to know how I
am; and whether I *am* at my place. I *am* very well, and I *am
very well satisfied.* I have no complaints to make whatever. I
am very glad of the instruction that I received from the Refuge.
I can plough and harrow; and I expect to mow next summer. It
is getting cold now, and we are about to go to the *woods* for the
fire wood; we shall be steady at it all winter, but when there are
any spare days I shall have time to play. We have a fine pond,
and my Boss'es son John and I will be skating whenever we
have time.[4]

The letter continues in the same vein.
As far as I can determine, none of the personal histories, except for the
success-story letters, appear in the person's own words. It seems that
the authors of the reports do not even understand what this would mean.
One boy's case is introduced thus: "His history as recorded from his own
mouth, follows, which will show the cause of the first trouble he gave us,
after which a letter corresponding with one of his former inmates in the
House, which will also show his talents and the firmness of his mind in the
good cause." But the "recording" is a summary statement made by
someone other than the boy. The case has an ending typical of these

reports, with the boy telling "in public religious meetings that he has been an unusually wicked boy, and how much he is indebted to the grace of God and the House of Refuge for his salvation."[5] The same pattern is found in the annual reports from similar institutions of the day, notably those in Boston and Philadelphia.

These pamphlets are transparent in their rhetorical intention, to attract public notice and contributions to these charity organizations by showing off their good work: "They will be read with pleasure and satisfaction by the virtuous and good, who have always at heart the interest and well being of the whole human family."[6] They were also promoting a vision of bad environment, especially bad parents, as the causes of delinquency, and they did this to make credible their artificial environment, a "home" to prevent and cure delinquency by instilling discipline and religion into young people. In discussing similar case histories appended to the 1829 and 1830 reports of New York State's Auburn Prison, David Rothman has written: "New York officials accumulated and published biographies because this technique allowed them to demonstrate to legislators and philanthropists the crucial role of social organization."[7] Colonial Americans had been "preoccupied with the sinner himself. Convinced that the corrupt nature of man was ultimately at fault, they did not extensively analyze the role of the criminal's family or the church or the general society. Furthermore, they shared a clear understanding of what the well-ordered community *ought* to look like, and this too stifled any inclination to question or scrutinize existing arrangements."[8] Rothman also alludes to the shift from examining only the crime to considering the criminal, a shift both Clay and Mayhew were also calling for: "Nor did these vignettes show the Revolutionary War generation's concern for legal reform. Officials now looked to the life of the criminal, not to the statutes, in attempting to grasp the origins of deviancy. They presented biographical sketches, not analyses of existing codes."[9]

In other words, if legal codes, utopian ideals, and moral or religious imperatives may be characterized as realities that *transcend* individuals, biography in this case encouraged a move in concepts of delinquency away from transcendental or absolutist causes that *should* control action and toward experiential or environmental causes that *do* (allegedly) determine behavior. Implied in this move was the possibility of social reform to change those causes, according to a more realistic view of what should happen. Biography presented evidence of the need for reform—the creation of institutions—that biography helped to bring about by publicizing those institutions. And insofar as the chief culprits themselves—parents— received a warning from these reports, "critics would inspire the family to a better performance. The biographical sketches, then, were not only investigations but correctives to the problem," according to Rothman,[10] though it is doubtful whether many parents, especially poor people, read them.

By the 1850s the first thirty-year cycle of innovation and decay in American institutional measures for delinquency control had run its course, and a new alternative to the old methods came into being. The houses of refuge were primarily adult penitentiaries for children, with strong emphasis on discipline. Quoting Rothman again: "It would not be a simple matter to distinguish between the corrections of a sadistic keeper intent on terrorizing his charges and the punishment of a benevolent superintendent trying, in the fashion of the day, to rehabilitate them."[11] One development away from the refuges was the reformatory schools, which emphasized education more than the refuges had done and which were less regimented. Another maneuver was the Children's Aid Society, founded in 1853 in New York City and led by C. L. Brace.

Bracing Methods

Charles Loring Brace (1826–90) was a minister who saw his destiny in following the example of Christ, to "go down among those who have no friend or helper."[12] While at Yale and at Union Theological Seminary he manifested "an intense earnestness in whatever he undertook," according to his daughter.[13] Brace believed the refuges could not reform delinquents, but could only temporarily affect their behavior. A few months' experience convinced him that work among deprived adults was also hopeless, so he turned to working with children in the slums of New York City. Brace's daughter writes that, after hearing reports about 1850 of increased delinquency in the growing metropolis, he and other philanthropic gentleman "organized 'Boys' meetings,' as they were called, to be held on Sunday evenings, and designed to draw the roughest class of loafers from about the docks, and to reach and influence them by stories and allegories." That is, "to reach those wild hearts through eloquence"[14]—eloquence that was uncharacteristic of any aspect of the refuges. These meetings led to the opening of the Children's Aid Society, which operated schools and lodging houses for New York street children and "placed out" boys and girls to farm families on the western frontier—Ohio, Michigan, Indiana, and Illinois. This was probably a more benevolent form of "transportation" than that practiced by the British or by the refuges: the latter sent incorrigible boys on whaling voyages.[15] By 1872 Brace could boast that his society had placed between twenty and twenty-four thousand children. He admitted very few failures.

As with the refuges' reports, the main function of Brace's and the society's publications was to promote the Children's Aid Society, and the format of presentation was identical to that of earlier annual reports. After an opening text, appendixes were given in smaller type documenting the

year's accomplishments. These included "incidents" or brief case histories, usually taken from the "office-journal," and letters from the masters or employers of placed-out boys and girls, as well as from "prominent
gentlemen, clergymen, bankers, farmers, judges, and lawyers, through
the West, where the main body of these poor children have been
placed,"[16] and letters from the children themselves. Excerpts from the
diaries of staff and volunteers, who kept their own journals, were printed
by the society; this had not been done by the refuges. And there is even an
occasional brief life story presented in the words of the youth. A cluster of
these appears in the 1859 report (pp. 60–66) as extracts from the office
journal: "Some incidents in the little histories of the children were
saddening, others amusing. The story of a 'Circus Child' was particularly
interesting, and was told with affecting naiveté, and ingenuous frankness."

THE CIRCUS CHILD

CHARLES B—— is an American orphan, and has not
yet numbered twelve years. His features were lighted by a
lively keen eye.

"I was so young," said he, "when I lost daddy and mammy,
that I can't recollect much about them, only that they were like
well to do, for I was well cared for. I don't know if I had friends
or relations anywhere; if so be as I had, I don't know anything
about them. Father died, and mother, and the next thing I
remember is, that somebody gave me up to a Frenchman as
kept a circus. This man had twenty large horses, and three
little ones. I had to care two or three of them, big and little. I
was the only boy he had, but he had men. 'Twas too much for
me, and I didn't like this kind of life, but I didn't know what
else to do. He had a wicked mare, and I was always afeard of
her, for she always kicked about so when she seed me, that I
sometimes thought she had a grudge like against me. She got
worse when she had a young colt, and chased me one day out
of the stable, and nearly killed me.

"I was more than a year with the Frenchman when this happened," continued CHARLEY, "and a few days after, while I
had partikler charge of this wicked mare, I lost her. I'll tell you
how it was. The beast went to look for her colt, that was snug
in the stable all the time, and when I missed her I went to look
after her; you could almost have heard my heart beat, I was so
scared, for I was afeard of the Frenchman, for he had a voice
like the big trumpet one of the circus-men used to blow o'
horseback. I couldn't fetch up the mare anyhow. The Frenchman got his dander up, threatened to lick me, and told me to
clear off. I didn't wait to be told twice—so, though I hadn't a
place in the wide world, that I might call a home, nor a friend to
give me one, I showed my back to the Frenchman and his

circus. I guess I was lonesome then; and when I seed other
boys with nice clothes on 'em, who had fathers and mothers
(poor CHARLEY had none), maybe I didn't cry as I went round.

"At last, when I got very tired from walking, and sleeping
in coal-boxes and old wagons, that sometimes looked nearly as
broken up as myself, I was taken notice of by a good woman,
who had seen me round in a street where she lived herself. 'So,
Bobby,' says she to me, says she, 'han't you got no home?'
'No, ma'am,' says I, so then I told her what I knew of myself,
and maybe she didn't cry like myself for compassion for me.
So she took me home with her, and there I stayed for a time;
but the good woman was poor, and I couldn't feel like staying
with her. I didn't like to go round any more, and so I told her,
so she went with me to the poorhouse, on Long Island, and I
was in one of the houses for homeless children for about a
month, and found my way, at last, to this Society."

Following this, another boy tells his story even more briefly and "very
innocently," and reference is made to a "beautiful Irish girl": "Her story
is among the sad histories," but is not given. "The Runaway" is next, the
only rather full oral history I have found in these reports, and it, like the
shorter sketches, is not from a delinquent, though some people might
have called a boy delinquent if he ran away from someone he had been
bound to as an apprentice; at least this was viewed as a seed of actual
delinquency. But there was also sympathy for the child with a cruel master, and the term "delinquent" was not applied in these 1859 cases. The
story of the runaway resembles the briefer story of the circus child. It
begins with a description reminiscent of Mayhew:

He appeared to be about fourteen years old, and had quite a
good-humored, well-looking face, and a merry twinkling in his
blue eye. His attire was very simple, almost consisting of a
primitive garment something like a coat with long skirts; the
original color was quite gone, several greasy hues having taken
its place, and it was fastened near the neck with a piece of
twine. His yellow skin appeared through a rent or two in the
sleeves—the remark is superfluous that linen was invisible.
Before he told us his story, he desired something to eat, "for I
han't had nothing to-day," said he, "an' I never likes to talk
with a hungry mouth." His story is here set down in the very
words in which he delivered it.

This boy says that one day when he was a very little boy in Philadelphia
he followed some soldiers marching down the street and got lost. Apparently he landed in the Philadelphia House of Refuge and from there was
placed with a farmer in Delaware. John voices complaints about the

farmer's treatment of him and the credulity of the inspector from the house of refuge:

> When the Superintendent of the Refuge came around, every-
> thing was made to show fair. Then we had something like a fine
> time; for we all ate at the same table [otherwise the placed-out
> boys did not eat with the family], and we had meat with our
> cornbread.
>
> Mr. M—— would tell the Superintendent (there was a new one
> every year; the only one I know was Mr. A——), how much
> we were improved; though we never had a chance of goin' to
> school, or any place else where we could improve the least.
> We dursn't speak a word to the Superintendent, for fear.

Score one against the houses of refuge, even though the Children's Aid Society inspectors were probably no better. And score one for the society: after running away several times from farmer M's "hard grip" and working on a transatlantic steamship, John finds his way to the society, and his story ends with his departure for the West:

> He was the merriest of the party—all smiles and good
> humor—and gave three cheers, and hip, hip, hurra! for the
> Children's Aid Society, in a voice that drowned every other, as
> they entered the stage which was to take them to the ferry-
> boat. We anticipate good news from him soon.

After his ordeal with the Delaware farmer and a year on the open sea, why is John so eager to join an unknown Ohio farmer? Obviously rhetoric has been exercised on him as much as it was being used on the reader of his story.

Probably the most moving story Brace told was about a girl who had prostituted herself. Though only an incident in her life, not her whole life, presented in dialogue form, it is a stark revelation of character and circumstance, perhaps more directly affecting as well as effective in so-liciting attention than an oral history might be. Brace quotes the account in his *Dangerous Classes of New York,* from its original appearance in his 1854 report of the society:

THE TOMBS

> "Mrs. Forster, the excellent Matron of the Female Depart-
> ment of the prison, had told us of an interesting young German
> girl, committed for vagrancy, who might just at this crisis be
> rescued. I entered these soiled and gloomy Egyptian arch-
> ways, so appropriate and so depressing, that the sight of the
> low columns and lotus capitals is to me now inevitably as-
> sociated with the somber and miserable histories of the place.
> "After a short waiting, the girl was brought in—a German

girl, apparently about fourteen, very thinly but neatly dressed, of slight figure, and a face intelligent and old for her years, the eye passionate and shrewd. I give details because the conversation which followed was remarkable.

"The poor feel, but they can seldom speak. The story she told, with a wonderful eloquence, thrilled to all our hearts; it seemed to us, then, like the first articulate voice from the great poor class of the city.

"Her eye had a hard look at first, but softened when I spoke to her in her own language.

"'Have you been long here?'

"'Only two days, sir.'

"'Why are you here?'

"'I will tell you, sir. I was working out with a lady. I had to get up early and go to bed late, and I never had rest. She worked me always; and, finally, because I could not do everything, she beat me—she beat me like a dog, and I ran away; I could not bear it.'

"The manner of this was wonderfully passionate and eloquent.

"'But I thought you were arrested for being near a place of bad character,' said I.

"'I am going to tell you, sir. The next day I and my father went to get some clothes I left there, and the lady wouldn't give them up; and what could we do? What can the poor do? My father is a poor old man, who picks rags in the streets, and I have never picked rags yet. He said, "I don't want you to be a rag-picker. You are not a child now—people will look at you—you will come to harm." And I said, "No, father, I will help you. We must do something now, I am out of place"; and so I went out. I picked all day, and didn't make much, and I was cold and hungry. Towards night, a gentleman met me—a very fine, well-dressed gentleman, an American, and he said, "Will you go home with me?" and I said, "No." He said, "I will give you twenty shillings," and I told him I would go. And the next morning I was taken up outside by the officer.'

"'Poor girl!' said some one, 'had you forgotten your mother? and what a sin it was!'

"'No, sir, I did remember her. She had no clothes, and I had no shoes; and I have only this (she shivered in her thin dress), and winter is coming on. I know what making money is, sir. I am only fourteen, but I am old enough. I have had to take care of myself ever since I was ten years old, and I have never had a cent given me. It may be a sin, sir (and the tears rained down her cheeks, which she did not try to wipe away). I do not ask you to forgive it. Men can't forgive, but God will forgive. I know about men.

"'The rich do such things and worse, and no one says any-thing against them. But I, sir—*I am poor!* (This she said with a tone which struck the very heart-strings.) I have never had any one to take care of me. Many is the day I have gone hungry from morning till night, because I did not dare spend a cent or two, the only ones I had. Oh, I have wished sometimes so to die! Why does not God kill me?'

"She was choked by her sobs. We let her calm herself a moment, and then told her our plan of finding her a good home, where she could make an honest living. She was mistrustful. 'I will tell you, *meine Herren;* I know men, and I do not believe any one, I have been cheated so often. There is no trust in any one. I am not a child. I have lived as long as people twice as old.'

"'But you do not wish to stay in prison?'

"'O God, no! Oh, there is such a weight on my heart here. There is nothing but bad to learn in prison. These dirty Irish girls! I would kill myself if I had to stay here. Why was I ever born? I have such *Kummerniss* (woes) here (she pressed her hand on her heart)—I am poor!'

"We explained our plan more at length, and she became satisfied. We wished her to be bound to stay some years.

"'No,' said she, passionately, 'I cannot; I confess to you, gentlemen. I should either run away or die, if I was bound.'

"We talked with the matron. She had never known, she said, in her experience, such a remarkable girl. The children there of nine or ten years were often as old as young women, but this girl was an experienced woman. The offense, how-ever, she had no doubt was her first.

"We obtained her release; and one of us, Mr. G., walked over to her house or cabin, some three miles on the other side of Williamsburgh, in order that she might see her parents be-fore she went to her new home.

"As she walked along, she looked up in Mr. G's face, and asked thoughtfully, Why we came there for her? He explained. She listened, and after a little while, said, in broken English, 'Don't you think better for poor little girls to die than live?' He spoke kindly to her, and said something about a good God. She shook her head, "No, no good God. Why am I so? It always was so. Why much suffer, if good God?" He told her they would get her a supper, and in the morning she should start off and find new friends. She became gradually almost ungoverned—sobbed—would like to die, even threatened suicide in this wild way.

"Kindness and calm words at length made her more reason-able. After much trouble, they reached the home or den of the poor rag-picker. The parents were very grateful, and she was to start off the next morning to a country home, where, perhaps finally, the parents will join her.

"For myself, the evening shadow seemed more somber, and the cheerful home-lights less cheerful, as I walked home, remembering such a history.

"Ye who are happy, whose lives have been under sunshine and gentle influences around whom Affection, and Piety, and Love have watched, as ye gather in cheerful circles these autumn evenings, think of these bitter and friendless children of the poor, in the great city. But few have such eloquent expressions as this poor girl, yet all inarticulately feel.

"There are sad histories beneath this gay world—lives over which is the very shadow of death. God be thanked, there is a Heart which feels for them all, where every pang and groan will find a sympathy, which will one day right the wrong, and bring back the light over human life.

"The day is short for us all; but for some it will be a pleasant thought, when we come to lay down our heads at last, that we have eased a few aching hearts, and brought peace and new hope to the dark lives of those whom men had forgotten or cast out."[17]

Oddly enough in the light of the above, the cause of delinquency persistently urged in nineteenth-century America was the failure of parental discipline. Institutions, even the refuges, typically claimed to be a substitute or even a model for the American family. But Samuel Gridley Howe remarked: "The family must grow; it cannot be made in a day, nor be put together by rules and compass.... We have, at best, a make-believe society, a make-believe family, and, too often, a make-believe virtue."[18] The briefer the case history, the more plausible the family interpretation seems to be. The larger the scope of life that emerges from an oral history, the more the broader community and even political situation begins to appear.

Forces Opposing Oral History

Why are there almost no oral histories in the publications of the houses of refuge or the Children's Aid Society? In his book *The Nether Side of New York; or, The Vice, Crime and Poverty of the Great Metropolis,* journalist Edward Crapsey in 1872 put his finger on perhaps the chief cause: "The moral and physical destitution of these child-vagrants and the causes which produced them, are the topics chiefly discussed by these societies; but the statements of facts are almost entirely confined to the means of reclamation which they so constantly and unselfishly exert."[19] These organizations were interested in the person's background only to demonstrate the need for an alternative environment for vagrant and delinquent children and to show how difficult was their job of maintaining one. But the real crux was whether they successfully reformed anyone; it was precisely in that regard, where the most powerful rhetorical appeal needed to be made, that the managers and secretaries did indeed approach oral histories when they published letters from children they had placed out.

Of course these are always success stories. (Not surprisingly, Horatio Alger collected material for his books at the Newsboys' Lodging House, operated by the Children's Aid Society.) Elijah Devoe, a disgruntled former employee of the New York House of Refuge in the 1840s, called the refuges' claims of "unqualified success" "tautological eulogies and pompous puffs," "the testimony of one party." What did the inmates *really* think?[20] Devoe himself exposed some bad features of the places, in one instance quoting a boy gazing through the bars of a window at a desolate waterfront and saying, "with naive earnestness and a delectable lisp, 'That lookths good out there, Mr. D———.'"[21] As Robert Pickett points out, case studies of juvenile delinquents describe the observers as well as, or perhaps even more than, the subject: "In large part the Refuge story becomes a chronicle of the activities of those who controlled the institution, the Board of Managers of the Society for the Reformation of Juvenile Delinquents."[22]

At any rate, the circumstances for collecting oral histories were most unfavorable in the refuges. Cecile Remick describes the daily regimen at the house of refuge in Philadelphia:

> In the summer months, they arose at 5:00 A.M., worked 9
> hours, and attended school for only 3½ hours. Hence, one can
> see there was little time for idleness or free play in the lives of
> the children who were incarcerated in the House. This, of
> course, reflected the belief that idleness was evil or could
> cause evil actions.[23]

Collecting histories at the Children's Aid Society seems to have been more relaxed than at the refuges. Reference is occasionally made in these reports to young people coming into the office and telling their stories. Notes on these interviews were included in the daily office journal, and summaries of them appear here and there in reports. But apparently no one thought it important to record the lives of children in as concrete, continuous, and detailed a way as their oral histories would have provided.

Even worse, refuge authorities seem to be saying that children should be seen only as conspicuous objects of philanthropy, especially when the many foreigners and Americans visited the institutions; they should be heard only to fortify the spirits of the staff and the bank balance of the organization through the congratulatory letters that were published. Mennel wonders about "the degrees of duress applied" to get such letters: "saying and doing what was expected of juvenile delinquents who had been reformed, some of the refuge children became accomplices to the missionary purposes of the institution's founders."[24] Rothman has raised a similar doubt about the Auburn biographies.[25] On the other hand, institutional authorities could have been duped by manipulative youths: Children's Aid Society personnel were aware of fictitious stories, especially from runaways.[26]

Another impediment to oral histories was the image held by refuge staff of the "ragged and uncleanly appearance, the vile language, and the idle and miserable habits of great numbers of children."[27] But if children's language was too vivid for the refuges, it was less than vivid for Brace, according to his remarks in the unconventionally "eloquent" story reproduced above. Perhaps the stories of many (though surely not all) delinquents were in fact undramatic. The plodding reports of institutional authorities were hardly more exciting, but behind *them* lay a respectable social position and quantified accomplishments. All the children had to testify to was their reform: on that they were considered expert enough. On that they could even give speeches, such as the oration of the newsboy who whipped up his comrades to "make tracks for the West, from the Children's Aid Society."[28] The format of putting offenders' testimony in appendixes to institutional annual reports was followed by the more humanitarian Clay, but in the houses of refuge cases the segregation seems even more related to their belief that the delinquent was an inferior being. Then, too, one reads appendixes only after having been correctly oriented by authorities' reports.[29]

We may say that five basic terms of rhetoric are argument, character of the speaker, emotion expressed in the speech, style of delivery, and audience. Fundamental change has occurred, first, in the quality of emotion, comparing Brace's writing with the refuge reports. Brace's method is considerably more intense and expansive in emotion than the earlier case histories, and this is connected to shifts in the other rhetorical elements: the argument has moved from favoring centralized institutions to proposing programs more spread out in communities; youths themselves occasionally appear as enthusiastic speakers; the language in places reproduces dialect;[30] and Brace's audience seems to be broader than the group of people who received the refuges' annual renderings. After all, more volunteers were needed for the decentralized programs of the Children's Aid Society than had been required for the penitentiarylike refuges, where one person wielding a whip could keep a file of boys in line. In fact, every citizen could be considered a Children's Aid Society volunteer, looking out for potential delinquents and getting involved with them through the organization. Echoing Mayhew and Clay, Brace wrote: "I have hope that these little incidents related of their trials and temptations, may bring the two ends of society nearer together in human sympathy."[31] It appears that the move toward oral history and volunteerism opens up a structure of discourse or society to nonprofessionals.

Histories of delinquency in antebellum America often refer to this period's acceptance of Lockean epistemology, especially the notion that the child is not born with an evil or a good nature but is a tabula rasa that could go either way depending on nurture. An equally fitting Lockean principle is the distinction between primary qualities (shape, weight) and secondary qualities (color, smell). Refuge case histories do not expand much beyond certain "objective" atomic data, such as age, offense, and disposition of the case, leaving out, say, the views of youths themselves, which could be only "subjective." So long as the subjective/objective distinction is fundamental, oral histories will be suspect and avoided, because from this perspective they fall squarely in the lesser of the two categories. Though emotion has its own integrity in rhetoric, in this "scientific" mode emotion is opposed to cognition and is thus "merely emotive." Rhetoric is usually "mere rhetoric." For the Children's Aid Society, rhetoric functioned to attract public funds and personnel. With the arrival and rise to paradigmatic prominence of the science of criminology, in the second half of the nineteenth century, cognitive methods triumphed: the scientist's audience did not need to be aroused as the philanthropist's did, and emotion became an object of investigation rather than a quality of expression. However, not every criminologist was exclusively a scientist: research and reform became mixed together, as we shall see.

At midcentury there was at least a mild alteration in the direction of human feeling for the American delinquent, along with a corresponding increase in awareness of the social contexts of delinquency, an increase of emotion directed to an expanding middle-class audience, and the appearance of something more like oral history. Even Charles Loring Brace emerges as a personality (a "speaker" with an ethos) more fully than any of the refuge managers. According to Schlossman: "The theory of juvenile justice in the mid-nineteenth century thus embodied a broad reorientation in values. In the Victorian period, affect (in the psychological meaning) became the moral and pedagogical axis around which, ideally, religion, literature, architecture, education, child nurture, and juvenile corrections revolved."[32] Hawes says that Brace's stories "illustrate not only the continued viability of the Protestant Ethic and the self-help ideal, but also a growing humanitarianism. It was only a beginning, and often it was a case of one stereotype replacing another. While 'lo, the poor children' was kinder than the view of children as miniature adults, it was no more accurate and certainly not much more individualistic."[33] According to Mennel: "Brace never referred to children as 'convicts' or 'depraved young persons'—traditional refuge terms implying at least some degree of innate wickedness."[34]

Even Brace, however, had one foot stuck firmly in natural causes. When a child exhibited licentious habits similar to those of his or her parents and grandparents, Brace believed that "gemmules" were at work. Brace said: "The 'gemmules,' or latent tendencies, or forces, or cells of her immediate ancestors were in her system, and working in her blood, producing irresistible effects on her brain, nerves, and mental emotions."[35] If the child's environment pushed in the wrong way, downfall was inevitable. Just as Mayhew's scheme was flawed by gratuitous assertions about "wandering tribes," so humanistic environmentalism in mid-nineteenth-century America was confused by notions about a person's nature that were at once atavisms and premonitions of later hereditarian and genetic theories.

The trend was toward concepts of a changing environment rather than of a fixed nature, toward more emotive communications by personalities rather than reports of official automatons, toward appreciation of experience rather than insistence on hard data about a hard regimen for hardened natures, and toward decentralization of programs, making greater use of community volunteers. Nevertheless, these leaders in delinquency efforts were held back from a fully phenomenological grasp of their subject mainly by a lingering Calvinism that demanded obedience to a stern, transcendent figure: nothing but prayer or its secular equivalent in the literature of "rising"—the success story—was worth repeating, and unctuous piety drowned out the sharp, frank stories of youth.

Five

Snitching Bees and Talking Cures:
The Early Juvenile Court

Ben Lindsey and the Beast

Benjamin Barr Lindsey (1870–1943) believed that individuals are not by nature corrupt, but that environment is the main determinant of human behavior.[1] He was aware of social conditions as causes of delinquency and exposed these to the public: "The child is not bad," he said, "but conditions are bad—things are bad."[2] He was an energetic, exuberant man, full of the "bully" spirit of his friend Teddy Roosevelt. He had an innovative, even improvisational temperament: he developed a juvenile court in Denver, Colorado, in 1901, making use of a truancy law and his position as a county court judge, though he was unaware of the juvenile court that had opened in Chicago two years earlier. Lindsey's ideas came from his firsthand experience during the "weary after court hours and long evenings I have spent with the boys in the court, in chambers, in the jail, in the alleys, in the slums."[3] Just as Mayhew cast scorn on "arm-chair theorists," Lindsey boasted that his books were not "academic . . . not a swivel-chair product."[4] Also like Mayhew, he was oriented to action, not as a journalist meeting deadlines but as a judge "obliged by my office to express . . . conclusions in terms of action and by official verdict."[5] And, like Mayhew's, Lindsey's thought was somewhat unsystematic and inconsistent, richer in rhetorical amplification than in conceptual cogency.

Ben Lindsey exemplifies a typical humanitarian stance in other ways. He urged condemnation of the offense, not the offender. He would cut through bureaucratic and even legal red tape in the interest of helping people. People should be motivated to obey laws not out of fear of punishment, he felt, but because the rightness of the act has been pointed out to them with sympathy and kindness. He had a remarkable ability to empathize, and the boys who appeared in his court must have found it easy to identify with him: he was almost their height and had a childlike face. Mennel writes of his "warm and erratic personality,"[6] Larsen of his sense of drama: "Whenever he was in New York, Lindsey found time to see a great number of plays and subsequently amazed his friends with his ability to mimic actors and re-enact scenes."[7] He had gotten through law school by organizing mock trials, debating societies, and quiz classes.[8] He had both a flair for oratory and a sense of humor, which he exercised in his many speaking engagements around the country as the most visible national spokesman for the juvenile court. He found hypocrisy repugnant, especially that surrounding sex and marriage.[9]

Like Mayhew and Clay, Lindsey organized a "Juvenile Improvement Association" to gather statistics, call meetings, and publicize the needs of underprivileged children,"[10] though it seems that he did not emphasize the abilities of citizens to organize themselves, as Mayhew and Clay had. To get support for the juvenile court and related initiatives, Lindsey "carefully cultivated private charitable and religious groups as well as public agencies and lawmaking bodies."[11] In conveying his accomplishments to the public he was not satisfied with "a mere report of the text of laws and the numbers of children in court, their disposition, etc., [to show] what is meant by the Juvenile Court of Denver. Something of its character, meaning, history, and the purpose and spirit back of it must necessarily be referred to."[12] How is this spirit to be communicated? "A story is its own good excuse; and these experiences from real life convey in the form of action the human side of the ideas I have been setting down."[13]

Lindsey's writing is filled with anecdotes about his encounters with young people. Doubtless he had occasion to listen to rather extended stories about their lives as well as to visit their homes, see their surroundings, and talk with their parents. However, though Lindsey had some of the personal attributes for producing delinquents' oral histories, he did not do so. For us he is an important figure because he illustrates several forces opposing the genesis of oral histories.

Lindsey's chief source of youths' stories about themselves was "snitching bees," as he called them. These were events where boys would meet in his court or chambers and confess their offenses.[14] Since snitching on other people was disloyal and wrong, they were allowed to tell only on themselves. These conversations were regarded by Lindsey as privileged communications: on one occasion he was suppoenaed to reveal what a boy had told him in private about the murder of his father, for which his mother was on trial; Lindsey refused to violate the boy's confidence and was assessed a stiff fine. The boys were encouraged to persuade other boys to come in and snitch on themselves, which apparently did happen. "The only way to remove the spell of fear which gags them and holds them dumb is to create the right protective conditions, the right privacy, and the right sympathy."[15] Lindsey was effective in this because he offered the boys security from reprisal (unless they were so incorrigible that they had to be sent to the reform school, but even this was "for their own good") and because he trusted and respected them (he had an honor system for sending boys on the trip to the reform school

unaccompanied, carrying their own papers). He spoke their own language
and made the whole court process an adventure for them. Lincoln Steffens wrote:

> the Judge reaches out and seizing one [boy] by the shoulder
> pulls him up to him, saying:
>
> "Skinny, you've been doing fine lately; had a crackerjack
> report every time. I just want to see if you have kept it up. Bet
> you have. Let's see." He opens the report. "That's great.
> Shake, Skin. You're all right, you are." Skinny shines.[16]

Apparently the stigma of being present at the court was reduced by

> many fine-spirited girls and boys of high character . . . who by
> their presence in my court, or in my company, furnish the
> camouflage that protects from suspicion other young people
> whose relations with me are of a different sort because they
> have come to me voluntarily to be helped out of some diffi-
> culty. This circumstance makes it easy for those whose con-
> science would otherwise make cowards of them to come to me
> without fear of exposure or loss of self-respect.[17]

In addition, no records were kept on anyone. Lindsey was so effective
with boys that a rumor started that he used hypnosis: it *had* to be some
esoteric technique, since decency and respect would obviously be mis-
placed in these little devils!

As an example of humor in these boys' stories, Lindsey relates the case
of Mickey, who had been in trouble so often that the local policeman
would automatically pick him up if anything went wrong in his neighborhood:

> Sometimes Mickey's hard little pipe-stem legs would carry
> him to my chambers ahead of time when he felt, as he used to
> say, "Judge, I dun got in trouble again; en I thought I better get
> here before de cops do"; and his squinty blue eyes and his
> shock of Irish red hair were a familiar sight in the court house.
> It came to pass, therefore, that whenever there was mischief
> afoot, and the local cop had gone ahunting, Mickey would run
> the instant he spied him; and this he would do even if he was
> innocent, as sometimes happened. Flight naturally drew suspi-
> cion and pursuit, and Mickey would then be confronted by the
> difficulty of explaining why he had run if he "hadn't done
> nuthin.'"
> "Mickey," I said to him on one occasion, "when you are
> innocent, why not stand your ground?"
> A pained expression came into his face. "Judge," he said,
> "don't you know that you can't tell a cop nothin.' Judge, *when*

a cop is after yuh, he's agin yuh; and there's only one thing t'do—Ditch and Skidoo. If yuh don't yuh just naturally gits pinched."

"But, Mickey," I protested, "that's no reason why you should lie to the cop."

To my surprise he said, "Judge, I never lies to the cop."

"I don't know what you call it, then," I said, "when you knocked the props out from under that fruit stand, and you skedadled with the cop after you; and when he caught you you told him you didn't do it. Just now you told me you did do it. You told me the truth, and you lied to the cop."

Again he put on the air of injured innocence that he could assume to perfection when he wished, and then came back at me with this:

"Judge, dat ain't lyin' to the cop, dat's *stringin'* de cop. For yuh see, Judge, it's like dis. Dat guy had pinched me so much when I hadn't done nothin' dat when he pinches me for somethin' I done I says I didn't do it, so as to make up fer one of the times when he says I done it when I didn't. Dat's stringin' de cop. An' he's still got a lot o' string comin' to 'im!"

I defy anybody to show that Mickey did not there make an effective appeal to the elemental right of self-defense, or to show that the policeman had any right to expect the truth from his lips.[18]

Lindsey uses this anecdote to show that boys' humor is "nothing but a form of logic so honest and remorseless that it follows through to the bitter end."[19] "Reform," according to the "kids' judge," as he was called, "can come about only through a change in thinking. The boy doesn't wilfully think wrong; he does it because the premises of his logic are incorrect. Change that and you change the boy."[20] Lindsey's snitching bees were therefore a form of group therapy, and the main point of action and change was not in communicating the boy's story to a public but in the very act of the boy's speaking—speaking intimately in front of a representative of the law and thus encouraging a less fearful attitude toward authority. "When they deal with me," Lindsey wrote, "they get it off their chests."[21]

In this respect, Lindsey's practice was similar both to Clay's confessional and to Healy's talking cure, which we shall consider next: "Usually I find I am the first person who has ever afforded them this essential relief, —unless they happen to be Roman Catholics, in which event the Confessional, which is in many respects one of the most profoundly wise of human institutions, has helped them."[22] According to Lindsey, the Juvenile Court of Denver was a "hospital, a moral hospital. It deals with the sick and crippled of spirit. Its function, therefore, is

psychologically one of extreme delicacy."[23] Elsewhere Lindsey wrote
that a juvenile court "should more nearly approximate a doctor's office or
a hospital than the court of the present." That is, it should be under the
direction of "those scientifically trained and fitted to deal with the behavior and conduct of people."[24] Because of the insight and techniques he
had developed apart from academic work, primarily out of his own experience, Lindsey was much admired by adolescent and educational
psychologists of his day.[25]

The relevant "life speech" was, then, the utterance by the boy that he
had done wrong. This satisfied at once a legal requirement of focusing on
the offense (though in the nonadversary procedures of the new juvenile
court, not of proving that it had been committed) and the therapeutic
requirement of undoing suppressions and instilling trust. Since the
reformatory aspect of the utterance was its most important feature, it is
not surprising that when the stories were communicated to the public they
tended to be parables or success stories similar to the letters used by the
refuges and the Children's Aid Society. Lindsey also employed such promotional material in his many homilies to the boys. Lincoln Steffens
wrote:

> "Boys," he [Lindsey] begins, "last time I told you about
> Kid Dawson and some other boys who used to be with us and
> who 'made good.' Today I've got a letter from the Kid. He's in
> Oregon, and he's doing well. I'll read you what he says about
> himself and his new job."
> And he reads the letter, which is full of details roughly set in
> a general feeling of encouragement and self-confidence.[26]

One wonders to what extent Lindsey conformed to the advice Lyman
Beecher Stowe gave to William B. George when George was writing
Citizens Made and Remade (1912), about the George Junior Republics,
self-governing societies of young people:

> There are some minor inaccuracies which you will please cor-
> rect. There are, however, I imagine some inaccuracies which I
> hope you will let pass so long as the general impression is
> truthful. Remember, you are not writing a history or a biog-
> raphy of yourself, but merely interpreting the whole. Truth in
> details can and should be subordinated and even sacrificed
> when necessary to truth of impression which must be a bit
> colored to penetrate the brain of the ordinary reader. There is a
> kind of prose license as well as poetic license.[27]

Despite Stowe's reminder, George's three books, in which he defends his
version of an anti-institution institution, are largely autobiographical.

To summarize: oral history does not appear in criminological discourse when more emphasis is placed on the delinquent's offense than on the social context of the offender; when the act of individual confession or therapy is more important than the act of going public to promote social change; and when what is promoted and defended is the accomplishments of an institution in brief success stories rather than the need for institutions fitted to people who live certain kinds of lives.

Lindsey may have avoided recording the social backgrounds of delinquents also because he knew some of that reality at first hand and did not find it as interesting as might someone for whom deprivation was an alien experience. While growing up, Lindsey had suffered hardship caused by his father's financial difficulties and eventual suicide. While attending law school, he was overwhelmed by a sense of failure and tried to kill himself, but the gun did not go off. This experience left him with the feeling that he had no greater enemy than his own weakness; if he had faced his own death, he could face anything. Face opposition Lindsey did, and the fight with "the beast" of political interests and corruption increasingly occupied much of his life. Criminogenic social circumstances that might have been revealed by oral histories were obvious, at least to Lindsey, but behind those situations were their economic and political causes, and the attention of the public needed to be aroused not so much to the immediate life situations of the child as to those more fundamental causes. The effects of "the system" (his word) could be seen in people's lives, but the system itself could be changed only by fighting it directly. Lindsey said: "I saw, through the tears and misfortunes of these children, the defects and injustice in our social, political and economic system."[28] He began with the individual problems of children in trouble, and then

> I began to deepen and broaden that work, to peer from effect to cause. And across my range of vision rolled cotton mill and beet fields with their pitiable child slaves and the dance halls and vice dens of the underworld.
> And I found that these influences that were undermining childhood were in league with the capitalistic powers of Special Privilege, the real political masters of our city and state.
> In short, I faced a whole system and the System's State.[29]

When Lindsey visited the home of a boy who had been brought to his court for stealing coal, he discovered that the boy had stolen to heat the family's shack. His father had been working a twelve-hour day but was laid up with lead poisoning: "If society had done its duty by protecting him from the rapacity of his employer—by means of an eight-hour [workday] law and an employer's liability law—his son would not have been driven to steal."[30] According to Slater: "Lindsey went from juvenile problems to ever-widening areas of social concern, in a process which can be called 'ramifying reform.'"[31]

Some of the many initiatives Lindsey fought for were: a contributory delinquency law, the first of its kind in the United States, which gave the juvenile court jurisdiction over parents of delinquents; a revision of probate laws; jury reform; agitation for women's suffrage; and bills opening schools as social centers, increasing the number of probation officers, creating a minimum wage for women and minors, and establishing child labor laws. The cause that probably brought him the most notoriety was "companionate marriage," which included legalization of birth control, sex education, abolition of automatic alimony, and easier divorces for childless couples. One of the reasons that Lindsey, unlike probably any other juvenile court judge, became involved in such broader issues was that he had improvised the Juvenile and Family Court of Denver while still serving as a judge in the county court:

> At that time I also presided in a Court having jurisdiction of cases growing out of the political turmoils of a growing American city . . . . In these contests powerful business interests were seeking special privileges and were not particular how they got them. This brought me into intimate, personal contact with the truth about the political life of our cities.[32]

Finally these pressures and the Ku Klux Klan succeeded in removing Lindsey from the Denver branch in 1927, and he spent the rest of his life as a judge in California.

With regard to oral history and delinquency, let me make two points about Lindsey's political activity. Oral reports of delinquents' experiences may be put to a more effective use than storing them away in a book that politically powerful people may not have the time or interest to read. If the stories reveal especially outrageous conditions, such as children mingling with adults in jails (as they still did in Lindsey's Denver a half-century after Mayhew and Clay had complained about the situation in England) or being allowed free access to saloons, then inviting the police board or the governor and mayor to your courtroom, with newspaper reporters or clergy present, and subjecting them to the boys' testimony (which they may try to impeach) may shame these worthies into appropriate action, urged on by outraged ministers the following Sunday morning and by headlines every day of the week. This Lindsey did. Hence the most interesting story concerning delinquency was not the life history of any delinquent but rather the sensational exploits of the world's most famous juvenile court judge. In *The Beast* Lindsey wrote:

> It is a condition of this whole struggle with the Beast that the man who fights it must come out into the open with his life, conspicuously and with the appearance of a strut—like some sort of blessed little hero-martyr—while it keeps modestly under cover and watches him and bides its time![33]

In *The Dangerous Life* (which was about this celebrated foe of special privilege, not about a street gang member), Lindsey said:

> The truth is that what happened to the public official, Judge Ben B. Lindsey, is tragic—any other representation would be false. It is tragic to America. And that is what justifies this story of "The Dangerous Life." That is why it must be burned into the consciousness of my country.[34]

As Larsen has put it: "Since he believed that his actions were motivated by a highly developed sense of social idealism, he had the satisfaction of always being the hero in the historical drama that was perennially unfolding."[35] In this he resembles Saul Alinsky, whom I shall consider later as a pioneer of the recent political model in the juvenile justice system. Lindsey straddled the turn of the century not only chronologically but ideologically: he avoided oral histories because his work was related both to the earliest and to the most recent delinquency efforts in America.

Sore Spots: William Healy and the Medical Model

When Jane Addams visited London in 1883 she saw a newspaper series on the London poor entitled "The Bitter Cry of Outcast London": "The conscience of England was stirred as never before over this joyless city in the East End of its capital."[36] Thus four years before Henry Mayhew's death the images he had brought to life had long since vanished and similar revelations were taking their place. Addams also had some direct contact with the London poor and saw in operation a settlement house, Toynbee Hall, that became the model for Hull House, which she founded in Chicago in 1889. Like London in the decades before Mayhew, Chicago after the Great Fire in 1871 witnessed enormous population growth; from 1880 to 1910 the population increased by a half-million every ten years. Harold Finestone has written that the Chicago ethos of social philanthropy developed under three conditions: "1. the rapidity of the economic and population growth of Chicago, 2. the heterogeneity of its population, including considerable class, social, and cultural cleavages, and 3. the complex, confused moral quality of its life."[37] The same could be said of Mayhew's London.

One of the many reform projects pursued by the ladies of Hull House was to start a juvenile court in 1899, the world's first. According to Jane Addams:

> Children over ten years of age were arrested, held in the police stations, tried in the police courts. If convicted they were usually fined and if the fine was not paid sent to the city prison. But often they were let off because justices could neither tolerate sending children to the Bridewell nor bear to be themselves guilty of the harsh folly of compelling poverty-stricken parents

to pay fines. No exchange of court records existed and the
same children could be in and out of various police stations an
indefinite number of times, more hardened and more skillful
with each experience.[38]

At first it was believed that court appearances and probationary supervision would prevent further delinquency, but as Ethel Dummer, one of
the Hull House ladies, noted: "There were certain children who without
rhyme or reason repeated some one symptom of delinquency, either
stealing, lying, or sex offense. These were so abnormal that I urged scientific research concerning the causes."[39] Juvenile court judges, with
their legal training, were not qualified to make such inquiries, and Chicago
produced no official with the broadened sensibility of Ben Lindsey. William Healy, M.D., was selected as the first director of the Juvenile
Psychopathic Institute, later renamed the Institute for Juvenile Research
when it was taken over by the state of Illinois. Though several institutions
antedated it, the Chicago institute is usually regarded as the first major
child study and guidance clinic: Healy made the first systematic investigations of individual delinquents using medical and psychological
tests, and he devised some of the early mental tests. In preparation for his
work, Healy toured the United States in 1908, a year before the opening of
the clinic, but found little to help him: "As for any scientific studies of the
bases of children's behavior tendencies, it was said that we in Chicago
would have to blaze a new trail."[40]

One of the techniques Healy used to study delinquents was to obtain
the individual's "own story," as he referred to it, always in quotation
marks, perhaps to give the phrase an air of technicality and transform a
rather ordinary process into a professional ritual. In 1948 Healy remarked: "It seems ridiculous now, but it was a sign of the times that this
introduction of the 'Own Story' was regarded as my unique contribution.
Anyhow, this innovation in the study of cases aroused much general and
professional interest."[41] It would have seemed as ridiculous in 1848 as it
would have seemed in 1948 to claim that acquiring a child's own story was
innovative, since apparently this was done to some degree even in the
houses of refuge. "Own story" as an innovation makes sense only in the
context of the scientific fashions Healy confronted when he set about his
work, fashions that overshadowed the earlier philanthropic work.[42]

The scientific tradition in criminology began in the 1870s with publications by the Italian physician Cesare Lombroso. Lombroso, dissatisfied
with legalistic classifications of crime (as we have seen that both Mayhew
and Clay were),[43] began examining individual offenders, focusing primarily on the criminal's body. Lombroso thought the offender's body had
marks of a "born criminal," revealing him to be an atavism on the scale of
evolution. Healy, who held a medical degree from the University of

Chicago, tried without success to find such stigmata on the delinquents he examined. (Ben Lindsey had remarked that physical conditions may indeed be connected with delinquency: if a boy is hungry he may steal food.[44]) Thus Healy's turning away from physical facts to personal facts viewed through an individual's speech was, as it had been in the opening decades of the previous century, part of a move away from a concept of the offender as innately criminal and toward a concept of environmental forces impinging on a basically good or at least morally neutral character or ego. Lombroso, too, had listened to offenders talk about their lives, though he published little of that material. Neither did Healy reproduce many "own stories" in his publications, and on final balance Dr. Healy's and Dr. Lombroso's methods, as we shall see, merge into what has been called the "medical model."

Why did Healy consider the child's own story important enough to solicit? Underlying all other influences was Healy's emphasis on case study of individuals: just as Langdell had introduced the case study method into legal education at Harvard in the 1870s,[45] Healy is usually given credit for introducing it into the scientific investigation of delinquency. This was a culmination of trends in both science and reform. The psychologist G. Stanley Hall had called for "further study, by expert methods, of individual cases and their relation to the social environment."[46] Hall himself, an academic, quotes experts on delinquency but includes no cases in his masterwork, *Adolescence.* The second tendency came from the juvenile court, which gave Healy his mandate of "diagnosis before treatment" in order to help the judge decide what was best for the individuals who appeared before him. As Hawes put it: "Such a study was in keeping with the whole trend toward individualization of treatment for juvenile offenders—the trend which had led to the creation of the juvenile court."[47] Unlike Lombroso and the European criminologists of his day, Healy had no interest in constructing a theory. As Radzinowitz has put it: "In the face of the complications of an actual case, the generalizations of criminology tended to crumble away."[48] (However, like Mayhew, Healy did emphasize a criminogenic place.) The court provided a never-ending source of subjects, and the clinic—at first three small rooms in the juvenile court building across the street from Hull House—was a place where records could be stored and research data built up.

In the absence of "nature" (inheritance or body) as a region of evidence, obviously "nurture" was the place to look, and one obvious source was the testimony of the youths themselves. When John Burnham asked Healy how he hit on "own story," he replied:

> how I got them to come out with this story. Well, it was just a
> friendly inquiry with the youngster, if you are friendly with

them, ask them, "Do you know why you do this?" A good
many times they say they don't. "Can't we find out why you're
delinquent in these ways?" And so on. The child likes to talk it
out, much the same as a person who goes into psychoanalysis
who gets the idea that it's lots of fun talking about yourself . . . .
That's how it began and that's how you still do it with
youngsters.[49]

Another influence predisposing Healy to "own story" was his association with William James. William Healy (1869–1963) was born near London and came to Chicago as a child. Because of his family's poverty he
had to leave school at the age of thirteen, but he got a good education from
several well-read colleagues at the bank where he worked. One of the
people he met in Chicago was the brother-in-law of William James. James
helped Healy enter Harvard as a special student at age twenty-four and
became "the figure with whom William Healy identified, and this
identification (physician, psychologist, and philosopher) fixed the abiding
interests of Healy forever."[50] Though in 1875 William James had set up at
Harvard what has been called the first laboratory of physiological
psychology in the United States, his interest became more and more
phenomenological and against "brass experimentation." In 1886 James
gave the Gifford Lectures on Natural Religion, and though they were not
published until 1902, as *The Varieties of Religious Experience*, surely
Healy either read the lectures themselves or drafts of the book, or at least
through James came under the influence of the appreciation the book
shows for varieties of experience expressed in autobiographical form.

Gordon Allport has called *The Varieties of Religious Experience* "the
first great book in psychology to rest its case entirely upon the use and
interpretation of personal documents."[51] According to Allport, James
was drawn to *documents humains*, as they were then called, as a way of
getting firsthand at experience and finding out what "finite individual
minds [which James had defined psychology to be the science of] were at
their more complex levels of integration."[52] As James Olney has put it:
"When William James studied the mind in use, or when Henry Adams
studied *his* mind in use and W. D. Howells *his*, what each of them seemed
to discover was that there is no single, inviolable personality that accompanies the individual his life long."[53] Autobiographies demonstrate that
there is no single essence to delinquency, or to any other human topic.
When Julia Lathrop of Hull House sought James's guidance in selecting a
clinic director, he replied that he did not think that experience in a
psychological laboratory should be a qualification for the job: "It was the
'dynamic' aspect which he thought important—in other words, the general, clinical, personal study of the individual child." And he strongly
recommended Healy for the position.[54]

"Own story" was also a result of the fact that Healy was a physician. After leaving Harvard, Healy had entered medical school: "I wanted to go into psychology but didn't want to go in professionally. I thought I would learn more about human beings by knowing them in medical ways than in any other way—as a physician." "A physician gets into the inner life of people." He "gets under the skin" of his patients.[55] Before he started the Juvenile Psychopathic Institute, Healy's field of specialization had been neurology, in the practice of which it was routine to acquire the patient's statement of his troubles. "Own story," then, gives the doctor an entrée into the patient's mind:

> The "own story" affords the only means of acquiring knowledge of many facts concerning outside situations as well as factors in the mental life which may be active elements in producing that which we are studying, namely, the tendency to delinquency. There is much richer psychology concerned with inner mental life, memories, ideations, imageries, etc., with their emotional backgrounds than is dreamed of during an ordinary examination of a delinquent young person. And this is not material of theoretic or academic interest; it is most useful in its practical bearing upon what ought to be done in the case.
> Some of this material is so deeply buried that it requires considerable skill on the part of the inquirer to overcome inhibitions and forgetfulness so that underlying fundamental truths of the situation may be brought to the surface.[56]

Listening to a child speak could also be a way of checking the widespread belief that a large proportion of delinquents were feebleminded. In fact, at first Healy himself believed they were.[57] Eventually, standardized tests were devised that sent the feebleminded theory packing. Another motive for letting the individual tell his or her story was that perhaps the child had not been able to talk in court, especially when the alleged deinquent was labeled dim-witted. Augusta Bronner, Healy's partner, discovered that when the clinic sent the court a finding of mental defectiveness on a girl sex offender, her testimony was rejected: "They were considered unable to tell a story." But Bronner says she could get a story from them: "It seemed to me grossly unfair in many cases that testimony should be rejected and the men go scot-free because the girl happened to be perhaps somewhat below average intelligence."[58]

Ever the pluralist, Healy insisted that all data could be useful in understanding an offender; put in terms of a political metaphor, all data should have a voice. But clearly data from one source were in Healy's constituency "privileged" (to use the existentialists' term)[59]—those from the "inner mental life" of the individual—though in some cases "own story" had "negative values," for it failed to reveal "deepset disturbing and conflicting elements" in the hidden mental life of a delinquent.[60] Or it might reveal emotions that distort an individual's performance on psychological tests.

In the process of exploring inner mental life, Healy found that some misbehavior stopped after a repressed emotional conflict was talked out. When it became evident that no plan of treatment for disturbed children was going to be carried out by the Chicago juvenile court, the importance of the therapeutic function of "own story" must have increased, since this nicely satisfied Healy's identities as research scientist and therapist, even when the cures were not so rapid as in the following example. In an early case, Healy asked a child:

> "What do you think of just before you take something?"
> "The name John. If I see it in my reading lesson, I must take something."
> Suddenly there poured out an experience which had evidently been repressed below conscious level. The stealing stopped from that moment. Releasing the subconscious repression of the motivating cause set the child free.[61]

Mrs. Dummer, whose report this is, concludes: "It was astonishing." Healy said:

> The feeling about the hidden experience was found to be the dynamic factor in the production of delinquency and other forms of unsocial behavior. Examples were some remarkable cases of pathological stealing, running away from home with acute suffering therefrom, and even one case of homicide.[62]

Perhaps Healy's most eloquent statement of this was the following:

> One of the chief regrets of my earlier work in Chicago is that I never gave time enough or was not skillful enough to get at the inner mental life of a capable boy who appeared over and over in the juvenile court, tight-lipped, always reticent to an extreme, and even in his physiognomy giving evidence of repressing something; a boy who was given most unusual chances in friendship and employment, but whose "Own Story" was never obtained by any of us; a boy who steadfastly set his path in antisocial ways, despite suffering and punishment, until he became a typical professional criminal—now for years in and out of adult correctional institutions with, undoubtedly, the old sore spot still unexplored, covered up, but remaining the original active agent in his career. One thinks of him in contrast to others, where the direct approach to mental life definitely unearthed some similarly potent feature of experience and reaction, and this gave rationality and at once the check to delinquency.[63]

Healy claimed that his discovery of the "talking cure" developed from his own contact with cases, independent of Freud:

> I of course knew something of Freud's work, but this stuff here wasn't discovered at all through the use of psychoanalysis. It didn't need necessarily greater interpretation . . . . The most striking thing that I found was youngsters saying, after they had dug it out of their unconscious, "Now I know." Kid after kid, either in those words or other words similar to them, told me that now for the first time he knew why he stole or ran away or something.[64]

Unlike Freud, Healy did not arrive at free association through hypnosis, for he quickly found that American youth would have none of that. Like Freud, he found the miracle cures of catharsis to be neither inevitable nor always permanently effective, and they do not have a prominent place in his work.[65]

The first publication by Healy of an "own story" of a delinquent was in a booklet "Printed for Use in the Harvard Summer School, 1912" entitled *Case Studies of Mentally and Morally Abnormal Types*. Case 1 does not include a presentation of "own story," but case 2 has an "own story" after several categories of information: first, a general description of a "Girl of 15 . . . . Mother says the girl is very unruly and has been giving much trouble . . . . Lies much . . . . No convulsions. Walked at 16 months . . . . No tea or coffee"; next, physical data: "102 lbs., 4 ft. 10 in., rather stoop shouldered . . . tired look about the eyes; everything else negative"; and, finally, results on a series of numbered tests. Next comes the "own story":

> "I know what I want and I want it. The trouble is mostly with father. He doesn't like me and I don't like him. He never liked me. He wanted me put in a Home when I was little and mother didn't want it. Not trouble every day, but it comes often. He has a bad temper, but he supports his family all right and doesn't drink. I have a bad temper too and get mad at the teacher as well as at father. I don't like where we live. Got a flat in a poor neighborhood and have nowhere to go. Mother says the street is no place for a girl, but she won't go out with me. She won't go unless father goes and he works nights and won't go. I just hate the house. I don't care where it is, but if she would only go out with me for a walk. She said I couldn't go to B. Park because that was too far. I got that settled for me anyway. Well, I've gone with some bad girls. (Names them with a snort.) Bad neighborhood all round there. I don't want to live at home, I ain't going to. Well, maybe now, but you just wait till I get older and work and save up some money. I go to

the dances at the I School on Wednesday afternoons. There is a party Wednesday nights, but she won't let me go. What do I like best? I like the gym best. Sure, I like it better out in the country. It's more fun out there. I like to climb around. We were down at B. in Ohio before we came here 4 months ago. My father moves all around. We just got the flat for the winter and he expects to go somewhere else.

"I remember the first thing I stole. It was a penny. A. was with me. A. she used to see pennies and nickels around and she said, 'Why don't you take 'em?' Mama got that $10 and the $5 back. Got it before I spent it. It was this way about that $10. My father got mad and said I had to leave. I got mad and she had the money in a trunk, and I got a key and opened it, but she got the $10 back and told me I would not have to leave, and that's all there was to that. When took some things from a store a girl was with me. Once she took some money and told me to take some postcards and run. That girl V. told me she used to do bad things with boys. I called her a liar and had a break with her. She moved away.

"Well, I eat a good deal of candy before meals and can't eat regular meals then. I don't like to go to school. I don't like to study. I like it out better. Like to go to work. Didn't like my teacher. I like Miss S. all right, but that school nurse I tell you I don't like her—don't like her looks."

These statements of cases were used in classroom discussion; there is no commentary on this case, but the facing page has been left blank for notes. In 1922, after Healy and Bronner had left Chicago for Boston, they published the *Judge Baker Foundation Case Studies.* Case 1, about a sixteen-year-old Greek immigrant boy, includes the "Boy's Own Story." This is not, however, in the boy's own words; the statement is a summary narrative without technical language.[66] These are two of the very few instances of "own story" that appear in Healy's publications. Case histories illustrating one point or another are scattered through *The Individual Delinquent,* his highly influential textbook of 1915, but the only extended quotation of the individual's own story in his own words in this book concerns a "verbalist type of defective," low on the scale of intelligence but deceptively eloquent.[67] The boy's language is reproduced only because his language is problematic. One reason for this absence of "own stories" may be that publisher's space is as limited as a busy doctor's time: *The Individual Delinquent* contains 823 cases presented in more than 800 pages, hardly room enough for discursive roaming.

Even more to the point is that for Healy the significance of the individual's story is not on its surface: its true meaning is in the underlying current of emotions that only partially appears on the verbal surface, and in the interpretation of an expert observer who does not share the speaker's psychic resistances. After all, physicians are taught to be "skeptical about second-hand, essentially unverifiable data such as the story told by the patient," as a recent author put it.[68] Allport reports a complaint by Healy "that even the classics of autobiography fail to tell what the modern scientific inquirer wants to know."[69] Presenting longer statements was superfluous; Healy's commentary said it all. Concern about privileged communication to a physician may have been an inhibiting factor, too: rather than disguise stories, why not simply transform them into diagnoses?

The other reason Healy did not publish oral histories is that he was not trying to attract a general public audience. He said: "If one had space and skill, many of these histories could be portrayed with the force and interest of clever romance."[70] Healy's audience already had an interest in delinquency and did not need captivating in this way. Teaching was the main purpose of these case histories.[71] Juvenile court judges and probation officers, doctors, lawyers, social workers, clergymen, and so forth who visited Healy's facilities did not need mock contact with delinquents through the pages of a book when they would meet offenders in person. What they needed was a discussion of exemplary cases, and "own story" apparently is specified not by presenting examples of it but by describing ways information from that and other sources could be integrated and interpreted. This pooling of data from various sources led to Healy's invention of the psychiatric case conference.[72]

Unlike Clay and Carpenter, Healy was not urging on the public the establishment of an institution; the juvenile court and the research institute already existed. Public relations were carried on by Hull House. Nor was he trying to show how successful those institutions were, as the houses of refuge and the Children's Aid Society had done. His task was to do research, and in fact, little treatment was even attempted by anyone in Chicago, according to Healy. In 1916 he left for Boston in search of better therapeutic facilities. From time to time he expressed a hope that through child guidance clinics the public would become better informed about children's problems; but the chief means of propagating this message seems to have been educating parents, who do not normally need oral histories to acquaint them with their own children.[73]

The group Healy influenced most was social workers. His work was important in professionalizing that field as it evolved away from earlier volunteer philanthropy. According to Lubove: "In the late nineteenth century, social agencies had delegated important administrative and treatment responsibilities to the volunteer; by 1930 her activities were often marginal or else closely supervised."[74] To the modern social worker there seems no good reason to preserve the client's own story in the client's own words, unless a problem somehow resides in the language itself—a stutter, perhaps. The important unit of discourse is the social worker's written assessment of the problem and decision about the kind of service to be rendered, noted down in a report that will be read by other social workers.

Though much has been made of Healy as an advance over Lombroso, these two physicians had much in common. In fact, both attended to delinquents' accounts of their own lives. Lombroso writes: "I have questioned [delinquents] and their answers and autobiographies proved to me how full even the better establishments are of the most infamous vices, such as pederasty, theft, and the Camorra, just in the case of the prisons."[75] (Note how autobiographies reveal social conditions in prisons.) In addition, both Lombroso and Healy often reproduced the offender's language because of features of that language itself, in the same way that the psychiatrist Aichhorn in his books quoted delinquents' letters and reproduced conversations to show the dynamics of therapy by pointing to latent, underlying meanings.[76]

Tattoos were one of Lombroso's passions, though not Healy's: Lombroso even found a woman who had tattooed her autobiography all over her body.[77] Also: "Walls, drinking vessels, planks of the prisoners' beds, margins of books, medicine wrappers, and even the unstable sands of the exercise-grounds, and the uniform in which the prisoner is garbed, supply him with a surface on which to imprint his thoughts and feelings."[78] What takes the place of oral histories in a geneticist system such as Lombroso's is photographs that "eloquently" suggest the natural depravity of individuals who were probably only intimidated by the photographer's flash and thus suggest the need for programs of eugenics. For William Sheldon, a more recent Lombrosian, photographs were essential: "Without photographs posterity will never be able to reconstruct what these men were— even grossly. A million measurements and a ton of verbal description, however well done, would not perfectly resolve even the gross outline of one human organism in three dimensions."[79] Surely the truth on this matter has been stated by Philip Rieff: "The body is an objective record only in a most limited sense; what is important about an individual lies in the historical dimension—in memory, whose complexity there is little likelihood the body can record."[80]

Nowhere does the similarity between Healy and Lombroso come out more clearly than in their focus on the individual—body or personality—to the neglect of the individual's social environment. Despite the profound differences between a tattoo, as an external bodily sign of delinquency, and a "sore spot" in a person's unconscious, both are simple, like an atom. Lombroso's terms were transcended by Healy in a movement of interiorization to become mental terms, in the same way that, according to Hegel, the *daimonion* of Socrates, which warned the philosopher to shun a course of action, was an interiorization of the "external" Greek oracles. Instead of dealing with tattoos on the bodies of criminals, Healy examined "criminalistic mental imagery."[81] The criminal body has been "sublimated" or "superseded."[82] Nevertheless, what Kurella says about Lombroso also applies to Healy: "He had a preference for observing and utilizing *states*—i.e., persistent facts—in place of observing and utilizing processes."[83] Thus the published "own stories," such as the one above, have a stacatto style, as if a narrative were a locus of points, a result of that "miniaturization" Richard Sennett has pointed out as a feature of the late nineteenth century—the minute scrutiny of persons for signs that expose personality.[84] In giving fuller attention to the personal contexts of delinquency, however, Healy is an advance over Lombroso.

For Healy, "own story" was a source of data, was placed among data, and was itself a datum. Even the therapeutic function derived from that, because the process of retrieving data from the unconscious overcame repressions and gave relief. Social data had to be included in any well-rounded case study, but Healy himself did not go into the community to obtain this data: a social worker or probation officer did that. The only social situation that Healy gave special attention was the family, because that was the scene of developing emotions. Parents visited the clinic, though family therapy was apparently not attempted. Healy's "place" was the clinic; the topology of his daily movements and the ecology of his concepts reflected each other. Thus his "own stories" are like contemporary photographs of street children posed in a studio with a blank or artificial background, as contrasted to photographs taken in the street.

From time to time Healy admits that much delinquency would be eliminated if social conditions were changed,[85] but that was not his goal:

> How the issues of general, social, political, and economic conditions tie up with what we discover concerning the basic factors of the problems of youth is very clear—so clear that I hardly need dwell on it. The knowledge of unfairness, of political trickery, of legal chicanery, and of graft rapidly filters through, as it were, to children in their teens and younger. We know this through autobiographical details.[86]

But Healy neither illustrated this point (note that he refers to abuses of office rather than to the distribution of power) nor used autobiographies for any purpose he would have admitted to be political. When asked about his political stance, he replied: "I have always been pretty independent in my feelings in politics. I have voted on both sides. I don't know that I have very strong feelings about it at all."[87] A far cry from Ben Lindsey.

But, curiously, this had the same negative result for oral history: what underlies as well as what transcends the individual's experience is antithetical to oral history's firm stand in phenomena.

However, the *practice* of "own story" does in fact politically transcend "own story." I need not repeat here the recent scathing critiques of the juvenile court for its forfeiture of juveniles' rights under the banner of a humane individualism. If what Healy claims about the miracle cures of therapy are correct, surely he benefited some *individuals*. But his major accomplishment in Chicago was to help set up the juvenile court *system*. Foucault has written: "The carefully collated life of mental patients or delinquents belongs, as did the chronicle of kings or the adventures of the great bandits, to a certain political function of writing; but in a quite different technique of power."[88] According to Foucault the essence of this technique is *surveillance:* "It is not on the fringes of society and through successive exiles that criminality is born, but by means of ever more closely placed insertions, under more insistent surveillance, by an accumulation of disciplinary coercion."[89]

What happened to "own story" as the psychiatric profession developed a professional identity and devised quantitative methods of investigation? In 1932 a psychiatrist on the staff of the Institute for Juvenile Research (IJR), responding more to the use of life histories by contemporary IJR sociologists than to anything Healy had done, wrote an article "Autobiography as a Psychiatric Technique," in which he concluded that "while autobiography is not a method which can be substituted in any part of the study of a psychiatric case, it often reveals facts which are not forthcoming in a particular examination and can be considered a valid supplementary method to reveal social, psychological, and psychiatric facts."[90] "Autobiography" has become crowded out by more specialized techniques into a subordinate position where at best it can only pick up leftovers. However, excerpts from autobiographies were used to give the public an entry into experiences of insanity by Carney Landis, a former worker at the Institute for Juvenile Research, in *Varieties of Psychopathological Experience* (1964). (Landis comments in his preface on the rare instances of cross-references in these autobiographies. The same may be said of delinquents' oral histories: most are written and published without any awareness that similar expressions have been made.) More recently, in the context of recognition by some of the most creative psychiatrists of the crucial influence of social realities on individuals' psyches, life history has taken on some importance in psychology. As Erik Erikson remarks in *Life History and the Historical Moment,* a person born into different historical circumstances would be a different person, and a "life history," even when it is biographical rather than autobiographical, should specify events that transcend the lone individual.

Six

"If Men Define Situations as Real, They Are Real in Their Consequences"

Human Documents from a Marginal Man

One morning about 1910, W. I. Thomas, professor of sociology at the University of Chicago, had to duck to avoid some garbage being tossed into an alley on Chicago's West Side. The bundle contained several packets of letters in Polish, which he was able to read. "In the sequence presented by the letters he saw a rich and rewarding account and in time he was led to pursue the personal document as a research tool." Thus states Morris Janowitz, claiming support for the anecdote's accuracy from Ernest Burgess, one of Thomas's students.[1] Thomas himself in 1928 traced the origin of his interest in human documents to "a long letter picked up on a rainy day in the alley behind my house, a letter from a girl who was taking a training course in a hospital, to her father concerning family relationships and discords. It occurred to me at that time that one would learn a great deal if one had a great many letters of this kind."[2] As Everett Hughes, who knew Thomas, put it in a letter to me: "Thomas was a great raconteur. He loved telling stories about himself as well as about others. He didn't tell them always in the same way." At any rate, the core of serendipity is the same in both versions, as is the emphasis on continuity or length of the letters—not to speak of the alley, perhaps itself a symbol of marginality.

At whatever moment Thomas began to realize the importance of personal or human documents, he certainly was the originator of their use by sociologists, especially at the University of Chicago, during the two decades following the publication in 1918–20 of the five-volume work that set off the fashion: *The Polish Peasant in Europe and America*, by W. I. Thomas and Florian Znaniecki.[3] (The first interest among anthropologists in publishing detailed life histories followed, under the additional influence of Paul Radin and Edward Sapir; this was also an extension of collecting oral testimony.) *The Polish Peasant*, which was also a pioneering model for empirical sociology in general, made what Gordon Allport has called the first scientifically critical use of letters, autobiographies, newspaper accounts, court records, and records of social agencies. Thomas considered all these *human* documents because they are concrete revelations of human action. But Allport omitted third-person records, such as the last three, from his category of personal documents, leaving only letters and autobiographies. My interest is even further limited to autobiography, though letters may have closely related functions, as we have seen. (I am also omitting diaries, such as that of a boy reported in the *New York Times* on 9 July 1973, in which he listed his crimes.) First-person accounts of lives are often called "life histories," though Allport and others occasionally use this term interchangeably with "case study" which "*may* be written in the first person."[4] The use of "life history" in ordinary language does not seem necessarily to imply self-expression, but, unless otherwise noted, "life history" and "oral history" will be used as synonymous here.[5]

W. I. Thomas is not known for contributions restricted to delinquency, but I include him because he was the originator of a social scientific paradigm that included oral histories. This means that the personal conditions of the genesis of delinquents' oral histories by other sociologists of the Chicago school—notably Frederic Thrasher and Clifford Shaw—were in the life of neither Thrasher nor Shaw (except insofar as through their university experiences they learned a preexistent sociological method), but in the life and character of W. I. Thomas. This is true also of the concept of social disorganization developed by Thomas in his study of the Polish peasant and used by others to explain juvenile delinquency. In addition, the epistemological status and problems of life history in general were explored more systematically in critiques of *The Polish Peasant* than in any of the later life histories or their critiques.

William I. Thomas (1863–1947) was born in Virginia, where he spent much of his youth "with a rifle, without a dog, shooting at a mark, regretting the disappearance of large game and the passing of the Indian and of pioneer life."[6] Images of hunting were favorites of Thomas and were often used in the 1920s and 1930s to describe the Chicago sociologist's activities: "One 'brought back' data, much as one would bring back game,"[7] according to Carey, a simile that recalls Plato's definition of the sophist.

Thomas began his rise to civilization after his father moved the family to Knoxville, Tennessee, site of the state university. There he was influenced by professors of Greek and natural history and one summer had a "conversion" toward becoming a scholar. After teaching foreign languages at Tennessee, Thomas studied in Germany, then became a professor of English at Oberlin College. He had a special interest in comparative literature, just as he later became interested in cross-cultural case studies. Thomas's humanistic background gave him an appreciation for languages, for the complexity of concrete human situations, and for the dramatic in human experience, and doubtless it developed his talent for literary expression.[8]

In 1893 W. I. Thomas, "driven certainly by the desire for new experience," became a student of sociology at the University of Chicago. The world's first academic department of sociology had been founded as part of the university when it opened in 1892. Robert E. L. Faris has said of this: "It was no accident that the new subject was put into the curriculum in a new organization, unbound by the traditions and vested interests which were to delay the development of sociology in many of the older universities in the Atlantic coast region." "None of the original faculty of the Chicago department was trained in sociology because there had been no department to train them. Thus there was still a large amount of uncertainty about what the task was to be—what sort of sociology was to be created. It was to be nearly thirty years before their successors could feel confident that they were at last on the true road."[9] Life histories thrived in this exploratory, marginal period in sociology. The publication of books using life histories was aided by another innovation: the University of Chicago had its own press.

Thomas began teaching sociology in the new department in 1894 and earned his doctorate in 1896. The merit of his studies, he said, was that he chose courses and did reading in areas "marginal" to sociology as it was then taught—biology, physiology, brain anatomy, psychology, ethnology. "It is, in fact, in this marginal region, where sciences meet and integrate, that productive ideas are most likely to arise," wrote Thomas more than thirty years before Arthur Koestler constructed a theory of creativity on a similar notion. Thomas also explored the city of Chicago: on one occasion Charles Henderson, a senior member of the sociology department, asked him to get some information about saloons. Henderson admitted that he had never entered a saloon or tasted beer. According to Edward Shils, "Thomas' readiness to observe directly, to collect 'human documents' of living persons, was supported by Small [the department chairman] and Henderson. They did not think it undignified for a professor or the professor's pupils to wander about the streets and interest themselves in 'low life.'" This differed from academic practice in Germany, where information about the working classes had to be obtained "from middle-class persons who in a professional capacity—for example, magistrates, clergymen, municipal administrators, and so forth—were in contact with the lower classes."[10]

However, the period to about 1904, apparently before he began to collect human documents, was a time of transition from old to new ways for Thomas rather than a time of accomplishment. His dissertation was "On a Difference in the Metabolism of the Sexes," and one of his essays concerned "The Mind of Woman and the Lower Races." Kimball Young describes Thomas's outlook thus: "The division of labor between the sexes rests upon the basic metabolic differences. Women, being anabolic

and reproductive in function, take naturally to more sedentary occupations. Men, being katabolic, take to more violent and active behavior."
Mercifully, Young adds: "Yet as Thomas worked over additional materials, he became more and more convinced that the differences between
the position of men and women in society rested upon historical and
psychological rather than on biochemical foundations." "This position of
inferiority, then, is rather an accident of history than something inherent
in the nature of the female," owing to "lack of opportunity, low cultural
standards, and isolation."[11] According to Burgess, Thomas gradually
"became much less concerned with ethnological subject matter, and
much more attracted by studies of the negro, the immigrant, the European
peasant, and the Jew"[12]—and, still later, by studies of the delinquent and
the child. Perhaps Thomas had been attracted to physical processes
underlying action as a way of putting a distance between himself and the
scholarly logomachies of the day, a way of bringing sociology down from
the heavens of bookish speculation to a closer contact with data. According to him, one of the merits of his education was, "I never became
influenced by philosophy as offering an explanation of reality."

Kimball Young claims that Thomas's shift away from his flirtation with
the biological was definite by 1904:[13] rather than the interaction of body
and mind, the interaction of mind and mind came into view. This would
mean that his appreciation for processes of social experience was well
under way before he discovered the usefulness of human documents, but
the timing of all this is unclear, to say the least.[14] In any case, the evolution of Thomas's mind must have been gradual and continuous, an ideal
subject for a complete autobiography, though he never wrote one.
Perhaps the best we can say is that life historical documents appear here,
as we have seen them appear before, at a conceptual turning point, in this
case in a man's career, away from "nature" to an appreciation for human
experience in an environment. Perhaps Thomas's discovery of human
documents thoroughly integrated into his character a tendency that had
been growing for at least a decade.

The objective function of oral histories in realigning the discipline of
sociology away from the physical (the success of natural science since
Newton had captivated all inquirers) as well as the transcendental (most
of the early sociologists had a religious background) will become clearer
as we proceed. But a similar function seems to have been at work in
Thomas's own evolution: human documents provided something more
concrete to get a hold on than the speculations of the founding sociologists—Comte, Spencer, Weber, Durkheim, Tarde, Simmel—as well as
the founders of the Chicago sociology department—Small, Vincent,
Henderson—and they also encouraged a move from the physicalistic tendencies of the early ethnologists to a grasp of personal traits.

This suggests that human experience and its expression may be located between the extremes of overarching or transcending ideas on the one hand and underlying entities on the other. In this way experience as an autonomous phenomenon is "marginal" to these two more solid-appearing realities. Perhaps it takes a mind steeped in marginality to perceive human phenomena for what they are in themselves. Elmer Barnes has written of Thomas: "His writings, like his interests, were marginal rather than central to systematic sociology."[15]

Thomas's marginality surfaced in another way when he was dismissed from the University of Chicago in 1918, the year the first volume of *The Polish Peasant* was published. The story is not at all clear, but it seems to have involved the threat of a morals charge concerning the wife of an American soldier stationed in France, with a great deal of adverse publicity in the *Chicago Tribune*, which made much of Thomas's earlier professional interest in sex.[16] Thomas left Chicago and spent the rest of his life writing, teaching at Harvard and the New School for Social Research, and working on research projects.

What sort of man was W. I. Thomas? In his memorial article "W. I. Thomas as a Teacher," Ernest Burgess wrote: "In contrast to his colleagues, William I. Thomas was at the same time a sportsman, artist, and scientist. He had his daily golf game, a habit he religiously maintained until within a few months of his death. He rolled his own cigarettes from a blend of tobacco of his own choosing. In his workshop he experimented with golf balls and clubs of his own fashioning. He had a great gusto for living; enjoyed food, drink, conversation, and people."[17] In the same series of articles, Znaniecki, his collaborator on *The Polish Peasant,* said of him, "Never have I known, heard, or read about anybody with such a wide, sympathetic interest in the vast diversity of sociocultural patterns and such a genius for understanding the uniqueness of every human personality. The famous statement of Terence, 'I am a man and nothing human seems alien to me,' expresses an ideal which few men have ever realized as fully as Thomas."[18] Janowitz writes: "As a person, he was immensely vigorous and stimulating. He maintained a wide circle of contacts with intellectual leaders in the other disciplines and thereby helped to disseminate the kind of interdisciplinary thinking out of which he grew." Janowitz speaks about Thomas's "pragmatic rather than dogmatic approach to theoretical constructs" and sums up his standpoint thus: "He essentially offered a synthesis of the anthropologist's or ethnographer's participant observation, the case study method of the social worker, and the content analysis procedure of the traditional humanistic disciplines."[19]

Thomas did not view himself as a theorist at all, at least in the sense in which the "older, armchair theories of unilinear social evolution" were

theories. Rather, he was a collector of reports, histories, quotations, and
of his own observations.[20] Janowitz calls him a "sociological 'pack
rat.'"[21] He invented a system of taking notes on four-by-six slips of
paper: bibliographical items on blue slips, extracts from books and articles on yellow slips, and his own comments on white slips. Robert Park
once declared this an invention comparable to movable type.[22]

Despite differences in their backgrounds, W. I. Thomas and Henry
Mayhew are similar figures. Both dived into the thick of social reality for
their material and scorned the host of contemporary "armchair
theorists." Each produced a magnum opus (2,169 pages from Mayhew,
2,244 from Thomas) that included oral histories (though Thomas used
mostly letters while Mayhew mostly conducted interviews), in some cases
touching on delinquency as part of the whole social fabric rather than
treating it as a separate subject, though both also later wrote books more
specifically about delinquency. Both were vigorous, gregarious, sympathetic men who did not quite fit the conventions of their day. After the
production of their great books, both turned to a study of prostitution,
then underwent something of a decline, though Thomas at least continued
to write books using the *Polish Peasant* method (without, however, the
scope of his masterpiece). It is interesting to speculate what might have
happened if American newspapers around the turn of the century had had
deeper social interests than muckracking or superficial human interest
stories and had attracted W. I. Thomas to head an investigative team, or if
British universities earlier had been willing to take on the functions of
surveying and evaluating social reforms in the way that has become institutionalized in the United States[23] and had been willing to hire Professor Mayhew to do the work.

During one of Thomas's many trips to Europe he met Florian
Znaniecki, a young Polish philosopher. Thomas was preparing a study of
Polish lower and middle classes as they underwent social changes in
Poland and after emigration to the United States. (Thus Thomas's subject
may be seen partly as a reflection of his own travels to Europe.) Znaniecki
came to Chicago in 1913 and helped Thomas with the study, acquiring and
translating documents and discussing substantive and analytic issues.
After *The Polish Peasant in Europe and America* had been substantially
completed, Znaniecki persuaded Thomas to include a long "Methodological Note" drafted by Znaniecki. The philosopher turned sociologist
had done so much work on the book that Thomas added his name as
coauthor. Robert Bierstedt has written: "It is doubtful indeed if either one
of them alone could have brought *The Polish Peasant* to fruition in anything like the form in which we know it or made it the sociological classic
it is generally conceded to be. Thomas's contribution was a psychological
penetration, a comprehensive curiosity, and a rare wisdom; Znaniecki's a

philosophical sophistication, an historical erudition, and a talent for systematization."[24] Znaniecki published an autobiography (not of himself) in Polish in 1923. He also translated Bergson's *Creative Evolution* and was so insistent about the continuity of social process that he opposed the notion of a social structure. No doubt Znaniecki easily joined Thomas in his taste for human documents, but commentators agree that the initiative for using them came from Thomas. Znaniecki, an extremely interesting figure in his own right, taught sociology in Poland, at Columbia University, and at the University of Illinois. Keeping in mind the comparison of Mayhew and Thomas, one wonders if the fact that the 2,244-page *Polish Peasant* was completed at all was attributable to Znaniecki. In any case, Znaniecki's contribution will be largely taken for granted in what follows.

Definition of the Situation

Throughout his career Thomas collected tens of thousands of personal documents. In a paper he wrote in 1912 he included in this category records of personal observations (especially those gathered while living with a family), as well as letters, diaries, newspaper stories, school curricula, handbills, almanacs, and court, club, and church records, addresses, and sermons. Volume 1 of the original edition of *The Polish Peasant* contains 754 letters arranged by family group in fifty sets on 800 pages, printed in small type, a typological convention something like the appendix style but set within the text. Thomas acquired most of these letters through an advertisement in a Polish emigrant journal, offering ten to twenty cents for any letter from Poland received by an immigrant to the United States. A second group of documents came from a Polish newspaper's archives, which Thomas bought around 1910. Thomas discovered that Polish churches in Chicago kept commemorative albums, and he also made use of these, along with records of Polish organizations in Chicago. Finally, a 312-page autobiography of a young Pole, Wladek Wisznienski, occupied most of the third of the original five volumes, one of several autobiographies that Thomas and Znaniecki collected. Wladek was paid for his work and seems to have been motivated by a desire to advance socially. As Paul Delaney has said in another context, "Vertical mobility seems to have been an ... effective exitant of the self-awareness requisite for autobiography."[25] All these documents, each sort used in a separate section of the work, are introduced by analytic introductions, occasionally quite long, and commented on in footnotes. Thomas intended to do a similar case study of Jewish social organization as a control group to the Polish study by making use of the *bintl brief,* immigrants' letters sent to the New York *Forward,* printed in Yiddish, but he was not given permission to use their files and he never completed the project.[26]

Concerning the use of such material, the authors of *The Polish Peasant* make a startling claim:

> We are safe in saying that personal life-records, as complete as possible, constitute the *perfect* type of sociological material, and that if social science has to use other materials at all it is only because of the practical difficulty of obtaining at the moment a sufficient number of such records to cover the totality of sociological problems, and of the enormous amount of work demanded for an adequate analysis of all the personal materials necessary to characterize the life of a social group. If we are forced to use mass-phenomena as material, or any kind of happenings taken without regard to the life-histories of the individuals who participate in them, it is a defect, not an advantage, of our present sociological method.[27]

Letters written with no thought that they would be used outside the correspondence situation had the advantage of spontaneity over autobiography,[28] according to Thomas, but "the extended life history has an obvious advantage over detached statements in that it reveals the sequences of experience, the total patterning of behavior, motivation, and change."[29]

Thomas articulated a sociological position on human documents better than anyone else ever has done, and no better statements than his could be made about it. The quotation most often repeated by other Chicago sociologists ends with the famous aphorism I have used to title this chapter:

> There may be, and is, doubt as to the objectivity and veracity of the record, but even the highly subjective record has a value for behavior study. A document prepared by one compensating for a feeling of inferiority or elaborating a delusion of persecution is as far as possible from objective reality, but the subject's view of the situation, how he regards it, may be the most important element for interpretation. For his immediate behavior is closely related to his definition of the situation, whch may be in terms of objective reality or in terms of a subjective appreciation—"as if" it were so. Very often it is the wide discrepancy between the situation as it seems to others and the situation as it seems to the individual that brings about the overt behavior difficulty. To take an extreme example, the warden of Dannemora prison recently refused to honor the order of the court to send an inmate outside the prison walls for some specific purpose. He excused himself on the ground that the man was too dangerous. He had killed several persons who had the unfortunate habit of talking to themselves on the street. From the movement of their lips he imagined that they were calling him vile names, and he behaved as if this were

true. If men define situations as real, they are real in their consequences.[30]

In another place Thomas wrote:

I am not suggesting that behavior can be adequately observed and recorded by the observational method or by statistical procedure. It appears, in fact, that the behavior document (case study, life record, psycho-analytic confession) representing a continuity of experience in life situations is the most illuminating procedure available. In a good record of this kind we are able to view the behavior reactions in the various situations, the emergence of personality traits, the determination of concrete acts, and the formation of life policies and their evolution.

There are undoubtedly insuperable difficulties in the way of perfecting the life record on the side of objectivity and reliability. It is introspective, the memory is notoriously treacherous, observation is defective, phantasy, fabrication and bias play large roles. Court testimony is the best example of the difficulties encountered in securing a complete and objective narrative of past events. But this form of data is capable of improvement and systematization, and will have valuable applications when considerable numbers of life histories adequately elaborated are employed in a comparative way in order to determine the varieties of the schematization of life in varieties of situations.[31]

A somewhat different statement appears in *The Unadjusted Girl:*

The "human document," prepared by the subject, on the basis of the memory is one means of measuring social influence. It is capable of presenting life as a connected whole and of showing the interplay of influences, the action of values on attitudes. It can reveal the predominant wishes in different temperaments, the incidents constituting turning points in life, the processes of sublimation or transfer of interest from one field to another, the effect of other personalities in defining situations and the influence of social organizations like the family, the school, the acquaintance group, in forming the different patterns of life-organization. By comparing the histories of personalities as determined by social influences and expressed in various schemes of life we can establish a measure of the given influences. The varieties of human experience will be innumerable in their concrete details, but by the multiplication and analysis of life records we may expect to determine typical lines of the genesis of character as related to types of influence. It will be found that when certain attitudes are present the presentation of certain values may be relied upon to produce certain results.[32]

Elaborating on the perfection or completeness of human documents, Thomas and Znaniecki wrote:

> An attitude as manifested in an isolated act is always subject to misunderstanding, but this danger diminishes in the very measure of our ability to connect this act with past acts of the same individual. A social institution can be fully understood only if we do not limit ourselves to the abstract study of its formal organization, but analyze the way in which it appears in the personal experience of various members of the group and follow the influence which it has upon their lives.... The development of sociological investigation during the past fifteen or twenty years, particularly the growing emphasis, which, under the pressure of practical needs, is being put upon special and actual empirical problems as opposed to the general speculation of the preceding period, leads to the growing realization that we must collect more complete sociological documents than we now possess. And the more complete a sociological document becomes, the more it approaches a full personal life-record.[33]

Obviously these assertions raise armies of questions and issues with which it is not fitting to do epistemological battle here. Nor will it be necessary in this case, since critiques of Thomas's actual use of his material point out the rather loose fit between these concepts and alleged instances of them in his work. This gap becomes more central to understanding human documents as they were actually used by Thomas (as was the case with Mayhew) than the details and abstract implications of his conceptual framework.

Nevertheless, some general features of his standpoint and method will illuminate the use of oral histories by Thomas, as well as by those of his followers who concentrated on juvenile delinquency. Some readers may find the following pages rather rough going. We shall have to follow these scientists into the thickets where they pursued a cognitive understanding of life history, but we should keep in mind that they did not achieve it. Thus the following expedition will open up a few perspectives on oral history we would have missed otherwise and lead to the conclusion that, though a "scientific" position cannot account for oral histories, a rhetorical method can.

Social Subjectivity

Desiring to establish a science of society, Thomas went so far as to state a methodological formula for "laws of social becoming": "The cause of a value or of an attitude is never an attitude or value alone, but always a combination of an attitude and a value."[34] An attitude is an individual's disposition to act; a value is a group's disposition to act. As Herbert Blumer pointed out in his critique of *The Polish Peasant,* this formula can be understood on two levels: first, that the subjective factor must be taken into account in any objective study of a social situation; second, that laws can indeed be discovered by using this formula. Blumer concludes: "The methodological formula as a device for securing laws of social becoming is fallacious; the fact that it is not seriously employed by the authors is further evidence of this."[35] The formula, however, is entirely sound on the more general level: the meaning of a social event resides both in social values and in individuals. This means, for example, that determining why one individual becomes delinquent and another does not requires looking at both sets of factors.[36]

The concept of value seems to have interested Znaniecki more than it did Thomas. Young says that Thomas was "concerned with the individual in his social interaction with his fellows rather than with the group as such."[37] According to Janowitz, Thomas's main interest was in the "subjective dimension of social organization."[38] Human documents preserve this subjective experience in an objective, repeatable form, just as the phonograph record and the moving picture film during Thomas's early period were beginning to preserve experience.[39] Ellsworth Faris attributes to Thomas the discovery of the scientific concept of social attitude.[40] "Now that the study of attitudes is taken for granted as a proper activity for sociologists, it is difficult to imagine how novel it must have appeared at the beginning of the century," says Madge.[41] One reason for the novelty of this inclusion of the subjective was Durkheim's exclusion of personal meaning from the category of social fact.[42] Thomas found it impossible to understand the dynamics of a social occurrence without looking at what the event meant to its participants. In this sense he was practicing social psychology, which he understood to be a broader field than either sociology or psychology alone. In retrospect, however, Thomas's social psychology appears to be a stage in the evolution of the empirical social sciences out of psychology toward a sociology of social structure.

Insofar as these attitudes are *social,* it is impossible to disconnect the person's "experience complexes," a term Thomas once used,[43] from their social objects. This is comparable to the claims by phenomenologists, also around the turn of the century (e.g., Husserl), that consciousness is *intentional:* that is, it is always consciousness *of* an object. Personality is both produced by and produces social realities in continual reflexive interaction. Indeed, attitudes and values are so intimate in Thomas and Znaniecki's analyses that in places it becomes impossible to distinguish which elements of the situation are attitudes and which are values, as Blumer points out. One side of this interaction is stated thus:

> Perhaps the greatest importance of the behavior document is the opportunity it affords to observe the attitudes of other persons as behavior-forming influences, since the most important situations in the development of personality are the attitudes and values of other persons . . . . It has been strongly objected, especially by the adherents of the school of "behaviorism," that this introspective method has no objectivity or validity. What they mean is that these records will not reveal the mechanisms of behavior, the process of consciousness, what is going on inside of us when we think and act, and with this we are in agreement. But the unique value of the document is its revelation of the situations which have conditioned the behavior, and concerning this there can be no doubt.[44]

Tension exists between the individual's desires and definitions and the definitions of situations imposed by society. Individualization, which preoccupied Thomas and played a part in his use of personal documents, "means the personal schematization of the situation and determining one's own behavior norms."[45] But, as Finestone has pointed out, morality requires that the individual respect the subjectivity of other people by imagining himself in their place.[46] In that respect, oral histories perform a moral function.

What this means is that oral histories make an appearance along with a vision of *social* realities, a vision the histories are good at representing from a personal viewpoint. Interest must remain on that personal viewpoint, for, if the locus of interest moves to the group itself as described by any number of viewers and with the aim of establishing general propositions, oral history is superseded. Thus oral history is situated in an area marginal to the purely personal on one side and the purely objective or social on the other. The creative oral historian is a person who adjusts these tensions to each other.

Quantification

Ellsworth Faris said that Thomas was "allergic to statistics."[47] In Thomas's later writing he gives credit to his second wife, Dorothy Swaine Thomas, for any statistical expertise, such as appears in *The Child in America* (1928). In writing this book, Thomas's contact with an abundance of data, research methods, and practical programs must have convinced him of the need for more mass-oriented, quantitative techniques:

> What is needed is continual and detailed study of case-histories and life-histories of young delinquents along with the available statistical studies, to be used as a basis for the inferences

drawn. And these inferences in turn must be continually sub-
jected to further statistical analysis as it becomes possible to
transmute more factors into quantitative form. Statistics becomes, then, the continuous process of verification. As it becomes possible to transmute more and more data to a quantitative form and apply statistical methods, our inferences will
become probable and have a sounder basis. But the statistical
results must always be interpreted in the configuration of the
as-yet unmeasured factors and the hypotheses emerging from
the study of cases must, whenever possible, be verified statistically.[48]

In this context, life histories function at the beginning and end of research:
they generate variables for quantitative processing, and they interpret the
results. Whether they have in fact ever been used in this systematic way,
however, is another question—and the answer is probably no. In the field
of delinquency in the 1930s the work of Shaw and McKay certainly comes
closest, but there is no evidence that the quantitative/qualitative dialectic
fits their research activities.

At one time it was thought that collecting large numbers of life histories
might be useful: Burgess warned that it was "harzardous to venture generalizations based upon data in a few case studies. For that reason Mr.
Shaw and his associates are now engaged in the task of obtaining a considerable number of life-histories of criminal careers."[49] Attempts were
made to collect large numbers of life histories for comparative purposes,
especially at the research institute Shaw headed, a nonacademic location
where delinquents dropped in and wrote their stories. The resulting collection of documents was the starting point for the project that led to this
book (see Introduction). However, no means was ever discovered to deal
with such an unwieldy mass of material, either in the 1930s or the 1970s.
The coup de grace on quantitative uses of life histories was a dissertation
written at the University of Chicago in 1930 by Samuel Stouffer: "An
Experimental Comparison of Statistical and Case History Methods of
Attitude Research." Stouffer proved that the same results in determining
attitudes of individuals and groups could be achieved by brief, quantifi-
able questions as by the much more resource-consuming life histories:
"The concept of social attitudes proved to be highly practical when,
through the labors of Thurstone, Stouffer, and their co-workers, it was
found that attitudes can be measured and the measurements proved accurate by statistical methods."[50]

In 1930 Clifford Shaw wrote: "Perhaps with the further refinement of
such techniques as the questionnaire and personality rating scales, many
aspects of delinquent behavior which we now study by means of personal
documents will be subject to more objective analysis."[51] With Healy,

"own story" gradually passed over into psychological tests. With
Thomas, human documents passed over into survey research and
marketing techniques. (Curiously, it was in each case the man's second
wife, working as collaborator, who moved research toward quantification:
Augusta Bronner and Dorothy Swaine Thomas.) Whether such techniques are more "objective" is an open question: that personal documents were replaced by more impersonal forms of discourse there is no
doubt, reflecting Whitehead's remark about the "canalization of curiosity
into professional grooves."

Continuity

One of the apparent advantages of oral histories is that they represent
continuities in experience, dynamics rather than elements or even a series
of static states. (Of course this can have aesthetic significance, as in the
melodic editing of Studs Terkel.) This is especially useful when the subject is change. Perhaps Thomas's sense of process came from
nineteenth-century sociologists' notions of social evolution, going back to
Hegel's magisterial march of concepts or Herbert Spencer's delineations
of social progress, or at any rate to the processual interactionism of
Thomas's University of Chicago faculty colleagues, George H. Mead and
John Dewey. (Thomas once suggested that he might have influenced those
philosophers more than they influenced him.)[52] Znaniecki's feel for the
flux of reality must have come in part from his work on Bergson. Life
histories should be especially useful in tracing "lines of genesis":

> The application of sociological generalization to social per-
> sonalities requires thus, first of all, the admission of what we
> may call *typical lines of genesis*. A line of genesis is a series of
> facts through which a certain attitude is developed from some
> other attitude (or group of attitudes), a value from some other
> value (or group of values), when it does not develop directly,
> and the process cannot be treated as a single elementary fact.
> For example there is probably no social influence that could
> produce directly an attitude of appreciation of science from the
> parvenu's pride in his wealth, no intellectual attitude that could
> directly lead an untrained individual to produce a scientifically
> valid concept from the data of common-sense observation; but
> by a series of intermediary stages the parvenu can become a
> sincere protector of science, by a more or less long training in
> theoretic research a student learns to produce scientific values.
> In such a series every single link is a fact of the type: attitude-
> value-attitude, or: value-attitude-value, and as such, if prop-
> erly analyzed, can always be explained by sociological law (or
> lead to the discovery of a sociological law), but the series as a
> whole cannot be subject to any law, for there are many possi-

ble ways in which an attitude can be developed out of another
attitude, a value out of another value, all depends on the nature
of the intermediary data.[53]

This sounds plausible enough, but in his critique Blumer could find no
instance of a line of genesis in Thomas and Znaniecki's commentary on
the life history of Wladek,[54] nor did the authors defend themselves on this
point.

It seems impossible to reconstitute a continuity in time once it has been
broken down into a series of discrete units, as Zeno's paradox of Achilles
and the tortoise demonstrates. But the fact of the matter is that Achilles
does not have to cover half the distance before he can start (or finish), and
half the distance before he does that, and so forth. He simply speeds
ahead and crosses the finish line. Likewise, the mind can understand the
dynamics of a complex situation by schematically integrating perspectives
on an object rather than adding up a series of atomic elements. Howard S.
Becker has written: "The life history, more than any other technique
except perhaps participant observation, can give meaning to the over-
worked notion of *process*. Sociologists like to speak of 'ongoing processes' and the like, but their methods usually prevent them from seeing
the processes they talk about so glibly."[55] Weintraub has pointed out the
connection of the idea of development with the idea of individuality:

He who traces a historical development has an implicit interest
in the precise moment, the constellation, the specific way in
which specific factors interact and result in a new configuration
of factors.... Only by telling the story could one account for
the continuous differentiation of reality into variable specifica-
tions of unique value, a logically undefinable quantity and
quality.[56]

Despite the claims of Thomas and others concerning continuity of process as a virtue of life histories, despite the apparent plausibility of this
claim, here too it does not seem that sociologists have ever worked this
out to any noticeable extent. Continuity is an attractive feature of personal documents, but it is not taken seriously: it is either left as it is,
without comment, or is ignored in the onrush to split reality into pieces
more easily handled in research projects.

Comprehensiveness
According to Janowitz, Thomas originally planned to study a variety of
Eastern European immigrant groups, but he came to see the need to
concentrate on a single one if he was to avoid superficiality.[57] Still,
Thomas's tendency toward comprehensiveness was manifest in his choice
of a large subject, the Polish peasant in Europe and America and social

disorganization generally, a broad analytic scheme rather than single-factor approach, life histories that represented schemes of dispositions rather than unit traits, and the use of all available techniques to get a well-rounded picture of an individual.[58] In *The Polish Peasant*, Thomas and Znaniecki aimed at comprehensiveness partly by "putting into the volume any and everything that we found ourselves able to say."[59] Or that others had to say! One way such comprehensiveness might open up a field is, as Read Bain put it, by setting up "grand hypotheses which, while being knocked to pieces, produce new valid scientific knowledge which later can be integrated into a more coherent and consistent theory."[60]

Janowitz makes two apparently contradictory statements about Thomas's expansiveness: "In his effort to be comprehensive he now appears excessively eclectic and his views too open-ended." "The decline in vigor of the Chicago school in its original format was manifested by a shift from what has come to be called macrosociology to an over-concentration of concern upon specific institutions and limited topics of sociological inquiry."[61] Put in context, these statements are not in conflict: in the context of proof, comprehensiveness tends to yield unsupported assertions, whereas in the context of discovery, comprehensiveness is needed to open up a new field.

Types

One way to organize and interpret oral histories and the multitude of processes that intersect in them is to perceive recurrent patterns and to propose them as types. The proposal of categories is conspicuous in the initial phases of a new field, and autobiographical material may appear in the same period, "grounding" those categories in experience. In his *Varieties of Religious Experience*, which was based on autobiographical material, William James distinguished the sick soul, the healthy mind, and the divided self, as well as four basic constituents of saintliness and six levels of asceticism. Usually the purpose of setting forth types is to aid perception of an otherwise chartless terrain: Weber's "ideal types" function as heuristic devices. However, such distinctions typically become hardened into a litany for the lazy-minded: they become stereotypes, even if the enterprise they are part of was initially meant to combat stereotypes. Thomas was disturbed to see the types he had proposed being used as if they were categories of things, and he began calling them "fields."

Thomas's most famous concepts, if one may call them that, were the "four wishes": desires for new experience, (social) recognition, mastery, and security. Later, mastery was replaced by response, in deference to the importance of sexual response. Thomas also proposed three personality types: the Philistine accepts conventional values, the Bohemian rejects them, while the Creative Man integrates a desire for new experience with a desire for security, neither accepting nor rejecting all norms, and creates new definitions of situations. A Thomistic autobiographical distinction, surely.

Delinquency

Thomas denied there was a "criminal type." The existence of a criminal type assumes a sharp break between the offender and the "normal" person, but that distinction is based on selecting a characteristic alleged to be found among criminals without checking to see how widespread the same characteristic might be among the noncriminal. (This lack of a control group is the typical fallacy of psychological research in criminology.) "Types have always seemed most clear-cut where only the deviating group has been studied, that is, where knowledge of the distribution of the typological characteristic among the general population is lacking."[62] Thomas's denial of criminal types resulted from his comprehensiveness and his insistence on continuity of personal and social process. He wrote:

> No part of the life of the individual should be studied dis-
> associated from the whole of his life, the abnormal as sepa-
> rated from the normal, and abnormal groups should be studied
> in comparison with the remaining groups we call normal. There
> is no break in continuity between the normal and the abnormal
> in actual life that would permit the selection of any exact
> bodies of corresponding materials, and the nature of the nor-
> mal and the abnormal can be understood only with the help of
> comparison.[63]

Court and prison records reveal people with a "high degree of imagination, ingenuity, constructive intelligence, artistic ability, and careers as long continued in crime as legitimate life careers in physics, engineering, or art."[64] Thus any human document could be used to illuminate unique features of an individual's or group's experience, or to illustrate common traits.[65]

Because of his preference for viewing the criminal offender in a broader context, Thomas resisted treating delinquency as a separate problem. Kimball Young has written about Thomas's view of the fallacy of particularism: "Categories such as 'prostitution,' 'crime,' 'war,' and 'education' are drawn upon with a view to solving the problems as isolated phenomena under the convenient stereotypes."[66] Delinquency does make appearances in *The Polish Peasant:* it is viewed primarily as a result of the breakdown of Old World values amid the exciting and commercialized attractions of the New World. The authority of immigrant parents was undermined in this new situation, while some of their children used illegal means to secure things they felt every true American should have, such as an automobile. The wish for new experience was intense, and the wish for recognition was satisfied by the child's peer group, perhaps a delinquent gang, not by the immigrant family.

Thomas never wrote a book about delinquency by itself, but he did make studies more restricted to delinquency than one might have expected, in *The Unadjusted Girl* and *The Child in America*.[67] The former concerns female prostitution after the First World War; the second is a review of theories, policies, and practices in the study and treatment of children, including delinquents. However, oral histories that Thomas collected from delinquents appear in neither book: the life histories show how girls were seduced or how young women took up "the life," but none is really about delinquency. *The Child in America* makes extensive use of Healy and Bronner's case studies, as well as cases from the journal *Mental Hygiene* and other books, journals, agencies, and researchers. One exception is a long excerpt from the manuscript of Clifford Shaw's *The Delinquent Boy's Own Story*, which was published two years later as *The Jack-Roller*.[68] In fact, after the mid-1920s, whenever Thomas made a statement about delinquency, he almost always used Shaw's work. The selection from Shaw that Thomas used describes the boy's life in detention centers, "houses of corruption" rather than of "correction," making the usual points about such places. Perhaps Thomas used this because it was the only selection Shaw gave him, but it might be because oral history is especially fitted to expose the futility of experience behind the walls.

In *The Unadjusted Girl* and *The Polish Peasant* (1918–20 ed.; chapters on "Vagabondage and Delinquency of Boys" and "Sexual Immorality of Girls"), when cases are clearly about officially recognized delinquents, records from the Cook County Juvenile Court are used, occasionally with a brief statement from the delinquent. Augusta Bronner said that while he was working on *The Polish Peasant*, Thomas used to visit the court and hear cases of Polish children. However, Thomas himself apparently never interviewed delinquents for their life histories. Perhaps this was because he preferred to use material he had not influenced (though clearly others had), or because of his lack of an institutional setting where he would encounter delinquents. But surely he could have arranged to approach young people firsthand had he wanted to. One has the suspicion that despite his advance in empiricism over his scholarly colleagues, he was able to reach only a certain distance from his academic literary beginnings, in which the written word is more sacred than the spoken.

Marginal Knowledge: Critique of *The Polish Peasant*

Several "critiques" of Thomas's work have been made; I shall examine these in the Kantian sense of determining limits, in this case of oral histories, at least as they were used by the generation of sociologists following Thomas in their studies of delinquency. One familiar point is the absence in a scheme laden with oral history of a direct confrontation with political factors. Janowitz puts this nicely: "Like much of the writing that was to come from the Chicago school, his [Thomas's] work neglects the political process per se as if it were a derivative aspect of society."

> He never developed an adequate set of categories for in-
> stitutional change, and in particular for dealing with society-
> wide political institutions. To some degree, this was the result
> of his interest in observing the raw material of the social scene.
> His direct observations made it more feasible for him to chart
> changes in social personality rather than changes in
> institutions—a state of affairs that still dominates sociology.[69]

That is, too close a dependence on human documents, with their inevit- able location of interest and subject matter in self and circumstance, prevents a student of society from tracing lines of genesis that transcend local experience.

But self and immediate circumstance themselves transcend other re- alities, such as early childhood experiences and the somatic substratum of experience. Even the psychologists who create theories in these areas have trouble including them in their own autobiographies. John Dollard complained that Thomas and Znaniecki should have been bothered be- cause the autobiography of Wladek started only at age six, by which time the individual's attitudes already have a background.[70] Dollard was also unhappy that the four wishes were not traced to their somatic sources; for example, how was the wish for security related to the emotion of fear? "We could hope for a more energetic and detailed analysis which would reveal how such a tendency as fear is attached to acts and objects in complex social situations."[71] If temperament is an organic given in an individual, and character is learned socially, "how temperament becomes character is the problem," according to Dollard, "and it remains a prob- lem throughout the discussion."[72] It is certainly not a problem that oral histories or even their interpretative schemes can begin to solve.

The most thoroughgoing critique of *The Polish Peasant* was made by Herbert Blumer in 1938 as the first in a series of examinations of books that had been most influential in the social sciences. The purpose of the Social Science Research Council in assigning these projects was to take stock of what had been achieved and to ask to what extent the social sciences were sciences. Thus the relation of human documents to *knowl- edge* preoccupied the participants in the seminar that followed Blumer's presentation of his paper. Blumer's analysis, plus pieces published with it—replies by Thomas and Znaniecki and a fascinating discussion among several prominent sociologists and psychologists—make up the locus classicus for discriminating the essential elements of the epistemological status of life histories.

No one in this discussion defended *The Polish Peasant* as containing an adequate or well-supported statement on any subject it treated. Blumer cut to the heart of the matter: "The basic terms 'attitude' and 'value' as employed by Thomas and Znaniecki are vague, ambiguous, and confused."[73] Regarding the letters, Blumer complained that the reader is not told how the authors collected them or selected which to use. Further:

> On the matter of adequacy, we are told virtually nothing concerning the life, setting, and background of the families or individuals; further, the content of the letters seems fragmentary, dealing with occasional and selected experiences and not covering the totality of interests of the writers. In the case of reliability of experiences cited, we are given no means of testing the honesty or truthfulness of the account. Finally, with reference to interpretation, there is no way of understanding how the interpretation was arrived at; nor are there any rules which would permit determination as to whether the interpretation is correct or erroneous, or the extent to which it is so.[74]

Blumer applied much the same criticism to the other varieties of human documents that appear in *The Polish Peasant*.

In fact, commentators have had something of a field day in pointing out epistemological inadequacies in *The Polish Peasant,* and some of these criticisms Thomas and Znaniecki agreed with. Dollard gave free rein to his imagination: "The authors do not, as it were, consider the material of Wladek's life on conceptual hands and knees; they take it rather in a general sense and do not take the trouble to argue very closely back and forth in constructing a theory of his life." "The 'fit' of their scheme of desires to the material does not seem very tight." "In most cases these interpretations seem to be affixed, like tabs in a manuscript, rather than to come organically out of the material."[75] Madge points out that Wladek's autobiography was moved from the middle of the first edition to the end of the second edition, and he concludes: "It is no detraction from the vividness and attractiveness of the narrative to state that it is somewhat difficult to tame and difficult to place."[76]

Some criticisms have demanded more than any book can give. During the panel discussion reproduced in Blumer's *Appraisal,* Max Lerner asked for *any* example of a sociological law or criterion of verification of a proposition; the implication was that in the most absolute sense of "knowledge" no one had established sociological knowledge, so that Thomas could hardly be criticized for not having done so.[77] Znaniecki's reply to the claim that "attitude" and "value" do not have fixed meanings was that their mistake had been rather in suggesting that the terms have any stability at all "in abstract isolation from other elements—just as, say, the substantial 'bodies' and the absolute movements of older physical theories," whereas "a concrete component of human active experience . . . is *infinitely variable*."[78] (How any statement at all is possible within this position is not clear.) On another point Dollard noted that Wladek "does not have to answer any questions other than those he chose to answer when he first wrote [his autobiography]. This must be viewed as a methodological weakness." "It is certainly a limitation of autobiography that you have to take it as given and cannot ask any questions about it."[79] However, as Socrates pointed out, this is true of *all* written things. At least the scholar is more open to questioning by peers—at meetings, in journals, and so on—than the scholar's subject is in an autobiography. Thomas was no recluse, and he could have answered questions had he been asked even before the late 1930s, when these critiques took place.

What, then, is the relation of oral history to knowledge? Obviously, reading such material can stimulate insights, hunches, and leads for further thinking and research, but it does not seem that human documents can ever by themselves validate a proposition. Can the epistemological place of oral histories be specified better than this? Louis Wirth, a member of the Blumer panel, commented: "I would like to raise the question whether there is not to be found a marginal field of scholarly, if not scientific, endeavor lying between the meaningful description of the unique and the formulation of invariant universal laws."[80] Read Bain located human documents and the mode of thought that accompanies them in *The Polish Peasant* somewhere between science and literary insight.[81] For Blumer, the letters in *The Polish Peasant* would not have been meaningful by themselves, and the theoretical analyses by themselves would have been abstract and dogmatic. But "the merging of the two does yield a concreteness and appreciative understanding that cannot be stated either as a mere illustration of the theory, nor as an inductive grounding of that theory. There seems to be involved a new relation, perhaps more in the nature of a psychological than a logical relation, that so far has not been stated or made clear." "There has been an interaction between theory and inductive material, but an interaction which is exceedingly ambiguous."[82] Allport asks if there is an "intermediate level of conception" "between the level that recognizes in broad manner that certain relationships prevail and the level of precise formulation of specific 'laws of social becoming.'"[83] In his own book on personal documents Allport notes: "The process of interaction between theory and inductive material which Blumer finds ambiguous is the essence of the methodological problem of personal documents."[84]

Curiously, this marginal area where the epistemology of oral history appears to be located has apparently never been explored, unless in poetics and literary criticism. Since my purpose here is to indicate the conditions under which delinquents' oral histories come into being, I need only point to this place as one such condition and leave it for future exploration or rediscovery.[85]

Thomas resisted writing about his own method, but the following was an exception:

> It is my experience that formal methodological studies are rel-
> atively unprofitable. They have tended to represent the stand-
> point developed in philosophy and the history of philosophy. It
> is my impression that progress is made from point to point by
> setting up objectives, employing certain techniques, then re-
> setting the problems with the introduction of still other objec-
> tives and the modification of techniques . . . . In all this, there is
> no formal attention to method but the use of some imagination
> or mind from point to point. The operator raises the question,
> at appropriate points, "What if," and prepares a set-up to test
> this query . . . . It is only, in fact, so far as sociology is con-
> cerned, since we abandoned the search for standardized
> methods based largely on the work of dead men, that we have
> made the beginnings which I have indicated.[86]

The kind of reasoning in this process is not different from that used in everyday life. Thomas wrote: "We live by inference. I am, let us say, your guest. You do not know, you cannot determine scientifically, that I will not steal your money or your spoons. But inferentially I will not and inferentially you have me as a guest."[87]

Inferences using human documents are not based solely on common human experience, however, but also on the special experience the reader of the documents brings to them. This experience is broader than that represented in the documents. Blumer is hard pressed to see how some of the interpretations Thomas and Znaniecki made came out of the documents they published. They must have had other documents they did not use, and we must take on faith that the omitted ones did not contradict those that appear. Moreover, behind their stated observations they had many of *their own experiences*. Blumer says: "They bring, so to speak, a rich 'apperception mass' based on an extensive and intimate acquaintance with Polish peasant life and also an appreciation and understanding of 'human nature' that is organized under the influence of a series of theoretical schemes. Their interpretation is grounded partly in the document, partly in their broad theoretical background."[88]

> In the authors, we have two excellent minds with a rich
> experience with human beings, with a keen sensitivity to the
> human element in conduct, with some fundamental notions
> and interests, with a number of important problems, with a
> variety of hunches, with a lively curiosity and sense of inquiry,
> with a capacity for forming abstract concepts—two minds, of

this sort, approaching voluminous accounts of human experience, mulling over them, reflecting on them, perceiving many
things in them, relating these things to their background of
experience, checking these things against one another, and
charting all of them into a coherent abstract and analytical
pattern. Perhaps, this is, after all, how the scientist works.[89]

The reader also judges the documentary material by relating it to his own
experience:

It is human material; you can assume the role of the person
whose account it is and thus arrive at some idea of how reasonable the interpretation is. Then, too, you bring your own
background of experience. If you are a person who has had a
lot of contact with human beings and understands human nature well, and particularly, if you already have a knowledge of
the particular people with which the authors are dealing, you
are in a better position to judge the reasonableness of the interpretation.[90]

Yet another interplay works among the letters themselves. Though
Blumer found the letters taken singly to be inadequate as data, "taken
collectively they fare much better. There is a large measure of verification
and support which the letters give one another; pieced together, they tend
to give consistent pictures."[91] Human documents and commentary in *The
Polish Peasant* mutually interpret each other: "The autobiography of
Wladek," in Blumer's view, "is not independently understandable; it has
to be viewed in the context of the Polish peasant social milieu as
established in the other volumes of this study by Thomas and
Znaniecki."[92]

But if one must depend on personal experience and internal interpretation, what prevents capricious judgments and the use of force to impose
judgments on people who do not share the same experiences or interpretations? Wirth asserted: "It comes down to the prestige or force of the
assertor as to whether a given proposition is valid or not. If that isn't the
case, then we obviously must look for certain other criteria of validity."
Max Lerner asked if the test should be the degree of acceptance, the size
of the following.[93] The answer is yes: that is in fact the way a science
operates, from the sociological point of view, a not unfitting viewpoint for
sociologists to take. A profession follows its most creative leaders, and the
profession—that is, the professional audience—legitimizes their creativity, even when they propose new methods of proof. Whether force is used
depends on the character of the organization, since force is not the only
alternative to airtight methods of proof. Persuasion is another alternative.
The epistemological status of oral history is not so much in that middle
ground between universal and particular as it is simply in the common

sense or special acquaintances and conventional acceptances of a document's possible audience.

Science and Rhetoric

My claim that the place of oral histories of juvenile offenders is in promoting social reform runs into an apparent counterinstance in W. I. Thomas's work with human documents. Thomas maintained that "from the method itself all practical considerations must be excluded if we want the results to be valid."[94] In their zeal, according to Thomas, reformers make unjustified assumptions, but it is the role of the social scientist to "check" these, in the senses both of examining and of restricting them. The scientist must pull away from action, must put a distance between himself and reform moves. Thus Thomas's human documents appear not to have had an direct intention to arouse an interest in social reform.

Thomas's writings, on the contrary, are filled with implications and suggestions for social practice. Concerning Wladek's autobiography, he and Znaniecki wrote: "It will make us realize also that the greatest defect of our entire civilization has been precisely the existence of a culturally passive mass, that every non-creative personality is an educational failure. It will show the sources of such failures and thus open the way for a more successful social education in the future."[95] Perhaps his most reformist book was *The Unadjusted Girl*. In the foreword to that book, Mrs. Ethel Dummer wrote: "Certain lines of research were undertaken, primarily to gather and interpret data which would lead to less unjust treatment than is at present accorded so-called delinquent women, by changing public opinion and especially altering procedure in our courts, jails, and hospitals." One of the reforms Thomas urged was the collection of more complete records on individual cases.[96]

Thomas's most principled suggestion for social reform came in the conclusion to the 1918–20 edition of *The Polish Peasant:*

> A country wide net of thousands, hundreds of thousands of small cooperative associations, with the activie participation of various nationalities, coming together on a basis of real equality and united by serious common aims would do incomparably more for economic self-dependence, for the prevention of demoralization, for the development of active solidarity, for a genuine Americanization of the immigrant than anything that has ever been done to achieve these aims. It would, besides, contribute in a measure to the solution of many of the most difficult problems which American society itself is trying to solve at this moment.
>
> The prevalent general social unrest and demoralization is due to the decay of the primary-group organization, which gave the individual a sense of responsibility and security be-

cause he *belonged to something*. This system has given way partly to the forces making for individual efficiency, and we have developed nothing to take its place—no organization which would restore the sense of social responsibility without limiting the efficiency of the individual. This new form is apparently destined to be the cooperative society, and all immigrant groups, among them perhaps preeminently the Poles, bring to this country precisely the attitudes upon which cooperative enterprises can be built.[97]

Thomas shows his appreciation for community autonomy in the following:

> It is a mistake to suppose that a "community center" established by American social agencies can in its present form even approximately fulfill the social function of a Polish parish. It is an institution imposed from the outside instead of being freely developed by the initiative and co-operation of the people themselves and this, in addition to its racially unfamiliar character, would be enough to prevent it from exercising any deep social influence. Its managers usually know little or nothing of the traditions, attitudes, and native language of the people with whom they have to deal and therefore could not become genuine social leaders under any conditions.... Whatever real assistance the American social center gives to the immigrant community is the result of the "case method," which consists in dealing directly and separately with individuals and families. While this method may bring efficient temporary help to the individual it does not contribute to the social progress of the community nor does it possess much preventive influence in struggling against social disorganization. Both of these purposes can be attained only by organizing and encouraging social self-help on the co-operative basis. Finally, in their relations with immigrants the American social workers usually assume, consciously or not, the attitude of a kindly and protective superiority, occasionally, though seldom, verging on despotism.[98]

Compare this with a similar statement by Mayhew:

> There is but one way of benefiting the poor, viz., by developing their powers of self-reliance, and certainly not in treating them like children. Philanthropists always seek to do too much, and in this is to be found the main cause of their repeated failures. The poor are expected to become angels in an instant, and the consequence is, they are merely made *hypocrites* .... It would seem, too, that this overweening disposition to play the part of *ped-agogues* (I use the word in its literal sense) to the poor,

proceeds rather from a love of power than from a sincere regard for the people. Let the rich become the advisers and
assistants of the poor, giving them the benefit of their superior
education and means—but *leaving the people to act for themselves*—and they will do a great good.[99]

Thus the principle of autonomy on which Clifford Shaw would build
community organizations was clearly present in Thomas's work, as it was
earlier in Mayhew's. That is, "the people themselves can do it" is a
reflection of "the people themselves can say it." John Madge has drawn a
related implication from Thomas's use of human documents, though it
appears that Thomas himself never made precisely this point:

> While the testing of rats in mazes may be a justifiable activity
> for learning about animal psychology, for testing people in
> real-life situations it is possible both to learn more and also to
> behave in a morally much more correct way toward your sub-
> jects if you take them into your confidence and if you take
> advantage of the fact that they can help you, as you can help
> them, toward a correct definition of the situation . . . . By taking
> subjects into your confidence, Thomas and Znaniecki rightly
> claim not only that you are acting correctly toward them in that
> you are respecting their human dignity but also that the result-
> ing investigations will be more realistic and fruitful.[100]

Though Thomas himself doubted it, others have insisted that his work
influenced social workers to be more aware of their clients' culture and
viewpoint. Wirth said: "I think [*The Polish Peasant*] has helped to rid
social workers of their moralistic approach and has helped them to con-
ceive of disorganization . . . in a more or less naturalistic way."[101]

Some of Thomas's pronouncements on matters of social policy were
exposed to the public, but his own predilection was not to address the
public, at least not after some early magazine articles before 1909.[102]
According to Thomas, the aim of science should be to improve the means
of "control": "It is recognized that the object of research in both the
material and the social worlds is control."[103] Blumer states: "The ultimate test of the validity of scientific knowledge is the ability to use it for
purposes of social control."[104] From this perspective the individual does
not seem to have such a large role in determining the process after all: the
means of social reform would not be so much persuading a broad public
audience to support a project or to volunteer resources as it would be
advising or "consulting" with a smaller group of social leaders to institute
new policies. The public might need a more spectacular form of motivation, but, "Scientifically the history of dull lives is quite as significant as
that of brilliant ones."[105]

Surely the large size of *The Polish Peasant* and the small number of copies distributed support the picture of a small audience of professionals. The first edition of 1,500 copies was exhausted in six years, and a second edition of 1,500 copies took a decade to sell out. The 1958 edition sold 3,000 copies in three years, "reflecting the great expansion of the sociological audience."[106] "The fact that all of Thomas' books were out of print during the later years of his life and that his articles were generally unavailable was of no serious concern to him. He was not even concerned that some of his most thoughtful writings remained in typescript or mimeographed form."[107] Thomas also exerted influence through his teaching and professional associations.

However, it does not appear that Thomas's human documents were intended to promote a social reform by vividly communicating to an audience. We may be looking in the wrong place for an instance of social reform, though, accustomed as we have been by the foregoing chapters to reform schools, houses of refuge, and juvenile courts. One of W. I. Thomas's main intentions was indeed to achieve a reform, and human documents were central to persuading his audience to adopt it. *That reform was the creation of empirical sociology itself.* Human documents communicated to potential sociologists the kind of phenomenon they should be dealing with. No other verbal device could do this so well: conceptual descriptions of "social phenomena" would risk merely falling again into overabstraction, of either the philosophical or the physical (hence numerical) variety, already endemic in the field. At a time when a professor of sociology wanted to write about saloons but had never been in one, an author would have to present something full-bodied and concrete in a book in order to direct attention to the *kinds* of things one could profitably investigate. Social phenomena may be difficult to focus on and hard to locate, for they are essentially marginal to physical things on the one hand and to ideas on the other. Experience with a number of human documents (another reason they are so voluminous) can evoke an appreciation for a proper and profitable subject matter of sociology or for a particular area: "Human documents may be very serviceable in aiding the student to acquire an intimate acquaintance with the kind of experience he is studying.... It is much better to develop one's theoretical judgments with the aid of such documents than to form them, extremely speaking, in a vacuum."[108] At the beginning of a new orientation in a profession, even the professional is a student; first Thomas himself, then his followers. Perhaps recent broad public interest in oral histories is also part of a major cultural reorientation.

This is not to say that *The Polish Peasant* did not yield substantive insights into social change and Polish life. However, the criticisms of that book insofar as it seemed to yield knowledge are unanimous and conclusive; yet the book was so respected and influential that it seems to call for a different means of judgment than the strictly "scientific." Blumer said of *The Polish Peasant:* "It is not a mere monograph on Polish peasant society. It is primarily an attempt to lay the basis for scientific social research and for scientific social theory."[109] It illustrates a "standpoint and method." It introduces concepts in proximity to events, and, if the fit between them is not close, further research will tighten things up. At least the concepts are not empty, the percepts not blind. Exploration and persuasion are two aspects of the same activity, since opening up a field or method requires persuading readers to follow the pioneer into that field. To use his own terms, Thomas was trying to redefine the situation of sociology. To do this, there was needed not a body of propositions or "laws," but general schemes of research analogous to those the individual uses for action:

> The individual, in order to control social reality for his needs,
> must develop not series of uniform reactions, but general
> *schemes* of situations; his life-organization is a set of rules for
> definite situations, which may be even expressed in abstract
> formulas. Moral principles, legal prescriptions, economic
> forms, religious rites, social customs, etc., are examples of
> schemes.[110]

"Schemes" are similar to the notes a speaker carries to the platform.

Indeed, the art of rhetoric is pervasive in Thomas: since the four wishes are present in all human beings and require satisfaction, they can be used in persuasion as "topics" (to use the technical term from classical rhetoric) that an orator can draw out of his repertory when it seems that the audience would be moved by a desire for new experience, security, response, or recognition.[111] From this vantage *The Unadjusted Girl,* an illustration of the four wishes, appeals to its readers by presenting material on the basic human desires, not to speak of the material on prostitution. The quality of continuity in human document material may be interpreted from this perspective as a rhetorical device, expressing Cicero's definition of eloquence as a continuous movement of the soul.

The richness of this human material, among other things, must have attracted a number of young people to pursue sociology at the University of Chicago. The vast land Thomas opened up was ideal terrain for later graduate students to carve up and cultivate piece by piece.

Seven
Chicago: The City as Laboratory

Chicago has been remarkably hospitable to oral history. Frontier Americans were virtuosos at "jawing" and at oratory: consider Abe Lincoln and, later, Chicagoan Clarence Darrow. A new, more naturalistic literary language originated in the writing of Chicago newspaper reporters such as Sandburg and Dreiser, who were part of the Chicago Renaissance in literature from the 1880s to the 1920s.[1] All the major figures of this movement wrote autobiographies, and much of the rest of their work has an autobiographical aspect: "Said Floyd Dell as editor of the *Friday Literary Review* to his apprentice writer, Margaret Anderson, 'Here is a book about China. Now don't send me an article about China but one about yourself.'"[2] As we have seen, Healy solicited the child's "own story." Following W. I. Thomas, the Chicago sociologists in the 1920s and 1930s collected thousands of life histories from hoboes, delinquents, gang members, confidence men, and other marginal persons of all sorts.

This autobiographical spirit has continued in Chicago. Richard Wright experienced human extremes in Chicago similar to those Mayhew saw in London: "There is an open and raw beauty about that city that seems either to kill or to endow one with the spirit of life. I felt those extremes of possibility, death and hope, while I lived half hungry and afraid in a city to which I had fled with the dumb yearning to write, to tell my story."[3] Studs Terkel, the nation's most conspicuous practitioner of oral history these days, grew up and works in Chicago, and most of the people who speak through his books seem to be Chicagoans. (After three major oral history books, Terkel wrote a sort of autobiography in *Talking to Myself*, the story of a professional marginal man.) The present dean of the Humanities Division at the University of Chicago, Karl Weintraub, has studied autobiography as a way of tracing the growth of consciousness of individuality as a value in the West. Howard S. Becker, at Northwestern University, is the sociologist today most associated with life history (see below, chap. 9), as the late Oscar Lewis (at the University of Illinois, Urbana, which stretches it a bit) was the anthropologist. There are other similar cases.[4]

An entire book could be written to describe and explain this. Here I can only suggest that the ubiquity of autobiography in Chicago, at least in the earlier period, seems to be connected to the pervasive individualism of the city, the push for success and the desire to read success stories—perhaps, too, curiosity about colorful personalities or genuine need for life guidance by reading about exemplary characters in a new, confusing world. None of this individualism implies much appreciation for individuality, the value of personal uniqueness, to use Weintraub's distinction. Nor would it explain interest in documents about social "failures," such as delinquents. In Chicago one cause of the greater willingness to view the ordinary or deviant person in his or her own concrete social setting was the absence of the aristocratic traditions that had accumulated in eastern American cities. Shils makes the same point about the universities: "The hierarchy of deference was weaker in the Midwest [than in eastern universities]; there was more equalitarianism, greater sympathy for the common life, more understanding for ordinary people, and, therefore, more readiness to be intellectually concerned about them."[5]

The Midwest did not yet have strong identifications based on either its land or its social positions, such as had already developed in New England and in the South. Chicago was a new city after the 1871 fire, with new styles of architecture. Two of the most creative architects during that period were Louis Sullivan and Frank Lloyd Wright, and it is not fanciful, I think, to compare the new architecture to the "new" form of documentary expression. Sullivan's solution to skyscraper design was to allow the building's inner structure to be expressed in its soaring exterior lines, rather than covering it with conventional decoration, a kind of visual logomachy quoting classical sources. Greater expanses of windows were installed in Chicago buildings, allowing "outsiders" to see inside, as oral histories permitted insight into the lives of strangers, though both varieties of spectator were kept at a distance.[6] Frank Lloyd Wright's prairie houses followed the contours of the flat Illinois prairie rather than stacking up traditional forms in the manner of Queen Anne houses, just as life histories allow a reader to follow the continuities and textures of someone else's experience, avoiding the application of one or another prefabricated theory. (Wright's Robie House, built in 1909, was adjacent to the University of Chicago campus, where W. I. Thomas might have passed it on his way to work.)

On the subject of "seeing through" and oral history, it is interesting to note that Mayhew wrote *London Labour* at the time of the great London Exposition of 1851, with its glass-walled Crystal Palace. This demonstration of technological innovation came after twenty years of profound social change in England. The Columbian Exposition of 1893 in Chicago, a few years before the juvenile court was founded, also came after twenty-two years of recovery from the Great Fire and almost thirty years after the Civil War; and its show of modern technology set Henry Adams's head swirling. The Century of Progress Exposition in Chicago in

1933 was almost contemporary with the publication of Clifford Shaw's major life histories.

These technological innovations caused social changes that affected the lives of children and the extent of delinquency. In the introduction to their book *The Child in America* (1928), W. I. and Dorothy Thomas made a statement that could have been written in any year during the century and a half now past:

> As a result of rapid communication in space, movements of population (concentration in cities, immigration), changes in the industrial order, the decline of community and family life, the weakening of religion, the universality of reading, the commercialization of pleasure, and for whatever other reasons there may be, we are now witnessing a far-reaching modification of the moral norms and behavior practices of all classes of society. Activities have evolved more rapidly than social structures, personalities more rapidly than social norms. This unstabilization of society and of behavior is probably no more than a stage of disorganization preceding a modified type of reorganization. When old habits break down, when they are no longer adequate, there is always a period of confusion until new habits are established; and this is true of both the individual and society. At present, however, it is widely felt that the demoralization of young persons, the prevalence of delinquency, crime, and profound mental disturbances are very serious problems, and that the situation is growing worse instead of better.

Gordon Allport in 1942 began his examination of personal documents by remarking on conditions for their appearance similar to the social conditions described by the Thomases:

> A decade of depression, war, and misery has had one benign effect. It has brought out upon the center of our cultural stage the struggles of the common man, the picture of his daily life, his courage, all his homely values. It has brought the documentary film into popularity, the public opinion poll, radio programs dealing with the common man's life—sidewalk interviews, "we the people"—candid cameras, autobiographies that give unaccented accounts of ordinary experience *(These are our lives)*. Journals like *Life* and *PM* have sprung into being with their featuring of the ordinary soldier, the ordinary baby, the ordinary school girl. The layman has become interested in the personal document: and so too has the social scientist, caught up in the general cultural tide.[7]

These publications were read by members of the burgeoning middle class, who also sent their children to universities to study sociology.

These were some of the conditions under which life histories of delinquents were produced in Chicago in the 1920s and 1930s.

From Rumination to Reform: Park and Burgess

The sociological standpoint and the empirical methods of W. I. Thomas were communicated to the next generation of sociology graduate students at the University of Chicago by Robert E. Park and Ernest W. Burgess. Neither made so extensive a use of human documents as W. I. Thomas had. Of the two, Burgess published more documentary expression than Park. The one book in which Park appeared to use human documents extensively, *Old World Traits Transplanted* (1921), was actually written by W. I. Thomas, whose name could not be attached at that time because of the 1918 scandal.[8] Why did Park seldom use life histories and Burgess often use them? Two factors: Park's philosophical background led to his interest in filling out a system of sociological research and knowledge, and oral histories themselves do not seem necessary to that task, while Burgess used life histories in his ventures of social reform. Nevertheless, some features of Park's life fitted him to appreciate and promote the use of life histories by other sociologists.

Robert Ezra Park (1864–1944) grew up in Minnesota, "an awkward, sentimental, and romantic boy" who published an amateur newspaper called the *Rambler*.[9] Having read a book with a mining engineer as its hero, he decided to go to the University of Michigan to study engineering, but under the influence of John Dewey, then teaching at Michigan, he took up philosophy. Studying Goethe's *Faust* hit him hard: "I made up my mind to go in for experience for its own sake, to gather into my soul, as Faust somewhere says, 'all the joys and sorrows of the world.'" The result was that he became a newspaper reporter from 1887 to 1898: "I lived the life of an intellectual vagabond. My program was to see and know what we call 'Life.'" "The yellow journals went in for reform, and I became a reformer." One of his projects was remarkably similar to Mayhew's discovery of the source of the Bermondsley cholera epidemic: "We had a diphtheria epidemic. I plotted the cases on a map of the city and in this way called attention to what seemed to be the source of the infection, an open sewer." As a reporter Park became familiar with many aspects of city life: "I expect that I have actually covered more ground, tramping about in cities in different parts of the world, than any other living man. Out of all this I gained, among other things, a conception of the city, the community, and the region, not as a geographical phenomenon merely but as a kind of social organism." In this way Park came to see that the newspaper might "make itself actually the powerful agency for education and reform that it had sometimes conceived itself to be."

But this "revolution" in journalism, as he called it, was slow in coming.

In 1898 Park went to Harvard University to work out an understanding of what "news" is: "I studied philosophy because I hoped to gain insight into the nature and function of the kind of knowledge we call news. Besides I wanted to gain a fundamental point of view from which I could describe the behavior of society, under the influence of news, in the precise and universal language of science." Park studied with Josiah Royce, George Santayana, and William James. One day during the period when he was writing *The Varieties of Religious Experience,* James read the class an essay, "A Certain Blindness in Human Beings." Park comments:

> The "blindness" of which James spoke is the blindness each one of us is likely to have for the meaning of other people's lives. At any rate what sociologists most need to know is what goes on behind the faces of men, what it is that makes life for each of us either dull or thrilling. For "if you lose the joy you lose all." But the thing that gives zest to life or makes life dull is, however, as James says, "a personal secret" which has, in every single case, to be discovered. Otherwise we do not know the world in which we actually live.[10]

Later on, one of Park's main interests was social distance: "An earthquake in China assumes ... less importance than a funeral in our own village."[11] One of his central distinctions was between knowledge about and acquaintance with, the latter yielding emotional insight.

Park went to Germany to continue his studies and wrote his doctor's thesis under the philosopher Windelband. It is entitled "Masse und Publicum" (The Crowd and the Public) and is preoccupied with what the subject matter of sociology should be. He returned to Harvard in 1903 as an assistant in philosophy for two years. "Any ambition that I had ever to be a reformer had quite vanished by that time," he later said, but he became first secretary of the Congo Reform Association, where he met Booker T. Washington. "Booker Washington gave me an opportunity such as no one else ever had, I am sure, to get acquainted with the actual and intimate life of the Negro in the South. I traveled all over the South; poked my way into every corner where there was anything that seemed instructive or interesting. I became, for all intents and purposes, for the time, a Negro myself." Richard Wright later wrote: "It was from the scientific findings of men like the late Robert E. Park ... that I drew the meanings for my documentary book, *12,000,000 Black Voices.*" Park, according to Wright, was not afraid to urge his students "to trust their feelings for a situation or an event [and to] stress the role of insight, and to warn against a slavish devotion to figures, charts, graphs, and sterile scientific techniques."[12] In 1911, while Park was at Tuskegee Institute, he met W. I. Thomas. Thomas said: "Park was not only ruminating all the time but imposing his ruminations on me, with eventual great profit to myself."[13] Thomas succeeded in getting Park an appointment as a lecturer in sociology at the University of Chicago in 1914, where he remained until his retirement in 1933.

Even this brief sketch of Park's life reveals something about his own "personal secret." Park was pulled in two directions, with most creative results: toward the adventure of new experience in the vast human world of the American city, and also toward an intellectual grasp of that experience. The tension between the two was so great because his immersion in each had been so thorough: twelve years as a reporter "tramping about cities," and seven years in philosophy, some of it with William James, who had a similar expansive curiosity about things human. This duality is typical in people who produce oral histories, but Park did not produce them because his desire for an intellectual grasp of social phenomena was stronger than his interest in representing or changing. them. Although Park remained keenly interested in the newspaper and in public opinion, he did not write about the communicative functions of human documents. One of Park's students, however, Helen MacGill Hughes, whose dissertation was "News and the Human Interest Story," played a central role in an autobiography we shall study in chapter 9.

In spite of his standard assignment to his students to write their life histories, Ernest Watson Burgess (1886–1966) apparently never wrote his own.[14] There may not be much to tell. Burgess has been called the first young sociologist, since he did not come to sociology after assimilating a broad intellectual culture: from the beginning of his career he was trained in sociology. He attended the University of Chicago from 1908 to 1913, when he finished his dissertation, "The Function of Socialization in Social Evolution." After teaching sociology at other universities, he returned to Chicago in 1916 and stayed until his retirement in 1957. Burgess had been a good student and early on achieved an apparently uncomplicated professional identity. Despite his studies of the family, he never married, a condition that he once jokingly remarked made him objective and prevented generalizations from one case; he lived with his sister. Although lacking worldly experience, Burgess was clearly committed to life histories, especially those of juvenile delinquents.

James F. Short, Jr., points out that the two abiding goals of Burgess's life were the amelioration of social ills and the development of sociology as a science. Of the former goal, Everett Hughes has said that Burgess was interested in "reforms, I suppose you would call them."[15] Burgess actively associated himself with social action organizations, especially with Clifford Shaw's Chicago Area Project. Thomas and Park (Park was twenty-two years older than Burgess) had pulled sociology back from direct involvement in social reform. They saw their mission as setting their own scientific house in order, clearing out humanistic Victorian bric-a-brac, before going out consulting. Park had a habit of throwing verbal darts at "those damned do-gooders"—social workers. This also accounts for Park's himself not publishing life histories, in spite of many features of his background and personality that fitted him to do so. Burgess did not experience these inhibitions of the reformist motive to the same degree: he did not feel that he had to fight against sociology as philanthropy. Rather, Burgess began with the sociological standpoint more or less established by Thomas in the early 1910s. He could feel more comfortable applying the results of that standpoint. Although human documents appeared in Burgess's writings for the same reason they appeared in Thomas's, to reorient sociology to the concrete, in Burgess they have the additional function of persuading nonsociologist readers to make specific social reforms. For example, in a report to the Illinois Parole Board, Burgess used case and life histories to illustrate four types of paroled men and thus to recommend different policies concerning each.[16] This appearance of a reformist tendency (though it had been present earlier as the desire to reform a discipline) will be important for our understanding of Clifford Shaw's use of life histories of delinquents, since Burgess was the guide and interpreter of much of Shaw's work.

To understand why life histories were no longer used in sociology after the 1930s, it is equally important to note Burgess's interest in advancing sociology as a science by developing quantitative methods of prediction, especially predicting success and failure of marriages and of people on parole. Just as the intellectual companions of Healy and of Thomas developed statistical devices that superseded "own story" as a means of studying mental traits and replaced human documents as a way of determining social attitudes, so Burgess's contribution of statistics speeded the move away from life histories. (Like Thomas, Park was averse to statistics.)

One final way Burgess differed from Park was that Burgess was not such an intellectual power. Shils has written: "When Robert Park withdrew from Chicago toward the end of his life . . . Chicago sociology faltered."[17] Burgess was less interested in laying out broad conceptual frameworks and generating new problems for inquiry than in designing schemes to organize data for the treatment of available problems and to organize agencies to solve those problems. The work of Clifford Shaw thus was guided more by imperatives of application than by the habit of continuous intellectual rumination that Park might have demanded of him.

Park and Burgess influenced their students through classroom and tutorial contact, but the content of their own thinking is known to us through their books and many professional articles. They collaborated on the *Introduction to the Science of Sociology* (1921), referred to as "the Green

Bible" because of its importance and its color. Robert Faris says of this book, "The direction and content of American sociology after 1921 was mainly set by the Park and Burgess text."[18] It is an edition of excerpts from writings by sociologists, something like a repertory of topics of memory or invention used in the rhetorical tradition.[19] In 1925 Park and Burgess published *The City,* with an article on social ecology by Roderick D. McKenzie. This book contains an essay by Park, "Community Organization and Juvenile Delinquency," that mainly repeats W. I. Thomas's views on the subject. The book opens with an essay by Park first published in 1915—"The City: Suggestions for the Investigation of Human Behavior in the City Environment"—which poses a long series of questions for research. Among these is one that also echoes Thomas: "To what extent in any given racial group, for example, the Italians in New York or the Poles in Chicago, do parents and children live in the same world, speak the same language, and share the same ideas, and how far do the conditions found account for juvenile delinquency in that particular group?"[20] This would become one of Clifford Shaw's central problems. Park ends this seminal essay with a declaration that "this is the place" for the Chicago urban sociologists of the 1920s:

> Because of the opportunity it offers, particularly to the exceptional and abnormal types of man, a great city tends to spread out and lay bare to the public view in a massive manner all the human characters and traits which are ordinarily obscured and suppressed in smaller communities. The city, in short, shows the good and evil in human nature in excess. It is this fact, perhaps, more than any other, which justifies the view that would make of the city a laboratory or clinic in which human nature and social processes may be conveniently and profitably studied.[21]

Burgess's most interesting contribution to *The City* was his diagram of urban growth, consisting of concentric circles expanding from the central business district. (Chicago, of course, was the model, but sociologists found the same pattern in other American cities.) This "zonal hypothesis" would be especially prominent in Shaw's discussion of delinquency. In 1923 Burgess wrote an article, "The Study of the Delinquent as a Person,"[22] in which he gives an evolutionary account of the history of delinquency concepts ranging from the abstract theories of Lombroso and his contemporaries to the "epochmaking" studies of the individual delinquent made by William Healy to, finally, the study of the delinquent as a person: that is, quoting Park's definition, "an individual who has status." "We come into the world as individuals," Park wrote. "We acquire status, and become persons. Status means position in society."[23] Burgess gives several case histories illustrating various means of maintaining social status. In one of these a caseworker relates: "She told me in her own way, which I should like to quote, but which would make too long a story, of the mother's being left a widow when Elsa was four years old; of the mother's poor health, their struggle with poverty, the mother doing what work she could with her little strength, the child at times almost starved, her lips bloodless."[24]

Burgess ends with the standard contemporary call for the development of a sociological science of delinquency using data the case histories had illustrated: "The study of the delinquent as a person opens up a fertile field. Materials in the form of case-records, personal documents, and life-histories, are now available for analysis."[25] Indeed, these materials had helped open up the field. At the very end of the essay Burgess gives a somewhat different interpretation to the phrase "the delinquent as a person," bringing in Thomas's "wishes" in a way that implies that the delinquent has a dignity also conveyed by Mayhew's oral histories:

> In conclusion, the point may be raised that this article deals with the sociology of personality rather than of delinquency. The criminal, however, is first of all a person, and second a criminal. Therefore, it is well to study him primarily as a person and secondarily as an offender against the laws of organized society. The basic fact to an understanding and control of the behavior of the criminal seems to be that the lawbreaker is a person, that is, an individual with the wishes common to all human beings and with a conception of his role in group life.[26]

1,313 Gangs

The concept of a juvenile delinquent as a person with conventional human wishes expressed in an unconventional society was advanced in studies of gangs by Frederic Milton Thrasher (1892–1962). Thrasher completed his Ph.D. dissertation in 1926 at the University of Chicago sociology department,[27] and it was published the following year as *The Gang: A Study of 1,313 Gangs in Chicago*. It contained 272 numbered entries in print smaller than the rest of the text, some of them statements of Thrasher's own observations, some giving evidence or illustration from interviews or other sources. About one-fourth (62 out of 272) of the entries are from a "gang boy's own story" or a "Ms. prepared by a former gang member." Forty-five are brief quotes of less than a page, but seventeen are a page or more in length.

Concentrated study of gangs is missing in Mayhew, as it is in other writers we have covered. To most students of delinquency, gangs seemed an effect rather than a cause. Healy thought gangs were less important than some researchers had made them out to be.[28] In any case they were difficult to investigate. Social workers and probation officers were still

explaining delinquency as a result of poverty or genetic inferiority when
Thrasher was doing his research (1919–26). Thrasher, however, "found
the boys to be psychologically normal, and the phenomenon of gang formation to be a natural sociological development."[29] Not all the gangs
Thrasher covered were delinquent: like Thomas, he was comprehensive
rather than specialized, and he included all kinds of gangs, from groups of
harmless little boys all the way up to criminal organizations. Like
Thomas, Thrasher was opening up a new field, a brave new world with
strange creatures in it.

One of the most useful concepts Thrasher introduced was the *interstitial* character of gangs. Gangs are interstitial both in time—"The gang is
largely an adolescent phenomenon . . . an interstitial group, a manifestation of the period of readjustment between childhood and maturity"[30]—
and in social as well as geographical structure:

> The most important conclusion suggested by a study of the
> location and distribution of the 1,313 gangs investigated in
> Chicago is that *gangland represents a geographically and
> socially interstitial area in the city.* Probably the most signifi-
> cant concept of the study is the term *interstitial*—that is, per-
> taining to spaces that intervene between one thing and another.
> In nature foreign matter tends to collect and cake in every
> crack, crevice, and cranny—interstices. There are also fissures
> and breaks in the structure of social organization. The gang
> may be regarded as an interstitial element on the framework of
> society, and gangland as an interstitial region in the layout of
> the city.[31]

Most gangs are found in "that broad twilight zone of railroads and shifting
populations, which borders the city's central business district on the
north, on the west, and on the south"[32]—that is, in interstitial areas.
According to Thrasher: "That the conception of the gang as a symptom of
an economic, moral, and cultural frontier is not merely fanciful and
figurative is indicated by the operation of similar groups on other than
urban frontiers."[33] In short, gangs were seen as transitional, interstitial,
or marginal groups, not unlike the Chicago sociologists who were trying to
establish scientific knowledge about them—and not unlike the human
documents that assisted in expanding the boundaries of inquiry.

That Thrasher's book is a classic of sociological exploration, no one
denies. According to James F. Short, "It stands . . . after more than three
and a half decades as the most comprehensive study of the phenomenon
of adolescent gangs ever undertaken. So complete was it that, at least in
part because of this fact, no other great survey of this type has ever been
undertaken."[34] Short also says: "The nature of the gang, in terms of

etiology and typology, ongoing process, and behavioral consequences still is unfinished business, but in Thrasher a significant beginning was made."[35] However, the book establishes no definite proposition about gangs. Short has made a critique of *The Gang* similar to the one Blumer made of *The Polish Peasant:* the material is unsystematic; not much information is given about any one gang; there is too little detail about episodes to permit group-process analysis; the study lacks analytic sophistication in holding variables constant; it does not set out to test hypotheses; age differences are not related to other variables; kinds of gang conflicts are not discriminated; some of the writing has a naive quality; statistical manipulation of more than 1,300 cases that had little in common was impossible beyond crude classification; and some of the interpretations are rather casual. In short, Thrasher did not do all the things later sociologists have done. We do not even know how he collected his material, how he chose his informants, or how representative they were.[36] James Carey relates a story from Norman Hayner, that Thrasher did magic tricks to gain boys' confidence.[37] No little magic carried over into his work, too.

If *The Gang* is unsound as science, what does it mean to say that it was exploratory? *The Gang* was one of the first in a series of monographs produced by the University of Chicago sociology department that promoted a new subject matter by illustrating it concretely in a particular area. Human documents or other case history material put before the eyes of potential and actual sociologists the sort of phenomena they could profitably focus on and investigate. They also communicated to people in other, older disciplines that sociology did indeed *have* a subject matter. The genuineness of the phenomena was conveyed by the variety of specific situations presented in the numbered entries. They could have been fabricated by Thrasher, but the sheer bulk gives them an authentic quality.[38]

Thrasher, like Thomas, also included human documents as a way of promoting the examination of the subjective aspects of social action. Long before "SOR" was coined (stimulus-organism-response), Thrasher insisted that between the observed stimulus and the observed response intervenes the "intermediate human nature factor," which he calls "this important middle term": "It is here that the delinquent 'boy's own story' assumes great importance." Taking the middle term into account is especially important in understanding children: adults, not excluding social workers, often fail to realize how the young person views programs designed for him or her.[39] "The additional development of this type of [autobiographical] material will serve to illuminate the whole field of juvenile delinquency and make methods of dealing with problem children

more intelligent and more effective."[40] In this regard Short points to
Thrasher's reformist tendencies and says his "chastisement of conventional institutions for their failure to provide socializing experience
consistent with the needs of the gang boys" is a problem still with us.[41]
That is, Thrasher promoted an expansion of awareness so that social
agencies would pay attention to the way the youth sees the agency. However, an entirely new institution to deal with problem youths did not
emerge until Clifford Shaw, a colleague of Thrasher's, set up the Chicago
Area Project.

One means of attracting new resources to existing programs was to
have *The Gang* read by a wider audience than sociologists. In his preface
Thrasher says that the book will "probably have considerable interest for
the general reader in that it deals with the relation of the gangs to the
problems of juvenile demoralization, crime, and politics in a great city."
The book presents "a general picture of life in an area little understood by
the average citizen."[42] One way to attract the attention of the general
reader was to put into the book some of the excitement that Thrasher
discovered as part of the gang itself: "To read these documents is like
drawing back a curtain upon the human drama. One gets an entirely
different picture from that presented by the statistical analyses of life in
the district and the rather formal statements and observations of outsiders."[43] "The city has been only vaguely aware of this great stir of
activity in its poorly organized areas. Gang conflict and gang crime occasionally thrust themselves into the public consciousness, but the hidden
sources from which they spring have not yet been understood or regulated.... This region of life is in a real sense an *underworld,* through
whose exploration the sociologist may learn how it develops...and ultimately he may be able to suggest methods for dealing with it in a practical way."[44]

> It is in such regions as the gang inhabits that we find much of
> the romance and mystery of a great city. Here are comedy and
> tragedy. Here is melodrama which excels the recurrent "thrill-
> ers" at the downtown theaters. Here are unvarnished emo-
> tions. Here also is a primitive democracy that cuts through all
> the conventional social and racial discriminations. The gang, in
> short, is *life,* often rough and untamed, yet rich in elemental
> social processes significant to the student of society and human
> nature.[45]

In his introduction to James T. Farrell's *Studs Lonigan,* Thrasher wrote:
"While in no sense autobiographical, [the book] is the *boy's own story,*
better than Studs himself could have told it."[46] Additional interest is
added to the text of *The Gang* by the inclusion of photographs; though

they are rather pedestrian photos, at least most of them were taken in the street, by Thrasher.

It has been remarked that being in a gang in the 1920s seems more fun than being recruited into one of the paramilitary gangs of the 1960s. Thrasher certainly plays on the romantic aspects of gang membership, the appetite for new experience, as is evident in the following excerpt, presenting "a gang boy's own story."

IMAGINATIVE EXPLOITS

"Be blythe of heart for any adventure" might well be the slogan of the gang boy. The sport motive provides one key to the interpretation of the behavior of the gang. The imaginative interest affords another. Exploits and activities which are nonsensical or merely mischievous to the adult have an entirely different meaning to the boy in quest of adventure.

THE ALLEY RATS KNIGHTS OF THE ROUND TABLE

48. The boys in my gang, which numbered about fifteen, have played with each other since we were wee little fellows. One day we discovered a large chicken coop in the alley behind the home of one of the boys. I saw immediately that it had possibilities for a clubroom, which had long been a cherished ambition of the gang. We moved in at once with such furniture as we could drag through the little three-by-four door. We became the "Polar Bears" and excited the envy of all the older boys in our suburban community. Our rivals now got busy and established a club of their own in the attic of a grocery store.

I thought I was pretty tough then. I smoked, shot with a revolver, and fought. When we had our gang fights we would make up a lot of stuff about armies. Most of the kids would stay away from home during the period of hostilities. We were interested in a lot of things besides fighting. One older boy, who was making an aeroplane, excited great admiration among us. He worked on it for four years and got everything just right. When he tried to fly it, it would not go in the air more than twenty-five feet. He used to fly along the ground. I think he was a-scared to go higher.

One day when we came back to our hang-out, we found the chicken coop nailed up. We found a new rendezvous in a basement under the old police station. We played in the old police cells and had a great time down there. We found a lot of stuff stored away, and helped ourselves freely. Among other things, there were flagstaffs, which we converted into swords for dueling.

We went to the movies about every other day, and it was from a picture that we got the suggestion for our new name—

"The Alley Rats Knights of the Round Table." Our new
hang-out was near a bakery where they kept a lot of pineapple.
We could get it from the kegs, and a lot of peaches and other
stuff, for our feasts. There were very few boys in the gang who
did not steal.

In the summertime we liked to cook our food in the open.
We would go out where there were not many houses and get
eggs and chickens every Sunday. One time the sister of one of
the boys swiped a chicken for us, and stuck it under her coat.
We took it to the foundations of an old house, where we
twisted its head off, made a fire, and cooked it. We ate it,
although it was hardly done enough.

At harvest time we'd go to a haystack and slide down and
climb around on the great piles of baled hay. We liked to make
little huts and we'd go out in the cornfields and build them out
of the stalks, so that we could smoke without being disturbed.
They are getting too many houses out there now—they spoil
the prairies.

We had certain special places that we liked to go. One of
these was Wasp Jones's gravel pit, where we liked to swim.
There was a big bull there, and we had a lot of fun with him.
We would always tie our clothes in the legs of our pants, so
that if we saw him coming, we could grab them and run. One
day the bull came before we got them tied up, and all seven of
us had to shin it up a tree.

Another place we liked to go to was a monastery near a pond
where the cows drank. After school we'd go swimming there.
We called it the "Pope's pond," and I had a bicycle on which I
would ride three boys, and we called that the "Pope's taxi."

Another favorite place was what we called the "Willows,"
near which was the haunted house. Inside, the wall was broken
in big cracks and the plaster was falling off. The first time I
went in, the boys tried to scare me. They slammed a door when
I was in the attic. I jumped out onto the roof and got away. We
liked to go in there for the man to chase us, but one day when
we came he had a gun. It was a lot of fun there; whenever the
plaster would fall it would scare you.

We used to flip the freights and go to the water-tower to
play. I ran away twice with some of the boys. We wanted to
stay on the freights, but we got caught at Waukegan and were
sent home. Mother does not want me to stay out at all, but one
day we ran away to Desplaines and slept there all night. We
took lots of clothes with us for a long trip, but a man with a star
saw us when we tried to catch a train, and told us to go back or
we would be put in Parental [School]. We went back half way
to Chicago, and then we got a freight that took us a hundred
miles the other side of Elgin.

The gang finally got caught and sent away for a robbing expedition.[47]

Thrasher makes no comment about the curious imbalance between the halcyon days atmosphere of this document and some of its more serious features, such as the use of a revolver.

Clifford Shaw: An Introduction

Clifford Ray Shaw (1895–1957) grew up in Indiana farm country. On one occasion he was caught stealing some bolts from a blacksmith to fix his wagon; instead of calling the police, the blacksmith fixed the wagon and thus provided the future sociologist with an anecdote about informal treatment of delinquents in rural areas. When he was fifteen he met a Methodist minister from Adrian College in Michigan who encouraged him to enter the ministry. Like Park and Thomas, at college Shaw underwent a conversion; in Shaw's case this was away from religion, which he began to consider "a barrier to the progress of humanity."[48] However, later in his life he led a social movement that had religious overtones; the speeches Shaw gave to promote his reform program sounded somewhat like sermons, and his followers believed in his message as a means of secular salvation, giving individuals and communities an opportunity to rise in a hierarchy of (property) values.

In 1917 Shaw was in the navy as a pharmacist's mate.[49] In 1919 he completed his A.B. degree at Adrian and went to the University of Chicago, where he took a full load of sociology courses through June 1922 and continued part time until December 1924. He never completed the Ph.D., either because he could not pass the foreign language exam or, some say, because he saw no need for it once he had already started his life's work. (Adrian College awarded him an honorary doctorate in 1939.)

Shaw "first became interested in juvenile delinquency as a result of courses offered by Professor Ernest Burgess. It was customary for graduate students of sociology to engage in specific activities related to the problems discussed in the classroom, which might also provide material for use in the preparation of theses."[50] Later on Shaw would be criticized for taking the problem of delinquency out of a broader context of social and political problems, but this specialization resulted in part from the need for students to concentrate on one or another aspect of the whole paradigm of the city that Thomas, Park, and Burgess had broadly schematized.

During 1921–23 Shaw worked part time with parolees from the Illinois State Training School for Boys at Saint Charles: "This work included the usual duties for investigating cases prior to parole, family visits, finding employment for parolees, etc. I was responsible for an average of 75 parolees."[51] From 1924 to 1926 he was employed as a probation officer at the Cook County Court: "My activities in this position included the investigation of cases, preparation of petitions and other legal papers, home visits, presentation of cases in court, etc. This work was citywide and brought me into touch with the various agencies which offered services to children. My experience at the Cook County Court was valuable because it gave me contact with hundreds of delinquents and a familiarity with the details of court procedure." In addition to this experience, according to Snodgrass, Shaw "lived in a settlement, 'The House of Happiness,' in an Eastern European neighborhood, near the inner city. The introduction to the slum sections served to awaken a consciousness of the starker realities of American social life."[52] Contacts with other students of delinquency must have been useful, too: Thrasher acknowledges Shaw's cooperation on *The Gang*.

The early 1920s were seminal years for Shaw's theories. Rice describes how Shaw formulated sociological hypotheses out of his experiences as a probation officer.[53] Shaw himself says the initial data-gathering for his publications of 1929 and after began in 1921.[54] Finestone points out that the later published life histories came from delinquents Shaw met during this period.[55] Likewise, the early 1930s saw the beginnings of the action program that emerged from the theories and the life histories.

In October 1926 Shaw became director of the new sociology research section at the Institute for Juvenile Research, the same institution William Healy had started in 1909. This new IJR division came about when "the Friends of the Institute for Juvenile Research," a group of private citizens, met in 1924 to begin fundraising to create the Behavior Research Fund; this fund allowed IJR personnel to do research, which heavy caseloads from the juvenile court and elsewhere had made it impossible for them to do. Robert Maynard Hutchins said of this group: "What was notable was that the fund was raised not by the generosity of a few wealthy donors in advance of their time, but by a community-wide response. I know of no other case in which a research fund into so basic and pioneering a field has been raised in so democratic a way."[56] Ernest Burgess, who was to become acting director of the fund in 1929 (to aid a merger with the University of Chicago, which fell through), persuaded the director of IJR and the Behavior Research Fund to include a sociology department in the new research arrangement. Doubtless Burgess also recommended Clifford Shaw as department head.[57]

Early in 1927 Shaw was joined by Henry Donald McKay (1899–1980).[58] When I first heard of this team I thought "Shawn McKay" was one person, so often are the two names spoken jointly, especially in references to the many books they wrote together. Snodgrass gives a typical characterization of the two men: "McKay was the professional scholar and gentleman—polite, kind, thoughtful—an academic out to prove his position with empirical evidence. Shaw was the more emotional practitioner, a professional administrator and organizer—talkative, friendly, personable, persuasive, energetic, and quixotic—out to make his case through action and participation."[59] Even though Rice describes Shaw as using statistics long before he met McKay, credit is usually given to McKay for the quantitative work and to Shaw for the life histories and the action program. The latter activity took up so much of Shaw's time that McKay, as he told me, did most of the work on the last life history book, *Brothers in Crime*. Even though this book was "the first detailed case study in which autobiographical documents written by a number of children in the same family have been used,"[60] it introduced no new concepts. The creative source of the life histories of delinquents at the Institute for Juvenile Research was clearly Clifford Shaw, who was also, it should be noted, the leader of the action program.

Though Shaw appeared merely to be applying W. I. Thomas's notions about human documents, he did so in the field of delinquency with greater skill than anyone else has ever done. Burgess wrote in the first edition to Shaw's masterpiece of this genre, *The Jack-Roller:* "In the document here presented and in a series of similar documents under preparation are set forth the findings of long-continued, sympathetic and patient observation through this new method which, if Mr. Shaw did not invent, he has perfected and rendered useable as an instrument of scientific research."[61] However, Shaw's activist personality introduced a dimension of meaning into life histories that was not present in the work of W. I. Thomas. To understand Shaw's activism we must first try to understand the theory of delinquency upon which it was based.

Delinquency Areas

Clifford Shaw entered the University of Chicago in the fall of 1919, after W. I. Thomas had departed, but he came under Thomas's influence through courses taught by Park, Burgess, and Ellsworth Faris. When Thomas visited Chicago, Shaw met him. Wirth said: "It is my belief that the notion of disorganization as a phase of reorganization in a new culture, and the putting of the personality into the context of a social milieu, of a cultural matrix, which is in a state of transition, has had a profound impact upon the mentality of people working in the field of crime."[62] Shaw assimilated these general features of Thomas's standpoint, and he advanced sociology by particularizing inquiry into the problem of delinquency. (Shaw's particularism makes it unlikely that he himself would have invented life history, since a large, opening comprehensiveness usually accompanies its initial appearance.) After the mid-1920s, Thomas often quotes Shaw on points having to do with juvenile delinquency, and in 1928

Thomas wrote: "I have now lived to the point where my most stimulating contacts are with the younger sociologists, such as Bernard, Burgess, Thrasher, Zorbaugh, and Shaw, some of whom have been my pupils."[63] Shaw and McKay's work stimulated much of the sociology of delinquency that came after them: since the 1930s, writers have typically acknowledged or opposed the Shaw-McKay position before setting up their own. Certainly the name of Clifford Shaw is more closely connected with life histories of juvenile delinquents than is that of any other person.

The general accomplishment of Shaw and McKay was to make a systematic empirical sociological interpretation of juvenile delinquency. Though hardly anyone was aware of it, Mayhew had made an unsystematic sociological penetration, but "Shaw had the advantage of being able to work within the confines of a body of social theory . . . which by virtue of its sophistication was superior to the somewhat primitive notions of such writers as Mayhew," as well as having access to more accurate data and more sophisticated statistical techniques than Mayhew had.[64] Early sociologists such as Gabriel Tarde had recommended sociological interpretations but had not done the empirical research to back them up. Healy had made case-by-case empirical *psychological* interpretations. In his first major work Shaw declared: "Although the individual delinquent has been studied intensely from the standpoint of psychological tests, biometric measurements, and emotional conditionings, comparatively little systematic effort has been made to study delinquency from the point of view of its relation to the social situation in which it occurs."[65]

Shaw and McKay were successful in communicating this point of view on delinquency, and their work became a model for research method on other subjects: "Empirical American sociology was perhaps popularized and transmitted to all corners of the world by the Shaw monographs more than by any other examples of this brand of research."[66] Here again life histories helped put before the eyes of the professional audience the concrete phenomena they would have to look at to produce a science of sociology. These may seem terribly familiar to us today (and indeed sociology no longer needs or uses such documentation), as they were familiar to Mayhew, but if the physical anthropology of Lombroso was still a vivid memory and Healy's psychologism a dominant approach in the field *at that time* (especially at the Institute for Juvenile Research, which is still dominated by psychologists), more than *argument* was needed: *demonstration* was required. Even Healy could agree with Shaw on the importance of environment to explain delinquency, though what Healy meant by environment never had the scope of Shaw's conception.[67]

The first major presentation of the Shaw-McKay theory appeared in

Delinquency Areas (1929). The first step in this, as in every other Shaw-McKay book, was to *localize* the problem of delinquency in certain areas of the city that had high rates of delinquency as revealed by official statistics: "With [the sociological] point of view, the study of such a problem as juvenile delinquency necessarily begins with a study of its geographical location. The first step reveals the areas in which delinquency occurs most frequently, and therefore marks off the communities which should be studied intensively for factors related to delinquent behavior."[68] The next step was to present a spot map of Chicago (as Breckinridge and Abbott had done in 1912 in *The Delinquent Child and the Home*), with each spot representing the home address of one male delinquent; a rate map, which showed the number of delinquents in the census area per hundred of persons of equivalent age; a radial map, showing rates along lines extending from the central business district; and a zone map, showing rates in Burgess's zones of city expansion. Delinquency rates were found to be highest near downtown Chicago, lowest at the edges of the city, and intermediate in between. Rates for female delinquents were found to be numerically lower but with the same distribution over the city. This pattern was later discovered in other American cities.

This was as plausible a beginning as any made by epidemiologists today. For Shaw and McKay it was a starting point suggested by Park, Burgess, and another Chicago student, Roderick McKenzie, who had set forth "The Ecological Approach to the Study of the Human Community" in *The City*. According to Park:

> The point is that change of occupation, personal success or failure—changes of economic and social status, in short—tend to be registered in changes of location. The physical or ecological organization of the community, in the long run, responds to and reflects the occupational and the cultural. Social selection and segregation, which create the natural groups, determine at the same time the natural areas of the city.[69]

In the city there are, Park said, "regions in which there is, as recorded by statistics, an excessive amount of juvenile delinquency, and other regions in which there is almost none."[70]

Shaw and McKay did indeed find that some areas of the city had higher official rates of delinquency, and that these were Thrasher's "interstitial areas," near the central business and industrial district, where residential property was poorly maintained in prospect of being sold to expanding commercial interests. "As industry encroaches on new areas a process of junking takes place [i.e., stripping off salable items]. Buildings constructed for residential purposes are allowed to deteriorate. Land is held for speculative purposes. Land values usually rise while rentals on the buildings tend to lower. This physical deterioration is paralleled by a declining population."[71] The very existence of high-rate areas reinforced the need for social interpretations of crime, because the individualist approach could not explain it. Nor could it explain the fact that "in approximately nine-tenths of the cases [of stealing appearing before the juvenile court] two or more boys were involved in the act."[72] Nor could psychologists account for the fact that delinquency rates had remained relatively constant in those areas no matter what group—German, Irish, Scandinavian, Polish, Italian—was living there, but rates for each group had gone down as its members gradually moved out toward the suburbs, following Burgess's scheme. This threw cold water on the notion of the "innate criminality" of national or racial groups. What seemed appropriate instead was a theory of culture conflict experienced by immigrants who lived in those areas. (From 1910 to 1930 the population of Chicago rose from 2,185,283 to 3,376,438; many of the new arrivals were from European and southern United States rural areas.)

The cause of delinquency was not the geographical features of the area or a person's mere residence in a certain place. Nor could other social factors present in abundance in those areas be causes by themselves: population change, bad housing, low educational standards, poverty, tuberculosis, adult crime, mental disorders, and so on. Though these could enter a person's life and contribute to delinquency, the overall cause of delinquency areas was alleged to be *social disorganization*. Thomas and Znaniecki had defined social disorganization as a "decrease of the influence of existing social rules of behavior upon individual members of the group."[73] Shaw and McKay explicate this rather nebulous concept thus:

> Under the pressure of the disintegrative forces which act when
> business and industry invade a community, the community
> thus invaded ceases to function effectively as a means of social
> control. Traditional norms and standards of the conventional
> community weaken and disappear. Resistance on the part of
> the community to delinquent and criminal behavior is low, and
> such behavior is tolerated and may even become accepted and
> approved.[74]

This is especially true in the immigrant's situation: "In the conflict of the old with the new the former cultural and social controls in these groups tend to break down. This, together with the fact that there are few constructive community forces at work to re-establish a conventional order, makes for continued social disorganization."[75] One of the chief tasks of Shaw's life histories was to exhibit the social disorganization of a delinquency area. The next chapter is devoted to a full examination of Shaw's life histories.

Shaw's beginning was both his strong and his weak point. Geographical placement allowed him to concentrate his attention in a way that had not been done by anyone before him. Even Thrasher's study of gangs was less focused and less productive of specific observations and hypotheses than Shaw's studies of neighborhoods. However, initial location of the problem in geographical, that is to say *physical* areas, using a terminology of *"natural* areas of the city" (meaning that no one planned them the way they turned out), prevented Shaw from connecting those smaller areas with social and political processes of the whole city, though this later gave thinkers the base from which to rise to the larger urban context.

The selection of life history material reinforced that localism, because life histories of delinquents are best at revealing experiences in a local area. Burgess could point to the increased mobility of youths outside their neighborhoods, made possible by the automobile, but this usually involved only quick expeditions; they still knew their own turf best.[76] McKay beautifully describes this "area of participation":

> The term "neighborhood" is used here as a general concept to describe the world of the child exclusive of his family on the one hand, and of the radio, newspapers, and other symbols of the larger community on the other. It is essentially the area known to him through participation—it is the area in which he works and plays.... The activities of the child in the neighborhood tend to be organized around basic institutions and groupings such as the church, the school, the playgrounds, and perhaps the movie theater. In addition it may include participation in teams, clubs, or other groups organized on the basis of interests, talents, or accomplishment. Collectively these groups may represent the most meaningful part of the child's social world.... The neighborhood of the child includes also institutions and activities in which he does not participate but with which he is familiar. Thus local lodges, taverns, clubs, and adult sport organizations are part of his world in a very real sense. In many but not all neighborhoods, other institutions and activities, such as picnics, carnivals, fights, weddings, funerals, and celebrations in which persons of all ages participate, are integral parts of the social life.[77]

It is almost impossible to know what "neighborhood" and "community" mean in the writings of Shaw and McKay, but these terms seem to refer to the world as a (typical?) youth is aware of it, an awareness that would be expressed by the child in a life history.

"To think of the neighborhood or the community in isolation from the city is to disregard the biggest fact about the neighborhood," proclaimed Ernest Burgess.[78] But for Burgess and Shaw this meant that one area should be located in relation to others in a scheme of urban growth, not that socially dynamic interrelations among areas should be studied, which would have certainly brought into the picture political aspects of the whole city's governance. Like W. I. Thomas, Shaw and McKay did not reach to the political level of analysis. What Janowitz has said about Park and Burgess also applies to Shaw and McKay: "This is not to deny their awareness of the political process that penetrated the local community. Rather they viewed these political elements as derivative or epiphenomenological. They could not see political institutions as having independent consequences." "The absence of an explicit macrosociology was a source of intellectual and analytic weakness."[79] Jon Snodgrass has been especially upset at this feature of the Shaw-McKay scheme:

> The interpretation was paralyzed at the communal level. . . .
> Instead of turning inward to find the causes of delinquency
> exclusively in local traditions, families, play groups and gangs,
> their interpretations might have turned outward to show politi-
> cal, economic and historical forces at work, which would have
> accounted for both social disorganization and the internal con-
> ditions, including the delinquency.[80]

Snodgrass makes Shaw out to be a villain by removing him from the historical circumstances he faced in the 1920s. Shaw's mission was to go beyond medical, psychological and psychiatric, and social work models and to open up the sociology of delinquency. To do this he used life histories to show nurture rather than nature, health rather than illness, social rather than individual conditions. This was the main thrust and to some degree the main accomplishment of his work, but along with it went concentration on the social world as experienced by the delinquent rather than the political and economic system of a whole city.

Shaw was aware of questions about the use of official arrest statistics to determine locations of "delinquency areas." He was aware that biased police attitudes and the better resources of middle-class families meant that a lower-class youth who broke the law was more likely to be arrested and sent to court. But Shaw said he saw no reason to believe that theft of automobiles was as high outside as inside a delinquency area, and he claimed that organized crime performed the same function of keeping young people from the slum out of jail as did psychiatrists in upper-class areas. In his preface to the 1942 *Juvenile Delinquency and Urban Areas,* Burgess held that *official* delinquency was the problem for the public anyway, not offenses that were not known by the police. This dis-tinction takes police procedures as givens not subject to study or change, and an unreported rape is still a rape. More recently, attempts have been made to survey the real incidence of delinquency by using self-report questionnaires, and theoreticians now locate the problem of delinquency not in a geographical area but in a social class structure. Concerning a major study of delinquency in 1960, Finestone writes: "Having 'placed' the problem [among lower-class adolescent males], the next step is an analysis of the special problems of adjustment confronting the young person and a demonstration that gang delinquency achieves a solution to them."[81] Life histories were not used in these later studies, perhaps because the variables—social class, for example—were too abstract or generalized to be explicitly exhibited by them.

The Chicago Area Project

The concept that social disorganization is the principal feature of delinquency areas has many conceptual difficulties. "Methodologically, the theory, at least as used by Shaw and McKay, was, as David Downes has pointed out, essentially descriptive and tautological: 'the rate of delinquency in an area [is] the chief criterion for its 'social disorganization' which in turn [is] held to account for the delinquency rate.'"[82] Carey claims that the Chicagoans tended to equate disorganization with its causes or consequences.[83] And, after all, the slum or ghetto is not so disorganized, as Whyte would later point out in *Street Corner Society* (1943), though it might appear that way to outsiders. Indeed, Shaw succeeded in organizing only those communities where there were already institutional structures of one sort or another (clubs, gangs, churches).[84] However obscure the term social *disorganization* is in itself, it suffers no impediments at all when it is used to justify community *organization,* as Burgess uses it here:

> All these factors [population change, bad housing, number of foreign-born and Negroes, tuberculosis, adult crime, mental disorders], including juvenile delinquency, may be considered manifestations of some general basic factor. This common element is social disorganization or the lack of organized community effort to deal with these conditions. If so, the solution for juvenile delinquency and the related problems lies in community organization.[85]

Since "disorganization" really meant only the absence of united community action, one wonders if reform (that is, initiating community action) was not the basic intention all along of sociologists in using this concept.

If the theory says that people eventually move out of the slum or ghetto toward the suburbs, why do anything about it? The process will occur "naturally." One answer is that an agency of state government, such as the Institute for Juvenile Research, was compelled by the nature of bureaucracy to generate a remedial program, just as the IJR psychiatrists and psychologists had their own therapeutic programs. At any rate, the Chicago Area Project (CAP) started in the early 1930s and was incorporated in 1934. The CAP consisted of community organizers on the IJR sociology staff who attempted, in areas with high rates of delinquency, to start groups of local volunteers who would take action to change neighborhood conditions thought to affect delinquency. They also worked directly with delinquents. In this context the spot maps directed action, and use of official delinquency statistics was justified because it was "the official delinquents who are of primary concern to the public,"[86] a rather dubious distinction, as I have noted. On the model of the Behavior Research Fund, the Chicago Area Project had a board of directors, wealthy or influential citizens who raised funds for the local projects but otherwise gave decision-making powers and credit for work done to local residents.[87] Saul Alinsky remarked about this: "You have to remember that concepts which are accepted today were considered wildly radical then—for instance, the idea that the local people have the intelligence and the ingenuity to work out their own problems."[88] The basic ingredient of the Chicago Area Project is usually claimed to be Shaw's experience growing up in an Indiana farm community,[89] where everyone pitched in when someone needed help. (This is the same sort of situation that Mayhew's oral histories were supposed to replace by reestablishing contacts between classes alienated in the cities.) But another source of influence was life history itself, which both by form and content encourages granting autonomy to a people.

By 1934 two of Shaw's three major life history books had been published; the third was in progress but did not add appreciably to the first two. Insofar as these books demonstrated the need for preventing delinquency by helping residents change their environments and work with delinquents on programs that diverted them from formal correctional institutions, life histories functioned to promote a social reform. By the 1960s this movement had indeed become influential in reorienting social programs so that they include participation by the people they affect.

The "indigenous worker" has been a central part of the CAP. Shaw tried to recruit as community organizers people who had grown up and lived in the community where they were assigned. This was done to draw into the process the actual inhabitants of the delinquent's or potential delinquent's world. That is, indigenous workers were people whose life histories, if they had written them (almost no one did), would have revealed a similar social world as life histories Shaw collected from delinquents. "It was assumed that the residents of these communities might have better access to the lives of young people, who were themselves part of the community, than could social agencies organized and managed from outside," since these latter "rarely if ever arise out of the wishes, hopes, and desires of the residents of these communities."[90] Shaw's organizers have been called "marginal men" because they "lived in two worlds but [were] not quite at home in either."[91] They were "ordinary" people working with children and adults in comradely fashion, but they were also employees of the state of Illinois through the Institute for Juvenile Research, working on an action-research program of delinquency prevention based on sociological concepts developed at the University of Chicago.

Community organizers were given a minimum of training, since their natural leadership abilities were supposed to see them through. This lack of training, in addition to the community-based model, brought Shaw into conflict with social workers, who were becoming professionalized during this period and simultaneously withdrawing their concern from environmental reform and turning to casework with individuals. "The indigenous worker was Shaw's answer to the professionally trained social worker. He believed that one of the reasons the social workers of his era were unable to enter into personal relationships with delinquents was because of the attitudes of expertise and superiority that they had absorbed during the course of their higher education."[92] Finestone adds that the Chicago Area Project "may be interpreted as a protest movement against the impersonality of the city." "These themes of the indigenous workers and others imply an attempt to reduce the impersonality of the situations in which services are provided to people in slum communities."[93] Shaw said: "We've got to change the emphasis of our approach from organizations and institutions to face-to-face human relations,"[94] relations of the type Shaw had experienced as a boy on an Indiana farm. The manner assumed by the collector of the life history, then, is a model of the respect with which one should view the delinquent as a human being. If violative activity is inevitable in a youngster who is neglected or despised as a person,[95] then restoring personality to the individual is a way of overcoming delinquency.

But the inward quality of all this, perhaps associated with the reflexivity of autobiography, determined that explicit connections with the broader society would seldom be made in action, as we have seen they were not in theory.[96] In McKay's words, the Area Projects were meant "to see to what extent the world of the child could be changed."[97] This was to be done by organizing adults surrounding the child so as to create new impressions on the child, not new "sensations" on city government. It was a rhetoric of persuasion rather than of conflict. Carey has said that sociologists in the 1920s believed sociology needed time to develop as a science and that too great a readiness to influence the political process could be self-destructive.[98] Rather than fight institutions and powerful men, the Chicago Area Project collaborated and cooperated with them. Indeed, all of the CAP ideology could be put in terms of *communication*. Social disorganization meant "lack of communication of conventional values from parents to children" or "communication of delinquent traditions endemic in a delinquency area," or, as Carey puts it, "absence of public opinion. This leads to a decline in the feeling of community solidarity and the institutions which function to support it."[99] The goal of the local CAP community committees in these terms was to open up channels of communication between local residents and representatives of local agencies, between adults and youth, and to educate people in "new behavioral perspectives from the larger world."[100] Need I add that life histories also depend on communication, not conflict, to promote social change?

Further insight into Shaw's character emerges from his Chicago Area Project activity. James Short has written:

> The history of the Area Project cannot be understood without reference to . . . Shaw's missionary zeal. His classroom presence was a rich combination of "hard data" and case materials, humanitarian ideology and political reality, but above all service in a cause—the cause of political and social self-determination by local neighborhoods and communities . . . . this was more than scientific effort or pedagogical technique—more even than humanitarian service. It was Shaw's "calling," and he served it well.[101]

Both Finestone and Snodgrass have pointed out contradictions in Shaw's character: "It was this fundamental ambiguity, this ceaseless tension between his heart and his head, his moral judgment, and his striving for the objectivity of the scientist, that rendered him so complex and vital a person."[102] The contradictions Snodgrass finds in Shaw are more contrived but point to the same effect:

> There are some amusing and puzzling contradictions in Shaw's biography. Never organized in his personal life, he persistently attempted to create organized communities. He was an agnostic trying to create Christian order, a pragmatist seeking an ideal, a former delinquent turned delinquent reformer, and a reluctant writer who tried to get almost everyone to write. He was an individual ardently against delinquency and crime with more than a hint of being a "legitimate" con man himself. No doubt in some respects Shaw was an enigma to himself.[103]

Shaw was both a practicing clinician trying to do therapy with paroled delinquents and a research sociologist: "The life history technique of research, which he did so much to advance, provided a felicitous medium through which he could synthesize and express both interests. Later when he ceased publishing life histories, his clinical interests found expression in the practical work with delinquents of the Chicago Area Projects."[104]

Even though Shaw seemed to Everett Hughes, as Hughes once wrote me, not to have had any academic ambitions, he taught criminology at various Chicago colleges. His promotional activities for the Chicago Area Project consisted not only in teaching but also in delivering a great many public speeches. In the following statement, made in a letter to Jon Snodgrass, notice how Henry McKay associates the rhetorical situation of speechmaking with that of acquiring life histories:

> If the published reports do not seem as voluminous as you had
> expected, it should be remembered that Mr. Shaw spoke or
> lectured to a very wide variety of audiences over a great many
> years. There is no written record of these addresses. However
> it is well known that he established rapport with audiences
> quickly and easily. I belive however that he was at his very
> best when interviewing juvenile delinquents, from whom he
> got "the whole story" very quickly without any duress. But he
> was almost as effective with large audiences. With delinquents
> I have never been sure whether he joined them or they joined
> him. At any rate many young offenders produced life histories
> for him some of which were published.[105]

According to Finestone, Shaw's "sense of justice was continually outraged by the treatment that the existing correctional system and other social agencies accorded the delinquent. It was, however, an outrage that he scrupulously sought to harness within the impersonal disciplines of social science and rational analysis."[106] Thus delinquents' oral histories were ways Shaw, like Mayhew, could express moral indignation and other emotional qualities while still maintaining the distance and image of the scientist.

If life history in the early phase of Shaw's work promoted the need for a program like the Chicago Area Project (a claim I shall examine in the next chapter), in the later phases, after the project had been set up, promotion was much more blatant. Shaw tried to get community organizers to write about their experiences, but only one did: Anthony Sorrentino drafted a manuscript about 1950, but it was not published until 1976, after I had edited it. It was first called "It's an Inside Job," but the publisher insisted on *Organizing against Crime*. What a gold mine a full statement would be of the decades of experience of this pioneering organization! Instead, Sorrentino's book is a not very illuminating look at some of what happened in starting and operating one community committee: the main intention of this book was to popularize the idea of the Chicago Area

Project and perhaps jar someone into writing a respectable history. Some early versions of the manuscript included several life history success stories that showed the effectiveness of the Area Project, but they were removed before publication in order to reduce the size of the book and the subsidy required to publish it.

The CAP was supposed to be an experimental program, testing new methods for preventing juvenile delinquency. In an effort to prevent "institutionalization," which meant that the CAP would become more protective of its reputation than critical of its methods, Shaw insisted on "a loose organization constantly in flux, amorphous in form, and unconventional in method, for he [considered] this pattern more alive and more closely in conformity with the ordinary life of the disorganized communities than a more formal one."[107] However, in the absence of explicit definitions of a community worker, not to speak of a professional identity, in the absence of Shaw himself after his death in 1957, and after a separation of the research and action arms of the enterprise, also in 1957, when the IJR and the CAP officially parted company, the Chicago Area Project did indeed become institutionalized to an extreme degree, in my estimation. "It had a distinctive rhetoric," Finestone remarks, "composed primarily of some frequently reiterated phrases and slogans, which comprised a rudimentary yet nevertheless quite effective ideology."[108] As less and less of substantial merit occurred in the CAP, promotional activities took up the slack. The introduction of personality into a public area, seemingly so promising for humanistic values, backfired. In Richard Sennett's words: "The attempts to create community in cities are attempts to make psychological values into social relations."[109] Collective being—who an individual is as a member of a group—became more important than accomplishing anything.[110]

Eight

Transmission of Delinquent

and Reformist Attitudes: Clifford Shaw

The following is an example of the shorter life histories that Shaw included in his works. It was the first life history in his first book, and he used it or parts of it more than once.

CASE 1

When I began to hang out with the gang of boys in our neighborhood who were robbing and doing the big stores in the Loop [shoplifting], I began to stay out of school. None of the boys in the gang went to school, and so I didn't go. . . .

We would bum around all day, going to shows and wandering around the streets. Every morning the bunch would come past my home about school time. We left home at this time to make our parents think we were going to school. It was easy for me, for my mother was working and didn't know much about me. [Boy's father had deserted the family.] We would wander around all day, going to the Loop and watching the crowds. This life was exciting and I was always seeing new things. I was greatly impressed by the sights I saw—the crowds and the big stores. . . .

I was only seven years old at this time and my companions were fourteen and fifteen. They had been shoplifting in the Loop and making lots of money. They talked a lot about stealing, but had never asked me to steal with them. One day, when we were bumming in the Loop, I did my first shoplifting. We went into the department stores and the 5 and 10 cent store. My chums were stealing from the counters, but it was new to me, so I didn't try at first. There followed many more visits to the Loop and finally I began to steal little trinkets from the counters, under my escorts' tutoring. They knew the house detectives and spotted them for me and showed me how to slip things into my hat or put my hat on the thing I wanted to steal and then take it with my hat. Within a few weeks I became an expert shoplifter. . . .

I liked the new game of stealing I had learned, and it really was a game and I played it with much zest and relish. I wanted to learn more about this new game and to indulge in it wholeheartedly, and I did this to the exclusion of all else. I forgot

about school, almost entirely. Compared to stealing and playing in the Loop, school life was monotonous and uninterest-
ing....

We would sneak a ride on the elevated railway, climbing up
the structure to the station, to the Loop. After getting
downtown, we would make the round of the big stores. If we
couldn't steal enough candy and canned goods for lunch, we
would go without lunch. I do not know of anything else that
interested me enough to go without a meal, but "making the
big stores" did. I do not know whether a good thrashing would
have cured me or not, as I never received one for stealing, just
the one my father gave me when he was mad. But, anyway, the
shoplifting experiences were alluring, exciting, and thrilling.
But underneath I kind of knew that I was sort of a social
outcast when I stole. But yet I was in the grip of the bunch and
led on by the enticing pleasure which we had together. There
was no way out. The feeling of guilt which I had could not
over-balance the strong appeal of my chums and shoplifting.
At first I did not steal for gain nor out of necessity for food. I
stole because it was the most fascinating thing I could do. It
was a way to pass the time away for I think I had a keener
adventurous spirit than the other boys of my age, sort of more
mentally alert. I didn't want to play tame games nor be confined to a school room. I wanted something more exciting. I
liked the dare-devil spirit. I would walk down between the
third rails on the elevated lines in the same daring spirit that I
stole. It gave me a thrill, and thrilled my chums in turn. We
were all alike, daring and glad to take a chance.

When we were shoplifting we always made a game of it. For
example, we might gamble on who could steal the most caps in
a day, or who could steal in the presence of a detective and
then get away. We were always daring each other that way and
thinking up new schemes. This was the best part of the game. I
would go into a store to steal a cap, be trying one on and when
the clerk was not watching walk out of the store, leaving the
old cap. With the new cap on my head I would go into another
store, do the same thing as in the other store, getting a new hat
and leaving the one I had taken from the other place. I might do
this all day and have one hat at night. It was fun I wanted, not
the hat. I kept this up for months and then began to sell the
things to a man on the West Side. It was at this time that I
began to steal for gain....

I became an expert shoplifter in time. I always followed my
chums. They would be walking in a store, me following, and
take a ring or two from a counter, or a bottle of perfume, or a
large carton of gum, stuff it into our belts under our coats, and
leave the store. We would then sell the things to a fence. We

could find fences who bought our goods; and then go to a show, buy something to eat, and there you are. I got so I could not only spot a house detective a mile away, but I could almost smell him. You can tell them by the way they act. If we did get caught, and we did several times, a few tears and a promise never to do it again would be enough to make him turn us loose and sometimes he would just lead us to the door and tell us to stay out of there. Being little and very small for my age, it was easy to win the sympathy of the detective when we were caught. So on I went; you know when you get by with it once it makes it a little easier to get by with it the next time. I became cocky and self-confident and had a real pride in my ability to steal.

When I was nine years old I was arrested and placed in the Detention Home, charged with stealing and truancy. Little did they know how many crimes I had actually committed. I got by because of my size and boyish appearance . . . .

In a place like the Detention Home and every place where delinquents are committed, anybody who feels sorry out loud for what he has done is openly jeered by his fellow inmates. You may feel sorry to yourself, but you dare not make it known. These ———— try to make you think that there is honor among crooks when it is really a case of "dog eat dog." A fellow will save himself first and his fellow inmates later. I've lied, and, using prison vernacular, double crossed everyone who has tried to help me. Why I have, I cannot say. I was on the wrong side of the wall from the start and could not get on the right side. From the very start, I learned about crime, liked it, and didn't know anything else.

Following my first experience in the Detention Home, I was brought back time after time for playing hookey from school and playing the big stores. Every time I was in the Detention Home I tried to get out by stealing the door keys, breaking through windows, or by some other way. I never wanted to do anything drastic, although I hated discipline and confinement. Several times I could have been in with fellows who wanted to tie up the guard, overpower him and black-jack him, but I didn't like that kind of work. I was inclined to figure out schemes to escape that way . . . .

At nine years of age I was sent to the Chicago Parental School for many truancies and much stealing. At the School I regarded the house officers as I regarded the police. I had learned to regard all authorities as natural enemies, the police and guards being the worst. I hated the military discipline at first but in about a month learned to like it. I liked to march and maneuver about to the beat of the drums and the blare of the bugles. I was in the dormitory squad. Every morning a group of us would

make the beds, sweep and dust the dormitory. Other groups had
other duties like washing dishes, sweeping the sidewalks, etc.
Each boy was given a small task that entailed about an hour of
work each day. The special privileged, as in every institution,
were allowed to do easy jobs like set the tables, clean the
officer's rooms and be officers. These were boy captains, boy
lieutenants, and shavetails. I didn't have a special position,
just a private, because I was only nine years old and older boys
were chosen to be officers. These boys who were officers had
free rein when the house father was absent. Most of the time
the power went to their heads and they became as much of a
tyrant as the rulers and kings of old. The other boys, me included, were so cowed and tattle-taled that we were always in
fear. When a boy officer or family officer struck you, you
almost had to say thank you. If you struck back you were put
in the cage for a week on bread and milk, and lots of muscle
grinders and squats every day. Everything was one-sided
against the boy. But all in all the boys had a good time playing
every day, sometimes two or three times a day, with lots of
good, clean food. This bunk that they got unwholesome food
that came out in that scandal a few years ago was a lie. All the
time I was there the food was good. But the punishment was
awful. You weren't allowed to smile any place, and turning
your head in line called for a bad mark. Anyone having marks
had to stand up in the cottage with his heels together and arms
behind. Four or five hours of each day is not a joking matter,
even for a man. It is not easy to take orders from a fellow
inmate, or let him make you squat for an hour or two, or make
you do muscle grinders. The boy-officer's word is always
taken against other boys, and he can frame boys left and right.
As long as a boy can be in the family officer's favor he can
frame others right and left and be protected. Just as soon as he
loses favor he will be framed by other boys. It seemed to me
that it was a game where the best liar was the overlord. It
didn't make any difference how much you tried to behave, the
great question was did you behave. The life in the Chicago
Parental School was worse than it is in Pontiac. I suffered from
the severe punishment and having boy officers giving me orders. When I first went to the Chicago Parental School I had
rosy cheeks and had a happy-go-lucky spirit. When I came out
I weighed more but my spirit was broken. The place changed
me but did not reform me. I felt revengeful, spiteful, and
dulled. I had more fears of the police and decided to be more
careful in the future. I didn't trust anyone when I came out. I
had been punished for something and then seen the family
officer and boy officers do the same thing. Somewhere in a

book it says that all men are liars. Well, I early learned that all men are hypocrites. Just one cheap skate, crooked hypocrite, among a hundred honest family officers is enough to give a boy a bad impression. It did me.

[In the following paragraph, omitted here, he continues to denounce disciplinary procedures at the Chicago Parental School—J. B.]

After I got out of the Chicago Parental School I couldn't, to save my soul, get used to the freedom and ease of the outside schoolroom. I felt out of place among the boys on the outside. I kind of felt strange and inferior about having come out of such a place. People distrusted me; I couldn't convince my folks that I wanted to go straight, attend high school and finally go to college. Everybody expected me to steal again. I had extreme trouble in finding something to talk about to my fellow students. I felt ashamed and then didn't know anything that was going on to talk about. Conversation had not been permitted in the Chicago Parental School except out in the yard. In the cottage and school you were compelled to keep absolute silence. I hardly ever had a heart to heart conversation with anyone while I was there. I can imagine the slaves before Lincoln's time afraid to hold conversation with one another lest the other person might be ready to tell the master if the tongue by any chance revealed something that was treason to the master. The Chicago Parental School kind of made a clam out of me and put a sort of inferiority and shameful feeling in me. I have never since been able to rid myself wholly of the feeling. I kind of felt I was unpopular with everybody, that people were afraid of me and distrusted me. I thought that perhaps by spending money and being a good sport I could gain favor with my chums. I would hardly dare to disagree with anybody for fear of discovering that I was not like other boys. I began to bum around. I was returned to the Chicago Parental School for another term. After being paroled, I stayed out of the Chicago Parental School only five weeks. I was so disgusted that I didn't even start to school, so I was returned to the Chicago Parental School where I stayed fourteen months before I finally got out again.

Returning home the third time I entered High School. When I started, the only suit of clothes I had was on my back. It was not good and I didn't feel right in it. One day I discovered a large trunk full of men's furnishings in our home. It belonged to an uncle who was living with us. Every few days I would take something from the trunk and sell it. I bought school supplies but most of it I spent on my chums. I took about three hundred dollars' worth of things, when my uncle opened the trunk one morning and discovered the theft. I was at school at the time and my father and uncle came there, calling me out of my class. My father slapped my face out in the corridor and in front of all my school mates. I never returned to school, not even to get my school books and other supplies. My father took me home and said, "I can't have my own brother staying in my house without being robbed." He was angry enough to kill me, but I ran away. My uncle has never spoken to me, nor I to him since then. I have never said much to my father since that time. My brother was also angry at me so the only friend I had at home was my mother. For the next few months I bummed around, working a little but never going to Continuation School. I was not interested in anything and nobody seemed interested in me. I began to bum around with some of the boys in the old bunch. We started to make the big stores in the Loop again and to break into stores. We stole and bummed all the time. I can't tell how many times we stole. If you multiply the times I have told about, by a figure with three numbers and use your imagination you will not be far off. Nobody interfered with us in our stealing. As long as we didn't get caught we were all right.[1]

Life History Sandwiches: Values of "Own Story"

Shaw's three books that consist mainly of one or more longer life histories are: *The Jack-Roller: A Delinquent Boy's Own Story*, which illustrated the value of "own story" in the study and treatment of delinquents; *The Natural History of a Delinquent Career*, which showed the differences between public fantasy reaction to a case of rape and the realities of an offender's life; and *Brothers in Crime*, life histories of five brothers that represented the problem of "culture conflict," in the way W. I. Thomas had first formulated it.[2] Shaw had contact with the brothers for sixteen years and with Stanley and Sidney, chief characters in the two earlier books, for six years each. Stanley and two of the brothers had earlier been examined by William Healy.[3] Shaw also developed three manuscripts that were never published: "Companions in Crime," with Saul Alinsky as coauthor, "Professionals in Crime," and "The Bartzon Brothers." Short statements or excerpts from longer documents appear frequently in Shaw's writing. Interviews were printed as such in four instances: three were with a delinquent and his family, among the most lively pages in Shaw's works, and one was of a social worker and a girl.[4]

Shaw originated neither the term "own story," which he used more often than "life history," nor a theory of its uses. The word was Healy's: perhaps Shaw used it to identify his work more closely with the psychologists at the Institute for Juvenile Research, thereby showing his institutional loyalty and playing down the competitive aspects of the sociology-psychology controversies. Shaw's theory of life histories is mainly a collection of quotations from Healy, Thomas, and Burgess. In general, Shaw's originality was his application of other sociologists' concepts in an unprecedentedly complete and concentrated form to the study of delinquency. According to Shaw, "own story" "reveals useful information" on the point of view of the delinquent, the social and cultural situation to which the delinquent is responsive, and the sequence of past experiences and situations in the life of the delinquent (*JR* 3). In addition, the person's "own story" may be a useful first step in devising a plan of treatment.

Viewpoints
In justifying the use of life history, Shaw occasionally says that, even if the boy's statement is inaccurate (was the Jack-Roller's stepmother as mean as the boy claims?), the document is valid if it expresses the boy's attitudes (he *believed* she was mean and acted on that belief—or was this an excuse?). In Burgess's words: "The truth of the materials in the document . . . is not so much the reliability of the events as portrayed, but the validity of the attitudes of the writer of the document" (*NH* 239). Shaw elaborates: "It is in the personal document that the child reveals his feelings of inferiority and superiority, his fears and worries, his ideals and philosophy of life, his antagonisms and mental conflicts, his prejudices and rationalizations" (*JR* 4). "So far as we have been able to determine as yet, the best way to investigate the inner world of the person is through a study of his revelations of himself through a life-history" (*DA* 9). Although the delinquent's view of the world appears in the documents, the inner world of imagination barely does. Emphasis is on the person's behavior, not his emotions separate from his actions. And usually even that is a single monolithic feeling of elation, resentment, or despair. None of Shaw's boys are introverts, and this fits well with Shaw's theory: "The subjective factors arise in the process of interaction between the person and the social world in which he lives" (*DA* 8). Krueger even refers to life histories as behavior "in the same sense as any phenomenon (in chemistry, physics, and psychology) is behavior."[5]

Social and Cultural Worlds
Shaw used excerpts from life histories and shorter documents to illustrate "the spirit of delinquency areas" (*SF* 109 ff.). The longer life histories illustrated the evolution of delinquent careers, but these also mainly depicted the delinquent's immediate surroundings. Here again one cannot even begin to present Shaw's account of life histories without pointing out

limitations, because Shaw simply does not in fact do all that his theory of life history implies. Rarely is there a glimpse of community life beyond the young person's companions, and a complete life history picture of the community as a whole is never given. Finestone has written:

> His data for the cultural level of the local community were entirely restricted to his case studies of delinquents. Such case studies provided indispensable sources of information of the social organization of the local community, but they were inadequate in themselves to provide the data from which the social organization of the local community could be constructed . . . . Shaw did not possess data adequate to the task of presenting a realistic depiction of the local community.[6]

Shaw wrote: "The relationships between the community situation and the development of delinquent behavior trends is suggested in the excerpts from the life-histories" (*DA* 204). However, none of the documents explores the social or cultural conditions of *adults* living in a delinquency area. In fact, the most prominent and recurring "community situation," or feature of a "social and cultural world," or "spirit of an area" evident in the documents is precisely what oral histories showed so well in both Mayhew and Clay: transmission of delinquent practices from delinquents, especially groups, to future delinquents, made possible when the two came into contact in certain places—low lodging houses, prisons, or delinquency areas. And the function of life histories was to *transmit that message*. Thus the theme of transmission appears in both the content and the method of life histories.

W. I. Thomas had written: "Perhaps the greatest importance of the behavior document is the opportunity it affords to observe the attitudes of other persons as behavior-forming influences, since the most important situations in the development of personality are the attitudes and values of other persons" (*JR* 8).[7] Two of Shaw's typical assertions are:

> Delinquency and criminal patterns arise and are transmitted socially just as any other cultural and social pattern is transmitted. In time these delinquent patterns may become dominant and shape the attitudes and behavior of persons living in the area. Thus the section becomes an area of delinquency.
> [*DA* 206]

"The manner in which the boy in the high-rate areas is exposed to delinquency values and assimilates them through his group contacts is more clearly revealed in autobiographical documents" (*JD* 176). That is to say, the idea of a delinquency area is also transmitted socially.

Sequences

In like manner, what *demonstrating sequentiality* actually means, as manifest in the life histories, is the way individuals first come into contact with delinquent groups and evolve into more and more advanced forms of crime by further participation in those groups. "In many cases it is possible to describe the continuous process involved in the formation and fixation of the delinquent-behavior trend" (*JR* 14). "Delinquencies appear not simply as isolated acts but as aspects of dynamic life-processes" (*BC* 143). "The material of the case history reveals...that the habits, attitudes, and philosophy of life underlying these criminal acts were built up gradually through successive social experiences of the offender over a period of years" (*NH* xiii). (However, for Sidney of *The Natural History of a Delinquent Career,* the sequence led up to a rape, which was the focus of public outrage, even though the rape was neither planned nor something Sidney habitually did but was an offshoot of a robbery.) The goal of presenting continuity of events is the reason for encouraging writers to "be as spontaneous as possible and always follow the natural sequence of events in [their lives]" (*JR* 22). It was also the reason for suggesting they use a chronological list of events to help guide their writing.

In addition, the study of life histories enables a researcher to formulate hypotheses to explain those sequences:

> They not only serve as a means of making preliminary explorations and orientations in relation to specific problems in the field of criminological research but afford a basis for the formulation of hypotheses with reference to the causal factors involved in the development of delinquent-behavior patterns. The validity of these hypotheses may in turn be tested by the comparative study of other detailed case histories and by formal methods of statistical analysis. [*JR* 19]

But Shaw never used personal documents in a systematic way to generate hypotheses. In any case, he devised only one hypothesis, or one cluster of closely related ones: the concept of a delinquency area, which essentially amounts to a group of delinquents communicating criminal "values" to initiates.

Treatment

Treatment therefore would be a process of substituting communication of "conventional values," to use Shaw's term, for unconventional "values." To do this intelligently requires listening to the attitudes the individual already has: "The first step in the course of treatment is the approach to the boy, not by sympathy, but by empathy. Through his life-history his counselor is enabled to see his life as the boy conceived it rather than as an adult might imagine it" (*JR* 194). But Burgess's distinction is obscure: "Sympathy is the attempt through imagination to put one's self in another person's place with all the fallacies which are almost necessarily involved" (*JR* 195). What those fallacies are, Burgess does not say. In another place he wrote: "The reader [of a life history] is able to enter vicariously, in greater or less measure, into the same experiences, and even perhaps be, for the moment, the same person" (*NH* 253). The best that probably can be said summarily here is that the reader moves somewhat closer in imagination to the writer, on that median ground between them.

According to Shaw, "You can't get under the kid's skin with the old probationary and social work methods. You can't come at the boy as a functionary of an institution. You've got to meet him as a person."[8] In this way the oral history might be an ideal model of the object one should perceive in the delinquent, recalling Augustine's "I love you; I want you to be," an affirmation of the individual's existence by contemplating an expanded vision of the person's life rather than looking through him to some further use. Restoring self-respect in this way is doubtless therapeutic, but it would be naive to ignore the utilitarian features of this as actually practiced. Other than serving as a guide to an expanded art of counseling, the life history may be used to devise a plan to bring the delinquent under social control. However, "What part of Mr. Shaw's admittedly intelligent treatment of the boy was due, differentially, to the 'illumination' of the life-history document? Could not any patient, well-trained probation officer have achieved equally good results?"[9]

Therapy for Shaw consisted partly in giving the young person an opportunity for emotional relief and partly in allowing him to get his own life into focus by writing or talking. But more important, as Shaw said in a speech he delivered in the early 1950s, "therapy . . . is inherent in and finds its expression in certain kinds of human relationships . . . . Now the people in the community welcome him . . . . They try to get him involved in their own enterprise [a community committee] in relation to other people in the community." That was the therapeutic maneuver of the Chicago Area Project. Before the Area Project was under way, the writers of the published life histories were "treated" by foster home and job placement. The Jack-Roller felt out of place in an upper-class family and ran away—an example of failure to look at his situation though his eyes—so he was then placed in a middle-class home and later became a mostly legitimate salesman. Sidney of the *Natural History* became an assistant to a Chicago criminologist. In 1973 Henry McKay told me that, of the five Martin brothers, the oldest was dead, the next was a successful businessman, and the other three "get along."

It should be noted that before the Chicago Area Project existed, the individual was encouraged to change "careers" by putting him into a different environment, not by changing a delinquency area itself. The initial meaning of "the need for a change of environment" was individualistic, only a step away from Healy's interpretations. The need for changes in the environment was suggested by the life histories, among other things, but, once an organization was established, life histories offered no guidance.

Transmission

What do Shaw's life histories do? They enable a reader to *see* the process of transmission of delinquent practices from one person or group to another and the gradual evolution of those practices through further participation in delinquent groups. Life histories give "concrete and vivid" pictures or illustrations (*DA* 124) or "focus attention upon the manner in which the child's social groups may be involved in his various behavior problems" (*SF* 4).[10] They perceptually demonstrated the very *existence* of certain social phenomena, especially to people who had no exposure to them. Burgess wrote:

> In the biological sciences, the invention and use of the microscope has made possible many, if not most of the scientific discoveries in the study and treatment of disease. For the microscope enabled the research worker to penetrate beneath the external surface of reality and to bring into clear relief hitherto hidden processes within the organism.
> In a very real sense, the life-history document performs an identical, or at least similar, function for the student of personality. Like a microscope, it enables him to see in the large and in detail the total interplay of mental processes and social relationships. [*JR*, 1st ed., xi]

According to Dollard: "The emotional forces bound by community life are seen near at hand through the telescope of the life history."[11]

Burgess pointed out that the materials could be interpreted variously by various students (*JR* 17), but this was not really encouraged by the texts themselves. Lest perception get out of focus, the life histories were published with rather extensive interpretation at the front and back of the books, which makes them into life history sandwiches, with the meat of lives placed between layers of sociological bread. Prefaces by Shaw's state agency superiors or his academic superior Burgess, and prefaces, justifications of "own story," chronologies of an individual's legal processing, or descriptions of a delinquency area by "the author" (Shaw) precede the history. Summaries of treatment and psychiatric, psychological, and medical comments follow it. All this supplementary material supports Shaw's claim that he used only cases that had been thoroughly researched (*SF* v), and interpretations were always made not only with the life history but also with other records (*JR* 2). The outcome is almost as much commentary as oral history: the three life history books contain 389 pages of interpretation and 454 of autobiographical writing. To use an image from John Updike, these were "escorted" histories.

The nonsociological commentary is perfunctory and perhaps was inserted to placate the psychologists who headed the Institute for Juvenile Research. At the same time, since no psychological abnormalities turned up, these reports indicated a need for sociological rather than psychological interpretation and therapy. The life histories themselves conveyed the message—both in form and in content—that delinquents are not mentally deranged but are capable of deliberate action, even rational action, considering their circumstances. Nowadays this may not seem an important point (because Shaw and others succeeded in making it). But in 1934 Sutherland pointed out that psychiatrists at one Illinois reformatory had classified 99.5 percent of the incoming inmates during 1919–29 as mentally pathological.[12] In that context the point about psychological normality could have an impact: "A more forceful mode of presenting the force of circumstance in the molding of human lives would have been difficult to devise."[13] One reviewer of *The Jack-Roller* put this message in terms of the absence of a criminal nature.[14] In another publication that included a few oral histories from delinquents, Walter Reckless stated:

> If there is any moral in these case studies it is simply that they support the growing notion that the juvenile offender is not an abnormal child. Our cases show, besides, that he is not necessarily a thoroughly bad child. It is surprising that we find children brought before the Juvenile Court who really have few bad habits. In this respect at least the "six boys in trouble" compare very favorably with boys in general—those who are not called before the court.[15]

Critiques of Shaw's Life Histories

Four major critiques of Shaw's life histories have been made, each from a different standpoint: Dollard from the psychological, Stott from the literary and journalistic, Snodgrass from the political, and Finestone from the sociological.

John Dollard's "Criteria for the Life History"

From a study of various instances of the genre, Dollard derived seven criteria for producing or judging life histories and applied them to six books, three of which were first-person life histories, including an auto-biography from *The Polish Peasant* and Shaw's *Jack-Roller*. Shaw gets high marks, with a few reservations, on five of the criteria:

1. A subject must be viewed as a specimen in a cultural series.
3. The peculiar role of the family group in transmitting the culture must be recognized.
5. The continuous related character of experience from childhood through adulthood must be stressed.
6. The "social situation" must be carefully and continuously specified as a factor.
7. The life history material itself must be organized and concep-tualized.

On two of the criteria Shaw fails abysmally:

2. The organic motors of action ascribed must be socially relevant.
4. The specific method of elaboration of organic materials into social behavior must be shown.

The latter demands are consistent with Dollard's assertion: "In the life history the body is what we have to go on; it is the primary unit of naive perception. The life history must begin with it and stay close to it during the whole of its course" (*CLH* 24). According to Dollard, what is missing in Shaw's work is "a really clear discussion of how culture patterns hook on to the organic man" (*CLH* 202–3). However, Allport says in his cri-tique of Dollard: "The framework of [his] study is acceptable only to those who share the author's intellectual biases." "All are the author's personal predilections, not scientific axioms."[16] There seems no good reason to demand that organic factors have a central role in a life history document of a delinquent. Reflections on the "hookup" of physical with nonphysical experiences are certainly not primary units of naive percep-tion but require a good deal of sophistication. Even Montaigne rarely does this. It is interesting to note that Dollard himself attempted to apply all seven criteria in his *Children of Bondage* (1940), but his book was in no sense as pioneering and influential as the six life histories he judged to be deficient in one respect or another. (Though he rated Freud high through-out, surely Dollard overestimated Freud on social and cultural criteria.) It appears that innovative work in oral history, at least in this modern period of specialization, is done by emphasizing (and promoting) a restricted area of experience, rather than by attempting to cover all bases. At any rate, Dollard covered only those areas that had already been opened up: he failed to cover political and economic factors.

Dollard complains that in their commentary Shaw and Burgess do not explore the formation of Stanley's personality, nor is his personality evo-lution evident in the autobiography itself. An especially glaring omission, says Dollard, is the absence in the text of any event before the boy's fifth year of life, in spite of Burgess's astonishing admission that by reading life histories he had been led to the tentative "hypothesis that the main outlines of the personality pattern are fixed in the early years of the child's social experience and are subject to only minor modification in youth and manhood" (*JR* 191). Dollard calls this "certainly a dubious inference" (*CLH* 210), and, considering the method used to make it—a perusal of documents that do not well represent the earliest years—I must agree. Allport notes: "There is something exceedingly elusive in mental *origins*. Actually, even the best autobiographies seem to leave beginnings in the dark." "It seems that methods supplementary to the autobiography must be used to determine the origin and development of attitudes."[17] But even here Shaw fails, for, as Dollard points out, "So far as we can see the additional records here accessible [in *The Jack-Roller*] have not played any great role either in the interpretation of the case or in the treatment program; what seems to ring the bell is the life history of the subject, defective as it is, and the light that this history throws on the social milieu" (*CLH* 222).

Dollard also complains that Shaw "shows why the Jack-Roller became a criminal but not why he became just the kind of criminal he did" (*CLH* 282). Stanley's life history does not explain why the boy became such a self-justifying person or why he remained so low in the criminal hierarchy (*CLH* 193). (Similarly, critics of *The Professional Thief* have pointed out that "Conwell" was a small-time confidence man, not the "complete" thief with experience in many rackets. Perhaps it is easier to get this sort of person to tell his life story than the more universally experienced.) According to Dollard, Shaw is good at showing what kind of social interaction produces typical delinquent attitudes and actions but not how a delinquent's other personal attitudes are generated (*CLH* 204). "Persons who do read the text carefully will hardly notice that [the authors] do not treat the actual personality-forming situation which they posit in theory did exist" (*CLH* 209). Even Healy can jump in here. In an essay in 1942 he wrote:

> One of the great strides forward in sociological research has been made by taking over from psychiatry the technique of case studies. Notable in this respect are the criminological studies of Clifford Shaw. But I submit that what is missing in these case studies are facts that modern psychiatry would demand and interpretations that psychiatry could offer. For example, in *Brothers in Crime* we have very good accounts of the environment, of the overt facts of the family life, and, so far as they go, the "Own Stories" as told by these young criminals ring true. But what we miss is factual material and interpretations concerning the emotional reactions provoked

by interpersonal relationships, particularly the father-son relationships in these cases, the significance of the lack of an
ego-ideal and of frustrations and hostilities developed within
the family circle—all these so overwhelmingly important for
the formation of patterns of personality structure and behavior, including criminality.[18]

One reviewer of *The Jack-Roller* went so far as to predict that Stanley
would regress to "his basic personality pattern (i.e., running away from
reality) upon the recurrence of a crisis or in the presence of a difficulty."[19]
Another reviewer stated flatly: "the psychological knowledge displayed
by the authors is distinctly weak."[20] Dollard also points to the lack of
substantial mention of the Jack-Roller's father, a point that casts doubt on
whether Shaw did indeed satisfy criterion 3, about the family. Snodgrass
says "Shaw-McKay had no psychology nor explanation as to how pathological social factors affected the individual.... [their] work is generally
inconsistent and ambivalent about the nexus between community and
individual."[21]

We can take our leave of Dollard with his affirmation that *The Jack-
Roller* "is less a life history in the sense of an account of the socialization
of a person than it is an inside account of the gangland culture" (*CLH*
188). However, one should remember that Stanley saw little of gangland
culture as a lowly jack-roller. Dollard says he would not have been
bothered by more interpretation from Shaw and Burgess: "Certainly the
life history of Stanley is an enigmatic document with many situations
inadequately defined and with many interrogations that beg for further
light from the writer" (*CLH* 187). Dollard even wonders if this life history
is as "clean of influence" from Shaw as it seems: "For example, there
arises the suspicion that Stanley's constant transference of blame to the
environment was not unwelcome to a man who approached Stanley's life
with a vivid concept of the culture area" (*CLH* 220). Thus the exteriority
of social fact demanded by Durkheim is to be found in an excuse-giving
personality, but no one has wondered whether this might have had something to do with Stanley's idealism.

William Stott's "Documentary Expression and Thirties America"
Stott's critique of Shaw appears on pages 199–200 of this book:

Both histories [*JR* and *NH*] are interesting and very like pulp
confessions of the time; the central character tells of his sins
(gloatingly), his capture and punishment, and his true repentance. Like Macfadden products, these narratives seem less
self-explorations than performances. It is evident they were
written, and written as they were, not to please their writers so
much as to please others (the jack-roller's reformation was so

convincing he won parole). Their motives apart, the narratives
are of dubious scientific value. The sociological generalizations
the editor draws from them in his footnotes are thin and superfluous. The rapist said his crimes began when, as a boy, after
much hesitation he stole an apple from a fruit stand; the editor
commented: "This is a vivid description of Sidney's first experience in stealing. Many careers in juvenile delinquency and
adult crime originate in precisely this manner."

Stott does not support any of these judgments. It is not clear what he
means by saying the histories are "interesting." Nor can we tell how they
are "like pulp confessions of the time," nor in what passages of the texts
any character views his offenses as "sins" or "gloatingly" exposes them.
Krueger admitted that the motives behind confessional life histories and
those in *True Confessions* (and other magazines such as Bernarr Macfadden produced) were the same—to help others and to relieve tension,[22] but
none of Shaw's life histories is in the confessional mode. As for performances versus self-exploration, an example from Stott would have
helped: it is not clear that Stanley's writing his life history had anything to
do with his being paroled from the House of Correction. One would also
like to hear Stott support his claim that the documents are "of dubious
scientific value": apparently this was not the opinion of a good number of
social scientists at the time, including Dollard, who called for more commentary by Shaw, not less, as Stott seems to want. The footnotes may
seem superficial today partly because their messages were successfully
communicated: in a period when as many as 88.3 percent of all Illinois
prison inmates were classified as psychopathic personalities (and 48.9
percent as "psychopathic personalities of the egocentric type") (*NH* 262,
n. 1), a demonstration of how a normal person gets involved in crime must
have come as a revelation to some people. This demonstration is apparently lost on Stott, however, who calls Sidney "the rapist" despite the
fact that Sidney stumbled into the one rape for which he was incarcerated,
and in any case the effect of reading the whole life history should have
been to prevent the use of labels. Finally, Stott does not specify what is
wrong with the comment by Shaw that he quotes: Is it false? If it is true
that many delinquent careers begin this way, should that not be stated?

Stott makes a number of contradictory remarks. On the one hand he
maintains: "Social scientists now consider most research of the period
sensational and lacking objectivity; these faults were in large measure the
result of the participant method—of too much involvement with the subject" (*DE* 170). But, on the other hand: "To read one case is to have read
them all. When every case history is chosen as typical, the generalizations
drawn from them are vapid and obvious" (*DE* 156). The life histories are

criticized both for lacking objectivity (though Stott does not say who the social scientists are who claim this) and for having so much objectivity that one will represent many. Stott also complains that the "case histories in books [of the Chicago school] run so long that they obscure the reason they were introduced. At times they take on such a life of their own that the social scientist resuming his analysis seems an interruption" (*DE* 160). From this perspective the reader is not tyrannized by generalizing commentary.

Nevertheless, Stott is getting at something. In a letter to me (12 February 1974) he wrote: "The best life histories—like O. Lewis' work, or Terkel's . . .—do not lead to simple generalizations of the kind soc sci seeks; they lead, instead, into greater mystery, psychological complexity, and human ambiguity." Surely "best" in "best life histories" is ambiguous, but Stott is correct in the sense that after reading one of Shaw's delinquents' life histories a reader of any of the others learns nothing basically new. After whatever initial impact has been made, I find them rather monotonous. But I am hardly a typical reader, having read hundreds of delinquents' oral histories. It is difficult to know the experience of people in the 1930s who read only one history. Burgess said: "Those who have read this life history in manuscript have all been astounded at its vivid and dramatic style" (*JR* 187). Perhaps the histories seemed more striking in contrast to the otherwise straitlaced, dull professional discourse of that period.

Burgess goes so far as to refer to "literary excellence," and Snodgrass, usually so negative about anything of Shaw's, rates *The Jack-Roller* "a good piece of literature on its own merit."[23] Now, the Jack-Roller is an adventurous character whose bouyancy is attractive, and his eloquence in places is remarkable if somewhat posed:

> I went to bed that night with spirits that were rare. I felt like an heir who had come to his fortune. I had a swell home, a good job, clothes, and friends. Dame Fortune was indeed smiling on me broadly. The kindness of Mrs. Smith, her son, and daughters was like a sweet balm. I was a quivering deer that had just escaped from the clutches of a lion. [*JR* 170]

Even Sidney, of *The Natural History,* occasionally rhapsodizes:

> The man responsible for the food is Finkley. Like a hangman he always walks alone and speaks on familiar terms with only those who are of his own kind. For years he has robbed our stomachs. His face bears the confession of his guilt. His soul is as drab as the clothes he wears and he himself as cheap. His heart is as small as the amount of food he feeds us and as unsavory. [*NH* 217]

But literary excellence is nowhere to be found in these works. Rarely is there an incident or characterization in any of Shaw's life histories that remains bright in the mind after the book has been laid aside. Shaw's histories are neither so literary as Burgess and Snodgrass have characterized them nor so flat as Stott has made them out to be. They are in the middle range of this spectrum, possessed of rhetorical attractiveness for an uninitiated but interested audience.

Jon Snodgrass's "The American Criminological Tradition"

One of Snodgrass's criticisms is that Shaw's life histories do not explain the origins of delinquent traditions; delinquent practices are passed on from one group to another living in a delinquency area, but how did they start in the first place? (*ACT* 166). Here again, "origins are elusive" for oral histories and the interpretation that accompanies them. Snodgrass makes a much more striking observation when he points out:

> Had Shaw-McKay's intention been to reveal the human-like
> qualities of the delinquents, they might have devoted portions
> of the life-histories to illustrations of their human-like qual-
> ities. . . . One knows a great deal about their background, but
> not about the boys themselves, not about their personal inter-
> ests and special abilities. There is little description of their
> non-delinquent traits; there is little discussion of their conduct,
> other than their delinquent conduct. [*ACT* 202]

Shaw's life histories are not what Allport called "comprehensive autobiographies" that cover "a relatively large number of lines of experience, giving a picture of variety, roundness and interrelatedness in the life."[24] Usually "topical autobiographies" (on a single topic) exist in collections of shorter documents, and indeed some of the shorter narratives, such as the one reproduced above, make the same basic points and impressions as the book-length documents. (Perhaps the books were published to reach a larger, less professional audience than a journal article would have reached.) This results in some obscuring of the person's whole life: "The danger of both topical and edited autobiographies is that they throw the investigator's interest sharply into focus only at the expense of throwing the subject's life badly out of focus."[25] Burgess justified this elliptical quality on the basis of space: "No life-history can be complete, in the sense that it records all events in a person's life; if so a library of books rather than one volume would be required. And where there is selection, there must be factors influencing the selection" (*NH* 241). We might think that the life history writers themselves did not have much experience outside their delinquent careers, but in fact this is doubtful: Stanley says he sat around one afternoon with Shaw and McKay getting "a great kick keeping them laughing about the funny experiences I had in prison" (*JR*

168). Those humorous experiences are nowhere given to the reader of the book. This limitation may have resulted from the use of a questionnaire that stressed problems, delinquencies, and arrests, or it may have come from the restricted context in which Shaw encountered most of the boys once he had set up shop in an office at the Institute for Juvenile Research. (Stanley, however, seems to have been a special favorite of Shaw's and saw him often both at IJR and in Shaw's home.)

Snodgrass also faults Shaw for calling himself the author of the life history books, at least half of which were written by young people. (In fact, Korn says the Jack-Roller "at times sounds more like a criminologist than Shaw [and] their collaboration set an early high-water mark for two way communication between the social scientist and his subject."[26]) Speaking of Sutherland's *Professional Thief,* Snodgrass remarks: "Although Jones [the thief] wrote the book, Sutherland got most of the credit.... This common oversight is only one of the many ways in which criminologists have traditionally slighted and subordinated the main subject of their studies, the criminal."[27] And in a footnote Snodgrass applies the same point to *The Jack-Roller.* Since the real name of the thief or delinquent is concealed, one might wonder what would be accomplished by listing a pseudonym on the book's title page. It could, however, emphasize a belief in the talent of the offender and an essential equality of offender and criminologist.

Only "essential" equality, not total? Snodgrass writes:

> There were ever-present reservations about the full endow-
> ment of the offender—he was always "basically," "funda-
> mentally," "essentially," not completely, wholly, totally
> human. There is also a limit on the extent of identification and
> subjective interpretation—they draw close but still maintained
> a distance. There was sympathy, but not empathy. The extent
> of "normality" was also restrained—delinquent behavior was
> normal only within certain bounds. [*ACT* 181]

Surely there was social distance between Shaw and Stanley, Sidney, and the others. That sociologists were trying to be "scientists" created an endemic elitism, but that does not mean there was lack of respect on either side. Of course Shaw did not approve of theft, assault, or rape; moral evaluation will always limit appreciation of common humanity in oral histories of criminal offenders. Snodgrass goes on: "The life-history documents Shaw-McKay considered useful for devising a plan of treatment, to be used in the conversion to conventional persons. The perspective which seeks to alter or transform the subject one studies, interrupts, if not eliminates, a sympathetic appreciation of the subject" (*ACT* 202). Shaw and Burgess made it clear that they were not interested in changing the egotistical *personality* of Stanley, only in changing his *social type* from a jack-roller to a position they thought he would succeed in—a salesman. But Snodgrass reports that "Stanley" was not successful in this job: "The Jack-Roller apparently did not hold this, or any other job, for very long. Later, after having three children, he was divorced. He spent the remainder of his life travelling from city to city, gambling heavily, incurring debts and occasionally being jailed" (*ACT* 151). However, Stanley did not develop the adult criminal career that seemed inevitable for a boy who spent so much time behind bars as a youth. Perhaps Shaw may be faulted for promotionally emphasizing the sociological approach at the expense of other therapeutic strategies, though other methods were represented in Shaw's books and clearly had been tried on the boys themselves. In any case, Stanley does not seem to be a failure, or a failure of Shaw's. Shaw realized that former delinquents often remain marginal characters, such as Stanley has indeed been.[28]

Harold Finestone's "Victims of Change"

Finestone's criticisms of Shaw's life histories resemble those Dollard made forty-one years earlier, though Finestone puts more stress on sociological factors. Finestone points out that, despite Shaw's statement that "own story" yields useful information concerning the youth's point of view, "Shaw made no attempt to pursue the implications of *The Jack-Roller's* idiosyncratic point of view for an understanding of his involvement in delinquent conduct" (*VC* 101). To throw Stanley's point of view into focus, his story might have been set in contrast to other viewpoints, perhaps using the technique of "triangulation" that Denzin recommends, but Shaw did not do this. Indeed, Burgess shows how *representative* Stanley is. Finestone, who worked with Shaw for several years, says: "In his practice [Shaw] revealed himself as extraordinarily sensitive to the role of idiosyncratic meanings in the experience of the individual, viewing cultural elements as these are reflected in the individual's personal experience. In his theory he appears to have gone along with Burgess in emphasizing the patterned nature, rather than the distinctiveness of the individual's experience" (*VC* 103–4). Another deficiency of the Shaw-Burgess scheme was that it "allowed no place for possible contingencies and turning points during which individuals might abandon deviant pursuits" (*VC* 106).

When it comes to accounting for crucial intersections, Finestone finds Shaw and Burgess wanting. Shaw "tended to avoid the methodological issues of how to synthesize his ecological and his case study data" (*VC* 111). "The presuppositions of each of these research techniques were diametrically opposed" (*VC* 108). One stresses cultural determinism, the other the influence of personal "definitions of situations."[29] Ultimately, cultural determinism won out in Shaw's system, and this was one reason Shaw did not publish life histories in the last two decades of his life. Likewise, in making a distinction between personality type and social type, he eliminated the possibility "of viewing the person as a whole interacting with others. Unfortunately, it was a distinction that remained central to the interpretation of Shaw's life histories of delinquents" (*VC* 102).

Several other criticisms could be made along these same lines. One of the most glaring flaws in Shaw's scheme is the absence of any account of youths living in delinquency areas or even in nondelinquency areas who do *not* turn to crime. Angell has written: "It is likely that all the factors predisposing to delinquency, now known, are present in the lives of many children who do not become delinquent. It will be necessary, therefore, to secure equally detailed personal documents from nondelinquent children for the further testing of hypotheses."[30] Why did Sidney become delinquent and his brother become a model citizen? (cf. *NH* 233–34). On one occasion Shaw refers to a comparative study he had made of delinquents and nondelinquents, but this unique study was not reported in detail and was never repeated, so far as I know.[31] Shaw only made gestures toward explaining such effects: he says Bernard Glueck gave him the following notion: "A 'factor,' whether personal or situational, does not become a 'cause' unless and until it becomes a 'motive,' and whether it will become a motive for one form of behavior or another depends upon the constitutional and acquired make-up of the individual."[32] But nothing is made of this distinction, an echo of Mayhew's inconsequential definitions. Burgess goes so far as to ask whether Sidney might have become delinquent because he had a *predisposition* toward it rather than because he was socialized by group participation (*NH* 231). "One might argue that 'delinquency areas' do not cause delinquent behavior but merely release it," remarked Dollard.[33] Without proof, which is probably impossible to obtain, nothing will stop the environmentalist position from sliding back to a "criminal nature" position—nothing except the reinforcement of belief.

According to Finestone, "One of the key enigmas of [Shaw's] life, and an issue that challenges any attempt to understand his work, is to account for the reasons why he made such little theoretical use of these case studies" (*VC* 94). Shaw did not address many questions that emerge from his life histories, yet the histories seem to be an essential part of his accomplishment. What were they good for? Shaw was not much interested in *theory,* which became so popular in sociology after World War II; rather, this activist was interested in attacking *practical* problems by means of appropriate action and rhetorically effective discourse.

Life History as Predispositional Device

What efficacy do Shaw's life histories have? They *illustrate* a certain kind of social process. They explore neither the somatic, psychiatric, and psychological regions that underlie that process nor the communitywide or political processes that transcend it. Nor do they pose problems of interrelations among these areas. To say "illustrate" or "show" is to imply an audience: illustrate or show *to whom?* Shaw's life histories come out rather badly when judged even by his own criteria (viewpoint, world, sequence). As *devices of communication* the histories fare much better. Rhetorical functions of life histories are mentioned briefly in Shaw's works, most often by Burgess. Apparently the rhetorical interpretation was not elaborated at that time because it might have made the documents appear less scientific than leaders of this budding profession wished. Allport admitted that personal documents could have this function: "Social progress may come about through the employment of vivid stories of personal experience (just as it may come about through socially-oriented novels of the order of *Uncle Tom's Cabin, Oliver Twist,* or *The Grapes of Wrath*)."[34]

Shaw's life histories had three audiences: professional sociologists, the public at large, and a group comprising social workers, reformers, volunteers with community organizations, students of sociology, and so forth—that is, people not so concentrated in interest as sociologists nor so amorphous as the general public, but interested enough to buy a book on this subject and be open to a more or less novel vision and scheme of interpretation. Apparently Shaw did not view delinquents themselves as an audience.[35] Life histories served to predispose these audiences in favor of a scheme of action—the Chicago Area Project. The CAP came into being immediately after the first two major life histories had appeared. (*Brothers in Crime* was also under way in the early 1930s.)

While the histories themselves show how a boy becomes disposed to commit one and then further delinquent acts, their presentation predisposes readers in favor of CAP principles: less formal treatment of delinquents, understanding rather than punishment, environmental change rather than individual treatment, community corrections rather than institutional confinement. The life histories do not blare forth these messages, as promotional literature began to do once the Area Project had been established and was looking out for its own interests. The need for these measures of "delinquency prevention" are voiced quietly by relating criminogenic situations concretely. If readers of Shaw's life histories believe these situations are real, then they are real in their consequences: they will support the Area Project or a similar initiative. Perhaps the best way to get this message across is to let someone merely tell his life story:

since the story is placed in a context of social science, theoretical questions arise about the relations of individual and society, psychology and sociology. But these questions are inappropriate to the document as persuasive device, and that can be understood as the reason Shaw did not pose them.

Two things support this rhetorical approach to Shaw's life histories. First is the character of Clifford Shaw and his generally nonacademic, activist orientation. Stuart Rice calls attention to this "telic element":

> The teleological element frequently found in "social science" appears in a typical manner in the work here analyzed. The problems to which the author devoted his attention arose in the course of telic endeavor. That is, the desire to prevent delinquency and to change the behavior of boys now delinquent was the presumptive social raison d'etre of his activities. In order to accomplish these and other humanistic aims more adequately, additional knowledge of the nature of delinquency, and of the processes involved in its causation, became necessary. The ultimate purposes for which the results of his inquiries would be used were thus replaced in the author's individual interests by more immediate aims of a scientific and factual character. It is unknown and irrelevant to what extent interest in the latter has been or is shared in the author's mind with telic interests of the more ultimate character. He himself would doubtless be unable to say. There is general agreement with the view that the two interests, if both exist, should not be allowed to interact in such a way as to affect the actual procedure employed in a given inquiry. Moreover, when once engaged upon the scientific study of relationships, any desire for the discovery or demonstration of particular kinds of relationships should be rigidly restrained or set aside.[36]

Shaw and McKay were profoundly committed to fighting prejudice against racial and national minorities. This came out most strongly in the unpublished manuscript "Nationality and Delinquency" and is apparent in their reply to Jonassen, who had criticized technicalities in their concept of succession of nationality groups in delinquency areas: Shaw and McKay's reply was to ask what the alternative would be—"the notion of the innate superiority of some peoples over others?" A rhetorical interpretation is not at all out of place applied to works from persons with such motives.[37]

Another justification for a rhetorical treatment of Shaw's life histories is the curious repetitiveness of excerpts from the life histories in his published works, as in Mayhew, as well as the redundancy of the various life histories. Shaw collected thousands of pages of manuscript from delinquents, yet the same examples appear over and over again in his writing, as if he were trying to get a single message across by reiterating the clearest, simplest stories: it was as if he were giving a speech rather than making explorations by diversifying examples or spinning out variations on themes, introducing subtleties of interpretation or working toward types of individual or community. Six of the seven subjects of the major life histories were Polish males (Stanley and the five brothers), two of the books are about residents of the West Side of Chicago (*Jack-Roller* and *Natural History*), and despite high rates of delinquency among Italians and the availability of long documents from Italian boys (most destined for the unfinished "Companions in Crime"), no major story from an Italian was published. The father of every one of the major life history heroes was an alcoholic. The repetitiveness of these publications may account for their low sales figures, especially the books that came after *The Jack-Roller*.

Professionals as Audience

McKay has said that his and Shaw's contribution to the Wickersham Report was the most influential of their books among their colleagues, because Burgess bought a large number of copies and distributed them to sociologists. That Shaw thought this was an important part of his audience is indicated by the professional journals where the life history books were advertised.[38] Insofar as sociologists read Shaw's life histories *as* sociologists, their interest was in the alleged facts and the sociological viewpoint. Quotations from and references to Shaw and McKay's writings have appeared often in sociological literature. The notion of a delinquent subculture can be traced back to the life histories, though Shaw and McKay hesitated to make the separation of deviant group from conventional society that this implied, preferring a more continuous rather than a discrete relation; this was the sort of relation between conventional society and delinquent to be found in the life histories themselves. Certainly the principle of criminal genesis enunciated by Edwin Sutherland—"differential association"—was suggested by the "transmission" concept. (Note that Sutherland was much less interested in life histories than Shaw—*The Professional Thief* was really a professional monograph—and he was a professor and the author of a widely used criminology textbook, not the leader of a reform movement.)

Professionals other than sociologists read Shaw's life histories, but one can imagine that they were not easily converted to the sociological way. They had their own training and habits in individualist modes of analysis and treatment, and they were in competition with sociologists for scarce resources from private sources and, later, the government. Everyone protects his own turf, even in the delinquency business. Foremost among the competitors of the Chicago Area Project, and indeed their enemy of choice, were the social workers:

> The social workers and their allies among the local elites were more open to sociological explanations—but only because these explanations appeared to suggest that more resources be made available to helping professions for family tinkering. In short, they did not reject sociological explanations; they misunderstood them.[40]

Shaw and Burgess hoped to get social workers to see more clearly the viewpoint of their clients before prescribing what *they*, the social workers, in their wisdom knew to be best for the delinquent. Burgess explores this in detail in his article "What Social Case Records Should Contain to Be Useful for Sociological Interpretation":

> The first requisite necessary to reveal to social worker and sociologist the person as he really is to himself would be to enter the record in his own language. To enter the interview in the words of the person signifies a revolutionary change. It is a change from the interview conceived in legal terms to the interview as an opportunity to participate in the life history of the person, in his hopes, in his attitudes, in his own plans, in his philosophy of life .... What are the facts for sociology and social work? They are certainly not descriptions of the mere external behavior of applicant and of social worker. They are rather, as we have seen, the life history of the applicant, his scheme of life, and his attitude to the problem in question. [p. 527]

However, Burgess admits that to prevent the record from running to enormous length the social worker must select what to include; this allowed Frank Bruno to make the following rejoinder:

> Selection of the significant statements introduces exactly the element of possible error which their interpretation in a third person recital involves, namely, the recorder is using his judgment with respect to the entire material.[41]

Also, Bruno pointed out a mechanical difficulty in a period when tape recorders were not in use and the interviewer did not take shorthand: "Personally I have not found any greater accuracy in my own personal memory in the verbatim method of reporting than in the narrative."[42] Yet surely life histories put before the eyes of receptive social workers, trained to perceive individuals in families, the reality and influence of neighborhood social life.

Once the broad outlines of the sociological approach to delinquency were laid out by life histories, sociologists did not work on further life histories but turned to investigations of specific areas, which they almost always reported in their own prose. With the advancement and popularity of sociology after World War II, life histories fell out of the central place they had occupied in sociology. It is almost as if life histories were rural, like the backgrounds of the pioneering sociologists who used them, calling for a more relaxed, contemplative ambience than the fast-talking sociologists of more recent times have cared to create.

The General Public as Audience

As we saw in our study of Mayhew, the voices of oral history speakers may be so delightful that they attract readers who would otherwise have no interest in the subject. Though the Jack-Roller is breezy in places, I doubt that many people have ever picked up his story as general reading, unless they thought they saw a connection with popular crime films of the day, such as *Public Enemy* (1931) or *Each Dawn I Die* (1939), or even the 1949 film *Knock on Any Door*, in which Humphrey Bogart defends a Chicago hoodlum by declaring that society is to blame for the slums that create criminals. After all, people around the world were very much aware of crime in Chicago, a circumstance that more than one reviewer of *The Jack-Roller* mentioned. But Shaw's histories simply do not have the impact on the imagination that Mayhew's histories have; rarely does Shaw reproduce dialects of *spoken* speech. (An exception is Sidney's father, whose dialect is reproduced: *NH* 49). No obvious stylistic variations appear in the different life histories. Other Chicago sociology monographs may have been more popular. Faris reports that *The Gold Coast and the Slum* was a best-seller in Chicago: "The wide circulation of the book may have aided sociology by stimulating public interest and understanding of urban studies at the university."[43]

Juvenile court judge Bartelme expressed her wish that Shaw's books be read widely:

> I wish every citizen would be required to read Shaw's description of [Sidney's] experiences in the correctional institutions to which he was committed. . . . Let us hope that the case of Sidney, which is a sad and vivid picture of the neglect of childhood, will stimulate in all of us a more active interest in the problems and welfare of our children. . . . In the final analysis, the problem of delinquency and crime is a community responsibility and must be met by the intelligent and concerned co-operation of all the citizens who are vitally concerned with the problems of human welfare. [*NH* 258–60]

Surely Shaw thought he would have a better chance of reaching the uninitiated public with life histories than with mere statistical compilations or even with his own uncomplicated prose. Shaw's secretary of many years, Helen Prendergast, once told me that Shaw often asked her to read over what he had written to make sure it was free of jargon and intelligible to a lay reader. In *The Gang* (1926), Thrasher refers to *The Jack-Roller* as *A Problem Boy* (p. 357): the title was changed, probably as a way to attract a broader audience than merely professional problem-solvers. That these documents are reproduced in the first person makes it easier for a nonprofessional audience to identify with the delinquent. *The Jack-Roller*'s dust jacket makes the appeal that the book is "complete, vivid, authentic. It is a graphic story of social causation, demoralized neighborhoods, preying and preyed-upon crime. Its terms are colorful, self-justifying, rebellious, but withal, accurate." The advertisement in the *Chicago Tribune* trumpeted that the story is "authentic, vivid, a rebellious record of the roots of crime." Rebellion does seem to be a good come-on in this area—or wanderlust, as in Thomas Minehan's *Boy and Girl Tramps of America* (1934), which contains some dialogue and photographs but no oral histories. In a letter to Normal Kiell (3 February 1961) granting permission for use of excerpts from *The Jack-Roller* in a book on adolescent experiences,[44] Henry McKay wrote:

> It was Mr. Shaw's hope that he might contribute somewhat to a broader and better understanding of the offender by the public. In line with this policy he always was glad to give permission to quote from his publications. And because the Jackroller was more successful than any of the other writers in making the reader a vicarious participant in the world of the offender it was, I am sure, the most significant of the case studies. The thought that parts of this book were to have a wider circulation would, I am sure, have pleased Mr. Shaw.

One of Shaw and Burgess's intentions in publishing life histories was to combat public labeling of the criminal by newspapers: "While such dramatization of a criminal act may serve to promote the financial interest of the newspaper, it contributes little to an understanding of the nature of the act" (*BC* ix–x). "The newspaper usage of the term 'the moron' calls up emotional reactions of indignation and vengeance; the phrase 'the natural history of a delinquent career' invites a scientific inquiry into the causes of the behavior" (*NH* 235). Burgess might not have said this had the title originally planned for the book been used, as reported on the dust jacket of the original edition of *The Jack-Roller—The "Moron": The Natural History of a Delinquent Career*. One newspaper columnist urged his readers to "read *The Jack-Roller* and you will have a much clearer understanding of the things you see in your daily newspaper."[45] In this connection the remark by Shaw's institutional superior in the foreword to *The Natural History* (p. viii) was especially damaging: "It is my opinion that the major portion of the story is true but students who read this book must constantly bear in mind that the attitude of the individual is warped and his expressions of opinion must be accepted as the product of such a mind.''

In a 1958 article, Joseph Lohman, who had been a community organizer with the Chicago Area Project, presented a few "ghosts that should have been interred long ago but bedevil the public yet":

1. "All delinquents are alike."
2. "Severe punishment is the ultimate effective deterrent."
3. "The delinquent has been effectively treated if he is removed from our sight."
4. "The first offender should be merely admonished and thus given another chance."
5. "There is a single and simple solution of the delinquency problem."[46]

However, only ghosts 2 and 3 are shooed away by Shaw's histories; 4 is not so prominent in them, and Shaw gives an impression that there *is* a single, if not very simple, solution to delinquency—community organization—and that all delinquents are essentially alike, though not alike in being evil, the public's usual view. This is an indication of how concentrated—or limited—Shaw's life histories are.

Burgess echoes Mayhew's hope that extremes of society will be brought closer together by their meeting in the life history space:

> Life histories of criminals secured for this study were used not only to check the material obtained from other sources, but also to find out how the *gangster* looks at his own life . . . .
> While the good citizen has grown up in an atmosphere of obedience to the law, the gangster has lived his life in a region of law breaking, of graft, and of "fixing." Because they have been reared in two different worlds, they have never been able to understand each other. The stories which the gangsters tell should enable good citizens to deal more intelligently and therefore more effectively with the problem of organized crime. When the public once realizes how deep rooted and widespread are the practices and philosophy of the gangster, it will not be content with merely punishing individual gangsters and their allies, but will be moved to make a frontal attack upon the basic causes of crime in Chicago.[47]

That is, good citizens will support the Chicago Area Project.

The Marginal Audience

The most important audience for these life histories was people already interested to some degree in the problem of juvenile delinquency, people whose approach to this problem might be swayed by seeing the sociological vision. This included the captive audience of students in sociology courses, some of them on the way to being professional sociologists, and social workers discontented with casework. It also included reformers, especially those in Chicago, the sort of upper- or upper-middle-class persons who started the Behavior Research Fund or who sat on the board of directors of the Chicago Area Project. According to Carey, during the 1920s a small group of reformers were the most active sponsors of sociological research in Chicago: some were from old established families, some were newly arrived businessmen, and some were professional people.[48] But Shaw does not seem to have had much success in communicating the substance of his theory to this audience. According to Carey, sociologists were least successful in gaining acceptance for their explanations of crime and delinquency. Though the more sophisticated reformers rejected simplistic notions of crime causation, such as poverty or broken homes, little understanding of concepts such as "culture conflict" had been achieved.[49] Does this account for the fact that, in the latest of the life histories, *Brothers in Crime,* Shaw returned to the concept of culture conflict, even though that was the oldest concept in the Chicago paradigm of delinquency and life history? One would have thought it had been adequately covered already, but apparently the audience had not yet been reached. Carey says that two reasons some people rejected sociological interpretations were that they dimly perceived requirements for major social and economic reorganization (though Shaw did not draw out these implications, perhaps to avoid scaring anyone off), and that no clear-cut program seemed to flow from his ideas.[50] The nontraditional, nonbureaucratic character of Shaw's delinquency prevention program must have been as difficult to grasp as his concept of culture conflict.

How did the life histories create a predisposition in favor of the Chicago Area Project? If the implications of the story were not clear enough, the "sandwich" commentary and the footnotes showed the way. Hugh Kenner has pointed out that footnotes allow a book to speak in two different voices:[51] spatially and intellectually "underlying" the boy's own voice on the page was the interpretive voice of Clifford Shaw. (One reviewer called these "offstage comments." Shaw had allowed the boys to "upstage" him, to use the word Humpherys applies to Mayhew, and the footnotes seem to support this process rather than undercut it.) Of the 227 footnotes in the three major life history books and the longer history in the Wickersham Report (*SF* 360–79), 52 *generalize* a point in the narrative (stating that a practice—truancy, junking, stealing fruit from stands—is common among boys of the area), 57 give *supplementary information* (such as the age of the boy at a certain event), 42 indicate how a passage illustrates the value of "own story" (usually by expressing the individual's attitude toward some object), 46 explain a *sequence* in the individual's life, and 30 are comments relevant to the *Chicago Area Project.*

The CAP comments fall into three categories: a call for less formal modes of treatment, the counterproductive results of incarceration, and the need for community-based programs of delinquency prevention. A recurring point in Shaw's commentary and occasionally in the remarks of others in these books (e.g., the juvenile court judge in *NH* 255) is that without information about the delinquent's situations and attitudes, "the worker's relation to the case is necessarily more or less formal, and the treatment consists chiefly of attempts to gain control and effect adjustment through threats of arrest and punishment" (*JR* 18). Shaw's attitude toward the Brothers in Crime is the kind of treatment he encouraged his workers in the CAP to give to the delinquent:

> personal relationships of a friendly, informed, and confidential character have been maintained with the brothers. When they had work difficulties, desired small sums of money, needed medical assistance for themselves or for members of their families, they came on their own initiative for aid or advice. They were always regarded as persons who could make an adjustment if given the necessary facilities. [*BC* 349]

The wrong approach to the delinquent was epitomized by the aloofness of the father in the Wickersham Report (*SF* 293 ff.) and the stiffness of the social worker in *Delinquency Areas* (*DA* 144–52). Both of these are vividly presented by reproducing interview transcripts. The wrong attitude was most likely to dominate in "correctional" institutions. Finestone has pointed out that the selection of cases for major life histories reflected Shaw's preoccupation with these institutions, since all the boys were "identified as recidivists, who had repeated contacts with the whole gamut of official correctional agencies."[52] Shaw noted:

> Unfortunately very little effort has been made to secure reliable data concerning the social processes which go on within detention homes, correctional schools, and penal institutions, and the influence of these processes upon the attitudes, personality, and philosophy of life of the inmates. Most studies of such institutions have been concerned primarily with the physical equipment and the formal administrative organization. [*JR* 11]

If there is any single point that is forcefully communicated by these life histories, it is the futility of imprisoning delinquents. Shaw clearly was advertising this in these documents, though in several places he somewhat neutralizes the structural point by attributing specific abuses to previous administrations (cf. *JR*, 1st ed., viii). Some reviewers of *The Jack-Roller* came down especially hard on the stupidity of authorities in allowing

Stanley to be in and out of their institutions so many times, and one reviewer in 1932 expressed a position that strikes a more current chord (demonstrating that exceptions to dominant paradigms are always possible):

> The reviewer is not impressed by the theory that living in a "delinquency area" is to be blamed for inducing a criminal career. The responsibility for continued delinquencies in this case appears to rest not upon an impersonal area, but on the incompetence of the court authorities. It is obvious that living within the jurisdiction of a juvenile court that does not function must be a good cause of continued delinquency.... The pressing need today is not the re-education of the criminals, but the re-evaluation of the makers and administrators of the law.[53]

Rather than reform the reformatory institutions—it would be impossible to transform them into anything resembling life outside the walls, anyway—Shaw's recommendation was to stop treating delinquency case-by-case and to organize local communities for delinquency prevention. Though this recommendation appears here and there in the life histories (cf. *JR* 196–97), it appears most often in the last of the three, *Brothers in Crime,* published four years after the incorporation of the Chicago Area Project:

> The wide ramifications of these experiences suggest the need for developing treatment and preventive programs of a community-wide character.... It appears that to bring about a substantial reduction in the volume of delinquency in these areas it will be necessary to develop an effective organization of conventional sentiments, attitudes, and interests as a substitute for the present situation in which socially divergent norms and practices prevail.... There is reason to believe that more satisfactory results might be achieved by programs in which primary emphasis would be placed upon the responsible participation of the local residents, as contrasted with the traditional practice in which the responsibility for determining policies and planning programs is vested in groups residing outside the community. [*BC* 359–60]

However, apart from the principle of autonomy they manifest, the life histories show neither the possibility nor the actuality of any community organization.

It is interesting that Whyte, in his autobiographical appendix to *Street Corner Society,* admits his interest in having social workers read the book to promote the use of indigenous leaders in therapeutic programs.[54]

Whyte, however, rarely used oral histories but often included participant-observer reports, some in the words of local people themselves. Whyte differed from Shaw methodologically in using participant observer reports rather than oral histories and substantively in discovering social organization in the slum, where Shaw had seen only disorganization. The participant observer method of inquiry and style of presentation captured those organizational structures better than Shaw's oral histories could, a reason the former replaced the latter in the 1940s. Shaw and Whyte together could be contrasted with the noted social worker Miriam Van Waters, who insisted that workers have a thorough "scientific" training concerning delinquency; when she turns to "the community," her proposals advance the claims of one or another type of agency, not participation by community residents themselves.[55] Shaw's insistence on the indigenous worker came to fruition in the 1950s, with the introduction of "detached workers," that is, people who did not stay in an office but worked on the streets with gangs, and in the 1970s with the growth of community organizations.

Rice claimed that Shaw's desire to prevent delinquency (that is, to set up the CAP) did not bias his theory. We can see that Shaw's scheme clearly has a pattern in which theory and practice reflected and reinforced eath other. Family life was not extensively explored in the life histories, and it was the psychiatric/social work mode of family therapy that the community-based model opposed. Burgess's "theoretical" distinction between personality traits, which cannot be changed, and social type, which can be, is only too pat in justifying measures of social therapy. The absence of economic interpretations of delinquency in Shaw's thought, as Snodgrass pointed out,[56] is consistent with the nonpolitical character of the Chicago Area Project. A theory that was more politically and economically astute would have demanded a different sort of action, but it would have found life histories insignificant, as we shall see in the next chapter.

Nine

The Political Paradigm: Saul Alinsky, Howard S. Becker, and the Autobiography of a Girl Drug Addict

Small-Time Confessions

Saul Alinsky became known in the 1960s as "the professional radical," an organizer and teacher of strategies for social and political change. In an effort to establish due process procedures in the juvenile court, Patrick Murphy and his colleagues during the early 1970s practiced "Alinsky law—using a variety of legal actions (some valid, some spurious), investigations, and intelligent use of the media to try to move, embarrass, and change bureaucracies."[1] But Alinsky did not begin his career as a political agitator. From 1931 to 1940 he worked under Clifford Shaw as a research sociologist at the Institute for Juvenile Research and a community organizer with the Chicago Area Project. As part of this work Alinsky collected a number of life histories of juvenile delinquents. However, when he started publishing his own writing he never used what he later called those "small-time confessions." The following brief survey of Alinsky's early career will add to what we know about Shaw's operation, and the contrast of Shaw and Alinsky on substantive matters will again bring out the political insignificance of delinquents' oral histories.

Saul Alinsky (1909–72) was the son of Russian Jewish immigrants who lived in a Chicago slum. One of the urban antagonisms he experienced was the conflict of the Poles and the Jews: on one occasion a friend of his was beaten up by some Poles, and in the revenging fracas Alinsky was arrested. It was not the last time: like many revolutionaries, Alinsky profited from his time in jail to do writing that helped disseminate his message. (No one else we have studied spent any time in jail as an inmate.)

Like Mayhew, Alinsky was hostile toward his father, and like Mayhew he expressed opposition toward those who exercised political power. The future organizer made a profound discovery about rhetoric, the art of image-making, in the following way:

> My father was far from permissive and I'd get my share of
> beatings with the invariable finale, "You ever do that again and
> you know what's going to happen to you!" I'd just nod,
> sniffling, and sulk away. But finally one day, after he'd really
> laid into me, he stood over me swinging his razor strap and

repeated, "You know what's going to happen to you if you do
that again?" And I just said through my tears, "No, what's
going to happen?" His jaw dropped open, he was completely
at a loss, he didn't know what the hell to say. He was absolutely disorganized. I learned my lesson then: power is not in
what the establishment has, but in what you think it has.[2]

Note that being "disorganized" is not an undesirable quality here, as it
was for Shaw: one wants to disorganize power structures, to throw them
into confusion.

When he was thirteen years old Alinsky's parents divorced, and he
began moving back and forth between his mother in Chicago and his
father in California. In 1926 Alinsky graduated from Hollywood High
School and entered the University of Chicago to study archaeology:

It was all very exciting and dramatic to me. The artifacts were
not just pieces of stone or clay. My imagination could carry me
back to the past so that when I stood in front of an old Inca
altar I could hear the cries of the human sacrifices. You need a
lot of imagination to be a good organizer. Today when I go into
a community, I suffer and resent with the people there, and
they feel this. It's a big thing in my relationships.[3]

At the same time, Alinsky took sociology courses from Robert E. Park
and others, but he became disdainful of most academic sociology. While
at the University of Chicago he plunged into social action with southern
Illinois coal miners who were fighting John L. Lewis and the United Mine
Workers. Later Lewis became Alinsky's model.

Alinsky graduated from the University of Chicago in 1930 with a major
in a field that was, during the depression, "as dead as its subject matter."
He was rescued by a fellowship in criminology at the University of
Chicago: "My assignment as a graduate student was to get insight into
crime. I figured the way to do this was to get inside." He hung around the
hotel headquarters of the Capone gang but was repeatedly kicked out.
One day he listened to a mobster telling a story his cronies had already
heard many times. Thus Alinsky became their audience, a sociological
stranger, both an insider and an outsider, a marginal figure. The mob did
not fear his turning informer because "they owned City Hall. They owned
the federal agencies."

From the Capone gang Alinsky learned the importance of primary
relationships: why, for example, the mob had to get an out-of-town killer
to do a job—because a local man might know the victim and not be able to
pull the trigger. Later, when he worked at a prison, Alinsky learned that it
was difficult for the warden to pull the switch putting to death someone
known to everyone in the prison. In the same way, perhaps personal
documents make murder or capital punishment a little less likely to occur.

This personalization also accounts for the pain we experience in viewing a television presentation such as "One Woman's Story," about a woman dying of cancer, shown on public television stations in January 1980: through the film we become so intimately acquainted with Joan Robinson that we experience her death as a personal loss.

On 21 December 1931 Saul Alinsky joined the staff of the Institute for Juvenile Research, in the sociology research department. Apparently Shaw wanted him to continue studying the Capone gang, but Alinsky felt he had done all he could and wanted to move on. He began to work with a gang of delinquent Italian boys on the Near West Side of Chicago. Toward the end of his stay at IJR a book was planned, to be titled "Companions in Crime," using materials Alinsky had gathered from this gang and following the format of Shaw's previous life history books.[4] Alinsky's departure in 1940 is probably the reason this volume was never finished.

Alinsky had met one of the gang members at Saint Charles State School for Boys. Thomas, a fourteen-year-old native-born American of Italian descent from Chicago's West Side, had been committed in 1929 for burglarizing public schools. The following are excerpts from the draft of the "Companions" preface:

> The rigid routine of institutional life, its strict discipline, and the formal, uncompromising attitude of the staff, made an overture of friendship acceptable to him. During this visit Thomas was asked if he would like to write his life history. The purpose of the plan was two-fold. It was hoped that the writing of the document might relieve some of the tedium of incarceration for him, give him some insight into the sequence of events which led up to his being committed to St. Charles, and possibly furnish us with material which might help to throw some light on the causes of delinquency of the type in which he had engaged. The boy readily accepted our suggestion.
>
> Through Thomas the writers later met three of his friends who happened to be incarcerated in the same institution, and a friendly relationship was established with them. The three boys came from Thomas's neighborhood and were all members of the same delinquent gang.

The boys suggested that Alinsky meet their friends in the neighborhood, and soon the sociologist was acting as a courier taking personal news back and forth. When one of the boys was paroled from Saint Charles,

> He came almost immediately to the office and asked us to accompany him to his neighborhood. There we met other members of his gang. One evening this boy and some of his friends came to the office. The boys were quite without restraint or diffidence and talked freely of the things in which they were interested. Before they left we suggested to them

that perhaps they, too, would like to write their life histories as Thomas had done. At first they were hesitant about setting down on paper the events of their lives, but one boy was so insistent that it was 'O.K.' that he overcame their reluctance. These life histories did not really take shape, however, until the same relationship of confidence and friendship was established between the writers and the boys as existed between the boys themselves. From this time on we were in constant association with the boys of this group. Scarcely a day passed without our spending some time with them in the neighborhood, engaging in their leisure-time activities, eating with them, taking them for rides, sharing with them our cigarettes.[5]

One must doubt that the relationship between the writers and the boys could be the same as among the boys themselves. At any rate Alinsky, and perhaps Shaw, became intimate with gang members by doing them such favors as giving a spaghetti dinner and arranging to have a photograph made of a boy killed in an attempted robbery: since his mother had no picture of her son, the police photographer touched up a picture taken in the morgue. "The news of what we had done spread quickly through the community and did much to strengthen our position in the neighborhood." Perhaps no single statement demonstrates more emphatically the ambivalence of life history activity in general: while helping the delinquent, a delinquency-prevention organization is strengthened.

Alinsky worked full time with the Kip gang during 1932–33 and kept up with them throughout the 1930s. He helped a brother of two gang members attend the University of Illinois. While driving the boy to Urbana, Alinsky stopped the car at a crossroads near Joliet and said dramatically: "That road leads to the state prison; the other one goes to the university. Which is it going to be?" The boy went to the university and today holds an important position in government.

From 1933 to 1936 Alinsky worked at the state prison in Joliet (now the diagnostic depot) as a staff sociologist and a member of the classification board. In his first published article, "A Sociological Technique in Clinical Criminology," he described ways to persuade convicts to confide in an interviewer. Two essential components of this technique were, first: "To know your community is to know your delinquent."[6] "The newly committed inmate, miles away from home in a strange penitentiary who suddenly meets some person who knows such intimate details of his community usually responds with an excited flow of conversation."[7] And second:

> The usage of delinquent vocabularies characteristic of the inmate's community is of great value in the establishing of closer rapport. To illustrate, if the question, "Have you ever

been chased by the police while you were in a stolen car and
have the police shoot at you" is phrased "Have you ever been
in a hot short and got lammed by the heat and have them toss
slugs at you," a warmer and more responsive answer usually
results. Furthermore, the usage of delinquent terminology may
serve as a criteria in analyses of degree of development of
delinquent attitudes.[8]

(Compare Mayhew's use of language to show how a formerly well-off
person had come down socially.) According to Alinsky, this life history
technique produces a deeper and more comprehensive diagnostic view of
the individual than professionals can usually obtain.

Working at Joliet, Alinsky felt he was beginning to be "institutionalized—callous." "I would be interviewing an inmate and I no
longer had any real curiosity as to why this particular guy did what he did.
I knew it was time for me to get out."[9] In addition, he was annoyed by the
narrowness of criminologists' minds: "They never read anything outside
of their own field." Alinsky was marginal to professional criminology. His
mind was elsewhere:

As a kid was telling me of an A&P store he robbed and another
of a gas station he heisted, Hitler and Mussolini were robbing
whole countries and killing off whole peoples. I found it difficult to listen to small-time confessions. Most of my time was
spent in anti-fascist and CIO activities.[10]

Concerning his early community organizing, he said: "I went in there to
fight fascism; delinquency was just incidental, the real crime was
fascism."

During 1936–40, Alinsky was a community organizer with the Chicago
Area Project, beginning in late 1938 mostly in the Back of the Yards area
of Chicago, Upton Sinclair's "jungle." Alinsky eventually left Shaw (or
was fired) and began organizing this area on his own. While still at IJR he
apparently continued to collect life histories and to assist community
committees in organizing self-help projects. But until the Hitler-Stalin
nonaggression pact of 1939 he says he identified with the communists
more than with anyone at the Institute for Juvenile Research, though he
delivered speeches on behalf of IJR to various groups in the city, with
titles such as: "The Basis in the Social Sciences for the Treatment of the
Adult Offender," "Chicago Area Project," "How Delinquents Are
Made," "Community Organization and Delinquency," and "Crime
Prevention—Juvenile Aspects." His separation from what had become
conventional criminology was thus a gradual one. He says:

So I started doing my job as a sort of sinecure, I quit right
when quitting time came and I got involved in raising money
for the International Brigade, for the share-croppers down

South, helping stop the evictions of city people who couldn't
pay rent, fighting for public housing. Wherever you turned you
saw injustice.

Alinsky saw injustice. Shaw saw social disorganization, and in his efforts to organize communities Shaw encountered powerlessness, which, in
a democracy, implied injustice.[11] But, since Shaw wanted the organizers'
experience to arise from concrete local situations rather than dictates
from downtown, he never wrote about the experience of organizing,
never drew out the specifically political implications of this model, which
had come out of the application of his sociological theory. Alinsky pushed
forward the evolution of criminology by employing many of the same
concepts of community organizing that Shaw had developed: for example,
using the indigenous worker and developing confidence in local residents
that they had the talent to act. Alinsky broke sharply with Shaw, however, over the use of cooperation versus conflict strategies as well as over
the target of that activity. For Alinsky, concentrations of political and
economic power outside the local community must be attacked, not cooperated with:

> The two major defects in the traditional community organiza-
> tion movement are (1) that it views each problem of the com-
> munity as if it were independent of all other problems and (2)
> that it views the community as a social, political, and economic
> entity which is more or less insulated from the general social
> scene . . . . This appears to be true of both those agencies who
> are concerned with some one special problem of the local com-
> munity as if this problem were isolated and those who claim to
> be interested in the development of a program for such a local
> neighborhood as a whole, without recognizing that the life of
> such a neighborhood is shaped by forces which far transcend
> the local scene.[12]

One consequence of this kind of strategy was that Alinsky became more
publicly prominent than Shaw had ever wanted to be—even nationally
known. Shaw had remained in the background of projects and let local
residents take credit for accomplishments. But in a battle against concentrations of political power, which may have a national base and be found
in the national media, identification of actions with individual leaders is
more useful than it is on the local scene. (Shaw's complaint about Alinsky
on this point does not seem to grasp the distinction in these two models.[13])
Thus one reason Alinsky shunned life histories after he left IJR on 15
January 1940 was that he became the hero in all the epics he initiated, like
Ben Lindsey. Moreover, in the Alinsky political paradigm, disseminating
life histories, "small-time confessions," was a well-intentioned waste of
time. Alinsky did write a biography of John L. Lewis that quotes the labor

leader extensively, but this was the history of an exemplary political leader whose life might guide other activists in their efforts to change economic conditions and structures that are alleged to produce, among other things, delinquency.

Has Alinsky's method been more successful than Shaw's? *Reveille for Radicals* (1945) is full of glowing optimism and hyperbole—Moses leading the multitudes to the Promised Land. It was an outburst of the exuberance of innovative youth. But by the 1960s it was not clear that Alinsky's agitation had been any more successful than Shaw's "within system" work. In an assessment of Alinsky's the Woodlawn Organization (TWO), John Fish wrote in 1973:

> TWO, although successful in building an organization, was unable to address some of the systematic causes of the social problems Woodlawn faced. On a week-by-week basis TWO was most successful in what might be termed little issues that affected a relatively small number of people and could be pursued to a successful outcome with relatively meager organizational resources. A boy was kicked out of school, a woman was cheated by a merchant, a slum lord turned off the heat. These were bread-and-butter issues that helped build the organization.[14]

This did not differ from Shaw's accomplishment. Toward the end of his life Alinsky himself was discouraged about what could be accomplished by organizing, but his beliefs and methods live on in a variety of organizations. More recently, among the Chicago public the initials CAP have stood not for Chicago Area Project but for Citizens' Action Program.

The Politics of Autobiography

Since *The Fantastic Lodge: Autobiography of a Girl Drug Addict* is not about a delinquent and does not contain an interpretative framework within the text itself, it might seem not to qualify for inclusion in this study. It is included here because the book came from the Institute for Juvenile Research and was connected with delinquency research there and elsewhere, and because the problems encountered in producing it are well documented, constituting an inadvertent interpretative framework (which includes the issue of whether to include expert commentary along with "Janet's" own story). In the process of telling that history, some political aspects of publishing personal documents will come to light, as well as what happened to an innovative institution in delinquency research as it aged. Just as Alinsky's organizations were fighting political power during this period, so sociologists began to examine ways those in power create and maintain classes of "deviants"—drug addicts, delinquents, homosexuals, and so forth—so that from this theoretical point of view delinquency and drug addiction did not differ generically. Finally, another objection to including *The Fantastic Lodge* is that the book is not an oral history as I have defined it but an autobiography: that is, the book has a greater development of character and action than a two- or three-page document. Granted. However, I shall treat it not as autobiography, but as a means of learning more about delinquents' oral histories by studying several of its circumstantial features, chiefly the power an institution wielded to prevent its publication, features that could also circumscribe oral histories.

The tape recordings from which *The Fantastic Lodge* was edited were made by Howard S. Becker (b. 1928). Becker, now a professor of sociology at Northwestern University, received a Ph.D. in sociology from the University of Chicago when he was twenty-three years old, having taken courses from Ernest Burgess, Everett Hughes, and Herbert Blumer. But Becker was unable to find a teaching position that paid more than he was making for playing the piano in Chicago taverns.[15] At the same time, during 1947–53, the Institute for Juvenile Research was conducting a study of drug addiction among young people in Chicago, under the direction of Clifford Shaw and Solomon Kobrin.[16] Kobrin and Becker met at a meeting of the American Sociological Association in 1951, and Becker suggested that IJR hire him to do a study of marijuana users, employing the method of analytic induction that Lindesmith had used in studying opiate addicts.[17] IJR had some funds available, so Becker was hired. One of the early interviews was with the girl friend of a fellow musician. Becker has said: "The minute she started talking I knew it was going to be something special. The tape was quite dramatic, full of information, and beautifully stated."[18] "Janet" was also a heroin addict. (In the French translation this comes out "heroïne.") When Becker played the tape of her interview for Kobrin and McKay, they agreed that she was so observant and articulate that it would be useful to interview her further in order to put together a complete life history.

"Janet Clark" visited Becker's home about once a week for four to six months, except for interruptions such as the time she spent in jail, and recorded her story on tape. She had wanted to be a writer, and she hoped to use the royalty money to pay for psychotherapy. In addition, these sessions were an outlet for the rage she felt against the criminal justice system. Janet was the ideal life history speaker: she told a well-organized story without needing to be asked many questions:

> Janet smoked incessantly as she talked, sitting bent forward, cross-legged or with her knees pulled up under her chin. She punctuated the story with abrupt, nervous angular gestures. She often gave nasty, but accurate and amusing imitations of the characters in her drama. Occasionally, her narrative would

revive feelings so unpleasant that she would ask for a recess to
recover her composure and courage.[19]

She had an egalitarian relationship with Becker: "She would go to his
house, gossip with him and his wife about mutual acquaintances in the
jazz world. Then he would get out the recording machine and they would
settle down to an hour or two of work on the story, he putting questions
and she talking."[20] In 1951 Janet was twenty-two years old, Becker
twenty-three. (Shaw was twenty-six, the Jack-Roller about sixteen when
they met in 1921.) Both Becker and Janet were white and middle-class,
and Becker occupied a position like that of Janet's boyfriend in the music
business.

During the 1950s Janet remained interested in the project, carting
around copies of the transcripts in a shopping bag. At the same time the
University of Chicago Press also was interested in publishing her autobiography, as it had published the earlier IJR books. But Janet never saw
her book in print. She took an overdose of drugs and died on 9 January
1959. The cremation permit gives her age as twenty-nine. Two years later,
after ten years of wrangling, the book first came out in Boston.[21] What
follows is a detailed account of that wrangling.

The first reference to this project in files of the Institute for Juvenile
Research is a letter dated 24 September 1952, from Morton Grodzins,
editor of the University of Chicago Press, reviewing a meeting the previous day with Shaw, McKay, Solomon Kobrin, and Anthony Sorrentino.
A number of projects had been discussed: the ill-fated "Nationality and
Delinquency," Sorrentino's "It's an Inside Job" (published under the
title *Organizing against Crime*), a possible revision of *The Natural History of a Delinquent Career,* a book about the Chicago Area Project, and
"the narcotics study by Sol Kobrin and others," which Grodzins divided
into two parts: the "comprehensive report" and "Becker's case history."

Apparently from the first Shaw emphasized that this life history had to
be viewed as part of the whole drug study, just as the earlier published
documents had included social ecology statistics and interpretations. But
Grodzins remarked that he thought Janet's story was "a fascinating
document standing alone," and thereby one of the issues was joined. He
added that if the "case history" were published before the larger study,
the former might attract attention to the latter and make its publication
easier to finance. Scientific reservations about the idiosyncrasy of this
single case, Grodzins said, could be met by including an essay by Solomon Kobrin relating Janet's experiences to those of other addicts and a
second essay by Kobrin or Everett Hughes putting her story in the larger
context of urban alienation and urban pathology. (Hughes, a University of
Chicago sociologist, "transmitted to the post–World War II generation of

Chicago sociologists W. I. Thomas' tradition of intensive social observation," and had also, along with his wife, Helen MacGill Hughes, been close to Robert E. Park.[22]) The book might appeal to a trade market as well. Grodzins concludes by saying that this book would symbolize a renewed academic interest in the "whole man." No one could have known at this time how innocent such hopes were in relation to imminent developments.

The worm was already in the apple: Shaw sent Grodzins's letter to the director of the Institute for Juvenile Research, who replied that he was impressed by the interest such a discriminating publisher showed in Shaw's work. As a sociological researcher in a state-supported structure dominated by psychologists, Shaw was concerned about the very survival of the IJR sociology research department, which he had kept alive during a depression and a world war. Could it survive Senator McCarthy too?[23] The general public had not been exposed to the subject of drugs to the degree it now is. Indeed, it was not until the period when *The Fantastic Lodge* finally came out that two other books about drug experiences were published: *The Addict in the Street* (1964) and *The Drug Experience: First-Person Accounts of Addicts, Writers, Scientists and Others* (1961). Once drugs became a middle-class topic, publishers became interested, because that group is their market. (Two earlier ice-breakers were the book (1949) and the movie (1955) *The Man with the Golden Arm* and Billie Holiday's autobiography, *Lady Sings the Blues* (1956), about which David Ebin has remarked: "Written by a woman, a rather rare occurrence in drug-experience literature."[24])

On 12 May 1953 Alexander J. Morin, then associate editor of the University of Chicago Press, wrote to Shaw, responding to a recent conversation with Kobrin during which misunderstandings over the "Life History of Janet" had surfaced. Morin said the Press was waiting for the essays by Kobrin and Hughes before submitting the manuscript to the Board of University Publications. He was convinced, he said, of the scholarly value of the document, and he even appeared to be trying to persuade Shaw on this point. Kobrin had been worried about the suggestion by the Press designer that a hypodermic needle be shown on the cover of the book; Morin reassured Kobrin that IJR would be consulted on how the book would be presented to the public. (The dust jacket of the cloth edition does have sketches of drug paraphernalia.)

Morin said he recognized that the Area Project owned the materials, but he emphasized that Howard Becker had until then done the principal editorial work on the transcripts and had been acting for Janet with the Press, so he should be included in any discussions. Morin called Becker's participation "inevitable," since until then the issue had been mainly the preparation of a manuscript that no one knew better than Becker. Kobrin had encouraged Becker, who was no longer on the IJR staff, to seek a publisher, hoping that a publisher's interest might nudge Shaw toward publication. However, Kobrin apparently did not tell Shaw and McKay he had given Becker this permission, and the feeling developed at IJR that Becker had taken matters into his own hands. Shaw already was uneasy with Becker, whose self-assurance he saw as arrogance (according to Kobrin), and to this day Becker suspects that Shaw impeded publication because he wanted his own name to appear as author on any IJR book. (Kobrin has denied this, pointing to articles he published, as did Finestone, without Shaw as coauthor.)

Janet had been paid five dollars an hour by the Chicago Area Project to make the recordings. This seemed to establish ownership rights for the Area Project. But the way they saw things going must have alerted Shaw and his associates to the need for more solid ground. The next month, on 26 June 1953, Janet signed a legal document giving the Chicago Area Project all rights to the material on the condition that her real name not be used in any publication of it (it never has been) and that royalties be paid to her. At that time she received only ten dollars, and that was all she ever got.

A few days later, on 1 July 1953, Shaw wrote to Morin expressing his agreement with Morin's assessment of the scholarly value of this life history, since it illuminated urban institutions and other aspects of human behavior: an essay by Janet's psychoanalyst was considered for inclusion. Now that the Area Project clearly owned the material, Shaw said, publication could be seriously considered. On 6 July Morin replied saying that Everett Hughes's introductory essay had been delivered to Kobrin—"a short, graceful and suggestive piece of work," only fragments of which finally appeared in the preface to the published work. Morin ends his letter with the hope that the book would appear in early spring 1954.

Exactly what happened at this point is not clear. Not all the documents are available, and not all that are available are dated. Two factors stand out: first, Shaw and McKay became indignant over the efforts Becker had made apart from them (though not, in fact, apart from Kobrin) concerning the manuscript; and, second, they were beginning to have misgivings about possible repercussions of publishing this material. In a letter to Grodzins, probably in the fall of 1953, Shaw reemphasized that no part of the total research design for the study of drug addiction should be viewed apart from the whole—that if Janet's story were to be published separately it could not be done until the entire study was complete. Shaw said that they had four other life histories that illuminated the problem of addiction better than Janet's: they were by delinquent males, who, they said, made up the largest single segment of the city's drug addict population.[25] Janet was one of the "minor social types encountered among youthful opiate addicts."

Furthermore, though Shaw had earlier embraced a book about urban life in general, he now retreated: IJR and the Area Project investigated problems that were publicly defined, Shaw said, such as delinquency, emotional disturbance in children, and drug addiction—not the processes of urban social life in general. In sum, insofar as Janet's story illustrated addiction, it had to be part of the larger study of addiction; insofar as it illustrated larger contexts, it had no place in a publicly supported institution whose work was officially defined. Shaw wrote:

> Nor are we free to divest ourselves of responsibility for whatever use other parties may make of such material. Should this publication become an object of controversy our release of it for uses other than those which are central to official function would place us in an indefensible position.

Consequently IJR decided to withhold the document from publication. In their defense it should be repeated that addictive drugs were not as important to the then middle class as they are now. Public awareness of the entanglement of a state-supported institute with addicts might have given the *Chicago Tribune* a juicy scandal, following the precedent of that newspaper's hounding W. I. Thomas out of the University of Chicago.[26]

A "Memorandum on the Janet Document," probably written by McKay about this time, confirms this official outlook. The desirable procedure, it says, would be to pick out sections that might be useful to them in preparing their drug study, then return the remainder of the material to Janet so that she might use any royalties to finance psychotherapy in a private sanitarium, just as earlier delinquents whose stories had been published by IJR had benefited in various ways. IJR would not publish the whole document because Janet was not typical and because "the editing of the manuscript to eliminate libelous materials as well as materials which are offensive to a sense of propriety represents a formidable task." (There was considerable profanity in the transcript.) "Certain aspects of our work might be jeopardized if we published this document even after careful editing." Later McKay said they feared the department would have been "wrecked" by publishing it. However, there were also reasons not to give Janet the material: she might relinquish her rights for a "negligible consideration," and, if she was not going to profit from it either way or if the manuscript proved unmarketable, IJR might as well keep it and avoid *any* complications. Also, her "friends" might publish her story, misrepresenting it as that of a "typical junkie." If the transcription were to be transferred to Janet, the right of IJR to publish the excerpts they wanted to use would have to be protected, and: "The Chicago Area

Project and the State of Illinois should be relieved of any responsibility for events resulting from publication.''

A few months later, Shaw received a letter dated 12 February 1954 from Howard S. Becker, then at the University of Illinois in Urbana. Becker asked what the status of the manuscript was:

> If it is true, as I hear in roundabout ways, that you have decided to forbid publication of the document, I would be greatly interested if you would indicate the reasons for such unilateral action in an area where, after all, others do have interests, both legal and moral.

The words "both legal and moral" have been crossed out, but they are still legible and should be revealed, for they point to an important aspect of this case: a dimension of action transcending conventional institutional interests is being appealed to. McKay shot back a reply emphatically denying that Becker had any rights whatever in the matter. The manuscript "belongs to the Area Project Corporation," and that was that. Kobrin added that he questioned the utility of using life history materials "divested of a carefully elaborated interpretative framework." Becker had argued for the value of the uninterpreted expression for teaching purposes, Kobrin says. (At one time Becker had proposed that the transcript be published straight from the tapes without any editing, in order to put general readers in closer contact with the material and to give specialists an untampered-with text to interpret, as Kluckhohn had advised.) Kobrin also said there was no reason to maintain that the person who made the tapes should be the one to do the editing (cf. John Clay and Mary Carpenter). Helen Hughes, who eventually served as editor, met Janet once at the home of Alfred Lindesmith when he was teaching in Chicago.

Becker replied that Kobrin had indeed given him oral permission to seek a publisher, but that he had not gotten it in writing. Becker apologized for his misconception of the Chicago Area Project as an organization devoted at least in part to carrying out sociological studies and, whatever they might be, making public the results. "My third misconception was that you might have seen, as others have, that there were rights other than purely legal ones involved here. But this assumption was also not based in fact." Becker concluded by thanking them for the great deal he had learned from the experience.

Later in 1954 Janet herself visited Shaw, and he agreed that publication would be possible if IJR and the Area Project were divorced from the book. Janet also paid a visit to the University of Chicago Press. A subsequent reader's report on the manuscript began: "Since the usual form for manuscript reports does not fit this manuscript very well, I will simply

discard it and express my reactions." The main problem, the reader declares, is that the *purpose* of publication had not been faced: "It looks to
me as though these rich interviews fell into their laps and their reaction
was 'let's publish them.' I don't believe it's quite as simple as that"—a
typical problem with this kind of material. Shortly thereafter the Press
again brought up using Becker as the editor, which McKay vetoed both
because Becker had been associated with IJR and because engaging a
better-known social scientist would attract more attention to the book and
would thus help Janet more. (Ironically, when a reissue of Shaw's *Jack-
Roller* was planned in 1965, the University of Chicago Press invited
Becker to write a new preface: when McKay learned of the Press's
choice, he said he believed they had chosen wisely.)

On 10 June 1955, Morin wrote to McKay that Everett and Helen
Hughes had agreed to edit the book. Neither was officially connected with
IJR or the Area Project, both were well known in sociology, and both
were associated with the Chicago tradition of life histories. The Hugheses
were not aware of the political and legal worries of IJR: they were professionally interested in an unusually fine life history, and they thought
such a tragic story should be told so that it might warn young people about
starting on drugs. Helen Hughes, who did most of the editorial work, also
thought the book would give Janet some reason for pride.

In October 1955 Shaw agreed under these conditions to relinquish rights
to the material *back* to Janet. Everything looked encouraging. But apparently the lawyers of the University of Chicago advised that the publisher
of this manuscript would become involved in "nuisance suits" and that
even the Area Project might be sued. In none of this correspondence does
anyone make specific references to what aspect of the text might stir
anyone up: all the names were changed, and though Janet's perception is
of a unique quality, one would think the events and persons she describes
are general enough to make identification impossible. There was no precedent of a lawsuit against any of the Chicago sociologists, who had, after
all, conducted and published many investigations.

In August 1957 Clifford Shaw died. At about the same time the Chicago
Area Project split off from the Institute for Juvenile Research and became
a part of the Illinois Youth Commission. (Today the community organizers are staff of the Illinois Commission on Delinquency Prevention.)
The action and research functions began to pull apart, and some of the
pressure to write about problems only as they are defined by government
bodies began to ease. The political atmosphere of the early 1950s no
longer existed, and the public had even been exposed a little to drugs. In
December 1958 Everett Hughes wrote to McKay asking for permission to
use Janet's interviews in a microfilm series to be circulated to libraries. In
his reply on 2 January 1959, McKay agreed that Becker's name should be

included on any publication of Janet's life history. The project was being revived, but a week later Janet was dead.

Helen Hughes had already edited the manuscript and sent it to a New York publisher, who lost it. She acquired another copy from IJR, on which she says she did a much better job of editing, removing a great deal of profanity. Sometime during late 1960 the University of Chicago Press lost interest. Helen Hughes showed the manuscript to David Riesman, who, like the Hugheses, had moved from Chicago to Cambridge, and one evening in 1961 he showed it to an editor at Houghton Mifflin. The next day it was accepted for publication. After a flurry of more legal activity—collecting death certificates of Janet and her father, locating her mother, signing contracts—the book was published in 1961. It came out with no interpretation, only a brief preface by the Hugheses, a glossary of terms that might be unfamiliar to readers, such as the word "pot," and a post-script by Becker. There has never been a hint of legal action concerning it. What very little royalty money it has earned has gone to a Chicago Area Project research fund.

The title *The Fantastic Lodge* was suggested by Everett Hughes, who noticed it in the following passage, referring to Janet's experience at the federal hospital in Lexington, Kentucky:

> I sat and listened mostly to them quack on, tell about the glamour of their outside lives, and outside junk histories. It's amazing! They don't become any less junkies, at all, for being in the place. All is junk, and that's all, you know; that's the way it is. This identification of yourself as a junkie. After the first six, eight months that I was making it, I never said, "Well, I'm a junkie," as an excuse or as anything. But now I say it constantly. I always refer to myself as a junkie, even when I'm not hooked or anything. And when you're introduced to some-body for the first time, the first thing you find out is whether he's a junkie or not. It's like belonging to some fantastic lodge, you know, but the initiation ceremony is a lot rougher.[27]

***

> I don't think anyone has written an article yet about how the junkie feels, you know, toward the whole of this legal setup. First of all he fears it, naturally, and is completely suspicious of it from the lowest nab all the way up to the judge because he feels he's getting cheated. He has this tendency to feel that he's a sick person in quotes, and not a criminal. And some-times it's just a cheap excuse, but he's still right, you know, in every sense. It's funny, the fringe group and some of the people who hang around the music world and so forth—like a

guy that told us somebody shook him down in the john at one of the joints, real proud of the fact. Nobody had! He was making it up, you know, a little story. He wanted to be busted, too.

The setup usually is that, first, you are picked up. If you're a fay this is by mistake almost always. With spades it's a persecution thing. And I think it's becoming more that way with fays, even so. These cats saying they want to help, they want to fight the problem, and really, it's almost too much to take. If you can pay off the nab in the first place who picks you up, solid, all the better. You know you're going to have to spread a little money around later on, even if you don't have to pay a lawyer and all the rest.

All this time I was asked absolutely no questions about my source of supply, about what was happening in the town, what I knew about, where junkies hung, anything. Anything that would have anything to do with the enforcement of the narcotics law. When I was down at the Main Station we talked about everything, the weather or how I started using junk, maybe, or how I felt about life or anything, but never, never anything that was going to do them any good.

On the lower level—the uniformed nab, the squad-car nab, the guy who's driving the paddy wagon, the small-time matron—the junkie is somebody you can kick the life out of and nobody can do anything to you because they're nowhere; they're junkies, you know. When you get up on the higher levels, at the Narcotics Unit itself, and when you get to the point where there is more information about junk, there's more tolerance and the attitude becomes one of "Oh, well, we have to do this. The public is down on everything. There's a lot of publicity and a lot going on. But, oh, what a drag." I don't think anyone really wants to be bothered enough to do anything genuine that's going to help anything. They pick up junkies as regularly as possible and book as many as they can as much as they can and send them away for as much as they can. Then they can say in their weekly statistics, "Four out of five junkies sent up for a year," or something.

But the people at the very top, the judges and the rest who should know most and who should be attempting most, after seeing these thousands and thousands of cases and not having a real understanding of any of them and just expecting them to straighten up after they get out of court and seeing them come back again, time after time, they've developed a tremendously cynical attitude. I mean, their philosophy about junk and junkies is very definitely that the junkie is no good to anyone, has no feeling toward anyone, and that maybe something more should be done for them; but under the existing laws that all they can do is—"two years!"

There's only one of that bunch that I consider had even a kindergarten knowledge of the problem. His attitude is sort of a "Well, I hate to be here and it really is too bad. But why don't you kids straighten up now, so we don't have to pick you up?" And he is aware of some of the significant things that have to do with drug addiction, like what the withdrawal symptoms really are and things like that. Most of the rest of them don't really know. They've absorbed the terminology; like in court now, you'll hear "spike," "fix," "junkie," "stash," "pad," things like that, coming right out of the nabs' mouth themselves; but they haven't absorbed what those words mean, the full significance of them, at all.

About the worst of the bunch, because he's in a position to do more for or against the average junkie coming up in front of the judge, is the prosecutor. He is out to get anything and everything that he can get. First of all, he'll take anything in the way of money, if it's large enough and pretty enough and pleasant enough, and if he doesn't have to screw around too much. Second, he's playing God twenty-four hours a day and that's a very heavy job, you know. He's the great avenger. These people have sinned, you know, and he's going to show them, that's all.

And the judge himself, I think somewhere deep down inside he must feel sort of badly about the whole thing. I mean, I don't think that *he* can kid himself that he's avenging the crimes that have been committed against humanity in the name of junk.

But the man I condemn most is the psychiatrist, because here is a man who supposedly is a court psychiatrist, supposedly should have enough understanding of human behavior to realize that these are definitely sick people and that something has to be done. If he were just, well, tough. But he's corrupt. And his pay-offs are much more organized than I think anyone else's in the whole setup.

And finally, I think the whole attitude in general, the court and the whole bunch, you know, is, once they have disposed of your case—in the best possible manner, of course, for instance with a two-year sentence, jail—this is supposed to take care of you. They wash their hands thereof—"Don't ever let me see you again in court!"—that's the idea. Or, "Don't let us ever pick you up again, because we've done it now. This is it. This is what we have to offer you, two years and make it."

So that's why it's not only going to fail and fail miserably but it's going to and has already made the problem far worse than it

was before they ever started it, because they have never succeeded in knocking off enough of the big peddlers or enough of
the syndicate. And they never will because they don't want to,
because this is their big source of money and because they look
at it as they do gambling. Exactly the same way. "Well, we'll
pick them up. We'll raid occasionally and get the little bas-
tards. But you know, so-and-so, the head of the syndicate, he's
a good guy, got a nice house"—and so forth and so on. And
that's the way it is.

But the general public, now they *do* feel abhorrence; the
junkie frightens them, I think. The junkie frightens them because they realize that this is something that no human is prepared to cope with at all; that even they, with a warm, normal
home and lovely background and a setup in society and so
forth, could somehow be hooked in the end. And it's true.
That's another reason why I'm very suspicious of those people
and of their feelings, because, actually, in all these loud pro-
testations about "Throw them all in jail! Get rid of them, preying on society!" et cetera, et cetera, all I can see is the terror
underneath it. And all that terror indicates to me is that they
have eyes [that is, *they* are interested in drugs—J. B.] almost,
in a weird sense. I could never trust anyone with an attitude
like that, ever. Not simply because of what they can do to you,
some pretty horrible things, but because they have just as irra-
tional an attitude as the junkie has.[28]

***

Outsiders: The Deviant and the Sociologist

There is no doubt that Shaw, McKay, and Kobrin worried about the
political repercussions of publishing *The Fantastic Lodge*. But there is no
way to account for the rapid change of IJR's attitude toward this project
after Shaw's death other than to attribute the earlier hesitancy to Shaw's
bias against Becker, or against the way the book was to be presented,[29] or
perhaps even somehow against the subject of drugs itself. On this last
point, though the book is hardly a manifesto in favor of drug addiction, the
"acceptance phenomenon" inevitable in oral history may have unsettled
Shaw: that is, the way a person speaks of certain things as normal within
his or her frame of reference, especially clear in a speaker with as strong a
skeptical voice as Janet's. Much of Shaw's thinking was based on acceptance of "conventional values," but Janet's sardonic glance somehow
calls all that into question as Shaw's life histories had not.

What is certain is that after World War II, when the profession of
sociology in general and sociology research and community organizing at
the Institute for Juvenile Research in particular had become established,

life histories were no longer widely used by sociologists. They had served their purpose of giving the profession and its reformist intentions a boost into the academic and philanthropic establishment; after that they were abandoned. But Howard Becker was not well established. He was in an "interstitial area" of his career, and he was definitely a marginal person among the IJR dramatis personae: he was not one of the inner circle around Clifford Shaw. For one thing, Becker was much younger than Shaw and his associates. For another, Shaw was never a participant in the community life he studied from a distance through life histories, whereas Becker's work as a pianist brought him into contact with the people he interviewed for his drug studies. In one place Becker says of his interviews: "Where it was possible and appropriate, I used the jargon of the [drug] user himself."[30] But Becker was not totally on "the other side"; he was somewhere in between. Like the William Whyte of *Street Corner Society,* Becker was a "college boy" and not dependent for survival on playing in jazz bands. Everett Hughes has said: "Becker was not a person who ever had any of the personal difficulties of the people he was working with and describing."[31] Becker's collegiate identity did not stand out so much because "many musicians were taking advantage of their benefits under the G.I. Bill, so the fact that I was going to college did not differentiate me from others in the music business."[32]

Since there is so little interpretation in *The Fantastic Lodge,* there is no evidence for any pattern of thought Becker might have had in working on it. (In fact, Becker did not construct a theory of addiction in this book and perhaps could not have done so at that point in his career: in this context the autobiography may be a way for a young—or even an older— sociologist to make an expert statement short of the full-fledged requirements of professional discourse.) But Becker's later thought contains ample evidence of the commonplaces we have found clustered around oral histories. These are especially evident in a paper Becker delivered in 1971 entitled "Labelling Theory Reconsidered." Some sociologists had interpreted labeling theory to mean that deviance was caused by law enforcement agencies' labeling a person an addict, a delinquent, or whatever. Becker sought to deny this simple interpretation. Rather, this position "*enlarges* the area taken into consideration in the study of deviant phenomena by including in it activities of others besides the allegedly deviant actor" (emphasis added). That is, rather than accept official arrest records of delinquents as given, one should question the activities of those who hold power over young people: parents, teachers, physicians, police, and court personnel. These moves, which are clearly manifest in *The Fantastic Lodge,*

> by making moral entrepreneurs objects of study as well as
> those they seek to control, violate society's hierarchy of credi-

bility. They question the monopoly on the truth and the
"whole story" claimed by those in positions of power and
authority. They suggest that we need to discover the truth
about allegedly deviant phenomena for ourselves, instead of
relying on the officially certified accounts which ought to be
enough for any good citizen.... They make it impossible to
ignore the moral implications of our work.[33]

Furthermore, labeling theory is not a theory: "I never thought the
original statements by myself and others warranted being called theories,
at least not theories of the fully articulated kind they are now criticized for
being." Labeling theory, according to Becker, is "a way of looking at a
general area of human activity, a perspective whose value will appear, if
at all, in increased understanding of things formerly obscure." Becker
then proceeds to use the term "interactionist theory of deviance." (After
all, "theory" and "theater" come from the same Greek root. In recent
years Becker has become immersed in studies of photography.)

In his article "Labelling Theory Reconsidered," Becker admonishes
his audience to look at "the mundane things people are actually doing":
"We ignore what we see because it is not abstract and chase after the
invisible 'forces' and 'conditions' we have learned to think sociology is all
about." Sociologists should be concerned if the people they write about
are not able to recognize themselves in their reports: that is, viewpoint
and language should not stray too far from the subject's (or object's) own.
This call for the concrete rather than the abstract also characterized the
early period in sociology, especially in W. I. Thomas's work, but the
recent period has seen no comparable use of oral history as an antidote
to abstraction, mainly because interest has centered on an area—the
political—that is not amenable to phenomenal penetration by the conventional life history.

Becker claims, as oral history demonstrates, that motivations of "deviants" are not dissimilar to motivations of socially conventional persons:
"They do what they do for much the same reasons that justify more
ordinary activities." On the whole, such groups cannot be psychologically disturbed because, "We see that activities thought deviant often
require elaborate networks of cooperation, such as could hardly be sustained by people suffering from disabling mental difficulties."

The most conspicuous contrast of *The Fantastic Lodge* with Clifford
Shaw's life histories is the absence of sociological commentary in Janet's
autobiography, which is "framed" merely by brief essays that set the
scenes of her work on the book and her death. This has political significance, for it means that an institution did not impose its interpretation on
the speaker's own words and her version of things. Not that IJR did not

want to do that: indeed, one of the reasons the book contains little sociological prose is that Shaw and his colleagues had asserted their rights to the material for so long that in the end everyone settled for publication, for whatever moral or public enlightenment effect it could have, even without a theoretical framework.

At any rate, Janet's story did not need annotation as the earlier ones did. For one thing, her narrative alternates between description of her feelings and experiences, observations on individuals and places, and reflections on various topics, as in the excerpt above. Shaw did the generalizing for his boys in footnotes and in his text; Janet, on the contrary, like all eloquent life history speakers, makes her own generalizations. She is, as the French edition puts it, "pleine d'invention,"[34] full of invention, the translation of the "resourceful" used in the English text. In addition, unlike Shaw's delinquents, who lived in "delinquency areas," which most readers had never visited, Janet moved from place to place in the urban environment: herself from a white, middle-class background, she encountered black musicians on Chicago's South Side, made contact with people in jails and at the federal drug treatment hospital in Kentucky, and interacted with students and professors at the University of Chicago. Except for her experiences with drugs, her life was not unfamiliar to anyone who had grown up in a large American city. Neither could her story have been accompanied by chapters on her arrest record, since she had not been arrested before the events depicted in the book itself.

Nor could some latter-day Burgess (or Burgess himself, who lived until 1966) have written about how typical Janet was, since she was not typical of drug users in Chicago, though her story was prophetic of the expansion of drug use among the white middle class in the 1960s, a social change that eventually provided a market for the book. Thus, to use a suggestion offered by Michael Connolly, she was not *typical,* but her story *became relevant.* She was *not representative;* autobiographical material is not good at determining or representing typicality anyway. Janet was *a representative:* she spoke for others about their common experiences, especially the experience of the ignorance and ineffectiveness of law enforcement personnel in dealing with addicts. As William James well said: "I took these extreme examples as yielding the profounder information. To learn the secrets of any science, we go to expert specialists, even though they may be eccentric persons, and not to commonplace pupils."[35] Is it likely that readers who begin with the notion that all addicts are dumb (in both senses) will come away from reading such a book with the notion that all are as acute as Janet? Surely the effect is altogether to diminish stereotypes through identification with an individual, not to replace one stereotype with its opposite, as if overcompensating. Rather than limiting the book's usefulness, the lack of interpretation and the delimitation of representativeness seems to have expanded it.[36] This is the only document we have encountered that has been translated into another language, in a *collection femme* (a series on women), edited by a friend of Sartre and Simone de Beauvoir.

This voice is as much clearer than the voices of Shaw's delinquents as the high-fidelity recordings of the 1950s are than the 78 r.p.m.'s of Shaw's day. To switch metaphors, it is a voice uninterrupted by "commercials" for the true sociological way or for community-based programs of delinquency prevention. (This, too, may have inhibited Shaw from supporting publication of the book.) The eloquence of the book lies partly in its continuity, if we recall Cicero's definition of eloquence as *motus animi continuus*—the continuous movement of the soul. *The Fantastic Lodge* even eschews chapter titles. From this viewpoint, and recalling the repetitiousness of Shaw's life histories, it appears that there is a stereotype of the delinquent's life history, despite the power life histories might have to dispell certain stereotypes. (The same may be said of lives of saints.) *The Fantastic Lodge,* on the other hand, transcends stereotypes and achieves a picture of a unique individuality.

"Janet" stands out as an individual also because she relates a broader range of her experiences than does Stanley in *The Jack-Roller.* (Recall Snodgrass's criticism.) Surely the drug experience is more likely to encourage introspection than the experience of beating up drunks. Dollard's complaint against Shaw about the absence of somatic references is partially overcome in *The Fantastic Lodge* also because of the nature of drug experiences. Janet's sexual life is included, too, while sex is for the most part omitted in Shaw's work, even though it is prominent in some of IJR's unpublished material. Janet explores her childhood and early youth more convincingly than Shaw's delinquents did, enabling a reader to get a better hold on this individual, a closer identification from the start. Like Mayhew, Janet was capable of metaphor, speaking in one place of "hurting colors" (p. 211). She was also capable of paradox and irony, humor, even if sardonic, and wonder:

> I used to lie in bed at night and talk to the baby after I felt
> movement. The first time I felt movement was a whole new
> world, a whole new feeling because now it wasn't just a hunk
> of something inside of me that I was carrying around but it was
> something that was moving, alive. It's a feeling approximating
> wonder, I think, at first.[37]

In the paperback edition of this book, a selection of Janet's poems appears. Here is one:

There were but two once
We were crowded
In the shell of me
But took turns
Polite as those in a public toilet.
Split centerwise I grew strangely.

I uncovered vast numbers
Of identities in me tonight
What I had thought only
A doubled departure
Smashed to an indefinite series
Sheaves of the forms
Flew like small white pigeons—
When I touched myself.

Do I like it?
No—(I don't know what other answer could be told)
But they are locked within me
And I must collect community taxes
For my multiplied society.

Of course, another contrast with the earlier documents was the tortuous path to publication. The only mention I have found of getting a life history writer to sign a release is in Krueger's "Autobiographical Documents" (p. 256), where advice is given to secure permission as soon as the document is finished, since the author may have second thoughts later on. Henry McKay has told me that there were never any such difficulties with the Jack-Roller or Shaw's other life historians. They were proud to be showing off. Shaw may have given some royalty money to Stanley the Jack-Roller, on a friendly basis, and when the American Antiquarian Booksellers reprinted *The Jack-Roller* (plus the other two life history books) in 1950 Stanley was sent $66.67 in royalties. In 1971 Stanley contacted the University of Chicago Press asking for royalties from the 1966 edition, but the Press replied that, since the copyright had not been renewed during the renewal year (1957–58), the book was in the public domain, though royalties were being paid to Shaw's widow. These life history publishing arrangements are never so innocent as they seem—not any more.

Though it is impossible to say definitely what effect *The Fantastic Lodge* has had, the aim of the book was clearly to generate appreciation in readers for the life of the drug addict. The Hugheses wrote in their preface: "Addicts live on one of the more secret margins between the respectable world and the underworld. Communication with ordinary people is not easy for them." Communication was one of Janet's motivations, and she excelled at it: "Perhaps the story would create more public understanding of people in her situation." Janet said:

> I suppose it's because no one can really understand what it's like to be locked up until they are locked up. I know people who haven't been locked up but they could still understand the sensation, you know. And, well, Roy the piano player, he was never locked up but he got me out in the end and he knew that I *had* to get out. Those people, there's something horrible about them, there must be, you know. And as I laid in the bed and I cursed every one of them. I cursed them until I couldn't talk any more. And that's when I felt most like a junkie—then. Everyone labeled me for one thing. But more than anything else, when you see everything the jail represents and the authorities represent and you see how they feel, the animosity they feel toward helpless, sick people, you know—you feel maybe the junkies aren't so bad after all; that maybe they're the cool ones and the nabs are the ones that are the wrong ones.[38]

Many of the words that had to be defined in the book's glossary are now commonplace. Is that an indication of social acceptance? If the deviant is put at a social distance from conventional society, to what extent does an autobiography narrow that gap, if only as an *image?* The main accomplishment of this book is to portray the image of a human being with a consciousness that no institution could bring into focus. The mode of *listening* that a reader might bring to the book might have been the ideal mode of treatment, but Janet never encountered this in the places she passed through. Haunting this book is the image of a consciousness that was doomed.

The Decline of Oral History in Sociology

After World War II life histories no longer held the prominent position in sociology they had occupied since the publication of *The Polish Peasant.* Sociology had become more theoretical, specialized, professionalized, and political, qualities that do not encourage the production of oral histories. Oral history has not utterly disappeared, however; it has assumed minor roles subordinate to sociology's dominant qualities: occasionally oral histories illustrate theory, open up new special areas, make important points outside professional discourse, and promote reforms. Although oral history has again begun to thrive, delinquency has not thrived as a subject in any of these popular or professional movements. The chief rhetorical means for attracting resources in "the juvenile justice system' today is not the oral history; it is the grant proposal.

The trends opposing oral history have been of two species: one narrowing, the other transcending. Specialization and professionalization have narrowed the scope of subject matter and the audience for any piece of social science writing. The subject area of the earlier life histories—the interstitial area between person and local environment—fit the psychological sociology of the time, but recent sociology has insisted on analysis of social structures in themselves, which oral histories hardly ever represent well. With a growing population of social scientists competing for recognition in a period of "normal science," to use Thomas Kuhn's term (each "hypothesis" connected with the name of its "supporter"), scientific inquiry has turned to smaller and smaller areas and problems. Howard S. Becker has written: "As sociology increasingly rigidifies and 'professionalizes,' more and more emphasis has come to be placed on what we may, for simplicity's sake, call the *single study*."[39] Becker points to the journal article, the Ph.D. thesis, and the research grant proposal as media crucial for sociologists today but uncongenial to life histories. (However, life histories did appear in the first two in the earlier period.) Social scientists are less interested in directly influencing nonprofessionals: influence flows through "programs" established by outside funding rather than through "readers." Even community programs are more likely to attract support by putting someone on the payroll than by cultivating the philanthropic volunteer, as in earlier times.

In any case, the science of sociology and efforts at social reform, which functioned together in Burgess and Shaw, have parted company. The older experiential sociology, stated in "categories that seemed most relevant to the people" being studied,[40] was replaced by a sociology with more systematic, self-referential, and self-coherent categories. The relevant language became not the everyday talk of an ordinary person, but rather a more artificial symbolic language probably not even intelligible to such a person. Concreteness is built into the discourse not by life histories but by surveys and references to fieldwork. The marginality of life history in the earlier period, when both sociology and in many cases its subject were interstitial, became, under the demands of theoretic accountability, contradiction and ambiguity that could not be tolerated. Oral histories cannot prove those hypotheses out of which the wall of science, to use Becker's image, must be built. The time had passed for new worlds scouted out by life histories.

At the same time that sociology was narrowing its focus by specialization and professionalization, it was also transcending its earlier method toward greater theoretical sophistication (which often seems sophistic) and its earlier subject matter toward study of societywide systems of power. (Both these moves were toward "system," with interest centering on justice; the result was a term not seen in the earlier period—"the juvenile justice system.") Students of society during this period were less likely to find Shaw's "delinquency area" problematic than they were to locate criminological problems in the distributions of social and political power. This required questioning those "conventional values" that Shaw had accepted. In 1943 C. Wright Mills wrote: "There are few attempts to explain deviations from norms in terms of the norms themselves, and no rigorous facing of the implications of the fact that social transformations would involve shifts *in them*." "If the 'norms' were examined, the investigator would perhaps be carried to see total structures of norms and to relate these to distributions of power. Such a structural point of sight is not usually achieved."[41] But today this structural viewpoint has taken command, both in theory and in action like Alinsky's, and oral histories have not seemed crucial to it. Data are located not in a geographical area but in class or economic cleavages, and therapeutic programs undertake the organization of areas larger than neighborhoods, larger than a young person is likely to be familiar with.

The problem of "labeling" delinquents by state personnel and procedures continues to be mentioned, as it was by Mayhew and Shaw,[42] but the process is studied in more detail. Political and legal problems in producing oral histories have increased, as evidenced by *The Fantastic Lodge*, and the most innovative work on delinquency has occurred in the juvenile court, where setting legal precedents to protect minors' rights is more important than attending to an individual's own story or even one person's testimony. The vocal event is not the oral history; it is the discourse of the advocate. This image of advocacy has even seemed to some to be at the center of the youth's own perception:

> The new image of the delinquent typifies these new trends. It is that of the delinquent as "aggrieved citizen." What is striking about this new image is that unlike the images associated with previous stages, this one represents an effort to view his world from the perspective of the delinquent himself. The image of the delinquent as "potential pauper," as "disaffiliated," and as "frustrated social climber" in contrast are all designations from the perspective of the reformer or the sociologist.[43]

But one must question whether any of these images of "the delinquent" are self-perceptions of the majority of delinquents; all appear to be categories imposed on experience by sociologists or reformers, with various tones of presumption and good intention, not least the "aggrieved citizen" strategy.

Oral histories of delinquents have not entirely disappeared, however. Their uses follow the trends above, the two most frequent being to illustrate theory and to promote reform. Analytic points are occasionally il-lustrated by brief quotations, usually abstracted from interviews on a specific research question rather than on a whole life. Longer documents may appear in a textbook, such as the fifteen-page "Gang Boy" in Dressler's *Readings in Criminology and Penology* (1964). These usually follow and thus instantiate statements of theory in a text. Contrast this with Angell's position on illustration:

> Several documents of some length may often serve as an in-troduction to the subject to be analyzed. They give the reader some orientation, what we call a "feel" for the scientific analysis to come. Such documents indicate in a broad way the type of situation with which the investigator was faced when he started work. In that sense they enable the reader to follow the various steps of the investigation intelligently.[44]

An ambitious effort to use a long life history to illustrate theory is Rettig's *Manny: A Criminal Addict's Story,* a book "written expressly for an academic audience with interests in deviance, crime, correction, and criminal justice."[45] "Although this book has as a central feature a provocative life history, our purpose in writing it has been to provide students with an academic exercise in examining the interrelationships of theory and the 'real world.'"[46] However, the fit between theory and experience in this book is rather loose: the last chapter attempts "an integrated theoretical perspective" on delinquency, but it makes no ref-erence to Manny's experience until the end, where it admits that Manny's adolescent gang activity was not delinquent. Perhaps theory seems to capture experience adequately only when experience is not presented in any full way—that is, when it is forgotten.

Many of these exercises in theory have political overtones. Rettig writes: "And if this book leads its readers to contemplate the types of social change that might ultimately minimize recurrences of the Manny Torreses in our society, it will have accomplished a very special objec-tive."[47] Denfeld claims: "Communication from 'inside,' that is from the offender's perspective, sensitizes us to the criminal nature of American society."[48] According to Chambliss:

> It is, as Harry says in chapter six, the police, the prosecuting attorneys, the fix and the judges who benefit most directly from professional theft. The thieves end up impoverished and in prison. It is only when the situation changes that we will see the death of professional theft. American society and Ameri-can criminal law being what they are we are not likely to see any profound changes in that regard unless, of course, there is a revolution.[49]

However, authors of such books apparently never consider who will read the book, what effect it might have in the direction desired, and what a new system might be.

Other uses of youths' own stories aim at sensitizing readers to the sufferings of young people, without specifying reforms that would in any case probably become tomorrow's jails or other means of confinement. In *Children in Jail*, Thomas J. Cottle says: "For me, the act of befriending, and inevitably working on the *child's* behalf, is the noble experience."[50] Cottle skillfully interweaves his own description with quotations from young people, but these are almost always anecdotal rather than comprehensive: that is, the account is altogether too much under the control of Cottle's perspective for one to call these oral histories. At the same time the focus of each account is not the community area but the individual and the family situation that causes suffering. In another book, *Private Lives and Public Accounts*, Cottle claims that "political ideology is all pervasive and influential,"[51] but Cottle does not make explicitly political interpretations in his texts. Nevertheless, his dialogue or conversational format is suited to interventions by an interpreter, manifesting meanings not obvious in a story itself.

Oral histories may also be present in marginal contexts of professional communication. Bruce Jackson has put this well in a personal communication:

> Human documents permit a sociologist to say things he couldn't say otherwise without a terrific amount of documentation. To say something in my own voice as a university professor requires, in the coin of the academic realm, that I supply certain stylized documentary evidence. What can be terrific about these "human documents" is they free the reporter of the responsibility of objectivity. How can you be condemned for being non-objective when you're merely presenting raw data? One's professional competence, one's political orientation, one's writing style—none of these matters in this kind of work, because there is always the fallback position: "It's not me talking. It's them. You've got to listen to what they say."

However, Jackson himself in publishing personal documents surely has not been free of the responsibility of objectivity, and perhaps has had even more responsibilities and other moral concerns than in simply presenting his own views. His statement does give one reason life histories are absent from sociology. Nevertheless, his locating life histories on the margins of professional discourse indicates their usefulness in opening up terra incognita, though not the whole of the sociological field as life histories did in the 1920s.

In *Love and Commitment,* the most recent life history to come from the Institute for Juvenile Research, Gary Schwartz and Don Merten use quotations from a series of life history interviews to shift from materialistic and psychological interpretations of love to a cultural exploration. Their account is organized by four "models," three "perspectives," and three "modes of consciousness," loosely discriminated topics of a sort familiar in oral history inquiries. Like Bruce Jackson with his *Thief's Primer* and Becker with *The Fantastic Lodge,* this project was not planned as such but grew out of another activity.[52] That is, originality may emerge from the marginal position in which one finds oneself and from the sometimes considerable efforts necessary to make sense out of a recalcitrant document that one is determined to publish.

Another example of the marginal use of life histories is Annabel Faraday and Kenneth Plummer's recent efforts to open up the field of sexual deviance to sociological rather than psychological inquiry. Thus life histories are again both exploratory (what they call the "ad hoc fumbling around" method) and "displacers" of subject matter toward the sociological. In an article characterizing their work, many familiar concepts make an appearance, apparently not so much out of familiarity with the literature we have covered as because of characteristics of the material itself.[53] They speak of the need for "sensitizing concepts" and ordering life histories by means of "themes," and one of their "social" goals is to destigmatize sexually stigmatized groups "through providing them with a platform." They offer the caveat that life histories cannot locate the truth of experience in larger structures, and they contrast themselves with "armchair theorists." In addition, Faraday and Plummer comment about the methodological marginality of life histories and the professional marginality of sociologists who use them, especially those who study such social marginals as sexual deviants. What is new in Faraday and Plummer's article, as well as in the writings of Thomas Cottle and Carl Klockars, is a greater willingness to reveal the sociologist's own activities in acquiring personal documents and to reflect on relevant ethical issues: indeed, perhaps these are two aspects of the same problem, each calling for the other. The appearance of these issues, however, indicates how little we know about processes of collecting life histories of delinquents, especially in the earlier period.

Ten

Conclusions: Genesis, Function, Accomplishment

Which images convey which realities and which fail to convey them or mystify and obscure them? Which realities are susceptible to such images and which are not? Which realities get communicated through the language and which are somehow lost?

Steven Marcus

The "economy" of discourses—their intrinsic technology, the necessities of their operation, the tactics they employ, the effects of power which underlie them and which they transmit—this, and not a system of representations, is what determines the essential features of what they have to say.

Michel Foucault

Probably each art and science has often been developed as far as possible and has again perished.

Aristotle

Persuaded of the wholly human origin of everything human, a blind man eager to see who knows the night has no end, he is always in motion. The boulder rolls on.

Albert Camus, *The Myth of Sisyphus*

In the beginning was the Word; shortly after came the Record.

Joseph Gusfield

If the past is a guide to the future, it is unlikely that criminologists will use history to guide their thought and action, the problems being so urgent and the public so resistant to too long a detour into expertise to reach solutions. Thus they will not build on the past but will repeat it in some areas. Add to this tradition of amnesia in criminology the typical resistance of "scientists" to admitting and thus refining their rhetorical intentions. The result is that the following summary of the uses of delinquents' oral histories, as schematic as it must be given the few examples available and the obscurity of some of the material, is probably a fairly accurate picture of future uses, perhaps in the developing nations of Asia and Africa, growing out of indigenous oral traditions.

I began with three basic questions, to which I shall now try to give coherent answers: Under what conditions do delinquents' oral histories come into being? How do they function? What have been their accomplishments?

Conditions of Genesis
Social Conditions
The most basic social condition for the genesis of delinquents' oral histories is rapid urban growth, both in size of population and in complexity of life, resulting from industrialization. This gives rise to a larger urban lower class with increasing rates of juvenile delinquency, to a middle class growing both in numbers and in power, and a cleavage between lower and middle classes in which the lower-class delinquent is exiled from the sight of the middle-class public. It is this split, this obscuring of visibility, that delinquents' oral histories seek to overcome.

Delinquency in the middle and upper classes does not as a rule appear in oral histories. Perhaps the middle-class audience (or perhaps merely the publishers) thinks that the life of the middle-class youthful offender would be familiar to them; or they may not want to look at their own delinquency; or obtaining such documents might be more difficult than obtaining information from slum or ghetto youths. Efforts to force the middle and upper classes to admit criminality in their own ranks are more likely to use conflict strategies, a different rhetoric entirely. Clearly there are exceptions to this, as well as examples that combine rhetorics. But the major instances of delinquents' oral histories have been and are likely to be about life "on the other side," not in the middle-class reader's own living room.

Despite the separation of classes, which had had closer contact in rural areas, another condition for the genesis of delinquents' histories is an individualism and ferment that pervades the whole society. Conventional values are not effectively communicated from parents, who may have grown up on farms, to offspring growing up in an urban slum. The child is drawn instead to "getting his" out in the fantastic, booming city, a city being created by highly competitive capitalists pursuing their fortunes in the absence of absolute monarchy, dictatorship, or even restrictive legislation. The result of all this individual initiative is a mass society that is, oddly enough, opposed by increased individualism, evident in the rise of autobiography, as well as in a new wave of writing about crime and famous criminals and detectives and in new interest in the "common man." The punishment thought fit for criminal offenders is loss of freedom, which entails having one's personal movement limited and being removed from the sight and hearing of the public. The offender is deprived of his personality, that is, his *persona,* the mask a Greek actor in antiquity used to amplify his voice and character before an audience. (In reestablishing the offender's personality before the public, the oral history is an escape from the essential meaning, if not from the walls, of a prison.)

Individualistic innovation occurs everywhere in this type of society. Louis Cazamian called the years 1830–50 in England "a creative and fecund period, during which theses and movements were adumbrated of which the following years saw the success and expansion."[1] This also applies to the years 1920–40 in the United States; each period has been called an "age of reform," and both saw major appearances of delinquents' oral histories. There were innovative attempts to study and prevent crime and to reform both criminals and the reforming institutions. Professionals began to pay attention to the individual offender—to listen to the delinquent's own story and even to publish it as a demonstration that "the criminal" does indeed have individuality, personality, and talent as well as to support the claim that the fledgling criminologist does indeed have a viable subject matter.

Programs of private voluntary philanthropy were created by clerics seeking to retain power by secularizing a waning religious motive, by women seeking power in acceptable ways, and by other social activists trying to make a society work but avoiding government interference. Terence Morris has written:

> The enforcement of social reform which does not depend
> wholly on idealism, requires compulsive legislation, but such is
> anathema to the advocates of *laissez faire,* who abounded in
> the warm climate of unrestricted capitalist expansion in
> America, just as they had done in Britain some three-quarters
> of a century earlier.[2]

The existence of such vigorous philanthropy is probably the sine qua non for the genesis of delinquents' oral histories. Since one of the functions of these publications is to attract volunteers to philanthropic programs, the relative absence of these associations outside Anglo-American societies may account for the apparent lack of such histories in countries besides England and the United States.[3]

Rhetorical Conditions

Rhetorical conditions for the genesis of oral histories of juvenile offenders, and of course of many others, are also social, but they relate more directly to the context of persuasion. First, distance: Insofar as people have *direct* contact with delinquents and their environment, there is less of a role for the artificial contact brought about by oral history, though such documents may serve to initiate students or to reorient caseworkers toward an expanded, more sociological view of a life.

Second, motivation: One can imagine a variety of motives that might attract a reader to a delinquent's oral history: voyeurism, a desire for vicarious adventure and even criminality, philanthropic benevolence, or an interest connected with one's profession or course of study. But it seems unlikely that these histories would exist in the numbers they do in Mayhew's and Shaw's works if the public at large were not uneasy over the growth of crime, perhaps even afraid of the prospect of revolution. The histories appear to be a way of heading off a rush to the barricades by setting up a channel of cross-class communication, though this at best consists of alternating speeches rather than dialogue, and though only a miniscule part of "the public at large" ever sees one of these histories. Instead, the histories promote various programs in which professionals take a position between middle and lower classes: thereafter, communication flows through increasingly self-protective institutions.

Third, receptivity: Conditions must be right for persuasion to take place. The audience cannot be so fearful of or even repelled by a subject that they refuse to consider it. And institutions and criminologists cannot fear reprisals from the public or a specific audience—whether or not they are right to do so—as happened with *The Fantastic Lodge*. In addition, it does not seem that oral histories of delinquents or other "deviants" will be at the very beginning of any movement: a society, an audience, or a reader must be prepared, "warmed up," before coming to the oral history. When Mayhew wrote, a series of novels and government reports had begun to remove stigma and strangeness from the poor. Before Shaw, psychologists had opened up the possibility that a delinquent might have not only a normal body but also a normal mind, though perhaps a disturbed one. Behind these developments were political outbursts: revolutions in France, watched uneasily by Englishmen; a revolution in Russia, predisposing Americans toward preemptive measures. The reason for this tardiness of oral history lies in the facts of its publication: as innovative as a document may appear, as effective as it may be in creating or at least expanding an audience, a publisher is unlikely to invest in it unless a market is already there—and the market must be opened up by something other than oral history. In the social movements in which they have recently appeared (the black, women's, and gay movements), oral history and autobiography have come at a second stage, after more overtly political action.

Fourth, credibility: The receptive audience must believe in the authenticity and truthfulness of the presentation. A published story is credible insofar as it is backed up by a reputable publisher and a respected criminologist. Everything here is image, and the images can dim or brighten unexpectedly: after writing three books to demonstrate that he was innocent of a murder, and despite the endorsement of so influential a public figure as William F. Buckley, Jr., Edgar Smith finally admitted his guilt after all. With this as precedent one might be wary of any offender's "story." On the other hand, during the radical movement in the United States during the late 1960s and early 1970s, in some circles criminal offenders were more likely to be respected and believed than criminologists. The normal situation is for the middle-class criminologist to vouch for the delinquent: the middle-class reader identifies first with the criminologist, then with the offender.

Finally, the pistic conditions (from the Greek *pistis,* meaning "belief"): Even assuming all the potentialities discussed above, oral history will not actually be used unless it is needed to work some change of perception or belief on its audiences. Delinquents' oral histories are most effective when the beliefs of potential audiences are either transcendental or physical, either "above" or "underlying" phenomena. That is, a social, environmental picture comes into being at those times in history when the public holds (but is receptive to letting go of) absolutist moral notions about the evil of delinquents, or when researchers hold (but are tiring of the intellectual fashion of) abstract theories about delinquents; or when the public or professionals have focused on physical or psychological characteristics or an alleged "nature" of delinquents without having resolved certain contradictions of explanation or overcome failures of therapy. The function of the oral history in these cases is to bring the perception of delinquency *down* from moral judgment or abstract speculation, or *up* from the nature, body, or unconscious of a delinquent, in each case realigning perception to the region of social action and speech. Thus oral history does not arise conspicuously when, as today, the fundamental paradigm of delinquency is not of those alien varieties. I shall return to this configuration of positions below.

Personal Conditions
Oral history also requires the presence of a criminologist with certain characteristics. Perhaps the most prominent trait of people who have collected delinquents' oral histories is their revulsion against hypocrisy, their irreverence, even their subversiveness. E. P. Thompson's reference to Mayhew's "glorious irreverent statements of the patterers, street sellers," and so forth was echoed by Allport in 1942: "The recent surge of interest in life documents is, in part, a protest against the laboratory emphasis and against the aridity of behaviorism. To a certain degree, therefore, enthusiasm for the personal document is deliberately an act of scientific irreverence."[4] More recently Howard S. Becker wrote: "Everyone knows that responsible professionals know more about things than laymen, that police are more respectable and their words ought to be taken more seriously than those of the deviants and criminals with whom

they deal. By refusing to accept the hierarchy of credibility, we express disrespect for the entire established order."[5] Another noteworthy quality of the oral history collector is a compassion and kindness that encourages people to open up and tell the stories of their lives. The collector of oral histories is an egalitarian who is even willing to let others "upstage" him, though more or less within the framework of his own drama.

The inventor of the oral history, such as Mayhew, Clay, and Thomas, may be an inventive person overall, interested in languages and oratory. He (or she—a reminder) may have had some experience with a medical or physical science, which strengthened empiricist habits. In essential respects he may be self-taught. Partly as a result of that, the specific background is typically marginal to the mainstream of a profession. Or the profession itself or the person may be in a transitional phase in relation to more established fields or careers. If one were in a central position of power, either in government or in an academic discipline, one would employ a less ambiguous rhetorical medium, such as a law (which Joseph Gusfield has recently treated as a means of communication) or a journal article. But the social scientist or the innovator in sociology must first attract an audience, a need oral history may help meet. That is, it seems unlikely that oral histories would make a major appearance unless called into being by a "maverick intellectual," as Philip Rieff has called the first generation of psychoanalysts, the sort of people who "invariably fill the ranks of a new discipline until it becomes economically respectable."[6] Once in the mainstream, criminologists may use oral histories or similar material to express reformist positions that do not seem adequately supported by scientific evidence. The oral history works at the margins of what is professionally possible.

One result of the criminologist's marginality is that he identifies more easily with delinquents than would a more institutionalized person, and they with him, though one must question just what such "personal relationships" involve. What Blumer called an "apperception mass" from broader experience is also essential: one could hardly devise a position on delinquency having merely read about delinquents, even if one had read a great many of their oral histories. Mary Carpenter and Helen Hughes, who used oral histories collected by someone else, had had direct contact with "the real thing" and had experience beyond the literary to draw on in their writing. On the other hand, the marginal criminologist should not have had so much experience with delinquents that his initial freshness of perception has been replaced by theoretical concepts or the need to defend a reformist strategy.

Another constituent of the criminologist's marginality is an unconventional comprehensiveness of vision. Robert E. Park once wrote about the ethnically marginal man: "Inevitably he becomes, relatively to his cultural milieu, the individual with the wider horizon."[7] This quality was most clearly present in the two outstanding inventors of oral history we have covered, Mayhew and Thomas. Each was more interested in opening up a new world of phenomena and action than in organizing a system of concepts. (Thus marginal knowledge is another genetic condition of delinquents' oral histories.) The person who *specializes* in delinquency may come after the pioneer has laid out a whole scheme of society in which delinquency is only a part, or the pioneer himself may turn to this particular problem at a later phase of his career. At any rate, the criminologist who specializes in delinquency may depend on other specialists for background information about areas adjacent to his, as Becker has pointed out that the Chicago sociologists did, and he may depend on the supplemental expertise of a partner, probably a statistician. The large vision has begun to be divided up, a process that ultimately leads to the disappearance of oral history, because oral history is not pinpointed enough for a specialization. Oral history is the pincushion.

The most intriguing feature of those who invent or make extensive use of delinquents' oral histories is contradictions in their characters that are resolved not analytically but productively: they are the sources of vitality and originality in their work. Humpherys has said of Mayhew: "All the best of Mayhew's writing had in it this subtle tautness between art and science, the general and the specific, engagement and distance."[8] The criminologist alternates between formulating general statements about society and showing, treating, and helping individual offenders. For example, Shaw did not resolve or even try to resolve questions about the connection of his ecological statistics with his case histories, to use Finestone's terms, but he found the tension between a science of society and the reform of individuals and communities productive. Or the criminologist may be ambivalent about conventional middle-class values. In some cases this reflects contemporary shifts of opinion, but it may relate more directly to his acceptance of all the values of his audience except their beliefs about the treatment of delinquents. The major conflict arises from his dual role of thinker and activist: he sees himself as a "scientist" who puts forth a "theory," but the need for action seems much more urgent than the speculations of "armchair theorists." Oral history itself seems to be a "bisociation," to use Koestler's term, or a scientific outlook and a reformist motivation that turns a theory into a message. Furthermore, oral histories depend on the prospect of reform, not on its achievement: a different form of narrative is appropriate to show successes of a program. Of course, the danger is that the dialectic among these various elements will sag into mere confusion.

If our criminologist takes a place marginal between thought and action, science and literature, theory and reform, individual and society, particular and general, conventional and unconventional, proposal and achievement, then he himself cannot take any of the extreme positions, outlined above, that audiences may hold. These positions can be divided into two species: (1) a theological or moralist position would produce prescriptions for what ought to be rather than dealing with what is. A legal position would propose appropriate punishments rather than making plans for social reform. A theoretical system would find little place for oral history's "lower level" of discourse. Action toward changing a political system would bring to the fore a charismatic leader whose autobiography could be used as an exemplary guide. (2) Neither would a criminologist produce oral histories if he held that offenders are innately criminal or that delinquency is inherited, or that all delinquents are mentally ill. That is, positions that transcend individual experience (1) and those that underlie it (2) are as inimical to the production of oral histories when held by a *criminologist* as they are essential when held by a *potential audience* whose opinions the criminologist will try to change. Each of these positions tends toward abstraction from experience, and in each case the speech of the expert or leader is the more significant discourse. Further, each position has its own genres of expression, with its own potentialities and genetic circumstances.

The criminological position most favorable to oral history tends toward a social psychology or psychologized sociology. Studies of psychic structure and social structure in themselves tend at best to include brief illustrative quotations. Just as language is a medium of communication between individuals, so oral history has as primary subject matter the interaction and communication of an individual with the persons around him. Its subject is the field of "symbolic interactionism." All this can be visualized by adapting a scheme of terms from the philosopher Richard McKeon:[9]

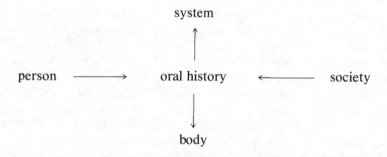

Take a standpoint in any one of the four surrounding "places" and you will be outside the region of oral history, though *system* may appear in oral history literature thematically transformed into comprehensive vision and *body* may appear as statistic. The region of oral history is not, however, the vertical or "ontic" axis (of transcending or underlying things), but rather the horizontal or "phenomenal" plane (of appearances), to use McKeon's terms, at the *intersection* of person and society. This place may be discursively located in one way or another, but whatever particular concepts are used to fix it, locating an inquiry in that place is an essential condition for the genesis of delinquents' oral histories. The consequences for subject matter and intention become all too obvious when one realizes that this horizon is constituted simply by the three traditional terms of rhetoric: speaker-speech-audience.

Technical Conditions
The essential technical or material conditions fall into two groups. In the context of *acquisition,* there must be a meeting place, an interviewer, and a juvenile offender. In the context of *presentation,* one needs a way to check truthfulness, to edit, and to publish. More specific conclusions here risk being "commonplace" in a pejorative sense. Not much is said here not only because I decided not to make these material conditions my main object of inquiry, but because there is little discussion of them in published histories. Although these criminologists see themselves as scientists working in a microanalytical tradition, they apparently assume that developing a personal relationship with a delinquent and transmitting urgent messages to an audience are more important than analyzing the many small causes that influence the acquisition and publication of those messages—more important than giving an autobiographical account of themselves. A little movement toward giving the reflexive account has taken place recently, apparently connected with an increased consciousness of ethical aspects of the process, but the evidence remains meager. Perhaps favorable conditions for the genesis of sociologists' oral histories are not the same as of delinquents'.

Despite this, a few observations may be made that are neither false nor trivial. The primary object in acquiring an oral history is a *continuous* flow of narrative, because that is the most important formal feature of the most readable documents. To the degree that the editor must create this quality by eliminating questions and contriving transitions, the authenticity of the document is diminished; the editor might just as well conduct and reproduce a dialogue. Thus the crucial task in an oral history project of this type is to find a person who is capable of speaking at length without being questioned frequently. In this case the speaker is a juvenile offender, probably though not necessarily adjudged legally, a person whose voice or viewpoint has a unique though not eccentric quality, who tells a story that "represents," even if it is not absolutely typical of, many other people. This speaker should have talent for relating information on specific points, narrating events, and pulling together incidents and observations under general perspectives or opinions. He or she will probably be about twenty years old, at some distance from the events. (The criminologist will probably not be a great deal older.) One may have to interview ten to twenty people to obtain a statement the length of Mayhew's and fifty to eighty to obtain a book-length autobiography. The main technical consideration in this process is simply to remove causes of anxiety or inhibition and to motivate the speaker, especially through the desire for self-improvement. The best interviewer is the "sociological stranger," someone who is curious and understanding but on the margins of the speaker's milieu (see below pp. 279–80).

Documents to be published must contain crucial points that can be checked against other evidence or testimony. Here again the process seems rather informal. In any case, verification of statements about internal matters, such as emotions and attitudes, is perhaps impossible, though consistency under repetition is reassuring. Without unedited transcripts it is impossible to study the editorial process: the criterion seems to be not to violate what one imagines to be an informed (not a deceived) reader's trust. An editor's addition of commentary, footnotes, italics, brackets, and so forth, creates a plurivocity, to use Paul Ricoeur's word, or a "choral testament," to use John Updike's image, that may have aesthetic value or political significance. Though the editor may include passages for general human interest, the aim is to avoid what Spinoza referred to as *res singulares*, radically particular items, and instead to trace a line of action that is like a plot. Since an oral history should not be distracted by too much small detail, it does not have the flexibility of participant observers' reports to cover a point at some length: this would impede the oral history's momentum. But what the history lacks in *detail* it should make up for in *presence*.

Finally, published oral histories need a favorable medium of publication, not a publisher ideologically resistant to the message or worried about recriminations. In the absence of a vigorous press (think of London newspapers about 1850, the University of Chicago Press about 1930), much less in the absence of widespread literacy, the oral history even where uttered would not reach beyond its utterance.

Limitations

The oral histories we have studied have been criticized for a variety of shortcomings, but, in the larger historical view I have taken, some of the faults seem to be inevitable limitations of a genre of literature. Before discussing the functions delinquents' oral histories might do well, let us examine those functions that it seems they could perform but that in reality they never have and probably never will.

Subject Matter

Surely realities that transcend individual experience—social, political, cultural, economic, and theoretic systems—and those that underlie it— somatic and psychic structures—may be inferred from the events of history, which are thereby diagnosed or interpreted. But the oral history does not directly present those states or processes. Not even the most sophisticated autobiographer is likely to linger over the somatic underpinnings of experience, unless they intrude, say, in the form of an illness. Psychologists have long complained about this deficiency of autobiographies, including those of psychologists, and the related absence of data on hereditary antecedents. In the study of delinquency, photographs have been the equivalent for physical anthropology of oral histories for sociology. In the other wing of the "medical model," psychiatry and psychology, oral histories do not give data about early childhood or the unconscious; they do not give an adequate picture of family interaction; they do not show evidence of much introspection, which is hardly encouraged in the environment the histories typically show; they do not provide a basis for explaining why some individuals are delinquent while others living in the same family or community are not, or why a youth turns to one form of delinquency rather than another.

Nor have delinquents' oral histories or even the commentary accompanying them demonstrated community organization, community organizing, or the operation of *a* community organization. Shaw's histories did not even directly explore the structure of community disorganization. Social disorganization was one cause of delinquency in an individual, but how did those "traditions of delinquency" in a "delinquency area" start, and what connection did they have with the larger society? In a sense, all the intentions of oral history are "political" in that they aim at persuading citizens and ultimately at changing institutional policies. But in the sense of manifesting connections of a delinquent's life in a neighborhood with the larger society and its networks of power, the oral history as it has been used has not been political. (One reason for this nonpolitical stance is that criminologists who have used oral histories have been so preoccupied with fighting a rearguard action against the concept of the delinquent as stupid or sick that they have not had the opportunity to expand their vision to the larger social and political area.)

In addition, the typical absence in oral history schemes of studies of power structures in delinquent gangs leads one to believe that those schemes simply do not have the conceptual tools to begin a political analysis: this is one reason the concept of a subculture is not developed, though it is clearly implied. This nonpolitical position gives little attention to questions about biases in procedures for the arrest and prosecution of juveniles. Even an oral history account of the juvenile court in terms of the youth's experience has yet to appear. For all the talk about individual attention, juvenile courts apparently do not enhance individuality or give an opportunity for an experience.[10]

If the oral history and its surrounding commentary do not explain that crucial point of police and court action at which an individual becomes "a delinquent," neither do they explain, or even give a means of explaining, other basic intersections that a comprehensive theoretic system might attempt to account for, such as interconnections among body, personality, neighborhood, and social and political systems. Nor do they resolve contradictions between appreciating an individual's unique perspective so as to enhance casework and letting an individual speak only as a reporter of local conditions in order to promote a plan of social change in which casework is considered beside the point. Probably the archcontradiction in these oral histories is the approach to changing a *system* by emphasizing *individual* experience: it sounds "humanistic" enough and thus a "good thing to do," but it seems to be a category mistake, a distracting and disastrous intrusion of personality into what should be understood and approached as a system that transcends individuals, a point Richard Sennett has made.[11]

Method

Participant observers' reports can provide more detail than oral histories. Though commentary accompanying the histories may compensate for this by filling out the context, this supplementary information usually merely supports the story rather than, for example, putting a speaker's perspective into relief by contrast with other viewpoints: Denzin recommends "triangulation" of viewpoints,[12] but that methodological refinement goes far beyond the usual practice of oral history in criminology. In some cases it is not even possible to determine historical factors in oral histories, since time, place, nationality, ethnic group, or other factors may have been removed to generalize the story.

The same detail is missing from accounts of the method of collecting and processing the oral history. Janet's gossiping with the Beckers, Stanley's telling Shaw and McKay the funny things that happened to him in jail, are nowhere presented, as they might profitably have been, to reveal concretely how the story came into being and to demonstrate human qualities by showing interaction in intimate situations. Criminologists who have not hesitated to relate delinquents' stories have failed to give any picture of their own lives or any narrative about their own procedure in verifying or editing documents or selecting which documents to publish. All these tasks have probably seemed informal and commonplace when perceived through the rhetorical lens they were in fact using: they were simply aware of getting a story told that obviously needed telling. But one might have thought that as scientists they would have turned their oral history scope on their own activities. Perhaps the requirement that the scientist be "nonsubjective" prevented this.

If not detail, can delinquents' oral histories provide proof? A researcher might collect a great many documents to test a hypothesis, but unless it is a hypothesis about oral histories, this would be a waste: other instruments could generate run-of-the-mill data more quickly and economically. Presenting a number of histories might have rhetorical functions, however, giving readers an impression of authenticity or of masses of people, especially when used in conjunction with statistics. Of course, a single piece of new information could come from an oral history, as from any other source.[13] But oral histories neither constitute nor easily support "knowledge," unless one means some sort of knowledge uniting the general and the individual.[14]

If oral histories cannot conclusively prove a theory, can they disprove one? According to Becker:

> The Jack-Roller can serve as a touchstone with which to evaluate theories that purport to deal with phenomena like those of Stanley's delinquent career. Whether it is a theory of the psychological origins of delinquent behavior, a theory of the roots of delinquency in juvenile gangs, or an attempt to explain the distribution of delinquency throughout the city, any theory of delinquency must, if it is to be considered valid, explain or at least be consistent with the facts of Stanley's case as they are reported here. Thus, even though the life history does not in itself provide a definite proof of a proposition, it can be a negative case that forces us to decide a proposed theory is inadequate.[14]

Becker goes on to point out that some sociologists accept exceptions to generalizations, so that a theory may be retained but reduced in scope of application. Or they may use exceptions as guides to further inquiry: "the negative case will respond to careful analysis by suggesting the direction the search should take."[15] Although more recent sociologists, of a more theoretical and sophisticated methodological bent than the earlier ones, may do this with the *cases* they encounter, this does not seem to be the way early sociologists operated with life-history *documents*. Both Healy and Shaw came to realize the inadequacy of then-popular theories partly through their contact with cases, but they perceived those inadequacies from the viewpoint of a new position that had been suggested by their background or taught as part of their training in a new field. In the context of established paradigms, life histories have not functioned well in evaluating theories, because the paradigm persists in some form, no matter what empirical attack it comes under. Lombroso was refuted, but genetic research into the causes of criminality still goes on. The psychological approach to delinquency was not successfully eliminated by the documents and ecological statistics that demonstrated the group nature of delinquency. Why are there delinquency areas? The psychologist cannot say. But the psychology of delinquency is still a thriving business. Following Thomas Kuhn, we must conclude that the evaluation of theories has not been so nonsocial as Becker makes it out to be in his *Jack-Roller* introduction.

Angell says that tentative sociological formulations using personal documents "are almost always influenced by pre-existing theory in a particular field. Thus they are both inductive and deductive."[16] Allport points to a "strange mixture of induction and illustration" in the use of personal documents.[17] One might even be suspicious that the ubiquity of the theme of communication in oral histories and the theories that use them reveals paradigmatic assumptions rather than a truth uncovered in the data. Doubtless this would be quite damning were it not that "truths uncoverable in data" is also laden with paradigmatic assumptions. Fortunately, each paradigm seems to capture a part of reality, in a way that philosophic inquiry has not yet resolved.

It appears that life histories have a central place in scientific innovation. Indeed, we have found them in especially innovative periods in the history of criminology, in what might be called interstitial periods. Becker claims that life histories may provide a basis for making assumptions about areas marginal to a main area of research, giving a "rough approximation to the direction in which truth lies." When an area becomes stagnant, life histories may suggest new variables, new questions, and new processes.[18] This is plausible. But has any criminologist ever used life histories this way, without that "apperception mass" or larger experience referred to above? Angell has put this point well:

> Personal documents may be employed as a means of securing conceptual "hunches." By immersing oneself in documents which are thorough and full of insight one may secure leads to the identity of the most fruitful angle of approach to a given problem, that is, the angle which will bring into focus those aspects of the phenomena that are particularly significant from a theoretical standpoint. This getting of new "slants" is a relatively rare occurrence because it takes an unusually curious and independent mind to break away from the traditional modes of conception. But nothing is more necessary to scientific progress. The Darwins and Einsteins are all the more precious because they are few.
>
> New conceptual "hunches" are few because they spring from breadth of grasp and flexibility of mind—a rare combination. When a person develops such a hunch it is probably a

2

product of his whole scientific and personal experience rather than any particular segment of it. Therefore we should hardly expect to say positively: "This came from studying personal documents." Even though the individual himself thinks that it did, he could hardly prove it. For our purposes it is enough if we can be satisfied that personal documents played some part in the development of his conceptual innovation.[19]

Oral histories have appeared at crucial turning points in the history of criminology partly because they express the criminologist's exploratory thought experience, but also because he uses them to communicate his new vision in order to attract adherents. Oral history itself has not rejuvenated a new field so much as it has expanded an audience, or urged a new audience or a new generation of workers to take the sociological viewpoint. Perhaps new beginnings, especially in certain fields, are made by the kind of person who would be interested in oral history: oral history represents that "pre-predicative" (rather than a "pre-test") mode of consciousness of which existentialists have spoken, which precedes and underlies the formation of propositions, otherwise known as hypotheses. The single terms that accompany oral histories, such as Thomas's four wishes, often have more a heuristic than a classificatory function, as John Dollard in 1935 wrote about the topic "culture and personality": "In the present state of social science the terms are used as a vague gesture in the direction of some unknown field of knowledge."[20]

Rhetoric
A third series of limitations contains not inadequacies of scientific subject matter or method but deficiencies of communicative capacity itself, limitations on what can be presented, as well as on how and to whom it is presented.

Though delinquents' oral histories are conspicuous advances over other means of communication in presenting "the delinquent as a human being," these narratives still fall short of reproducing the features of a unique person, and thus they do not stimulate in readers an intense perception of a delinquent's individuality. Instead, the histories with commentary give the impression that the individual can be very well captured and processed by the nets of the criminologist's theory. The individual character in the story is not fully given his freedom, in Sartre's terms, and the criminologist rather than the youth is often given as the book's "author"—Snodgrass's point. Furthermore, the narrative tends not to wander much from the person's criminal or other socially deviant activities, so that a more complete identification does not take place between speaker and audience on the basis of qualities, events, and experiences that are common to the human condition. On all these points autobiography advances further than oral history. Different genres and styles are appropriate to different lives: as Allport put it: "It seems impossible that an infinite variety of mortals . . . can or should be expected to represent themselves equally well through any one prescribed form of life-writing."[21]

An exhaustive picture of a life, in the sense of atomic detail, is out of the question; selection is inevitable. But one wonders if the editing that has been done on transcripts or manuscripts has been overdetermined by the audience editors envision, rendering this autobiographical genre essentially "other directed." If obscenity, repetitions, slips, misspellings, dialect, and sequences of spontaneous association and speech are all smoothed out in favor of an artificial, even contrived, narrative continuity and rhetorical presentableness, what has happened to authenticity? Doubtless we are forgetting our own position and the limits of rhetoric itself: a life is a life, but the representation of a life inevitably picks up some of its features from the representation as well as from the life. The editorial task is to maneuver within this marginal area of speaker, medium, and audience, each term limiting but not dominating the others.

If oral history in our account is midway between casework reports and autobiographies in capacity to represent individuality, it is also midway between those reports and other modes in capacity to represent conflict and tension. Oral history is able to convey drama, but not so conspicuously that it interrupts the continuity of the person's narrative or confuses it by introducing forces that the story's viewpoint cannot account for. Drama is conveyed better by an outside reporter or by a camera reproducing events in which opposing forces engage in dialogue or debate, such as Frederick Wiseman's "Juvenile Court" or the NBC television presentation "For the Child's Own Good" (28 February 1980). This more journalistic form of presentation exposes abuses more quickly than oral histories and creates more vivid, actual mental images, though probably more ephemeral ones—or more contradictory ones. The more dramatically the delinquent's painful experience is shown, the more the audience may feel a certain literary pleasure in watching it. Indeed, one area of an offender's experience that it seems structurally hopeless to represent in any medium (except the person's own memory) is the experience of penal *confinement*, because this experience contradicts a reader's or viewer's experience of *expanding* the boundaries of the self by identifying with another person in autobiographical works. The oral history is wrong even to attempt to convey the essential horror of incarceration, because the inevitable failure is concealed: the reader is deceived into thinking he has been "on the inside," whereas a candid and humble admission of the collapse of language before such extraordinary realities would be the only means of even beginning to gain imaginative entrance.

In general we must follow Kafka's paradoxes and conclude that the delinquent's oral history overcomes the distance between delinquent and reader only on condition that it establishes and maintains a distance.

Finally, since delinquents' oral histories neither demonstrate drama nor arouse conflict, they have little to offer to radicals such as Saul Alinsky, who called them "small-time confessions." If they do not interest the proponents of revolutionary change, neither do they reach the staunchest defenders of the status quo, who hold to their fantasies about "criminals" and thus need these oral histories more than anyone else, as do members of those repressive societies in which these oral histories do not even appear.

Functions

The chief function of delinquents' oral histories is a certain variety of communication, divisible into three parts: attracting an audience, putting phenomena before the eyes of the audience, and persuading people to hold certain opinions.

Attraction

Oral histories can interest people in a subject they might otherwise have ignored. They do this because the narratives offer the prospect of identification with a person who is essentially the same as but somehow different from one's self and thereby they provide the opportunity both to affirm and to transcend one's ego. Thus another condition for the appearance of these oral histories is some degree of social flexibility of personal identity, likely to be a concomitant of the widespread social changes set forth above as conditions for the genesis of these histories.[22]

To attract an audience by selecting and editing oral histories such as we have studied one must create a document that falls between two extremes: that of a narrative that may be abbreviated without much loss into scientific prose, and that of a narrative of the cops and robbers variety that does not lend itself to serious reform proposals. Each extreme fails to generate the interest necessary to lead a reader to new perceptions and opinions concerning delinquency. However, interest may arise precisely from a balance of these cognitive and voyeuristic appeals: the synthesis of the universal and the "peculiar" as factors in attracting an audience is a *unique* voice capable of representing *common* states of affairs; some common to mankind, others common to the criminological area at issue.

Perception

The dialectic between common and unique, identification and expansion that operates in attracting an audience to delinquents' oral histories also works in the experience of reading them. The reduction of distance between speaker and audience in the very act of beginning to read the story of another person's life is the genesis of a "primary relationship," albeit an artistic or artificial one. This is where the perception of the delinquent as less an outlaw and more a human being begins or is reinforced. The essential factor in the perception of the "personality" or "humanity" inhering in a delinquent is merely that the youth is able to speak coherently at all. (Surely this is a reason "freaks" are considered human—and interplanetary visitors might be—despite inhuman bodies, and a reason why there was doubt about the humanity of the Wild Boy of Aveyron, who never learned to speak.) The reader also perceives that the speaker is capable of initiating action and sustaining what Burgess called "social status," that is, a position among other people "just like us," made possible by communication. The delinquent is not "dumb" because he is not dumb. For this reason the words reproduced must be the youth's: the story must be told in the first person to show that the individual is capable of speech and, by inference, of the action conveyed by the speech. This is the beginning of acceptance of the person and, by a "halo effect," of his deviance. Thus begins the reincorporation of the deviant into the community, at least in the mind of the middle-class reader, who might subsequently act, or support action, or at least not stand in the way of appropriate action to bring the outsider in. The chasm of class alienation and criminal segregation that was a condition for the appearance of the histories is bridged, however tenuously. National, racial, or ethnic stereotypes are opposed. All this is made possible by metaphor, not only in the sense of verbal devices of comparing unfamiliar with familiar, but more generally as a principle of passing over in imagination from one place to another.

A caution: We must not be deceived by a kind of promotional humanism into believing that the delinquent in these oral histories is transformed into a person *simpliciter*. That way lies hypocrisy. If the delinquent (or other deviant) ceases to be the monster or outcast, neither does he become the "respectable citizen." He ends up somewhere between: neither all offender nor all "normal," he becomes and he remains "the delinquent," albeit the delinquent qualified in certain more human ways.[23] He is more emphatically marginal a character than even the outcast! If the delinquent became totally "normal," he would pass out of criminological focus and no message would be transmitted. Whatever else may be said about the personality conveyed by the deviant's oral history, in the way of damning or promoting it—and the extent of inquiry here could be considerable—in truth this "humanity" cannot be removed from its very constricting, and sometimes contradictory, rhetorical context.

The marginal person of the oral history, for all the fences installed around him, is at least a concrete object rather than merely the static

referent of an abstract account. The oral history is a "text," to use
Foucault's term, that orients perception toward actualities. The object
has actuality because, as Aristotle says in his *Rhetoric,* it is shown in
action. If the action seems too distant from the reader, it may lose its
vitality: for example, Mayhew's histories could not simply be dusted off
and used again today even if the conditions they revealed were the same,
because they would not exercise enough "presence." Another reason
Mayhew's histories would not work today is that the criminologist would
want to make the point not that the state of things now is the same as it
was a hundred years ago, but that specific reforms are needed today. And
the audience must believe it is seeing reality capable of change rather than
conditions beyond practical reach.

The impression made by these experiences is that neither "delinquency" nor delinquents have fixed natures; yet, for all that, the doors
of speculation are not thrown open to all comers. Attention is localized in
the interaction of the individual and the society that immediately sur-
rounds him. Perception is shifted away from physical states, ideals, systems, and psychic and extrapersonal structures, just as the activity of
collecting life histories may assist in turning a scientist from a position in
one of those to a belief in the reality and integrity of social phenomena.
The viability and respectability of professions and careers in this area may
then be promulgated by oral histories. More specifically, delinquents' oral
histories turn a spotlight on places of a certain sort—low lodging houses,
prisons, "delinquency areas." Appropriately enough, these are places of
human communication, though often described on the model of epidem-
iology, the communication of a disease. Once the reader's perception is
directed to those places, the criminologist begins to lobby for a reform
program.

Persuasion

The typical humanistic messages of criminological oral history are much
better demonstrated by a rhetoric in which the experience of speakers and
actors becomes, by art, the experience of readers than they would be by a
mere listing of hypotheses. Even those occupying opposed positions,
such as social workers, psychiatrists, and political activists, might "get
something out of" the narratives, "see some truth" in the position the
oral histories espouse, whereas the flat statement of that position would
more likely give rise to competition, controversy, and attempts at refuta-
tion. This way also lets an audience feel that they are formulating
these messages themselves, though this is somewhat deceptive given the
ubiquitous nudging of the criminologist.

The first of these propositions is: *Juvenile delinquents are not alien
beings.* They are not the devilish thugs of popular stereotypes, nor is any

person one hundred percent "delinquent," whatever that may mean. This seems innocuous enough, a result of the perception of personality, but it is the foundation of a profound moral principle: the imperative to apply to the recipient of your action the same relevant criterion you apply to yourself, versions of which are the golden rule, Kant's categorical imperative, and Alan Gewirth's Principle of Generic Consistency.[24] I need not discuss these principles here: my point is that there is a moral dimension to the very form of the oral history.

If individuals are not in essence delinquent, where does their delinquency originate? In their genes? In their unconscious? In those systems of power that label them? Not according to oral histories. The second propostion is: *The good person becomes bad by interacting in a criminogenic environment.* Thus we have the likelihood of an ecological scheme, as in Mayhew and Shaw. Attention concentrates on two places: the area where a person grows up and the institution where he is segregated after legal action. The latter is more frequently exposed and condemned, possibly because it seems easier to change, since it was more deliberately constructed than a neighborhood. But this is also because the jail, prison, or correctional school is inherently a violation of a principle of oral history: that is, the custodial institution removes the origin of speech and action from the person. Furthermore, there usually are many specific abuses to complain about: not only the delinquent has been removed from public scrutiny but the custodian also, with no one to monitor the exercise of custodial power except the very people whose status makes their testimony doubtful. The oral history seeks to reverse this "hierarchy of credibility," as Becker puts it.[25]

The third proposition that oral histories seek to persuade readers to believe is: *Delinquency can be prevented or eliminated in part only by changing or eliminating criminogenic environments, a process in which nonexperts should have a say.* In the oral history schemes we studied (Clay, Thomas) this reform program is mentioned only in the briefest way; but Clifford Shaw's Chicago Area Project is surely the best manifestation of the reformist assumptions tacit in delinquents' oral histories. (One of these assumptions seems to explain the lack of specifics: the expert provides only a very general framework so that nonexperts will be allowed to define their own program.) The reforms include local autonomy, personal rather than formal relations with young people, use of marginal workers who are able to function in two social worlds, social rather than individual therapy, and work with delinquents on their own turf rather than in institutions. Showing in an oral history that the delinquent has qualities of personality and autonomy suggests the feasibility of those programs,[26] even though no thorough analysis or evaluation of them has ever been made. The emotional appeal here is mild. A particular outrage might rouse a reader to action, but without that he will probably not take action because of an oral history unless he comes to it with an interest in, say, crime control, community organization, or a career in sociology, and unless that interest is expressible through extant or feasible institutions.

Accomplishments
What have delinquents' oral histories accomplished? Since they have appeared as parts of larger studies, it is impossible to discriminate their unique effect. In any case, it is very difficult to assess any action concerning delinquency because of the paucity of evaluations or adequate data, even about programs today, not to speak of the absence of agreement on certain political or moral issues and on what constitutes true scientific subject matter and method. From the perspectives of the transcendent and underlying causes I have noted, which are also "causes" of professional or activist allegiance, delinquents' oral histories seem to have achieved little or nothing of significance. Whatever accomplishment they have made lies in their effects on certain audiences and the institutions thereby promoted.

Despite their apparent capacity to reach nonprofessional audiences, it is evident that delinquents' oral histories have not reached a broad public, for they have been distributed in meager quantities: the number 2,500 seems typical for the most prominent books or newspaper series at the time of their publication. Editors at the University of Chicago Press in the 1950s were surprised by the sales figures of Shaw's books. The influence of those books, and others such as *The Polish Peasant*, depended on their being read not by a great many people but by a small group of philanthropically minded people, and one wonders if oral histories were essential to reaching that audience. Mayhew, working at the dawn of professionalization in the area of delinquency, doubtless reached a more nonprofessional audience than Shaw, but the best that may be claimed for Mayhew is that he "gave impetus to social amelioration," in Bradley's words. In view of the power of the rhetoric of crime and vengeance, any exposure to the human characteristics of juvenile offenders, any predisposing in favor of more humane treatment, is a conspicuous accomplishment, but those large commonplace claims about bringing extremes of society together are more wishful than practical thinking. In any case, union could take place initially only in the rather limited area of a reader's mind. Perhaps this form of literature is a symptom rather than a cause of the existence of institutions fostering cross-class communication. But generalizations here may be as far wrong as general assertions about "delinquents." One really does not know how much oral histories and other similar forms of publicity may have decisively altered attitudes and initiated action in particular cases.

Generally, there could be two effects of delinquents' oral histories: first, to attract new personnel and volunteers into delinquency prevention and treatment programs and, second, to stimulate reform of correctional institutions. In the letter to Howard S. Becker quoted above, Henry McKay wrote:

> The latent power of this educative device is illustrated by the fact that one very well known sociologist-educator, known to both of us, said in a public meeting a few years ago that his whole life orientation had been changed by reading the volume under discussion [*The Jack-Roller*] and the companion volume *The Natural History of a Delinquent Career.*

Life histories introduced them to a kind of situation they would later encounter directly, just as documents were used at the Institute for Juvenile Research as training materials. Concerning prison reform, Hermann Mannheim has written:

> There can be little doubt that many of these books by prisoners, even the less reliable ones, have provided useful stimulus for prison reform as they have been widely discussed in the daily press and professional journals and often forced the authorities to examine complaints and to take action.[27]

Oral histories may not be so effective in causing immediate changes as more spectacular exposés, say, in newspapers, but these often stimulate only minor alterations and are quickly forgotten, unless they influence legislation: for example, Louis Hine's photographs of children working in cotton mills, beet fields, and coal mines influenced legislators to make child labor illegal. Life histories have pointed to the need for alternatives to incarceration. Yet, for all the new blood in the form of enthusiastic young workers infused into the "juvenile justice system" and for all the agitation for prison reform and promotion of diversionary programs, plenty of correctional institutions still exist, and their problems are basically what they have always been. One can only reply to this criticism of oral history that conditions might have been much *worse* had such material never been published. How much, for example, has the continuing availability and influence of Shaw's life histories prevented regression to a paradigm in which the delinquent is bad by nature or is mentally ill? Surely the strength of the counterregressive force lies in the whole institution of sociology. How can one measure the part played by life histories in that?

In some cases oral histories may effect reform through appealing to public opinion in general, as when Clay tried to influence magistrates by printing his reports in local newspapers. But it seems more plausible to trace the influence of such publications through persons who undertake action rather than merely hold opinions. Did volunteers join Shaw's community committees as a result of reading the life histories? Someone may have joined the downtown board of directors of the Chicago Area Project through that route, though reading a book could have been only part of a larger process of personal contacts and public-spiritedness. The route to joining a committee in Little Italy on Chicago's West Side in the 1930s almost certainly did not pass through a book but rather resulted from hearing a speech delivered by Shaw in person or perhaps from reading a newspaper article or taking part in conversation.

The persons more likely to read a book that was, after all, in Shaw's case academic were professionals or marginal professionals. This latter group consisted of caseworkers dismayed with individualistic casework methods: some observers at the time believed that one effect of Thomas's and Shaw's work was to encourage social workers to notice and respect their clients' own viewpoints and values. (From this perspective their accomplishment was to give respectability to the subjective.) It was among this group of marginals, including students on the verge of their careers, that life histories probably had their greatest impact, for these people were in a position to be swayed and to act as a result of that persuasion. Among professional sociologists the accomplishment of life histories was to promote acceptance of a more productive subject matter than abstract ideas and physical traits. Among professionals outside sociology it was to promote acceptance of a new academic field.

Ultimately, the question about accomplishments of delinquents' oral histories demands evaluation of the institutions they helped set up. Here I can only give my belief, formed by study of some nineteenth-century programs and a somewhat fuller study of the history of Shaw's Chicago Area Project. The programs that oral histories help establish tend to be improvements over contemporary measures: they encourage a kinder, more personal attitude toward the young person. Even if they were part of a political instrument of "domination-observation" of which Foucault has written,[28] I do not doubt that they have helped some individuals live better lives. But the people who profit most from these institutions are those upwardly mobile individuals who join as staff or volunteers. In that respect the incorporation of the slum-dweller into the bourgeoisie by means of an oral history enterprise has been all too concretely accomplished. Furthermore, the initial lack of structure in these organizations, intended to keep open channels of community expression and sustained by the charismatic figure who used oral histories, becomes the condition for the evolution of a rigid structure in which "primary relations" become cronyism and marginality becomes xenophobia. This is aggravated when the charismatic person departs and the image-protectors take command.

The rhetoric of the success story replaces the oral history. It has happened more than once and doubtless will happen again.

Anabasis

The fate of oral history in a field such as criminology is that, after its appearance in the heroic early phase of inquiry into crime by a particular science, it is surpassed by abbreviated techniques. At first "own story" revealed mental traits to Healy, but mental tests got at those much better. For W. I. Thomas, life histories exposed social attitudes, but eventually opinion surveys did the same job more efficiently. Shaw could see the life of a social area through the telescope of life history, but W. F. Whyte saw it close up by using participant observation techniques. Some of the functions oral history seemed to perform, such as attracting an audience, became no longer necessary, since the profession had achieved legitimacy and could obtain resources from institutions as specialized as the profession had become. The "scenario" is such that, on the entrance of each new subject matter, oral history, in some form, risks being discovered all over again. As late as 1948 someone wrote:

> We have become so preoccupied in recent years with ab-
> breviated methods of inquiry that even the simple procedure of
> asking a person a question and then leaving him alone to an-
> swer it as he wishes, is greeted as a great novelty, discussed as
> a major methodological contribution and is honorifically
> named after a proponent of it. It is equally interesting to note
> that what nowadays is called an intensive interview is one in
> which the gag customarily placed on the subject is slightly
> loosened.[29]

Delinquents' oral histories have a certain staying power. Leon Radzinowitz has written: "Ecological studies and natural histories such as those undertaken by C. R. Shaw, H. D. McKay, F. M. Thrasher, will always remain significant whatever the future direction of criminological research and however attractive new hypotheses appear."[30] According to McKay, Shaw believed that this form of documentation was timeless: it shows processes that will always occur in the making of delinquents.

Certain features of the content of delinquents' oral histories also seem timeless. Jo Manton refers to children who "robbed drunken people who fell unconscious in the streets" in Mary Carpenter's day.[31] Jack-rollers may be found in Chicago today, though not in such numbers as earlier (partly because it is known that some drunks carry guns and use them when set upon), and they have turned up in the Soviet Union as well.[32] Wonder at a big city is a common experience: a sneak thief in Mayhew's *London Labour* said: "I remember on coming to this great city I was much astonished at its wonders, and every street appeared to me like a fair" (*LL* 4:302). Sidney in Shaw's *Natural History of a Delinquent Career* called downtown Chicago "that fairyland of pleasurable thrills."[33] Young people have perceived themselves as ragged, or they have dressed in flashy clothes. They have met delinquents in low lodging houses or on the streets of the slum or the ghetto.

One reads today in research grant proposals that at last a collection of data will be started that can be continuously built upon in the coming years. This view, with its naive notion of scientific progress, is utterly belied by history. No such universal timeless instrument will ever exist, because fashions and assumptions change. Shaw and McKay used delinquency statistics (from official sources) to prove that one national group is not more criminogenic than another. When they tried to publish these findings in "Nationality and Delinquency" in the 1950s, the book was rejected because the data were not recent; but they pointed out that statistics on national origins of delinquents were no longer kept. Oral histories might overcome this difficulty, since they seem to be more universal. But they must in fact be specific to times and places to perform their rhetorical functions; thus, along with recurring images are dated ones. And inquiries that assume certain positions would not likely use oral histories anyway, as we have seen.

Interviews or other oral-history-related presentations appear from time to time that illuminate an area or make a new point, such as the autobiographies of Piri Thomas and Claude Brown. Calls for oral histories of juvenile delinquents have been made during the past thirty years,[34] but no project of the scope of Mayhew's or Shaw's has been launched, perhaps confirming my position on conditions of genesis. To us in the United States in the 1980s, the concept of juvenile delinquents as human beings and the environmental context of delinquency are such commonplaces that it seems there would never be occasion to demonstrate them again. But remember that these were also commonplaces for Mayhew, who was nevertheless forgotten when the Lombrosian paradigm seized control of criminology. A spectacular discovery in genetic research during the next few decades might have the same effect, starting the cycle all over again. The current fashion in the most innovative criminology is the study of systems of power and the institution of antirehabilitative measures of punishment. These aim at overcoming the individualism that oral histories and related historical developments created. But their ultimate effect may be to eclipse some simple truths and thus set up conditions in which the messages of delinquents' oral histories are again new.

Appendix

Aspects of Technique:
Mayhew, Healy, and Shaw

Mayhew's Modus Operandi

Henry Mayhew's technique of acquiring oral histories was what we might expect: he located people who were closest to his subject—the poor and the workers themselves—and asked them questions about their lives and occupations. This was not what his contemporaries expected of a scientific investigator, as Mayhew made himself out to be. Authors of books on "picturesque London" might convey anecdotes picked up from "London characters," but Mayhew was expected to interview middle-class experts on the condition of the poor: for example, charity workers, and policemen. Whenever a controversy arose, Mayhew's opponent inevitably attacked "the disjointed lucubrations and melodramatic ravings of Mr. Mayhew's sentimental dragomen and poor artizans" (*UM* 39).

One of these controversies arose over Mayhew's claim that Ragged Schools—alternative schools of his day for children who could not attend ordinary day schools and named after the condition of the students' clothing—had not prevented delinquency but might have fostered it by providing places where nondelinquent youths could meet delinquents for the first time. Ragged School classes were taught mostly by middle-class volunteers. The secretary of the Ragged School Union, in an indignant letter to the editor of the *Morning Chronicle*, insisted that the teachers and the board of directors should have been interviewed, not the children themselves, who could give only "exterior evidence":

> One would have supposed that "the most experienced persons" for
> furnishing the information he desired would have been parties actively
> connected with the schools—those who, by years of self-sacrifice,
> unremunerated, had taught the children, visited them in their homes,
> watched them in the streets, and thus by actual experience had be-
> come acquainted with their habits and conduct: or if they were not
> sufficient, the gentlemen who form the local committees of the
> schools (whose names and addresses are published with every one of
> their reports), would have been the best authority to whom he could
> have applied. They are generally men of business, intelligence, and
> respectability, who are not likely to give their time, energies, and
> money for the support of institutions of which they know nothing.
> Many of them have property in the very localities of the schools,
> which, if "nurseries for criminals," would doubtless make them
> among the first sufferers.[1]

But neither were these ladies and gentlemen, including Charles Dickens at one time, likely to admit that their pet charity project was a failure. Mayhew said he was "impressed with the idea that the teachers believed Ragged Schools to be productive of pure unalloyed good,"[2] and he replied to the Ragged Schools secretary not only by printing letters from witnesses to the initial interviews—letters that confirmed Mayhew's claim that he had neither posed leading questions nor twisted their replies in his articles—but he also went on to print further oral histories of youths who had spent time in Ragged Schools, as well as other testimony, all of which supported the conclusion that the schools were indeed "nurseries for criminals."

Although Mayhew did not interview middle-class gentlemen to the exclusion of others, he did occasionally seek their testimony and almost always solicited their advice in locating representative members of the group he was studying. In other words, he descended through a social hierarchy starting with, say, an official of a charity institution, who would refer him to a gentleman who could give him practical information, and finally end up with the people at issue themselves—vagrants, street sellers, or artisans. Concerning the Ragged Schools, Mayhew had been directed to some of the boys by the secretary of the Ragged School Union himself, and later he was guided by "police authorities" to policemen familiar with the schools. The names and addresses of some students had been acquired at random from enrollment lists by one of his assistants. On other occasions, Mayhew would find a spokesman of the group of tailors or dockmen by consulting with a number of workers in that occupation or by asking trade union officials for "intelligent informants" (LL 1:301; UM 189, 236), as he called them. Of course, one person would lead to another, a "snowball" process.

Or he would simply run into someone in the street, ask him a few questions, and invite him to visit his home later on: if the interviewee failed to show up, Mayhew might go knocking at *his* door (LL 2:157). "When possible, the informants were seen in their own homes where they could talk most freely" (UM 63). Mayhew would pull up a chair and listen to an artisan talk while he worked (UM 109): "Later in the day Mr. Black became very communicative. We sat chatting together in his sanded bird shop, and he told me all his misfortunes" (LL 3:14). Sometimes he would knock on the doors of the first six or so houses on a street (UM 53, 108) or arrive unannounced "when there could have been no preparation" at a house he had arranged to visit (LL 3:261), or he would ask the first sixteen children he ran into in the streets whether they could read and write (LL 1:528). Sometimes informants would come to the *Morning Chronicle* office, and he held mass meetings of needlewomen (UM 167), tailors (UM 198), shoemakers (UM 236), ballast-heavers' wives (LL 3:295), residents of a cheap lodging house (LL 3:323–28), and boy vagrants (LL 1:466–71), at which he took statements from members of each group.

Some statements Mayhew received in writing (LL 1:39, 291). In his correspondence with readers he asked for "a brief account of the experience, privations, and struggles of those working men whose lives have been unusually checquered, and the publication of which is likely to be interesting or useful to their fellow-workmen, or the public generally."[3] But he took down a vast amount of oral material in notebooks, using some sort of shorthand or perhaps writing very fast: "The statements are always taken down word for word from the narrator, when possible."[4] In one of his oral histories he inserts: "[But don't, he expostulated, take it all down that way.]"[5] Sometimes this even included peculiarities of speech. Unfortunately, as Thompson says, "none of Mayhew's original notebooks have survived (it would seem)."[6]

Skepticism has been voiced over whether the statements that appear in Mayhew's works are indeed verbatim recordings of what the people said. Perhaps Mayhew conformed to Thucydides' practice: "It was in all cases difficult to carry [speeches] word for word in one's memory, so my habit has been to make the speakers say what was in my opinion demanded of them by the various occasions, of course adhering as closely as possible to the general sense of what they said."[7] Given the inevitable necessity of editing even tape recordings, one wonders if this is not what always happens. A problem for the student of oral history is to discover the particulars of this process, but that task is not easy.

To check the accuracy of people's statements, Mayhew used several common-sense devices. On occasion he would acquire official documents or even letters in an individual's possession:

> I hardly knew how to ask one whose narrative and manner bore so plainly the impress of truth, for proofs of the authenticity of her statements; still I felt that it would not be right, without making some inquiries, to allow the story of her sufferings to go forth to the world. I explained to her my wishes, and she very readily showed me such papers and official documents as put her statement as to birth and position of her husband utterly beyond doubt. [*UM* 158]

Mayhew's most recurrent means of checking was to question many people on the same subject: "The rest of the histories may easily be imagined, for there was a painful uniformity in the stories of all the children" (*LL* 2:174). If someone lies, someone else will either raise a doubt or reveal the speaker to be a liar (*LL* 2:565). No one who has seen the number of oral histories in Mayhew's works, well over two hundred of a page or more, doubts that he spoke with a great number of people, "some thousands," according to the preface to *London Labour*. He did so not only to test a person's truthfulness on particular points, but also to check an individual's more general claims about the class of persons under scrutiny. A most productive procedure for Mayhew, one seldom used today, was to call a group meeting, where the audience would immediately correct a speaker if they thought he strayed from the truth: "I charge you all to speak only the truth. You cannot benefit by any other course, and therefore be you a check the one upon the other; and if anyone departs from the strict fact, do you pull him up" (*LL* 3:443). "The gentleman who accompanied me assured me that the answers they would give to my questions would be likely to be correct, from the fact of the number assembled, as each would check the other" (*LL* 3:326).

In judging the truthfulness of an individual's statement in isolation, Mayhew's assessment of human character might come into play. When he spoke with a woman who had seen better days, he realized that she was "endeavouring to make her circumstances appear better than they really were" (*LL* 2:100). On another occasion Mayhew believed a man's statement true partly because "he did not appear to me to have sufficient intellect to invent a falsehood" (*LL* 2:157). The "earnestness and solemnity" of a girl proved her truthfulness (*LL* 1:49), even though Mayhew was always on guard against exaggeration (*LL* 2:42) and ran special checks on "the most incredible statements" (*UM* 147). He or one of his assistants also ran a kind of credibility check on people whose statements were to be printed, asking their neighbors if they generally were known for honesty. In his study of working conditions, Mayhew says that, when he checked his informants against written documents, he found the testimony of the employees always to have been more truthful than the assertions of the employers (*UM* 40–41, 145).

Mayhew was not alone in this work: while he was at the *Morning Chronicle* he had "an army of assistant writers, stenographers, and hansom cabmen constantly at his call."[8] Some, like R. Knight, would help locate informants; others, like Henry Wood and Mayhew's brother Augustus (Gus), took "statements" and gave them to the Metropolitan Correspondent to edit. Mayhew's wife took dictation from him and fended off the bill collectors.

Mayhew soon must have discovered that some people hardly need any prompting to get them started on what they know best—their own experiences— while others have to be continually primed with questions. He was receptive to both: "His statements, or opinions . . . were given both spontaneously in the course of conversation, and in answer to my questions" (*LL* 1:24). "The following statement of his business, his sentiments, and indeed, of the subjects which concerned him, or about which he was questioned" (*LL* 2:252). One girl curtsied after hearing each question (*LL* 1:47). Another girl "each time she was asked a question frowned, like a baby in its sleep, while thinking of the answer" (*LL* 1:572). In some instances Mayhew gives the questions and answers:

> Whilst I was present [at a House of Refuge for the Destitute Poor] there was among a portion of the male applicants but little hesitation in answering the inquiries glibly and promptly. Others answered reluctantly. The answers of some of the boys, especially the Irish boys, were curious: "Where did you sleep last night?" "Well, then, sir, I slept walking about the streets all night, and very cowld it was, sir." Another lad was asked, after he had stated his name and age, how he lived, "I beg, or do anything," he answered. "What's your parish?" "Ireland." (Several pronounced their parish to be the County Corruk.) "Have you a father here?" "He died before we left Ireland." "How did you get here, then?" "I came with my mother." "Well, and where's she?" "She died after we came to England." So the child had the streets for a stepmother.[*LL* 3:418]

In other places Mayhew "melts" his questions into the edited interview, to use Humpherys's term,[9] or perhaps the speaker went on at length without questions.

Informants were asked for data on, for example, their average rate of wages, and also for their opinions, on, say, the causes of the depreciation in the value of their labor (*UM* 105). But these oral histories contain much more life than that: "The character, thoughts, feelings, regrets, and even the dreams . . . are given in the narratives" (*LL* 1:439). "'I dream sometimes, sir,' the cripple resumed in answer to my question, 'but not often . . . . I never seem to myself to be a cripple in my dreams. Well, I can't explain how, but I feel as if my limbs was all free like—so beautiful'" (*LL* 1:78). (Cf. Studs Terkel: "Yet my experiences tell me that people with buried grievances and dreams unexpressed do want to let go."[10]) Some people objected to telling Mayhew anything about their youth (*LL* 1:77, 133; 2:277), but many gave rather full accounts of the major events of their lives. In the case of a runaway boy, "The only thing of which he cared to talk was his step-mother's treatment of him; all else was a blank with him, in comparison; this was the one burning recollection" (*LL* 1:525).

Since the London poor were usually not asked by someone from a class above them what they thought about anything, Mayhew's purpose was often misunderstood. At a meeting of parolees, he says:

> When I first went among you, it was not very easy for me to make you
> comprehend the purpose I had in view. You at first fancied that I was
> a Government spy, or a person in some way connected with the
> police. I am none of these; nor am I a clergyman wishing to convert
> you to his particular creed, nor a teetotaler anxious to prove the
> source of all evil to be over-indulgence in intoxicating drink; but I am
> simply a literary man, desirous of letting the rich know something
> more about the poor. (Applause.) [*LL* 3:440]

On other occasions Mayhew was mistaken for the truant officer from a Ragged School (*LL* 3:36) and for the dog-tax collector: "After I had satisfied him that I was not a collector of dog-tax, trying to find out how many animals he kept, he gave me what he evidently thought was 'a treat'—a peep at his bull-dog" (*LL* 3:4).

One way to avoid misunderstandings was to select people who were more likely to grasp what he was up to:

> I have found the intelligent artisan—who could easily be made to
> understand the purport of my inquiries—ready to give me the neces-
> sary information not only without reluctance, but with evident plea-
> sure. Among the less informed class I am often delayed by meeting
> with objections and hesitations. [*UM* 294]

One man, on being told that the information was wanted for the press, replied, "We are oppressed enough already" (*LL* 1:24). But Mayhew sloshed his way through objections and hesitations often enough; in only a few places does he introduce his oral histories as coming from a "more intelligent" informant.

Apparently Mayhew tried to explain to prospective informants that he was trying to relieve their oppression by telling their life stories to the public. At a meeting of needlewomen he had called, one of the speakers proclaimed:

> God bless the gentlemen, I say, who have set this inquiry a-going to
> help the poor slop-workers, and I hope that public attention being now
> called to these matters, the oppressed will be oppressed no longer,
> and that the Parliament House even will interpose to protect them.
> But I am sorry to say the good are not always the powerful, nor the
> powerful always the good. [*UM* 176]

Some people were eager to get the story of their sufferings before the world (*UM* 119), but surely some people turned Mayhew down entirely, an event we obviously cannot use the published texts to examine.

People were also motivated to answer Mayhew's questions by a small payment (*LL* 1:35; 3:449).[11] The metropolitan correspondent helped some find better jobs, most notably a "mud-lark," a young boy who had been a scavenger along the banks of the Thames, often getting nails stuck in his feet. Mayhew got him a job with a printer (*LL* 2:176). Some people became enthusiastic after seeing their words in print (*LL* 3:326) and doubtless promoted the enterprise. Some sinners relieved their guilt by confessing to Mayhew: a young girl forced into prostitution ends her statement: "I never stole anything in my life, and have told you all I have done wrong" (*LL* 3:396).

But people who had devised schemes to survive, often on the margins of society or beyond, were understandably hesitant to bare their souls to a reporter. One of Mayhew's colleagues says of a burglar he interviewed: "In the first part of his autobiography he was very frank and candid, but as he proceeded became more slow and calculating in his disclosures. We hinted to him he was 'timid.' 'No,' he replied, 'I am not timid, but I am cautious, which you need not be surprised at'" (*LL* 4:345). Mayhew is often at pains to show that he kept his promises of confidentiality. He did not print names of individuals (*LL* 1:283), and, since he was more interested in the conditions of a class than in the tale of an individual for its own sake, he says he altered particulars of stories so they could not be traced back to their sources (*UM* 155). (Like other oral historians who make this claim, Mayhew never gave details about this process.) He withheld from publication the signals that crossing-sweeper boys used to alert each other on the approach of a policeman (*LL* 2:562), and he promised not to reveal a ratcatcher's secret technique for catching fish with his hands (*LL* 3:14). Mayhew apparently developed personal relationships with criminals, receiving them into his home at all hours. But this does not mean he concealed the modes of dishonesty he encountered: "I have unsparingly exposed the rogueries and trickeries of the street people" (*LL* 1:531). He was a consumer advocate before his time. When a reader wrote to point out that Mayhew's exposé of a street seller's tricks would decrease the man's ability to make a living, Mayhew replied: "It is impossible to benefit any class or any individual by falsity.... It is the dishonest portion of the street-folk who injure the more honest members of that body."[12] How can the honest make a living if the dishonest use false weights?

None of this should be surprising to more recent collectors of oral histories. What is remarkable is that Mayhew developed this technique in a period of high Victorian respectability and class sneering, characterized in the works of Charles Dickens, who was born the same year as Mayhew and was acquainted with Mayhew through the *Punch* circle.[13] Mayhew was not devoid of middle-class smugness; it shows through on occasion, in the same way that Dickens alternated between humanitarianism and harshness in his views on prison discipline. But for the most part "it is clear that Mayhew was that rare creature, a natural democrat; his first thought, that is to say, was never 'This is an unfortunate wretch whom it is my duty, if possible, to help,' but always 'This is a fellow-human being whom it is fun to talk to.'"[14] Mayhew's enthusiasm, even enthrallment, must have been the most potent factor in his success in obtaining oral histories, as it is with Studs Terkel today. About the crippled street bird seller, Mayhew wrote: "The man's sister was present at his desire, as he was afraid I could not understand him, owing to the indistinctness of his speech, but that was easy enough, after a while, with a little patience and attention" (*LL* 2:77). To people who may have been accustomed to lining up and having curt questions fired at them (*LL* 3:418), patience, attention, curiosity, and appreciation must have felt like a gift. They repaid the metropolitan correspondent with the stories of their lives.

Mayhew's Art of Presentation

Mayhew's procedures in collecting oral histories have been duplicated, but the way he presented this material constitutes a unique art form, more concerned with dramatic voices than Clifford Shaw's life histories of delinquents, while also more concerned with the guiding intelligence or commentary critics have found missing in Studs Terkel's work.[15] The typical order of presentation in both the *Morning Chronicle* series and *London Labour* is to begin with a general description of an occupation or a place, which usually includes the numbers of people or items involved, often presented in a chart. In most cases Mayhew and his crew had to compile these statistics themselves. A general history may be given of the evolution of the object under investigation, with special attention to consequences of changes in economic arrangements. In volume 4, John Binny begins his discussion of thieves by noting their techniques, then he describes a visit he made to a locale where they were observed in situ and concludes with oral histories.

Mayhew's texts move predominantly from the general and abstract to the particular and concrete: after preparing the reader by setting forth facts about the subject, Mayhew then descriptively dives into a particular place, relates an event on a certain day, or gives an oral history: "The men shall now speak for themselves" (*LL* 3:287). Mayhew calls these "statements," "accounts," or "experiences" of someone—he does not have a technical term. (In vol. 4, John Binny calls them "narratives.") In one case he calls them "street-biography" (*LL* 1:393). Indeed, a major portion of *London Labour* is not about the poor so much as it is about the streets of London: "The statements are among the most curious revelations of the history of the streets" (*LL* 1:283). (Cf. his 179-page disquisition "The Streets of London" in vol. 2.) Occasionally he calls the statements "histories"; might Lewis Carroll have had Mayhew's histories in mind (perhaps the newspaper series or the 1851 booklets) when he wrote, about 1860, the Queen's invitation for Alice to hear the Mock Turtle's "history"?

But it is impossible to discover a formula for Mayhew's arrangement of material. The roving journalist will be treating one subject and stop to track down something else: "to avail myself of the channels of information opened up to me rather than defer the matter to its proper place, and so lose the freshness of the impression it had made upon my mind" (*LL* 3:322). "This unsystematic mode of treating the subject is almost a necessary evil attendant on the nature of the investigation," he says, and he apologizes for the "erratic and immethodic nature of my communication."[16] But the sequence that resulted when his fresh impression appeared in the newspaper is seldom any different from the order in the book he later put together from the newspaper material; not surprising, since he did not even bother to correct misprints he was well aware of. Sometimes Mayhew links an oral history with other evidence in what we might call a "trapeze device," much practiced by Studs Terkel: a person's statement may include several topics, but only one of them will become the subject of the text immediately following: the reader's attention seems to swing from one topic to another, not knowing until he grabs hold what will be there to meet him. (In Terkel's work this seems to be an expression of his underlying feeling for variations on jazz themes. He has called it "a sort of flow," a sequence of moods.)[17]

Mayhew's art consists in alternating oral history material with more comprehensive, summary statements; for example, juxtaposing the eloquent little girl seller of watercresses with a table showing the total quantities of greenstuff sold in London (*LL* 1:158; cf. 3:416). Statements by women follow those by men. Mayhew includes both long and short oral histories, doubtless partly because of the quantity of usable material he was able to collect.

Oral histories of juvenile offenders are not segregated from the main flow of presentation: they appear here and there, as crime itself appeared from time to time in some people's lives, and just as striking orations from law-abiding young people appear occasionally in *London Labour*. An exception is the "Narrative of a Mudlark," about a youth who "steals pieces of rope, coal, and wood from the barges at the wharves" (*CP* 46). This story appears in volume 4 of *London Labour* in a sequence of narratives by a thief, a pickpocket, and two burglars, and is followed by the story of an ex-convict. But none of this was put together by Mayhew; John Binny, who also took over writing *Criminal Prisons* after Mayhew abandoned it, was responsible for these.

Some of Mayhew's oral histories focus mainly on the life of a person. Others tend to report objective states of affairs, past or present. For example, accounts from juvenile offenders are included to show conditions in cheap lodging houses but always cover a broader area of the person's life than merely the time spent in those places. There are disquisitions on flies and rats, and other statements that would later be called "personal documents"—newspaper articles and quotations from experts and other observers, such as Dickens. Some histories are packed with data. Others are rendered in heavy dialect; for example, this from a London dustman:

> Father vos a dustie;—vos at it all his life, and grandfather afore him for I can't tell how long. Father vos allus a rum 'un;—sich a beggar for lush. Vhy I'm blowed if he vouldn't lush as much as half-a-dozen on 'em can lush noe; somehow the dusties hasn't got the stuff in 'em as they used to have. [*LL* 2:200]

Some accounts of experience are paraphrased in the third person, perhaps to create even greater aesthetic variety than if all people appeared in the grammatical first person. This assemblage of diverse forms of statement does not confuse the reader, because each section is long enough to bring us up close to the subject but short enough to keep our minds moving and our impressions fresh.

Among the most striking areas of Mayhew's texts are his brief prefaces to each oral history. Preceding the person's speech is almost always a vivid image of a person or place, "reproducing the scenes . . . in all their stark literality" (*UM* 116):

> He was a red-headed lad, of that peculiar white complexion which accompanies hair of that colour. His forehead was covered with freckles, so thick, that they looked as if a quantity of cayenne pepper

had been sprinkled over it: and when he frowned, his hair moved backwards and forwards like the twitching of a horse shaking off flies.

"I've put some ile on my hair, to make me look tidy," he said. The grease has turned his locks a fiery crimson colour, and as he passed his hands through it, and tossed it backwards, it positively glittered with the fat upon it. [*LL* 3:210]

When she spoke, there was not the slightest expression visible on her features; indeed, one might have fancied she wore a mask and was talking behind it; but her eyes were shining the while as brightly as those of a person in a fever, and kept moving about, restless with her timidity. [*LL* 2:571]

Surely Mayhew edited the interviews, at least by omitting material that did not seem relevant (e.g., *LL* 1:291; 2:13). After all, an undetermined proportion of the material was obtained in response to Mayhew's questions in the first place and could be summarized in the metropolitan correspondent's own prose. Despite the spiritedness that gives the statements a sense of continuity, it is difficult to make out how some of the published narratives could have been uttered in just the words that appear. Surely Mayhew's dramatic skill came into play here, and the momentum of reading tends to give a text more apparent continuity than can be discovered in a closer examination.

But no evidence suggests that in his editing Mayhew falsified any factual point. Despite the public exposure of his work, only in the Ragged Schools controversy did anyone allege that he had twisted testimony to suit his own prejudices, and Mayhew's defense against that charge seems conclusive—at least on the particular schools he was investigating, even if it was unfair to the movement as a whole. The secretary of the Ragged Schools Union claimed that when a policeman had said that students purchased Bibles with their money, Mayhew had exclaimed, "Never mind that; we don't want to put that down." Mayhew's assistant replied that he had been present at that interview and others: "In fact, I never heard him say so on any occasion—unless, indeed concerning some statement too personal, or utterly irrelevant."[18] Cursing was edited out, though not entirely: "'Why, who's insulting the old b——h?' says the woman, says she.... 'What the b—— h—ll do I care how she lives,' says the woman" (*LL* 1:181). Modern readers are not much disturbed by "bloody hell," but a nineteenth-century Englishman might have been. Also eliminated were "certain gross acts common to lodging-houses, which cannot be detailed in print."[19]

Mayhew used italics most frequently to ride his hobby horse about the settled and wandering tribes of mankind (*LL* 2:91, 137, 398, 508). His most effective device, apparently still unique to him, was parentheses and brackets, used about once in each oral history. These insertions might give supplementary information: "(This statement was taken in June 1856)" (*LL* 2:562). Or they might correct or explain a person's language: "You has to get up a sparapet (a parapet) of a house" (*LL* 2:83) or facts: "'At this time of year we knock off work at dusk, that is, at five [I am informed at the Commercial Docks that the usual hour is four] o'clock'" (*LL* 3:300). Or they might give evidence to confirm a speaker's claim: "Once my mistress knocked me down-stairs for being long on an errand to Pimlico, and I'm sure I couldn't help it, and my eye was cut. It was three weeks before I could see well. [There is a slight mark under the girl's eye still.]" (*LL* 3:395). Or they might translate: "'All a fellow wants to know to sell potatoes,' said a master street-seller to me, 'is to tell how many tanners make a bob, and how many yenaps make a tanner.' [How many sixpences make a shilling, and how many pence a six-pence.]" (*LL* 1:528). Or Mayhew may shift perspectives in the middle of a per-son's monologue, keeping before the reader's imagination an impression of the actual event of the interview, reminding him of the continuing presence of the interviewer:

> I have been in the Asylum a week, and tonight is my last night here. I have nowhere to go, and what will become of me the Lord God only knows. [Again she burst out crying most piteously.] My things are not fit to go into any respectable workroom, and they won't take me into a lodging either, without I have got clothes. I would rather make away with myself than lose my character. [As she raised her hand to wipe away her tears I saw that her arms were bare, and on her moving the old black mantle that covered her shoulders I observed that her gown was so ragged that the body was almost gone from it, and it had no sleeves.] "I shouldn't have kept this, she said, "if I could have made away with it." She said she had no friend in the world to help her, and that she would like much to emigrate.[20]

On one occasion Mayhew makes a curious use of italics and brackets together: "'*I would do anything but starve, to get out of this life; but what can I do?*' [Mr. Mayhew has put these words into italics, to point attention to them.]"[21]

It is primarily from such asides that anything of Mayhew's technique can be extracted from his writings. (Cf. Studs Terkel, who includes very little to reveal his movements, though his prefaces are personal memoirs and his interviews promoting his most recent book help us understand his methods.) If Mayhew had concealed his presence entirely, or if he had thrown all his advice on method into a separate treatise, containing perhaps more wishful thinking than actual practice, he would have been less honest than he was.

"The Good Doctor"

In spite of William Healy's contention that obtaining an individual's own story "requires more technical understanding and training than perhaps any other part of the study,"[22] he devotes almost no discussion to the technique: for example, no entry for "own story" appears in the index of *The Individual Delinquent*. Just as his identity as a doctor contributed to his hitting on the procedure of obtaining "own story," so his attitude and image as a doctor seem to have been the crucial factors in his practice of it: "In the first place he thought [physical examinations] often gave a very good entrée to establishing rapport with the youngster."[23] Healy speaks of the "friendly attitude of the family physician,"[24] who makes a different impression on the offender from that of a "detective who, according to the classic account, prefaced his interrogatory with, 'You know that anything you say can be used against you'";[25] or a judge ("Do you think that a judge sitting up on a bench is going to get into a close enough *rapport* with a kid?");[26] or the police, with their "brutal suspicion";[27] or institutional personnel:

"At no institution did the heads of it get next to the boys or girls to find out what they needed, to make friends with them, to show some love for them."[28] Healy insisted that the chief requirement of the "observer" is his or her[29] kindness, affection, and sympathy. It seemed to Healy that his type of work was based on a "combination of sympathy and scientific effort."[30] These two tendencies were balanced in Healy, but it appears that the former usually won out: "It is better apparently to believe a great deal, and preserve one's kindly attitude, than to spoil one's service in the case. The skepticism required is that of the scientist who asks a reasonable amount of corroboration."[31]

Healy's role as a doctor was always central to his technique: "A great deal that is most valuable in this work can never be done successfully except when the attitude and obligations of the family physician are assumed by the observer," Healy said.[32] The obligations included privileged communication with a doctor, which seemed to help a child open up.[33] But we should not overlook the rhetoric of such a situation, where the "good doctor," as Jon Snodgrass has called Healy,[34] is alternately a credible speaker and a trustworthy audience for the child. A vivid description of this situation appears in a book by Justice Jacob Panken, entitled *The Child Speaks:*

> Psychoanalysts put great stress in affording a patient the opportunity to "speak out." Admission of wrong-doing by a child, his recognition that he has inflicted wrong upon another, is important as part of a treatment towards rehabilitation. Not always is it immediately possible to have a child admit a misconduct; frequently the process takes time.
>
> No effective treatment can be administered until the child has first told the truth. Sometimes I approach a youngster in this fashion: I ask him to regard me as his doctor. Then I inquire whether he would tell his doctor that he suffers from a headache when in fact he had a heart ailment? Usually the child will say, "No." I then ask him whether, if I believed he had a headache, I would, as a doctor, give him a remedy for anything but that? And would medicine for headache cure his heart condition? The result, I suggest, would possibly be disastrous to him. Therefore, if he wants me to help him, he must tell me the truth about his troubles. I should say that in nine hundred and ninety-nine cases out of one thousand the child will then tell me the truth.
>
> Sometimes I ask him to write out what he would like to have his "doctor" do for him, or write a description of his ailment or trouble for his "doctor."[35]

Healy advised selecting subjects from among more youthful offenders: "With the development of reserve and self-containment characteristic of the adult, and particularly the adult who feels himself antagonistic to society, there is often difficulty in getting at some vital points."[36] (Contrast this with oral historians, who aim at getting a well-developed expression of the unique individuality of a person; for them, the speaker usually must be at least twenty years old and not, for all that, given to inhibition.) Concerning the place of observation, Healy says that "in the open" (Mayhew's place) has advantages, but scientific studies in psychology did not seem to him possible there.[37] Concerning timing, he says:

The offender must approach you willingly before you can do anything
for him. Now, when will he exhibit this willingness? Certainly not
when he is "on the outs," and feeling it quite unlikely that he will
recommit offenses or at least be caught again. No, the golden moment
is when he feels himself to be a problem, and his relatives feel it, and
all want a promising solution to the difficulty. It is after he has been
caught, and while he is either detained or on probation, and has not
already been sentenced that is the best time of all for inquiry.[38]

(Contrast this with John Clay's warning against interviewing anyone before trial.)
Normally, according to Healy, no third person should be present in the room
during the interview,[39] the exception being when a male doctor is with a female
patient.[40] Usually Healy interviewed the boys and Bronner took the girls,[41]
though just after Bronner joined the staff Healy took a leave of absence to finish
The Individual Delinquent, and Bronner was embarrassed by what she heard for
the first time, especially about homosexuality.[42]

How to get youngsters to reveal themselves? Healy says that they often started
by trying to find out the child's special abilities or vocational interests, a means of
establishing rapport and of providing material they did indeed need for diagnosis
and prognosis, material that also enabled them to pioneer in the study of learning
disabilities. In other instances, more devious methods were used:

We used various devices: if for instance, we were getting to some sex
problem and saw that it was difficult to have the youngster verbalize
it, we would make an excuse to go out of the room and give them
pencil and paper and tell them to write the words that bothered them
and fold it up and put it away. We often left the typewriter in the room
and let the youngsters play with it and sometimes got very interesting
material. I remember one boy who was terrifically hostile to his father
wrote over and over again, "I'll kill him some day. I'll kill him some
day. I'll kill him some day."[43]

Two standard procedures were employed: either an interviewer took notes and
later wrote up a report, which may account for their paraphrased form in publications, or the child was given pencil and paper and asked to write his autobiography, guided by questions given orally or in writing.[44]

Different individuals required different amounts of time for study. However, as
Bronner says: "In Chicago the cases were seen for the court in such numbers that
we didn't have too great time with any of them. I wouldn't be surprised if the
writing of the lists of words that bothered them was used."[45] Surely Healy and
Bronner did not "grind [their] interviews out according to a schedule from which
you never deviate."[46] But it is unlikely that Healy had the time to allow the child
to ramble on about his life, nor did he have the sensitivity for it: "That's one of the
quarrels I have with psychoanalysis: a lot of people keep on with it just because
they like to talk about themselves."[47] Instead, a battery of tests was invented, and
Healy attributes no importance to autobiographical expression in that invention,
though surely his conversations with young people had some influence on what
went into the initial tests. A temperament suitable to oral history had functioned in
Healy just long enough to establish a more abbreviated procedure. The well was
capped.

The Sociological Stranger: Securing the Life History

Clifford Shaw began collecting life histories from juvenile delinquents probably as early as 1921 (*DA* ix). From 1926 to the early 1940s (especially from 1929 to 1933, if the remaining documents are representative), Shaw and his associates at the Institute for Juvenile Research collected hundreds of life histories from delinquents on parole or probation, from older offenders (some of whom were "professional criminals"), and from other people, such as relatives of offenders. The most frequent procedure was the personal interview (*JR* 21). Burgess said, "A hidden stenographer often is employed," or a tape recorder was used, according to Burgess, though probably not in the 1930s.[48] The stenographic record was then edited into a continuous story. However, this editing risked betraying the original: after all, the reason for preserving the "own words" was to avoid introducing alien elements into the person's expression: "A translation of the story into the language of the interviewer would, in most cases, greatly alter the original meaning" (*JR* 22; cf. *SF* 5, n. 1). If the very words should be preserved, so should the subtleties of sequence; but transforming an interview transcript into an uninterrupted narrative may substantially alter meanings. (This is the reason a "life history interview" differs from other types of interviews: the speaker should continue to speak at some length without being prompted by questions that would only have to be edited out of the transcript to produce a continuous narrative.)

Other life histories, including all the major ones that became books, were acquired by having the individual write out his own story: "Usually these documents present a more coherent and connected picture of the boy's life than could be secured through a series of personal interviews" (*JR* 21). The process would begin with an interview to develop a list of the individual's "behavior problems, delinquencies, arrests, court appearances, and commitments. These experiences were then arranged in the order of their occurrence and presented to the boy to be used as a guide in writing his 'own story.' He was always instructed to give a complete and detailed description of such experience, the situation in which it occurred and the impression which it made upon him" (*NH* xi). If the first essay was meager, as it usually was, and Shaw thought he could get a more detailed account, the writer was encouraged to elaborate further.[49]

Often the only guidance given the writer would be not a questionnaire but examples from what he had already written. Burgess wrote: "From the standpoint of a document as a free and spontaneous expression of personality, the ideal would be to obtain it without questions or directions at all. At all events, only a few simple, unguided questions or directions should be given." Burgess understood this to be Shaw's procedure (*NH* 240–41). According to Krueger in his dissertation "Autobiographical Documents and Personality" (1925), "Life-histories can be secured without a questionnaire. Having lived chronologically, it is easy to write temporally... however, the questionnaire has distinct values.... It assists the person to organize his story into a more connected and more complete account... permits focusing upon specific problems.... It eliminates the problem of taboo and irrelevancy."[50] Shaw and company did use questionnaires in some cases, samples of which are in the files of the remaining life histories.

Life histories were "secured," as the phrase then was, in three places: in the offices of the Institute for Juvenile Research, out in the communities being worked by the Chicago Area Project, and in Illinois prisons. In the 1920s and 1930s, the IJR sociology department was at 907 South Wolcott Street, on Chicago's Near West Side next to the University of Illinois medical school. At that time the area was also filled with residential buildings. From their offices Shaw and McKay could look over into the backyards where children were playing. Shaw's position in a state agency (a division of the State Criminologist, who operated the Illinois prison system) made it possible for him to be assigned boys on parole from state institutions; thus Shaw had a constant source of "the real thing," which academic sociologists did not have. Neighborhood boys would drop by and Shaw or another staff member would give them pencil and paper and send them into another room to write about their experiences. Some wrote a great deal; others next to nothing. The more articulate ones were those who had spent time in detention; they were more outspoken and had more to say.[51] One of the brothers of *Brothers in Crime* sat at a corner of Henry McKay's desk and wrote one sentence at a time; after writing each one, he would turn to McKay for approval, then write another. Some wrote while they were employed as clerks at the institute under a Works Progress Administration program. (In fact, the employment of ex-convicts created quite a stir in this government agency, but Shaw stood his ground, since for him this was a matter of principle.) Some were given "candy money" for their efforts. All manner of confidence men were going in and out of the sociology department at IJR in those days. The wonder is that Shaw and McKay were never seriously robbed, though they probably made loans to needy people that were never repaid.[52]

In addition, life histories were collected by fieldworkers of the Chicago Area Project in those neighborhoods where the Area Project was active, even in the three years before it was incorporated in 1934. As a boy, the late criminologist Hans Mattick was encouraged (unsuccessfully) by Joseph Lohman, a worker for the Area Project, to write his life history. In fact, acquiring life histories from anyone who had something interesting to say about the city, the family, delinquency, crime, social deviance, and so forth was a preoccupation of a group of people beginning with Burgess at the University of Chicago, continuing through Shaw at IJR, and including Shaw's workers, who were in contact with neighborhood residents.[53]

Life histories were collected from former delinquents at Illinois detention facilities, primarily at the adult facilities at Pontiac and the Old Joliet Prison, and from delinquents at the State Training School for Boys at Saint Charles. (Almost no documents were collected from girls or blacks.) Prison officials in those days were unfamiliar with having sociologists interview prisoners, but they were accustomed to psychologists, so Shaw's worker usually operated out of the office of the psychologist. (Just as Healy found it convenient to use the image of a doctor, so sociologists made use of the familiarity of psychologists.) In addition, that IJR was part of the State Criminologist's office made it easier for staff and inmates to understand what sociologists were doing in prisons, where labels are so very important, and made it easier to get admitted in the first place. One of Shaw's staff told inmates he was a University of Chicago student—he was not, but he had been and it made sense that he might be.

Someone would drive down to the prison two or three times a week to pick up life histories that had been written and to arrange for the writing of more. Usually the first writer would be suggested by the psychologist, someone he had met while giving tests to inmates, or perhaps it might be the clerk in the psychologist's office. First the sociologist would interview him and tell him to write as much as he could about his life, though the main focus was on his criminal acts. The prisoner would write in his cell or in the psychologist's office. Word would get around among the inmates that no one was hurt by this activity, and one writer would recommend another. Many of these writers expressed a genuine desire to be of help in criminological research. Among these was Nathan Leopold: in 1930–31, at the urging of one of Shaw's staff, Leopold collected two life histories from "professional thieves" who were inmates at the Old Joliet Prison. None of this was done with a tape recorder, since the wire recorders of the day were too bulky and inefficient; Leopold took down his interviewees' words in speedwriting.[54]

In contrast to the sophisticated analyses of interviewing technique that have developed within the social sciences during the past thirty years (though not perhaps successfully for the life history), the most important part of Shaw's procedure, as of Healy's, was relatively commonplace: his own personality and the personalities of his workers. The boy who was the subject of Shaw's most famous and influential life history publication, *The Jack-Roller,* has said:

> As a boy of twelve, I just met Cliff, back in 1921. He worked then at the Juvenile Court as well as at the settlement house on 31st Street. I recall quite vividly his splendid bearing, being rugged of build, and tall of stature with a thick mane of dark hair, and quite handsome too. However, he particularly impressed me with his sincere manner and a geniality that at once captured my confidence, and that I must say was a big thing, since at that time I had spent over half of my twelve years in institutions and was very much on the defensive. Instinctively I knew him as a friend.[55]

Perhaps the image of *Dr.* Shaw had some influence here too, especially in the context of physicians at IJR; however, Shaw had no right to the title until his alma mater, Adrian College in Michigan, awarded him an honorary degree in 1939.

One of the most interesting notions in the 1920s about life histories was the concept of the "sociological stranger." As Krueger put it: "The comparative stranger with prestige and a disinterested object can as a rule secure better results than the investigator whose relationship with the subject is an intimate one."[56] An example would be a traveler who, while passing through a town, listens to stories a resident would never tell another resident. Or a prisoner may open up to a visitor sooner than to a fellow inmate. Surely the success of Studs Terkel is based partly on this factor, which makes Terkel's accomplishment less miraculous than it seems. The concept began with Georg Simmel:

> In the case of the stranger, the union of closeness and remoteness involved in every human relationship is patterned in a way that may be succinctly formulated as follows: the distance within this relation indicates that one who is close by is remote, but his strangeness indicates that one who is remote is near.[57]

In other words, the life history interview relationship lies somewhere between distant and close social distance: interviewer and interviewee approach each other as mutually marginal persons.

What motivated delinquents to tell Shaw the stories of their lives? From studying the documents collected by Shaw and others, Burgess concluded that they manifested four basic personality types: the chronicler, who listed external events and conventional explanations, the self-defender, the confessant, and the self-analyst (JR 190). Burgess also noted eight types of interview relationships affecting motivation: punishment (the legal situation), investigation, official, casual, friendship, confessional, professional, and research (scientific) (NH 241–43). The closer a particular case is to the last situation on this continuum, the less motive the interviewee has to lie. The five Martin boys of Brothers in Crime were motivated by "an interest in their own lives, monetary considerations, and a genuine hope that the documents might be useful in preventing other boys from becoming involved in delinquency and crime" (BC 143). Allport, Kluckhohn, and Krueger have listed other motivations.[58] The strongest interests of the boys whose stories appeared in Shaw's books seem to have been pride in participating in an important enterprise and the hope of making something of themselves.

Inevitably the question arises about juvenile offenders writing of their lives: Are the documents truthful? I am still amazed that young people who admit they seldom attended school could write so intelligibly and in places even eloquently. Burgess said about this:

> So far as the writer can judge, Stanley's style is not markedly superior to the run of present and former delinquents and criminals. Because of the forced leisure of confinement, convicts read quite as much as any other group in our population, with the possible exception of teachers, clergymen, and writers. Besides it seems to be universally true that one can talk or write best upon the subjects with which he is most familiar. Every person, we have been told, has the ability to write at least one book, his autobiography. [JR 187–88][59]

Still, their articulateness is remarkable, even though most of the written material came from older delinquents (JR 22) (the Jack-Roller was twenty-two years old when his life history was completed). McKay said in an interview (19 April 1973) that they did not keep the handwritten life histories once they had been transcribed by a typist; thus today it is impossible to confirm the authenticity of documents in the way Gottschalk recommends.[60] As for truth, certain points were checked against official documents and confirmed through further interviews with the writer and with people who knew him. However, as Sutherland pointed out: "The author of the book evidently cannot verify the smaller details of the offender's career, or the wishes, attitudes, and philosophy of the offender, which are said to be the significant part of an autobiographical method. At best the framework of the offender's career can be verified."[61] The "subtle aspects," according to Shaw, are often the most influential factors—not the gross points of, for example, family breakdown, but how family members view the event.[62] But Shaw does not consider the possibility of self-deception.

Burgess pointed out that a lie is a response to a punishment situation (JR 188), from which Shaw apparently, for the most part, successfully disassociated himself. Furthermore: "The more a man tells, as all criminal investigators know, the more he is certain to entangle himself in inconsistencies and contradictions, if he is attempting to deceive" (*JR* 188). This is as far as either Burgess or Shaw was willing to go on this issue. Perhaps they were demonstrating their trust in the boys.[63] More likely, in the many other documents they had collected they had ample confirmation of their central point—that delinquency is socially transmitted—and a host of other problems that might seem important to us, such as whether to leave spelling as it was written or whether the life history merely illustrated the life of an intelligent individual or fairly represented a group on every small point in the story, were more or less irrelevant to them.

But the question of editing does raise Allport's warning: "When many liberties are taken [in editing] it is clear that the personal document passes over into a third-person case study; and it is more candid in such instances to present it as such."[64] But what constitutes "many liberties"? If the document was not by a delinquent at all but promoted values and programs in the same way as an authentic document, would it have the same effect on an audience? Not if the audience were aware of the deception; the presentation would not function rhetorically if the conditions for instilling *belief* were absent. The number of liberties allowable in editing seems to be the number an editor can make without risking the violation of the informed reader's trust.

Handwritten life histories were transcribed by typists at the Institute for Juvenile Research, some of them on the WPA payroll, some of them embarrassed by what they read. These documents were then read by sociologists at the institute and filed away. Part of this collection was lost in various moves made by the IJR sociology department in the 1960s, though about one hundred have survived. Some histories were edited, footnoted, and mimeographed for use in training programs at the institute. (For a similar educational purpose, about ten copies of each of the published life histories were available at the University of Chicago library.) McKay claims that nothing was added to the stories, obscene language was removed, names and addresses were changed, and minor corrections in spelling and style were done to make the text read more easily. Thus the rhetorical intent is clear.

There are several other problems with Shaw's method of presentation. He says: "Since it is not possible to present the complete case-history, it may be stated that the boy's 'own story' is confirmed by verification obtained from independent sources" (*JR* 8). We are never given the slightest picture of this process, however, so we are really left with taking the whole enterprise on faith or dismissing it. Also, Shaw gives his readers no inside view of *his own* activities in acquiring the life histories. Kluckhohn remarked: "Particularly neglected in the past has been the responsibility of the anthropologist to report upon himself." Kluckhohn also noted that editing makes it impossible to see repetitions in the original, spontaneous speech or points solicited by the interviewer rather than voluntarily expressed.[65] Sutherland wondered if the impression given by the life histories "that the family and neighborhood are immensely important in the formation of delinquent careers and that the broader culture and social organization are relatively unimportant" is justified by the facts or is a result of Shaw's repeated requests for amplification of points that interested him.[66]

Furthermore, one wonders if removing "obscene" material is not a triumph of public prudery over scientific activity that, after all, viewed itself as improving on public ignorance. One of the mimeographed documents used within IJR stated: "Such incidents involving homosexual behavior are a matter of common practice among such delinquents groups" (file 58, p. 49). But I do not find homosexual incidents in the public writings. In *The Natural History* Shaw has put especially significant statements into italics "in order to draw the reader's attention to them" (*NH* 53). But the italics are distracting, and in no instance are they interpreted: a certain italicized phrase is flagged as being significant, but precisely what is its significance? In fact, italics were never used in the later life histories. Since some, though not much, punctuation and spelling is askew, it is impossible to distinguish a typographical error from a mistake the writer made, such as "carfare" (*NH* 114) or "carefare" (*NH* 113). Perhaps this is further evidence of Shaw's lack of interest in psychological interpretation. Finally, since birthdates are not given, one does not know the precise historical context of any of the events; nor does one know exactly which culture or nationality is undergoing "culture conflict" in America, since Shaw sought to generalize the process to avoid further stigmatizing of one or another nationality group.

Notes

Introduction

1. Norman K. Denzin, *Research Act*, pp. 226, 220.
2. Gordon Allport, *Use of Personal Documents*, p. xii; Herbert Blumer, *Appraisal of Thomas and Znaniecki's "The Polish Peasant,"* p. 28.
3. "Oral history" appeared as early as 1863, was used publicly in the 1930s by Joe Gould, a Greenwich Village bohemian, and was established by Allan Nevins in the Columbia University project. See Charles T. Morrissey, "Why Call it 'Oral History'?"
4. See Marvin E. Wolfgang, "Criminology and the Criminologist."
5. Cf. William James on autobiography in non-Christian religions: "Strange that a species of book so abundant among ourselves should be so little represented elsewhere" (*Varieties of Religious Experience*, p. 402). Though I have been assured by Daniel Bertaux that there has been no tradition or major uses of delinquents' life histories in France, *Biography and Society: The Life History Approach in the Social Sciences*, edited by Bertaux, covers uses of life histories in Europe; this may require alteration of my position. Unfortunately, I was able to see only the table of contents and a draft of the introduction of this book. See also Michel Foucault's edition of a life history of a nineteenth century French criminal: *I, Pierre Rivière*.
6. The earliest presentations resembling oral history were probably the speeches the Greek rhetorician Lysias (active in this work about 403–380 B.C.) wrote for his clients to deliver in court. Since lawyers were nonexistent and Athenian citizens were required to present their own cases, the practice grew up of using a *logographos*, or speech writer. Lysias is considered the first of these to express the character of his client in the speech he composed, and where appropriate he included events in the life of his subject besides those involved in the crime at issue. Momigliano has said: "The technique for winning lawsuits and making political propaganda relied generally on the ability to present one's own and somebody else's life in a suitable light" (*Development of Greek Biography*, p. 48). One of the foremost examples of this in an autobiographical mode is Isocrates' *Antidosis*, in which the author adopts the fiction of "a trial and of a suit against me," and in so doing gives "a true image of my thought and of my whole life" (*Antidosis* 7). The speeches of the Greek rhetoricians are one of the best sources of our awareness of everyday life in ancient Greece, preventing us from interpreting all Greeks as geniuses. This "localizing" of human reality in what Heidegger might call *Dasein*, or "being there," is a function of oral histories.

7. In an anonymous review of a book by Isaac d'Israeli, who had himself used the term "self-biography" (Arnaldo Momigliano, *Development of Greek Biography*, p. 14). Momigliano also points out that the *Grand dictionnaire universel Larousse* in 1866 remarked about "autobiography": "Ce mot, quoique d'origine grecque, est de fabrique anglaise."

8. Karl Weintraub, "Autobiography and Historical Consciousness," p. 821.

9. Karl Weintraub, *Value of the Individual*, p. 261.

10. G. W. F. Hegel, *Phenomenology of Mind*, p. 23.

11. Michel Foucault, *Discipline and Punish*, p. 74.

12. According to James Olney, when he wrote his *Metaphors of Self: The Meaning of Autobiography* in 1972, there were only a few books about autobiography, but more recently many articles and several books have been published. See James Olney, "*Autos, Bios, Graphein:* The Study of Autobiographical Literature," p. 113, and James Olney, ed., *Autobiography: Essays Theoretical and Critical.*

13. Everett V. Stonequist, *Marginal Man*, pp. 2–3. Cf. Robert E. Park, "Human Migration and the Marginal Man."

14. In a chapter of *Professing Sociology* entitled "Mainliners and Marginals," I. L. Horowitz distinguishes between "occupationalists" and "professionals": for the occupationalist "the 'image' of association instilled is that of other fields, usually of high prestige but low systematization. In the case of sociology: history, biography, and sometimes fiction.... There is an emphasis on autoconsciousness, on an awareness of the historical continuities of social problems and social forces." In the case of the professional, "the 'image' or chain of associations instilled is that of other professions, usually of high prestige standing. In the case of sociology: physics, mathematics, and sometimes engineering. Images are often linked to those areas that have achieved a high grade of systematization and quantification, and no less clear and distinct separation of theory-building from historical antecedents." The occupationalist "views the field as a calling rather than as a job," a field where "novelty, generalization, and new modalities of relations to the general public are countenanced if not encouraged," while professionals prefer to address their peer groups.

15. Momigliano, *Development of Greek Biography*, quotes one Johann Gustave Droysen to the effect that "the adventurer, the failure, the marginal figure [are appropriate] subjects for biography" (p. 2). Momigliano also makes some relevant observations about the Greek originators of biography—Skylax of Caryander and Xanthus, a Lydian, both Persians belonging to "Asia Minor, indeed marginal zones of Greek culture" (pp. 36, 33). During the fourth century B.C. biography "came to occupy an ambiguous position between fact and imagination" (p. 46). Aristoxenus, the inventor of Hellenic biography and a "strange personality," had been trained a Pythagorean but went over to the Peripatetics (p. 103). I mention these curiosities to suggest that marginality and biography in general may be essentially connected.

16. Michel Foucault, *Discipline and Punish*, p. 301.

17. For example, Edwin Schur has pointed out that Clifford Shaw, like James Baldwin, Claude Brown, Piri Thomas, and Oscar Lewis, conveyed "a sense of how it feels to live in and through situations that are quite remote from the lives of

'respectable' middle-class citizens," but only Shaw, with his explicitly stated theory, related "subjective reactions... to our systematic understanding of crime" (*Our Criminal Society*, p. 105).

18. Even though John Clay collected oral histories before Henry Mayhew, I shall begin with Mayhew. Mayhew is the archetype: his works display the pattern of marginality and rhetorical activity more clearly than any other writing. At any rate, Clay's influence was at its height on juvenile matters about 1851–54 through the reform efforts of Mary Carpenter, while Mayhew reached his apogee earlier, during his 1849–50 newspaper series.

Chapter One

1. John D. Rosenberg, ed., *London Labour and the London Poor*, p. vi. In an article in the *New Yorker* (8 January 1980), Whitney Balliett referred to *London Labour*, Mayhew's greatest work, as a "great nineteenth-century oral history." These statements are evidence that common usage supports my application of this term to the work of Mayhew and others like him.

2. Denis Brian, *Murderers and Other Friendly People*, p. 302; cf. Studs Terkel, *Working*, p. xiii.

3. Terence Morris, *Criminal Area*, pp. 63, 62. Nothing better pinpoints the similarities between Mayhew's method and that of sociologists of the Chicago school, to be discussed below, than his use, like theirs, of the term "natural history" to refer to human social experience: "the natural history, as it were, of the industry and idleness of Great Britain in the nineteenth century" (*London Labour* 4:4). Both Mayhew and the Chicagoans used natural histories to move from abstract to more concrete perceptions of social processes.

4. Anne Humpherys, *Travels into the Poor Man's Country*. Almost all of my writing about Mayhew was completed before I read this authoritative book. My contribution to the study of Mayhew is a discussion of delinquency and oral history in more detail than has been done elsewhere. Another work I read too late to include in this study is Alan Thomas's dissertation "Henry Mayhew's Rhetoric: A Study of His Presentation of Social 'Facts.'" Thomas is especially good at relating oral history material to its "surround," Mayhew's statistics and descriptive prose.

5. W. H. Auden, "A Very Inquisitive Old Party," p. 121. Auden attributes the title of his article to a prostitute describing her interviewer. However, this was not Mayhew, but appears to have been Bracebridge Hemyng (cf. *London Labour*, 4:221). The *New Yorker* has something of a tradition of glowing references to Mayhew: John Updike wrote (7 April 1980): "The interview as a tool of art and history is a fairly recent device, though Henry Mayhew's "London Labour and the London Poor" used it to construct a nineteenth-century masterpiece."

6. Eileen Yeo, "Mayhew as a Social Investigator," p. 94. Frederick Engels was also expressing an interest in direct experience at this time: he wanted, he said, "to see you in your own homes, to observe you in your every-day life, to chat with you on your condition and grievances, to witness your struggles against the social and political power of your oppressors." Quoted in Steven Marcus, *Engels, Manchester, and the Working Class*, p. 92. But Engels's investigations were more orderly than Mayhew's: more on this below.

7. Mayhew was not the only person calling for a system based on knowledge about individual offenders in order, for example, to treat the habitual thief differently from the first offender. There was a mixture of the two approaches—punishing for the crime and rehabilitating the criminal—in Mayhew's day similar to the situation today, except that for the most part we are now going in the opposite direction, reflecting our disenchantment with "rehabilitation."

8. See Alfred Lindesmith and Yale Levin, "The Lombrosian Myth in Criminology"; Yale Levin and Alfred Lindesmith, "English Ecology and Criminology of the Past Century"; and Yale Levin, "The Treatment of Juvenile Delinquency in England during the Early Nineteenth Century." Terence Morris has pointed out another pioneering effort of Mayhew and John Binny's *The Criminal Prisons of London:* it is "the only authoritative but non-official account of the early days of the new prison system which followed upon penal reform and the abolition of transportation" (*Criminal Area,* p. 62). "Transportation" refers to the practice of sending convicts to overseas colonies.

9. John L. Bradley, ed., *Selections from London Labour and the London Poor,* pp. xvii, xxv.

10. Quoted in E. P. Thompson, "The Political Education of Henry Mayhew," p. 44.

11. Later, when Mayhew had a falling-out with the newspaper's editors, a disagreement arose over who had originated the idea for the series. The *Morning Chronicle* had a history of social activism and innovation. John Stuart Mill, who had written for the newspaper, called an early editor, John Black, a major influence in breaking down the superstition that the British legal system was perfect (H. R. Fox Bourne, *English Newspapers* 2:13). Dickens's first published work, *Sketches by Boz,* appeared in the *Morning Chronicle.* The earliest use of the electric telegraph by a newspaper may have been by the *Chronicle* (ibid., p. 138), and its use of rough woodcuts led to the *Illustrated London News,* for which Mayhew also wrote (ibid., p. 119).

12. Andrews claims this experiment followed a similar one on the state of Wales but on a smaller scale, made by the *Times* (Alexander Andrews, *History of British Journalism,* 2:276).

13. *London Labour* (1851), vol. 1, no. 16, Answers to Correspondents.

14. Henry Mayhew, *Young Benjamin Frankin,* p. xiv. Andrews remarks that in his attempt to put together "that great Encyclopaedia of Industry and Idleness," Mayhew was "unaccountably and unfortunately defeated by adverse circumstances" (Andrews, *History* 2:277). Or by outrageously grandiose plans. The wrapper on one of the 1856 booklets announces that "The Great World of London" will be divided into the following parts: Legal, Medical, Religious, Commercial, Shop, Literary, Theatrical, Fashionable, Political, Military, Nautical, Market, Working, Serving, Locomotive, Street, Fast, Poor, Criminal, Exhibition, Musical and Artistic, Eating and Drinking, Scholastic, Foreigners, Refuse, Suburban, and Ancient London, as well as a General View of London. All this will cover "Its Hard Life, Its Easy Life...Its Highways and Byways and Slyways...Its Lions and Puppies, Sharks and Gulls, Big-Wigs and Small Fry, Philosophers and Fast Men...In Fine, Its Everyday and Out-of-the-Way Scenes, Places, and Characters."

15. This copy, now owned by Anthony Sorrentino, Shaw's assistant, unfortunately contains no marginal notes by Shaw. The Dover edition of *London Labour* is out of print.

16. Eileen Yeo and E. P. Thompson, eds., *Unknown Mayhew*.

17. For an excellent analysis of the ambiguities in Mayhew's subject, see Gertrude Himmelfarb, "Mayhew's Poor: A Problem of Identity." Mayhew himself admitted that the street folk constituted only one-fortieth of the population of London, but his characterization of them as strange "nomads"—in a book with such a title—seems to apply to London laborers and the London poor in general, despite the fact that Mayhew neglected to study those in the most populous occupations: domestic workers, construction workers, tailors, dressmakers, milliners, and shoemakers.

18. Tobias reports on a visit to London in the 1840s by a group of Ojibwa Indians, one of whom said: "We see hundreds of little children with their naked feet in the snow, and we pity them, for we know they are hungry.... You talk about sending blackcoats [missionaries] among the Indians; now we have no such poor children among us.... Now we think it would be better for your teachers all to stay at home, and go to work right here in your own streets" (J. J. Tobias, *Crime and Industrial Society in the 19th Century*, p. 86).

19. Cf. Robert Angell in 1945: "It is unlikely that all of a great many documents dealing with a certain set of phenomena would be biased in the same way" ("Critical Review," p. 181). "The more individual each worker's experience the more convincing was his information when it confirmed the figures about wages from another worker totally different in abilities, background, and individual station" (Anne Humpherys, *Travels*, p. 44).

20. One possibility is that, like John Clay (see below), Mayhew took his idea from the 1839 *Report on Establishing a Constabulary Force*. Mayhew obviously read this report, because one of his favorite explanations of crime was contained in it: "the temptation of obtaining property with a less degree of labour than by regular industry."

21. Alexander Andrews, *History of British Journalism*, 2:277.

22. John L. Bradley, *Selections*, pp. ix–x.

23. E. P. Thompson, "Mayhew and the *Morning Chronicle*," pp. 45, 12–13. For an even more eccentric collector of oral histories, see Joseph L. Mitchell, *Joe Gould's Secret*.

24. Alexander Andrews, *History of British Journalism*, 2:277.

25. In the preface to his biography of Benjamin Franklin, Mayhew deplored the existence of Tothill Fields Prison, where juveniles were kept, saying that if it were in Paris it would be torn down like the Bastille: "But here, good easy citizens that we are, we pay our poor-rates; we call ourselves miserable sinners, in a loud voice, once a week, from a cozy pew; our 'good lady' belongs to a district visiting society, and distributes tracts in the back slums; we put our check into the plate, after a bottle or two of port, at a charity dinner; and this done, we are *self-content*" (*Young Benjamin Franklin*, p. xv).

26. *Quarterly Review* 84 (December 1848): 173–74. Quoted in W. K. C. Guthrie, *Sophists*, p. 6, n. 1.

27. Eileen Yeo, "Mayhew as a Social Investigator," p. 73.

28. Henry Mayhew, *Wonders of Science*, p. xi.

29. Henry Mayhew, *Young Benjamin Franklin*, p. ix.

30. Eileen Yeo, "Mayhew as a Social Investigator," p. 57.

31. *Punch*, 9 March 1850, p. 93; quoted in Anne Humpherys, *Voices of the Poor*, p. ix.

32. Ibid., pp. xi, xiii.

33. Referring to criminals, Mayhew says: "Now, we have paid some little attention to such strange members of the human family as these, and others at war with all social institutions. We have thought the peculiarities of their nature as worthy of study in an ethnological point of view, as those of the people of other countries, and we have learnt to look upon them as a distinct race of individuals, as distinct as the Malay is from the Caucasian tribe. We have sought, moreover, to reduce their several varieties into something like system, believing it quite as requisite that we should have an attempt at a scientific classification of the criminal classes, as of the Infusoriae or the Cryptogamia. An enumeration of the several natural orders and species of criminals will let the reader see that the class is as multifarious, and surely, in a scientific point of view, as worthy of being studied as the varieties of animalcules" (*Criminal Prisons*, p. 45).

34. John L. Bradley, ed., *Selections*, p. xviii. Concerning the journal *Figaro in London*, Fox Bourne has written: "independent comic journalism was something of a novelty in 1831, when, on December 10, Gilbert Abbot à Beckett and Henry Mayhew commenced 'Figaro in London.'" Others were introduced, but only *Figaro* took the public fancy. The venture ended in 1839, but it was revived in 1841 as *Punch* (H. R. Fox Bourne, *English Newspapers*, 2:116).

35. Anne Humpherys, *Travels*, p. 14.

36. See *London Labour* (1851), vol. 1, no. 13. Humpherys doubts this book was ever written (*Travels*, p. 209).

37. Eileen Yeo, "Mayhew as a Social Investigator," pp. 86–87.

38. Clifford R. Shaw, *Natural History of a Delinquent Career*, p. xi. Cf. Steven Marcus, *The Other Victorians*, pp. 184–85.

39. Helen MacGill Hughes, "From Politics to Human Interest," p. 154.

40. M. D. Hill, *Report of the Select Committee on Criminal and Destitute Juveniles* (1852), p. 33, quoted in Levin and Lindesmith, "English Ecology," pp. 804–5. Hermann Mannheim remarks about Hill's claim that he "seems to have in mind a period prior to the age of Adam Smith, who regarded that 'silent but very efficient control' exercised by the superior classes over their low-class neighbors in big cities already as a thing of the past. In any case, however, what Hill regards as criminogenic is the crowding together of masses of poor people in certain city districts abandoned by the wealthy" (*Comparative Criminology* 2:552). The latter point also appears in Clifford Shaw's theory of criminogenesis. Richard Sennett has attributed the segregation of classes in early nineteenth century Paris and London to the building of new apartment buildings, investment in which seemed more secure if a homogeneous class population inhabited them (*Fall of Public Man*, pp. 135–36). Cf. Steven Marcus, *Engels, Manchester, and the Working Class*, pp. 174–75.

41. According to Anne Humpherys, the newspaper's readers knew something of the condition of the poor from several studies that had been made, but: "Nearly

all private and public investigations of the lower classes before 1849 concerned only those workers outside London" (*Voices of the Poor,* pp. ix–x).

42. Susan Sontag, *On Photography,* p. 57.

43. Of course many of these notions were commonplaces: John Howard wrote that *The State of the Prisons* "was not published for general entertainment; but for the perusal of those who have it in their power to give redress to the sufferers" (p. xxii).

44. Alan Cedric Thomas, "Henry Mayhew's Rhetoric," p. 41.

45. E. P. Thompson, "Political Education of Henry Mayhew," p. 43.

46. *London Labour* (1851), vol. 1, no. 15, Answers to Correspondents.

47. E. P. Thompson, "Political Education of Henry Mayhew," p. 57. The wrapper on *London Labour* (1851), vol. 1, no. 10, Answers to Correspondents, makes the same statement.

48. *London Labour* (1851), vol. 1, no. 22, Answers to Correspondents. This is the meaning of "advocacy" for Mayhew, not the securing of political rights by legal action, as it means in the juvenile justice system today.

49. Eileen Yeo, "Mayhew as a Social Investigator," p. 95.

50. *London Labour* (1851), vol. 1, no. 10, Answers to Correspondents.

51. The *Economist* wrote: "the rich are no more responsible for [the] condition [of the poor] than [the poor] are responsible for the condition of the rich; and if they cannot help themselves, all experience demonstrates that the rich cannot help them." Quoted in Thompson, "Political Education of Henry Mayhew," p. 49.

52. Peter Quennell has said that Mayhew "loved figures for their own sake, and welcomed every opportunity of drawing up vast ingenious tables" (*Mayhew's London,* p. 19). Terence Morris has pointed out that Mayhew's statistics are the least original parts of his work, since the maps and tables were already familiar in the writings of Guerry, Rousseau, Fletcher, and others (*Criminal Area,* p. 61).

53. Henry Mayhew, *German Life,* 1:xii.

54. Eileen Yeo, "Mayhew as a Social Investigator," p. 86.

55. This was not confined to England. Concerning the same period in the United States, Harold Finestone has written: "The point of view from which these reformers approached the problem of poverty was composed of an improbable blending of the moralisms of puritanism with the belief in the malleability of human nature and its responsiveness to environmental influences associated with the Enlightenment" (*Victims of Change,* p. 5).

56. Cf. "It is pleasant to note that Roman biography contributed to keeping emperors within the bounds of mortality" (Arnaldo Momigliano, *Development of Greek Biography,* p. 100).

57. John D. Rosenberg, ed., *London Labour,* p. vii.

58. William Gass, *On Being Blue,* p. 25.

59. Motlu Konuk Blasing, *Art of Life,* p. 158. For a recent example, see John Langston Gwaltney, *Drylongso.*

60. E. P. Thompson, "Mayhew and the *Morning Chronicle,*" p. 24.

61. W. H. Auden, "A Very Inquisitive Old Party," p. 133. Oscar Lewis makes the same point in his introduction to *Children of Sanchez.*

62. Introduction to Clifford R. Shaw, *Jack-Roller* (1966 ed.), p. xvii.

63. Wrapper on "The Great World of London."

64. For London spectacles of the time see Richard D. Altick, *The Shows of London* (Cambridge: Harvard University Press, 1978).

65. Henry Mayhew, *Story of the Peasant-Boy Philosopher*, p. x.

66. Thomas J. Cottle has made this point in a recent book: "Some claim that rendering portraits of poor people in even a slightly artistic fashion automatically turns them into the proverbial noble savage, thereby convincing one's readers that these people, as attested to by the beauty and majesty of their words, require no special political or economic support" (*Private Lives and Public Accounts*, p. 11).

67. Eileen Yeo, "Mayhew as a Social Investigator," p. 73.

68. *Magic of Kindness*, p. vi. This method was also espoused in *Mormons*, p. 16, though Charles MacKay, not the Mayhews, wrote this book, according to Anne Humpherys. For more on authenticity, see Alan Cedric Thomas, "Henry Mayhew's Rhetoric," chap. 7, "The Rhetoric of Authenticity."

69. Aristotle, *Rhetoric*, 1410a.

70. Henry Mayhew, *Young Benjamin Franklin*, p. xiii.

71. Susan Sontag, *On Photograpy*, p. 71.

72. *Punch*, 9 March 1850; quoted in Anne Humpherys, *Voices of the Poor*, p. ix.

73. To show how haphazard some of Mayhew's work was, the same illustration appears in *London Labour* (3:113) as "Coster Lads in Holiday Attire," and in *Criminal Prisons*, p. 33, as "Ticket-of-Leave Men."

William Stott has written: "The first-person life histories in Henry Mayhew's *London Labour and the London Poor* (1851–62) were illustrated with engravings which intensified the reality of the poor for readers of the times, but which, a century later, make the poor look almost as fabulous as Cruikshank's caricatures. Though Mayhew's narratives retain a great deal of their power, the illustrations do not. They are too glib and sentimental; they certainly do not strike the twentieth-century reader as authentic in the way John Thompson's 1870 photographs of London street people do. The engraving is a medium in which documentary would now seem to be impossible" (*Documentary Expression*, p. 75).

The propaganda use of photography by reform schools was soon to be explored: "Upon arrival at Dr. Bernardo's each child would have its photograph taken. Ideally a photograph would also be taken of the child when he or she left the home. A photograph ... was often ... used by Dr. Bernardo for publicity" (Gail Buckland, *Reality Recorded: Early Documentary Photography*, p. 93).

74. *London Labour* (1851), vol. 3, no. 39, Answers to Correspondents.

75. Henry Mayhew and George Cruikshank, *1851*, p. 154.

Chapter Two

1. *Morning Chronicle*, 25 April 1850.

2. J. J. Tobias, *Crime and Industrial Society*, pp. 44, 170, 255.

3. A. F. Young and E. T. Ashton, *British Social Work*, pp. 8–9.

4. Philip Collins has written in *Dickens and Crime* (p. 349) that "parallels to Oliver Twist occur on every page" of volume 4 of *London Labour*, which, however, was not written by Mayhew though it was almost certainly inspired and perhaps even planned by him.

5. Eileen Yeo, "Mayhew as a Social Investigator," p. 88.

6. This institution had been opened in 1834 and was quickly judged by an expert to be "a huge and costly blunder" (*Criminal Prisons,* p. 363). It was difficult to prove the age of an individual until the second half of the century, when compulsory registration of birth, started in 1836, began to have effects (cf. J. J. Tobias, *Crime and Industrial Society,* p. 12). This allowed some youths to claim they were younger than they were in order to be sent to juvenile wards, where they probably received better treatment than in adult sections.

7. Ibid., pp. 253–54.

8. Cf. Steven L. Schlossman and Stephanie Wallach, "The Crime of Precocious Sexuality."

9. "The same division obtained amongst the girls as amongst the boys, the less intelligent being prostitutes and beggars while their brighter sisters were primarily thieves who used prostitution merely as a means of taking strangers unawares" (J. J. Tobias, *Crime and Industrial Society,* p. 67).

10. *London Labour* (1851), vol. 2, no. 34.

11. Ibid., vol. 2, no. 38.

12. Ibid., vol. 1, no. 11.

13. J. J. Tobias, *Crime and Industrial Society,* p. 168.

14. Offenses that fell under vagrancy laws were begging or sleeping in the open air, disorderly prostitution, fortune-telling, gaming, indecent exposure of the person, abandoning families, being an incorrigible rogue convicted at sessions, obtaining money by false pretenses, and being a reputed thief, rogue, or vagabond.

15. *Morning Chronicle,* 31 January 1850, p. 5.

16. Ibid., 29 January 1850, p. 5.

17. Ibid., 19 March 1850, p. 5.

18. Quoted in Edwin H. Sutherland, *Principles of Criminology* (1934), p. 313.

19. *Morning Chronicle,* 19 March 1850, p. 5.

20. Fragment 184.

21. According to Yeo, "Lawyers like M. D. Hill and newly organized charity workers like Mary Carpenter saw the social causes of crime largely in terms of the troubled family environments of the perishing and dangerous classes but paid little attention to the economic constraints working on problem families" ("Mayhew as a Social Investigator," p. 89). However, neither did Mayhew, except insofar as this is implied in some of his articles on the slop system. His consciousness was not raised to make economic realities a permanent element in his interpretation of juvenile crime.

22. J. J. Tobias, *Crime and Industrial Society,* pp. 165–66.

23. *Morning Chronicle,* 22 January 1850, p. 5.

24. J. J. Tobias, *Crime and Industrial Society,* p. 100.

25. E. P. Thompson, "Mayhew and the *Morning Chronicle,*" p. 11.

26. E. P. Thompson, "Political Education of Henry Mayhew," p. 56.

27. Anne Humpherys, *Voices of the Poor,* p. xiv.

28. H. R. Fox Bourne, *English Newspapers,* 2:159. Humpherys says that the *London Labour* pamphlets sold about 13,000 copies weekly, a fact that emerged in a lawsuit between Mayhew and his publisher. By comparison, the fifteenth number of *Pickwick Papers* reached nearly 40,000 (Anne Humpherys, *Travels,* p. 24).

29. John L. Bradley, ed., *Selections,* p. ix.

30. *Morning Chronicle,* 25 April 1850, p. 6.

31. Ibid., 29 March 1850, p. 5.

32. John L. Bradley, ed., *Selections,* p. xxxiv, and Humpherys, *Travels,* chap. 6. The Reverend Miciah Hill used some *London Labour* material in his prize-winning essay on juvenile delinquency; otherwise the essay contains no firsthand observations, even from a second party, much less from Hill. See Wiley B. Sanders, *Juvenile Offenders for a Thousand Years,* p. 233; cf. p. 223, where Thomas Beames quotes Mayhew on London rookeries.

33. E. P. Thompson, "Mayhew and the *Morning Chronicle,*" p. 66.

34. Yale Levin, "Treatment of Juvenile Delinquency," p. 43.

35. J. J. Tobias, *Crime and Industrial Society,* p. 176. Philip Collins concurs with this judgment: "My study of the records and publications of the Ragged School Union, and of other contemporary reports, suggests that Dickens was shrewd and just both in his criticisms of the Ragged Schools, and in his praise for them" (*Dickens and Crime,* pp. 91–92).

36. J. J. Tobias, *Crime and Industrial Society,* p. 42.

37. Ibid., p. 215.

38. Ibid., p. 41.

39. Ibid. Elsewhere Tobias writes: "These comments on the Irish immigrants in the nineteenth century fit in well with subsequent experience elsewhere and with criminological theory. Adult immigrants are thought as a rule to stick to the types of crime familiar to them in their place of origin, while the second generation, the first to be born or brought up in their new homeland, are often unusually prone to crime. They reject the ideas and standards of their parents, it is argued, and enthusiastically adopt those of the people of the area in which they live" (ibid., p. 170).

40. One of Mayhew's correspondents wrote to complain that a young man had been dismissed from his job when his earlier criminal record came to light. In his reply Mayhew sides with the police, who had refused to reissue the man a license as a bus conductor, since they said they could not risk having dishonest people in positions they were responsible for. Mayhew says he knows about the essential honesty of the police because he has depended on them for information. However, he concludes that since he is in no such position of public responsibility as the police, he will do all he can to help the individual (*London Labour* [1851], vol. 3, nos. 41, 43).

41. Eileen Yeo, "Mayhew as a Social Investigator," p. 75.

42. In *Low Wages,* Mayhew said the political economists of his day "sat beside a snug sea-coal fire and tried to think out the several matters affecting the working classes, or else they have retired to some obscure corner, and there remained, like big-bottomed spiders, spinning their cobweb theories among heaps of rubbish" (p. 126).

43. E. P. Thompson, "Political Education of Henry Mayhew," p. 43.

44. *Children in Trouble,* by Howard James, based on a series of articles in the *Christian Science Monitor* in 1969, is similar to Fine's treatment, with briefer quotes from children.

45. Fine's book on delinquents was apparently so marginal to his career that it was not even mentioned in his obituary in the *New York Times,* 17 May 1975.

Chapter Three

1. In *Discipline and Punish: The Birth of the Prison,* Michel Foucault views the ghastly public torture-executions before the nineteenth century as exhibitions of the absolute power of the monarch to annihilate evil. Clearly, one condition for the genesis of oral histories in criminology is the absence of this political absolutism.

2. Clay was not the only pioneering prison chaplain. During the same period, John Luckey, chaplain at Sing Sing prison in New York, studied the personal histories of inmates by interviewing them and their visitors and examining their correspondence. W. David Lewis says: "He took down his findings in notebooks which were carefully indexed so that he could refer to a particular case at a moment's notice; by 1846, he had filled about fourteen of these with information, and as he counseled his charges he tried to apply the understanding he had gained from his research." "In a real sense he was New York's pioneer caseworker, using for the first time methods which were later to become staple techniques" (*From Newgate to Dannemora,* p. 213). In his book *Life in Sing Sing State Prison, as Seen in a Twelve Years' Chaplaincy,* Luckey presents numerous case histories in his own rather pious words, one exception being a straightforward memoir of a forger trained by the man's father (pp. 208–17), dictated the day before his execution: "I sent for you to relate, as far as my weakness would allow, those incidents in my criminal life which might, I hope, be a warning to my fellow-prisoners and others. It is all I can *now* do to atone for my numerous and vile acts against society" (p. 214). Like Clay, Luckey wrote annual reports but apparently did not use oral histories in them (cf. pp. 347 ff.).

3. "Report of Commissioners," p. 2.

4. Ibid., p. 17.

5. Ibid., p. 29. Humpherys quotes a character in a contemporary novel proclaiming about parliamentary reports: "I don't think one lady in a thousand ever looks into them, to say nothing of other classes. . . . What we chiefly want is to have some public information given about it, such as will be read, and may stir up the hearts of God's servants to succour us" (*Travels into the Poor Man's Country,* p. 199).

6. "Report of Commissioners," p. 30. Appendix 6 of the report also gives a long account of the practices of delinquents in London, written by an educated prison inmate convicted on a charge of arson, derived from conversations with "depredators in whose company he was unavoidably kept" (p. 30).

7. Mary Carpenter, *Juvenile Delinquents,* p. 42.

8. For example, the *Report from the Select Committee of the House of Lords on the Law Relating to the Protection of Young Girls* (London, 1881). Pages 110–13 contain some of what was later called "own story," and Appendix A has some "Cases in Illustration" that quote girls about their involvement in prostitution. "These statements were taken down by the Solicitor to the Treasury" (p. 130).

9. J. Arthur Hoyles, *Religion in Prison,* p. 44.

10. Margaret May, "Innocence and Experience," p. 12.

11. Clay, quoted by Mary Carpenter in *Our Convicts,* 1:74.

12. *Chaplain's Report* (1848), p. 74.

13. *Chaplain's Report* (1849), p. 43. A few brief quotes indicating the harmful-

ness of contact with books and plays about the celebrated criminal Jack Sheppard were recorded in the text itself of the 1841 report, pp. 12 ff.

14. Clay wrote to Carpenter on 25 August 1854: "I have in MS. the *very* bulky memoir of a young London thief. It is very striking, as laying open the state of things among the *accomplished* practitioners in crime, and I have been able to test its truth. Would you like to have the perusal of it?" (Walter Lowe Clay, *Prison Chaplain*, p. 620).

15. Mary Carpenter, *Juvenile Delinquents*, pp. 59–61.

16. Ibid., p. 62.

17. Ibid., pp. 65–70.

18. See Philip Collins, *Dickens and Crime*, pp. 141, 333.

19. For example: *Chaplain's Report* (1852), pp. 28–29.

20. *Chaplain's Report* (1848), p. 37.

21. This monotony casts doubt on Mary Carpenter's claim that Clay's oral histories show "that an immense variety exists among those who are already habitual offenders," though she may have meant here merely more variety of criminal techniques than the public was aware of (Mary Carpenter, *Our Convicts*, 1:19). For a recent collection of delinquents' oral histories emphasizing parental alcoholism, see Thomas Cottle's *Children in Jail* (1977).

22. *Chaplain's Report* (1849), p. 78.

23. One of the most influential and indefatigable agitators in the movement for reformatory schools, Mary Carpenter (1807–77) exhibited no ambiguity, contradiction, or marginality in her character, and she did not collect oral histories— some small confirmation of one of my claims, though she doubtless conversed with hundreds of delinquents who passed through the schools she operated. Her name was even put on three "autobiographies" of female prison inmates, but all three were written by Frederick William Robinson.

Carpenter's books are filled with quotations, most of them from middle-class authorities. Clay's oral histories of prison inmates are reproduced at length in two places in her works: chapter 2 of *Juvenile Delinquents*, and chapters 1 and 2 of *Our Convicts*. The first chapter of the former book treats several classes of delinquents, but Carpenter says: "We cannot reform whole classes as such." "The work of reformation is an individual work; for every one must bear his own moral burden, and by his own works shall each one stand or fall" (p. 50). The title of the chapter is "A Single Captive." Clay's documents also appear in the first volume of *Our Convicts:* chapter 1, "Who Are Our Convicts?" and chapter 2, "How Are Our Convicts Made?"

A reviewer of one of her works wrote in the *Edinburgh Review* (122 [1865] 337): "Miss Carpenter has at last supplied us with materials needed to qualify us so to understand the conditions of a life *altogether unlike our own*, as to perceive what sort of minds we have to deal with" (emphasis added). This was not Carpenter's view. She shared Clay's notions that delinquents are neither innately evil nor totally different from everyone else, but that they are developed in a certain kind of environment. Oral histories showed that the impact of that environment had been so deep that a short stay in a prison was not enough.

Her lifework was to get government recognition for schools of various types: Ragged Schools for nondelinquent children in the city areas in which they lived;

Industrial Boarding Schools for vagrant nondelinquents; and Reformatory Schools for delinquents. She herself operated examples of these schools, and she eventually succeeded in getting government recognition for all these types of institutions in England. Her work was one factor in the passage of the Education Act of 1870, which made school attendance compulsory for all English children. She was also influential in the development of reform schools in the United States (see Anthony Platt, *Child Savers*, pp. 50, 63–64, 68–69).

24. *Chaplain's Report* (1852), p. 45.

25. *Chaplain's Report* (1849), p. 51. Mary Carpenter in *Our Convicts*, 1:24, quotes Clay in his 27th report to the effect that oral histories of a gang of pickpockets "show too plainly, that the land, or at least the police, is unequal to a successful contest with such characters, and it may, therefore, be of service to exhibit to the public the amount of depredation they are exposed to, in order that they may obviate, by their own watchfulness, those losses which, if once sustained, can seldom be recovered."

26. Jo Manton, *Mary Carpenter and the Children of the Streets*, p. 121.

27. *Chaplain's Report* (1841), p. 10.

28. *Chaplain's Report* (1849), p. 43. Compare this reference to the "real state of society" with Engels's contemporary study of nearby Manchester.

29. J. Arthur Hoyles, *Religion in Prison*, pp. 26–27.

30. Indeed, Mary Carpenter found that "those who behave best in prison are more likely to do badly when they come out" (Margaret E. Tabor, *Pioneer Women*, p. 47). What consequences might this have for an oral history project conducted in jail? Lewis L. Langness advises the anthropologist to beware of the "marginal" individual who, having nothing else to do, presents himself to the interviewer, possibly with an idiosyncratic perspective on the group (*Life History in Anthropological Science*, p. 39).

31. Mary Carpenter, *Our Convicts*, 2:324.

32. Ibid., 2:368.

33. Quoted in J. Estlin Carpenter, *Life and Work of Mary Carpenter*, p. 407.

34. J. Arthur Hoyles, *Religion in Prison*, p. 46. Hoyles traces this back to the preaching of the Wesleys in the eighteenth century: "The new interest which was inspired toward the poor and the sick was extended to the criminal, and reform became inevitable" (ibid.).

35. Cf. Willard Gaylin, Ira Glasser, Steven Marcus, and David Rothman, *Doing Good: The Limits of Benevolence*.

36. Michel Foucault, *Discipline and Punish*, p. 192.

Chapter Four

1. Mennel says: "Of course, 'informed opinion' must take into account the unvarnished recollections of the boys and girls who, for one reason or another, were called delinquents. Their testimony, though hard to obtain, especially in the nineteenth century, is also included." Robert M. Mennel, *Thorns and Thistles*, p. xiv. Next to impossible to obtain would be more accurate, and Mennel includes very little of it. ("Unvarnished" is almost trite in this field—and inaccurate, since editorial varnishing always occurs.)

For a broader scope of information on all the developments in this chapter, see the books by Hawes, Mennel, Schlossman, Pickett, and Finestone.

2. Wiley B. Sanders, *Juvenile Offenders for a Thousand Years*, p. 345.

3. Tenth Annual Report of the New York Refuge (1835), p. 25. Brief case histories were given in some of the annual reports of British philanthropic institutions in the early nineteenth century: see Sanders, *Juvenile Offenders for a Thousand Years*, p. 97 and passim, esp. p. 242. On pp. 250–53, Sanders reproduces the questioning of a youth who had been chained to a wall, given little to eat, and forced to work at a crank in Birmingham jail in 1852.

4. Twentieth Annual Report of the New York Refuge (1845), p. 39.

5. Tenth Annual Report of the New York Refuge (1835), p. 36.

6. Fifteenth Annual Report of the New York Refuge (1840), p. 6.

7. David J. Rothman, *Discovery of the Asylum*, p. 70.

8. Ibid., pp. 68–69.

9. Ibid., p. 68.

10. Ibid., p. 71.

11. Ibid., p. 260.

12. Emma Brace, ed., *Life of Charles Loring Brace*, p. 154.

13. Ibid., p. 21.

14. Ibid.

15. David J. Rothman, *Discovery of the Asylum*, p. 225. A century later vagrant children worked their way westward on their own, and police departments would give them small sums of money to get them to move on or would chase them into the next state. According to an official of the California Youth Authority, quoted in Benjamin Fine's *1,000,000 Delinquents* (p. 103), when the waifs reached California they were rounded up and shipped back eastward in four trains a year. "At each key city enroute a passenger car is detached from the train, and the children are scattered back to their home communities" (p. 104).

16. Charles Loring Brace, *Dangerous Classes of New York*, p. 240.

17. Ibid., pp. 119–20. Page 123 has an illustration of a young woman at the edge of a pier gazing into the water; it is captioned "The Street-Girl's End."

18. Quoted in Steven L. Schlossman, *Love and the American Delinquent*, p. 48.

19. Quoted in Wiley B. Sanders, *Juvenile Offenders*, p. 429.

20. Robert S. Pickett, *House of Refuge*, p. 161.

21. Quoted in Robert M. Mennel, *Thorns and Thistles*, p. 28.

22. Pickett, *House of Refuge*, p. xvii. Pickett quotes Emerson: "The State must consider the poor man, and all voices must speak for him" (ibid., p. xix).

23. Cecile P. Remick, "House of Refuge of Philadelphia," p. 186.

24. Mennel, *Thorns and Thistles*, p. 24.

25. "These sketches reflected the ideas of the questioner, not some objective truth about the criminal." "Interviewers probably induced the convicts to describe, whether accurately or not, their early life in grim terms" (Rothman, *Discovery of the Asylum*, p. 70). However, Rothman admits (p. 64) that no record exists of how these case histories were acquired. (The same applies to the Children's Aid Society interviews.) As for the grimness, doubtless enough of the lives were so grim that duress need not have been applied to get enough material to publish.

26. 1859 Annual Report, p. 67.

27. Quoted in Wiley B. Sanders, *Juvenile Offenders*, p. 342.

28. Brace, *Dangerous Classes*, pp. 111–12.

29. Cf. William Foote Whyte says he placed his own autobiographical account "in an appendix because I feel it will mean more to the reader if he goes through the body of the study first" (*Street Corner Society*, p. viii).

30. Brace, *Dangerous Classes*, p. 172.

31. Ibid., p. iii. Of course, this is the commonplace of commonplaces. In 1884 George C. Needham wrote: "This evil [neglected and destitute children] is exposed by statement of fact, by illustrated narrative, and by statistics. If public attention is thereby arrested, and sufficient proof adduced to awaken an interest in child-life . . . I am persuaded the tragedies of which children form the chief part will materially decrease" (*Street Arabs and Gutter Snipes*, p. iii).

32. Schlossman, *Love and the American Delinquent*, p. 53. Schlossman refers to a related development in antebellum America: "Rather than being embodied in statutes, sermons, and biblical precepts, as in the colonial period, the newer views on child rearing were conveyed in popular printed form, through dozens of books and several widely read magazines."

33. Joseph M. Hawes, *Children in Urban Society*, pp. 260–61.

34. Mennel, *Thorns and Thistles*, pp. 32–33.

35. Quoted in Miriam Z. Langsam, *Children West*, p. 15.

Chapter Five

1. Lindsey's environmentalist position and the inconsistencies in it are set forth in Peter Gregg Slater, "Ben Lindsey and the Denver Juvenile Court."

2. Ben B. Lindsey, "The Delinquent Child" (address given to the First National Conference on Race Betterment, Battle Creek, Michigan, 1914).

3. Denver Juvenile Court, *Problem of the Children*, p. 7.

4. Ben B. Lindsey and Wainwright Evans, *Revolt of Modern Youth*, p. vi.

5. Ibid., p. vii.

6. Robert M. Mennel, *Thorns and Thistles*, p. 139.

7. Thomas Larsen, *Good Fight*, pp. 23, 43.

8. "Biographical Sketch of Benjamin Barr Lindsey."

9. Cf. Lindsey and Evans, *Companionate Marriage*.

10. Thomas Larsen, *Good Fight*, p. 42.

11. Ibid., p. 29.

12. Denver Juvenile Court, *Problem of the Children*, p. 7.

13. Lindsey and Evans, *Revolt of Modern Youth*, p. 267.

14. According to Larsen, "Girls' cases were usually handled by a woman who served as court clerk" (*Good Fight*, p. 45 n). In *Revolt of Modern Youth* (pp. 72 ff.), Lindsey is at pains to show that he did not closet himself with young ladies in his chambers; while he interviewed them, his doors were open at all times.

15. Lindsey and Evans, *Revolt of Modern Youth*, p. 75. On p. 338 of this book Lindsey quotes Emerson: "Do you think that the youth has no force because he cannot speak to you or me. Hark! in the next room, who spoke so clear and emphatic? Good heaven! It is he! It is that very lump of bashfulness and phlegm

which for weeks has done nothing but eat when you were by, that now rolls out those words like bell-strokes. It seems he knows how to speak to his contemporaries. Bashful or bold, then, he will know how to make us seniors very unnecessary."

16. Quoted in Larsen, *Good Fight,* p. 48.

17. Lindsey and Evans, *Revolt of Modern Youth,* pp. 72–73.

18. Ibid., pp. 328–29.

19. Ibid., p. 328.

20. Ibid., p. 327.

21. Ibid., p. 340.

22. Ibid.

23. Ibid.

24. Ben B. Lindsey, "Trial of Criminal Cases and Adult Probation in the Chancery Court," p. 14.

25. In a letter to Lindsey, Edward L. Thorndike, the noted educational psychologist, said: "I am writing to you in order to express my deep appreciation of the work that you have been doing. . . . If all of us had the knowledge of human nature which you have, both mental and moral education, in school and out, would be a simple matter." Quoted in Slater, "Ben Lindsey," p. 211.

26. Quoted in Larsen, *Good Fight,* p. 48. On one occasion Lindsey offered a prize for the best letter by a boy about what makes boys get in trouble. Under the heading "What the Boys Say," the replies of some of the winners are set out, alleging as causes bad companions, inattentive parents, financial need, and so forth. But the first-place winner explained it thus: "Because he does not obey the Ten Commandments and he turns his mind away from God and towards Satan and obeys him—what he puts in his mind. Hoping that I may win the prize, I remain. . ." (Denver Juvenile Court, *Problem of the Children,* p. 143). There is no indication that Lindsey was not the judge of this contest or the author of this report about it.

27. Quoted in Jack M. Holl, *Juvenile Reform in the Progressive Era,* p. 44, n. 22. This organization still exists.

28. Quoted in Peter Gregg Slater, "Ben Lindsey and the Denver Juvenile Court," p. 216.

29. Ben B. Lindsey and Rube Borough, *Dangerous Life,* pp. 6–7.

30. Ben B. Lindsey and Harvey J. O'Higgins, *Beast,* pp. 151–52.

31. Slater, "Ben Lindsey," p. 216.

32. Lindsey and Evans, *Revolt,* p. v.

33. Lindsey and O'Higgins, *Beast,* p. 5.

34. Lindsey and Borough, *Dangerous Life,* pp. 3–4.

35. Charles Larsen, *Good Fight,* p. 23.

36. Jane Addams, *Twenty Years at Hull House,* p. 63.

37. Harold Finestone, *Victims of Change,* p. 61.

38. Jane Addams, *My Friend, Julia Lathrop,* p. 133. This confirms Mennel's claim (*Thorns and Thistles,* p. 127) that the reason the juvenile court appeared first in Chicago was because Chicago had developed fewer facilities for child-saving than had other cities.

39. Ethel S. Dummer, "Life in Relation to Time," p. 9. Mrs. Dummer supported the first five years of this research, in addition to funding a number of

related activities. See her autobiography, *Why I Think So*. For a study of the reform elite in Chicago during this period, see Steven J. Diner, *City and Its Universities*.

40. William Healy, "Child Guidance Clinic: Birth and Growth of an Idea," p. 15.

41. Ibid., p. 27.

42. Alfred Lindesmith and Yale Levin, in "Lombrosian Myth in Criminology" (p. 669), refer to this as a seizure of power by medical people. In "English Ecology" (pp. 814–15) they write: "In the evolution of criminological theory, it would appear that the work of Lombroso [who was the originator of the medical model] was in the nature of an interlude and interruption."

43. See *London Labour*, 4:30. Also Walter Lowe Clay, *Prison Chaplain*, pp. 135–36. For Clay the outrage had to do with the contamination of first offenders by hardened criminals, with whom they were thrown together because they had committed the same offense, a procedure that ignored the great differences in their characters. Lombroso was influenced by Darwin, whose theories of struggle for life may be seen as metaphors of Victorian society.

44. Mennel, *Thorns and Thistles*, p. 137.

45. See Arthur E. Sutherland, *Law at Harvard*, pp. 174–79.

46. G. Stanley Hall, *Adolescence*, 1:342. Hall's theory that the individual recapitulates the race was abandoned by Healy, seeing as he did the variety in histories of individuals.

47. Hawes, *Children*, p. 256.

48. Leon Radzinowitz, *Ideology and Crime*, p. 75.

49. Healy Oral History, pp. 84–85. The source of most biographical information on Healy and his associate Augusta Bronner, who was also his second wife, is an oral history conducted by John C. Burnham, professor of history at Ohio State University, in 1960, when Healy and Bronner were in retirement in Florida. Copies of this document are available at the Houghton Library, Harvard, at the Judge Baker Foundation, in Boston, where Healy worked after he left Chicago, and at the Chicago Historical Society. Inquiries at the Institute for Juvenile Research and at the Judge Baker Foundation have failed to turn up any of Healy's correspondence or other papers.

50. George E. Gardner, "William Healy," p. 8.

51. Gordon W. Allport, *Use of Personal Documents in Psychological Science*, p. 5. Allport locates the origins of the personal document in psychological science in: "(1) the tradition of phenomenology and introspection which produced the great foundation stones of mental science; in (2) the growing influence of biological positivism that required the use of subjects (other organisms) for study and in (3) the discovery and featuring of individual differences in the late nineteenth century. With these major lines of influence lesser trends seem to have converged: (4) the flowering of interest in morbidity and genius, with its emphasis on autobiographical materials and in case reports—Krafft-Ebing, Lombroso; (5) the development of the psychological novel (Eliot, Dostoevsky, Melville); (6) the breakdown of Victorian reticence and taboo upon the revelation of intimate feelings in letters, diaries, and autobiographies—Havelock Ellis, Bashkirtseff" (ibid., pp. 4–5).

52. Ibid., p. 6.

53. James Olney, *"Autos, Bios, Graphein,"* p. 118. William James helped Clifford Beers publish *A Mind That Found Itself* (1907), which Allport says "led directly to the founding of the mental hygiene movement in America, and to the elimination of many of the institutional evils depicted in the story" (*Use of Personal Documents,* p. 11). From our point of view it is interesting to note Beers's purposes in writing this book: "First: I hope to rob insanity of its terrors—at least those that do not rightly belong to it . . . . Secondly: Books alone can never produce the desired results. But a society founded and endowed for the sole purpose of solving this stubborn problem can at least raise the standard of treatment to such a level that existing shortcomings will be forever done away with. . . . Thirdly: It is my hope that the beneficent rich may be prompted to come to the aid of the States and Nations by supplying funds for the erection and endowment of model institutions wherein mental and nervous diseases, in their incipient and curable stages, may be treated with the maximum efficiency" (Clifford Whittingham Beers, *A Mind That Found Itself,* pp. 4–5).

54. "A Life of Service," in *Welfare Bulletin* (Springfield, Ill.: Department of Public Welfare, November–December 1952), p. 4.

55. Healy Oral History, pp. 18, 46, 205.

56. William Healy and Augusta F. Bronner, *Judge Baker Foundation Case Studies,* ser. 1, pp. 29a–31a.

57. Robert M. Mennel, *Thorns and Thistles,* p. 163.

58. Healy Oral History, p. 195; cf. p. 198.

59. Cf. Jean-Paul Sartre in the introduction to *Being and Nothingness:* "The appearances which manifest the existent are neither interior nor exterior; they are all equal, they all refer to other appearances, and none of them is privileged."

60. Healy and Bronner, *Judge Baker Studies,* p. 31a.

61. Ethel S. Dummer, "Life in Relation to Time," pp. 9–10. For a formal research and therapy project using life histories of delinquents, see Ralph Schwitzgebel, "A New Approach to Understanding Delinquency."

62. Healy and Bronner, "Child Guidance Clinic," pp. 27–28.

63. William Healy, "The Psychology of the Situation," p. 45. See also Healy Oral History, pp. 85–87. An advantage of the talking cure was that it enlisted some degree of cooperation from the child, as contrasted with a physical cure, if such were possible, which probably would not (see Jane Addams, *Second Twenty Years,* p. 306). Lubove points out that "skilled, differential casework, emphasizing client participation, eliminated once and for all the patronizing overtones associated with philanthropy in the past" (Roy Lubove, *Professional Altruist,* p. 48).

Schlossman insists that the juvenile court movement must be understood in the context of progressive education "in which persuasion and conscious manipulation of children's native emotional resources became the key pedagogical tools of teachers, judges, probation officers, settlement workers, and boys' clubs and boy scout teachers" ("Traditionalism and Revisionism," p. 65).

64. Healy Oral History, p. 84.

65. Healy became increasingly interested in Freud's work: in 1929 he did some "analytic work" with Helene Deutsch, and in 1930, when he was sixty-three years old, he underwent a brief analysis with Franz Alexander, with whom he later

wrote *The Roots of Crime.* Moreover, in 1930 Healy, Bronner, and Bowers produced *The Structure and Meaning of Psychoanalysis,* which was intended to clarify and popularize the concepts of psychoanalysis in the United States. This it succeeded in doing, despite Freud's disdain and lack of cooperation. The story of Healy's attempt to approach Freud is given in Gardner, "William Healy," pp. 21–26.

66. In the presentation of this case, in addition to data from various physical and psychological tests, a piece entitled "Excerpts from Autobiography" is included, acquired when the boy was nineteen. He had been a good boy in Greece but had met with bad companions in America after his father, when drunk, began beating him. The court placed him in a better home and he improved. In a note to the document Healy admits that before reading the "autobiography" they had not known the boy's father drank.

67. Healy, *Individual Delinquent,* pp. 473 ff. Sophonisba Breckenridge and Edith Abbott in an appendix to their *Delinquent Child and the Home* (1912) stated that they wanted to acquire the child's own statement about his or her attendance at school "to obtain a clear indication of the child's command of the English language" (p. 333). Appendixes 4 and 5 contain "family paragraphs" relating to the delinquencies of one hundred boys and fifty girls. "It is believed that a study of these simple statements of fact will help the reader to see the delinquent child as a human problem and not merely as an abstract question of social policy." "The number presented is believed to be sufficiently large to enable the reader to test the conclusions that we have drawn in these chapters and to find the truth, if he wishes, quite independently of the writers' interpretation" (p. 267). In 1911 the Chicago Vice Commission, on which Healy served, used a few oral histories of prostitutes in *The Social Evil in Chicago.*

68. Stanley J. Reiser, "The 'M.' in M.D. Isn't 'Machine.'"

69. Gordon Allport, *Personality in Formation and Action,* p. 133. Among a certain breed of "scientific" author, this is a commonplace. L. M. Terman wrote in *A History of Psychology in Autobiography:* "My chief anxiety about these series of autobiographies is that so few of the authors will tell me the things I should like to know about their ancestry, their childhood and their youth" (quoted in Allport, *Use of Personal Documents,* p. 15).

70. Healy, *Individual Delinquent,* p. 6. Cf. Charles Booth: "The materials for sensational stories lie plentifully in every book of our notes; but, even if I had the skill to use my material in this way—that gift of the imagination which is called 'realistic'—I should not wish to use it here. There is struggling poverty, there is destitution, there is hunger, drunkenness, brutality, and crime; no one doubts that it is so. My object has been to attempt to show the numerical relation which poverty, misery and depravity bear to regular earnings and comparative comfort, and to describe the general conditions under which each class lives" (quoted in Robert E. Park, *On Social Control,* p. 7).

71. Floyd N. House, "Social Forces," p. 503.

72. John C. Burnham, "The Struggle between Physicians and Paramedical Personnel," p. 100. Cf. John C. Burnham, "The New Psychology," pp. 364–65.

73. Throughout the previous century parents had turned increasingly from clergymen to scientists for guidance (David Rothman, *The Discovery of the*

Asylum, p. 216). Robert E. Park once wrote: "While mothers are necessarily, and under all ordinary circumstances, profoundly interested and responsible to their children, it is notorious that they do not always understand them" (*Crowd and the Public*, p. 114).

74. Roy Lubove, *Professional Altruist*, p. 18. According to Lubove (p. 64): "Much of the extramural [outside a hospital or asylum] psychiatry and psychiatric social work of this early period was concerned with problems of juvenile crime and delinquency. The undisputed leader in this field was William Healy, and his work at the Juvenile Psychopathic Institute was probably more familiar to social workers than any other practical experiment. Through Healy, in large measure, the principles of social psychiatry entered the mainstream of social work thought."

75. Cesare Lombroso, *Crime: Its Causes and Remedies*, p. 309. An intriguing reference is made in a note on p. 310: "For detailed proof see the autobiographies and dialogue at the end of the 2nd edition of 'L' Homme Criminel,' Turin, 1878." Unfortunately, I have been unable to consult this edition. Two "autobiographies" appear in *Criminology* (1893), by Arthur MacDonald, an American follower of Lombroso. General criminology, according to MacDonald, should be supplemented with special criminology, in which a few cases are studied thoroughly, including acquiring written and oral statements from the offender. MacDonald provides autobiographical statements from offenders in a case of "pure murder" and one of "pure meanness." A case of pure murder he defines as one "in which the innate tendency to take human life is predominant" (p. 174); however, the only effect of the "Autobiography of 'A,'" in which a young man describes his father's murder of the boy's mother and his own assault on an old woman is to make MacDonald's references to purity ridiculous. MacDonald does appreciate social circumstances more than Lombroso: in addition to the autobiographies he gives reports from various employees in the institution where A was incarcerated. A girl, allegedly an example of "pure meanness," was so badly abused as a child, a fact evident from her autobiography, that only someone maintaining a thesis at all costs could overlook this and continue to refer to innate tendencies.

76. August Aichhorn, *Delinquency and Child Guidance*, pp. 44–47, 95.

77. Cesare Lombroso, *L'homme criminel: Atlas*, plate 34, fig. 6. Cf. *Tattooed Tears*, a film by Joan Churchill and Nick Broomfield: one of the boys featured in this film about the California Youth Training School tattooed one tear coming out the corner of his left eye for each year he was in the school.

78. Gina Lombroso Ferrero, *Criminal Man*, p. 300. Cyril Burt, in addition to including photographs, studied examples of handwriting in *The Young Delinquent*, appendix 1. This is the same Cyril Burt who was discovered in the 1970s to have fabricated data to support his claims about innate differences of intelligence among races, classes, and sexes.

79. William H. Sheldon, *Varieties of Delinquent Youth*, p. 752.

80. Philip Rieff, *Freud*, p. 148. Yet in some cases physical evidence may be all there is: "The much-criticized Spofford Juvenile Detention Center in the Bronx is the sort of place where signs and decorations tacked to cracked and dirty walls tell far more about its frustrated staff and young inhabitants than either group is likely to speak about directly" (*New York Times*, 4 August 1978).

81. Healy, *Individual Delinquent*, pp. 339 ff.

82. G. W. F. Hegel, *Phenomenology of Mind,* p. 164. Hegel's word is *aufheben.*

83. Hans Kurella, *Cesare Lombroso,* p. 135.

84. Richard Sennett, *Fall of Public Man,* p. 167.

85. Healy Oral History, p. 176.

86. Healy, *Twenty-five Years,* p. 5. Cf.: "if the roots of crime lie far back in the foundations of the social order it may be that only a radical change can bring back a large measure of cure . . . until a better social order exists, crime will continue to flourish" (Healy, Bronner, and Shimberg, "Close of Another Chapter in Criminology," p. 221).

87. Healy Oral History, p. 41.

88. Michel Foucault, *Discipline and Punish,* p. 192.

89. Ibid., p. 301. According to Foucault: "Our society is not one of spectacle, but of surveillance; under the surface of images, one invests bodies in depth; behind the great abstraction of exchange, there continues the meticulous, concrete training of useful forces; the circuits of communication are the supports of an accumulation and a centralization of knowledge; the play of signs defines the anchorages of power; it is not that the beautiful totality of the individual is amputated, repressed, altered by our social order, it is rather that the individual is carefully fabricated in it, according to a whole technique of forces and bodies. We are much less Greek than we believe" (ibid., p. 217).

90. Lowell S. Selling, "Autobiography as a Psychiatric Technique," p. 171. In "Reliability of Life-History Studies," psychologists Cartwright and French concluded from an experiment they conducted: "Each investigator uncovered some aspects of the personality which the other did not discover, with the result that the validity of each experimenter was actually greater than the reliability between them. The interests and biases of the investigators apparently operated as a selective factor determining which aspects of the personality were observed" (pp. 116–17).

Chapter Six

1. Morris Janowitz, introduction to W. I. Thomas, *On Social Organization and Social Personality,* p. xxiv.

2. W. I. Thomas, "Life History," p. 250. See below, note 6.

3. The first two volumes of *The Polish Peasant in Europe and America* were published by the University of Chicago Press in 1918. Volume 3, in 1919, and volumes 4 and 5, in 1920, were published by Richard G. Badger, Boston. Alfred A. Knopf issued a second edition of two volumes in 1927. This was reprinted in 1958 by Dover Publications. All quotations here are from the 1958 Dover edition.

4. Gordon Allport, *The Use of Personal Documents in Psychological Science,* pp. 18–19, xiii, xii.

5. When I arrived at an Illinois prison to "collect some life histories," the assistant warden was surprised that I had brought along a tape recorder. He was not sure permission had been granted for use of the machine as part of the life history project. How did he expect me to take down the person's own words? I asked. He had identified life history and case history. I was eventually admitted to the prison with the recorder.

An examination of the use of the term "life history" by sociologists would reveal anomalies: the most basic ambiguity is in the word "history," which may refer to the written account or to the events themselves. I am using "life history" to designate the account.

6. Unattributed quotations in the following are from Thomas's "Life History." This document was one of 258 autobiographies collected around 1927 by Luther L. Bernard, but most have never been published. (See Paul L. Baker's introduction to the Thomas document.) They are now at Pennsylvania State University. Therefore Janowitz's statement, in his introduction to Thomas's writings (p. ix), that no life history of Thomas is available is incorrect. Oddly enough, for a man who valued letters so much, Thomas did not save his own correspondence.

One of the proposals for a book on method in sociology was a series of "autobiographical versions of the growth of their scientific interests from distinguished scholars who have contributed to the development of social science." However, while such a venture had advantages, "it was regarded as impracticable because of the probable length to which such a series, if sufficiently comprehensive, would run" (appendix A, "History and Organization of the 'Case Book,'" in *Methods in Social Science: A Case Book*, ed. Stuart A. Rice, p. 733). Psychologists did follow through on such a plan in *A History of Psychology in Autobiography*. Janowitz has remarked that it is paradoxical that the Chicago school, "with its concern for the human document, never produced its own ethnographic chronicler, as Margaret Mead was for the Columbia anthropological group with her volume on Ruth Benedict, *An Anthropologist at Work*" (introduction to Robert E. L. Faris, *Chicago Sociology*, p. vii). One of the classic personal statements about sociological research was made by William Foote Whyte in the appendix to *Street Corner Society*. Whyte says: "There have been some useful statements on methods of research, but with few exceptions they place the discussion entirely on a logical-intellectual basis. They fail to note that the researcher, like his informants, is a social animal" (p. 279). In *his* appendix to *The Sociological Imagination*, C. Wright Mills wrote: "It is much better ... to have one account by a working student of how he is going about his work than a dozen 'codifications of procedure' by specialists who as often as not have never done much work of consequence" (p. 195).

7. James T. Carey, *Sociology and Public Affairs*, p. 155.

8. Howard S. Becker has written: "The life history is certainly not fiction, although the best life history documents have a sensitivity and pace, a dramatic urgency, that any novelist would be glad to achieve" (introduction to *Jack-Roller*, 1966 ed., p. v). An eminent sociologist once said to me, "Why do we need Studs Terkel as long as we've got Saul Bellow?" Lombroso might have said, "Why do we need Mayhew as long as we've got Dickens?" Surely this is sweeping with a rather large broom.

9. Robert E. L. Faris, *Chicago Sociology*, pp. 25, 9.

10. Edward Shils, "Tradition, Ecology, and Institution in the History of Sociology," p. 771.

11. Kimball Young, "Contributions of W. I. Thomas to Sociology," pp. 12, 13, 14.

12. Ernest W. Burgess, "W. I. Thomas as a Teacher," p. 123. Cf. John W. Petras, "Changes of Emphasis in the Sociology of W. I. Thomas."

13. Kimball Young, "Contributions," p. 123.

14. Janowitz (introduction to W. I. Thomas, *On Social Organization,* p. xxiv) remarks that Thomas had not thought to use documents written by subjects of a study because in his earlier ethnological studies he had been studying preliterate people. However, Bierstedt says: "Even before Thomas turned to this particular subject [the Polish peasant] he had encouraged his students at Chicago to submit to him their autobiographies, including their sexual histories, all of which he regarded as important data for sociological purposes" (introduction to *On Humanistic Sociology,* p. 12). Thomas himself complicated this when he declared that he did not think *The Polish Peasant* had had much influence on social workers: "This movement toward the collection of human document materials was going on inevitably, anyway, that is, in Chicago. So this work was merely another influence on the concrete trend in sociology" (Blumer, *Appraisal,* p. 130). Since Thomas included case histories as human documents, he probably has in mind here Healy's documentation, which Thomas frequently used. Fortunately, the larger pattern is clearer than the particulars.

15. Harry Elmer Barnes, "William Isaac Thomas," p. 796.

16. Janowitz, introduction to W. I. Thomas, *On Social Organization,* p. xiv. Janowitz, who writes about this intriguing incident more thoroughly than anyone else, is wrong about Thomas's being arrested by the FBI, which did not yet exist in 1918.

17. Ernest Burgess, "W. I. Thomas as a Teacher," p. 760.

18. Florian Znaniecki, "W. I. Thomas as a Collaborator," p. 766.

19. Janowitz, introduction to W. I. Thomas, *On Social Organization,* pp. xxvii, xxix, xxi–xxiii.

20. Kimball Young, "Contributions," pp. 3, 6.

21. Janowitz, introduction to W. I. Thomas, *On Social Organization,* p. xx.

22. Ellsworth Faris, "W. I. Thomas (1863–1947)," p. 759.

23. See Shils, "Tradition," p. 781.

24. Bierstedt, introduction to *On Humanistic Sociology,* p. 11.

25. Paul Delaney, *British Autobiography in the 17th Century,* p. 21.

26. See Marvin Bressler, "Selected Family Patterns in W. I. Thomas' Unfinished Study of the *Bintl Brief.*" An edition of these letters was published by Doubleday in 1971 under the title *A Bintel Brief.*

27. *Polish Peasant,* 2:1832. This mention of perfection sounds more like Znaniecki than Thomas. See Blumer, *Appraisal,* p. 133, where Thomas expresses some regret over the use of that word to describe life histories.

28. W. I. Thomas, *Unadjusted Girl,* pp. 250–51. However, on one occasion he said that the only reason letters were used so much in *The Polish Peasant* was because they were available, not because they were spontaneous productions (Blumer, *Appraisal,* p. 134).

29. Ibid.

30. W. I. Thomas and Dorothy Swaine Thomas, *Child in America,* pp. 571–72.

31. W. I. Thomas, "Relation of Research to the Social Process," p. 190.

32. W. I. Thomas, *Unadjusted Girl,* pp. 249–50. In a paper Thomas submitted to the Social Science Research Council in 1933, entitled "Outline of a Program for the Study of Personality and Culture," he listed a series of functions of life

histories (pp. 298–99): "Life histories and case records have hypothesis-forming importance, and provide data of the following character: *(a)* The systems of ideas and purposes of individuals as related to the general culture patterns of society, and the relative compulsiveness of the various specific cultural stimuli. *(b)* The trains of experience through which the individual's conception of his role in society is developed. *(c)* How organizations and institutions as they are (family, school, occupation, etc.) promote ·and interfere with individual adjustment. *(d)* Whether the personality is essentially structuralized in infancy, and later maladjustments in the adolescent period (schizophrenia, crime) date back to that period, or whether childhood maladjustments are to a degree self limiting. *(e)* What are the determining crises at adolescence and other periods of maturation and experience. *(f)* The incentives involved in personality development and what necessities of human nature (organic and social urges) must always and everywhere be satisfied as conditions of an adjusted personality. *(g)* The desire for intimacy, forms of intimacy, and the size of groups within which intimacies are possible, with special reference to the psychoses. *(h)* The different reactions of different individuals to the same critical experiences. For example, one may become insane, another commit·suicide, another commit a crime, another continue unchanged, another adjust to a higher level of efficiency. *(i)* To how many and what codes does the individual respond and what conflicts arise from this source.... *(j)* Differences between verbal and actual behavior."

33. *Polish Peasant,* 2:1833–34.

34. Ibid., 1:44.

35. Blumer, *Appraisal,* pp. 27–28.

36. Although William Healy was "scientific" in the sense of making diagnoses before prescribing treatment, he made no attempt to be scientific in the sense of constructing a series of general propositions about juvenile delinquency, not to speak of a general statement about "own story," though on both subjects he suggested emphases. As Floyd N. House has put it: "In the Judge Baker Foundation case studies, considerable emphasis is placed upon the *individualization* of cases. This principle would seem to involve the denial of all possibility of applying science in the diagnosis and treatment of such cases, for science is in essence generalized knowledge" ("Social Forces in Personal-Behavior Sequences Studied by the Judge Baker Foundation," p. 503). *Individuum ineffabile est.* The transcendence of the individual toward social realities (which reached only the social-psychological) and the transcendence of statements about individuals toward more general hypotheses (which were nevertheless accompanied by individuals' life histories) were aspects of a single move.

37. Kimball Young, "Contributions," p. 392.

38. Janowitz, introduction to W. I. Thomas, *On Social Organization,* p. viii.

39. Cf. Daniel Boorstin, *The Americans: The Democratic Experience,* chap. 42, "Making Experience Repeatable."

40. Ellsworth Faris, "W. I. Thomas," p. 758.

41. John Madge, *Origins of Scientific Sociology,* p. 53.

42. See Emile Durkheim, *Rules of Sociological Method.* See Madge, *Origins,* pp. 53, 86–87, for a comparison of Thomas and Durkheim. Cf. the behaviorism of James Watson, Thomas's contemporary at the University of Chicago.

43. Kimball Young, "Contributions," p. 268.

44. Thomas and Thomas, *Child in America,* p. 571.

45. Thomas, *Unadjusted Girl,* p. 86.

46. Harold Finestone, *Victims of Change,* p. 63.

47. Ellsworth Faris, "W. I. Thomas," p. 758.

48. Thomas and Thomas, *Child in America,* p. 571.

49. Clifford Shaw, *Natural History,* p. xii. Burgess also wrote that a life history "indicates behavior processes and personality types which may be analyzed when a sufficient number of detailed life histories have been accumulated for comparative purposes" (ibid., p. 253).

50. Ellsworth Faris, "W. I. Thomas," p. 758. However, Allport states two reservations about Stouffer's work: it dealt with only one point, the subjects' attitudes toward prohibition; and the task of writing on a limited topic (rather than about one's whole life) and responding to questions on that topic are too similar in the first place. Allport concludes: "Probably Stouffer's results should be considered representative of what can be expected under *simplified* conditions of research" (*Use of Personal Documents,* p. 25).

51. Clifford R. Shaw, *Jack-Roller,* p. 21. In *Social Factors* (p. v) Shaw wrote: "It should be remembered that the case materials are presented chiefly for the purpose of illustration. They serve also to focus attention upon certain aspects of delinquent behavior for which quantitative data are at present not available" (cf. Stuart A. Rice, "Hypothesis," p. 563).

52. Paul J. Baker, "Life Histories of W. I. Thomas and Robert E. Park," p. 245. Like Thomas, Healy, and Park, Mead also studied with William James.

53. *Polish Peasant,* 2:1839.

54. Blumer, *Appraisal,* p. 43.

55. Clifford R. Shaw, *Jack-Roller,* 1966 ed., p. xiii. Thomas and Znaniecki had written in *Polish Peasant,* 2:1834: "social science cannot remain on the surface of social becoming where certain schools wish to have it float, but must reach the actual human experience and attitudes which constitute the full, live, and active social reality beneath the formal organization of social institutions, or behind the statistically tabulated mass-phenomena which taken in themselves are nothing but symptoms of unknown causal processes and can serve only as provisional ground for sociological hypotheses."

Blumer remarked: "I question whether this reduction to simple situations in sociology, at least, does not really mean the loss of the original problem. I notice that when vague and indefinite concepts are broken down into very precise and definite terms that can be tested empirically, it frequently happens that those simple terms cannot be recombined to produce the original concept" (*Appraisal,* p. 162).

56. Karl J. Weintraub, *Value of the Individual,* p. 333.

57. Janowitz, introduction to W. I. Thomas, *On Social Organization,* p. xxiii.

58. In *Child in America* (p. 572), the Thomases wrote: "The total situation will always contain more and less subjective factors, and the behavior reaction can be studied only in connection with the whole context, i.e., the situation as it exists in verifiable, objective terms, and as it has seemed to exist in terms of the interested persons. Thus, the behavior records of the child clinics are contributing important

data by including the child's account of the difficult situation, the often conflicting definitions of this situation given by parents, teachers, etc., and the recording of such facts as can be verified about the situation by disinterested investigators." See also Thomas's comment in Herbert Blumer, *Appraisal*, p. 86 (also cf. p. 132).

59. Quoted in Janowitz, introduction to W. I. Thomas, *On Social Organization*, p. xxiii.

60. Herbert Blumer, *Appraisal*, p. 177.

61. Janowitz, introduction to W. I. Thomas, *On Social Organization*, pp. xxxi, viii.

62. W. I. Thomas, "Relation of Research," pp. 183–84.

63. W. I. Thomas, *Unadjusted Girl*, pp. 231–32.

64. Ibid., p. 240.

65. Cf. Marvin Bressler, "Selected Family Patterns," p. 564.

66. Kimball Young, "Contributions," pp. 244–45.

67. Might this onset of particularism have resulted from his departure from the University of Chicago, where he might have continued larger cultural case studies?

68. Thomas and Thomas, *Child in America*, pp. 96–106.

69. Janowitz, introduction to W. I. Thomas, *On Social Organization*, pp. xxxvii, xlii.

70. John Dollard, *Criteria for the Life History*, pp. 172–73. Cf. Murdock's remark in Blumer, *Appraisal*, p. 187: "In their use of human documents, they seem to me to lay altogether too little stress upon the early formative years of the life history, when the animal is undergoing social conditioning, when the foundations of character are being laid down, when, in short, the fundamental 'attitudes' effective in later life are being formed."

71. Dollard, *Criteria*, p. 167.

72. Ibid., pp. 36–37.

73. Blumer, *Appraisal*, p. 24. Part of this book was reprinted in Blumer's *Symbolic Interactionism*. See also Evan A. Thomas, "Herbert Blumer's Critique of *The Polish Peasant*."

74. Blumer, *Appraisal*, pp. 36–37.

75. Dollard, *Criteria*, p. 181.

76. Madge, *Origins*, p. 61.

77. Blumer, *Appraisal*, p. 117; cf. pp. 123–24, 112–13.

78. Ibid., pp. 93–94.

79. Dollard, *Criteria*, pp. 165, 181.

80. Blumer, *Appraisal*, p. 147.

81. Ibid., pp. 142–43.

82. Ibid., pp. 39, 38.

83. Ibid., p. 189.

84. Allport, *Use of Personal Documents*, p. 21.

85. The conceptual scheme in Kant's *Critique of Judgment* might be suggestive here. The faculty of judgment operates between the fixities of sense experience on the one hand and of reason on the other. Judgment is the interplay of imagination and understanding (particulars and generals) that is purposive yet without any definite purpose.

86. Blumer, *Appraisal,* pp. 166–67.

87. W. I. Thomas, "Relation of Research," pp. 189–90. More specific delineations of methods using human documents have been made, though this usually makes oral histories disappear. One of these methods, proposed by Znaniecki under the title "analytic induction," requires examination of a variety of contrasting instances of a thing in order to avoid errors arising from generalization from a single case. Blumer mentions that progress can be made by general critiques of concepts themselves, such as the theory of instincts (*Appraisal,* p. 112).

88. Ibid., p. 50.

89. Ibid., pp. 50, 76. Znaniecki pointed out that this background of experience "was not mere personal acquaintance with the facts, such as is derived from active participation in a collectivity. It was conceptual knowledge, the result of previous methodical studies made by Polish historians, anthropologists, ethnographers, economists" (ibid., p. 68).

90. Ibid., p. 146.

91. Ibid., p. 77.

92. Ibid., p. 145. Becker makes the same point about the various monographs written by Chicago sociologists in the 1920s and 1930s: "Much of the background that any single study would either have to provide in itself or, even worse, about which it would have to make unchecked assumptions, was already at hand for the reader of *The Jack-Roller*" (Howard S. Becker, introduction to *Jack-Roller,* 1966 ed., p. ix).

93. Blumer, *Appraisal,* pp. 148, 153.

94. *Polish Peasant,* 1:7. According to James T. Carey: "Before World War I, sociological interest in applying sociology and social reform had been expressed primarily by the individual as a citizen. Albion Small served in the Civic Federation of Chicago, W. I. Thomas in the Chicago Vice Commission [as had Healy], and Robert Park later in the Chicago Urban League" (*Sociology and Public Affairs,* p. 9).

95. *Polish Peasant,* 2:1908.

96. W. I. Thomas, *Unadjusted Girl,* p. 253.

97. *Polish Peasant* (1918–20), 5:344–45; (1927), 2:1826–27.

98. Ibid., 2:1526–27.

99. Henry Mayhew, *London Labour,* 2:298.

100. John Madge, *Origins,* p. 72. Of course this would not apply in a behaviorist system that seeks to go "beyond freedom and dignity."

101. Blumer, *Appraisal,* p. 131.

102. "All his popular writing falls in the years 1904–1909" (Kimball Young, "Contributions," p. 22, n. 50). Thus an interest in human documents arose about the same time as the popular writing ceased. Could the former have been a sublimation of the latter?

103. W. I. Thomas, "Relation of Research," p. 175.

104. Blumer, *Appraisal,* p. 70.

105. W. I. Thomas, *Unadjusted Girl,* p. 254.

106. Janowitz, introduction to W. I. Thomas, *On Social Organization,* p. lii.

107. Donald Young, foreword to Edmund H. Volkart, *Social Behavior and Personality,* p. v.

108. Blumer, *Appraisal,* p. 80. In the preface to *Varieties of Religious Experience* William James said: "In my belief that a large acquaintance with particulars often makes us wiser than the possession of abstract formulas, however deep, I have loaded the lectures with concrete examples."

109. Blumer, *Appraisal,* p. 69.

110. *Polish Peasant,* 2:1852–53.

111. There is an ambiguity in the word "scheme" that relates this to the scheming of sophists and confidence men. Thomas Kuhn's notion of a paradigm also depends on persuading a community of scientists to accept a paradigm or scheme. A crucial differentiating factor is the quality of moral purpose behind the "scheme."

Chapter Seven

1. Hugh Dalziel Duncan, *Culture and Democracy,* p. 51. See chapter 4, "Oral Art and American Vernacular in the Middle West," and chapter 5, "Chicago Journalism and the New Urban Speech of Chicago." Cf.: "[The research student] develops some of the traits of a newspaper reporter, especially those of getting people to talk freely about their experiences. He differs from a newspaper reporter, however, in that he is not after the 'news' but the 'olds'; he has time; he moves painstakingly; and he accepts data with scientific caution" (Emory S. Bogardus, "Personal Experiences and Social Research," pp. 297–98).

2. Bernard Duffey, *Chicago Renaissance,* p. 134.

3. Richard Wright, introduction to St. Clair Drake and Horace R. Cayton, *Black Metropolis,* 1:xvii.

4. Among other instances are Northwestern University sociologist R. Lincoln Keiser's edition of Henry Williamson, *Hustler! The Autobiography of a Thief,* and Todd Gitlin and Nanci Hollander's use of oral histories in *Uptown: Poor Whites in Chicago.* Alice and Staughton Lynd's *Rank and File* may be added here also. Chicago historian John Hope Franklin has edited a series *Negro American Biographies and Autobiographies* (University of Chicago Press). The Northwestern University philosophy department has been a center for studies in phenomenology: William Earle, of that department, has written *The Autobiographical Consciousness: A Philosophical Inquiry into Existence,* though it actually has little to do with autobiography. Perhaps some of the University of Chicago tradition is connected with the practice there in the humanities of reading original texts, out of which came the Great Books program (cf. *Philosophers Speak for Themselves,* ed. T. V. Smith). Harvard University has also had a sustained interest in human documents, evident in the works of William James, Gordon Allport, and Erik Erikson (who worked for a while with Healy).

5. Edward Shils, "Tradition," p. 780. For the more general point I am indebted to Terence Tanner.

6. Cf. Richard Sennett, *Fall of Public Man,* p. 217.

7. Gordon Allport, *Use of Personal Documents,* p. xi.

8. W. I. Thomas, *Old World Traits Transplanted,* ed. Robert E. Park and Herbert A. Miller.

9. Autobiographical statements from Park in the following text come from

Robert E. Park, "Life History," and from "An Autobiographical Note," in *Race and Culture*. Many of the writings of the Chicago sociologists have been republished by the University of Chicago Press in the Heritage of Sociology series.

10. James also made a comment on human documents in relation to his own marginality to theology in *The Varieties of Religious Experience:* "The *documents humains* which we shall find most instructive need not then be sought for in the haunts of special erudition—they lie along the beaten highway; and this circumstance, which flows so naturally from the character of our problem, suits admirably also your lecturer's lack of special theological learning" (p. 3). C. Wright Mills has emphasized James's compulsion to popularize concepts, such as pragmatism, especially in the many public speeches he gave (C. Wright Mills, *Sociology and Pragmatism*, p. 221).

11. *Crowd and the Public*, p. 111.

12. Richard Wright, introduction to Cayton and Drake, *Black Metropolis*, pp. xviii, xix.

13. W. I. Thomas, "Life History," p. 249.

14. The papers of Ernest Burgess are in Special Collections, Regenstein Library, University of Chicago. These include many fragments of life histories from his students.

15. Quoted in James F. Short, Jr., introduction to part 3 of Ernest W. Burgess, *On Community, Family, and Delinquency*, pp. 167–68.

16. Andrew A. Bruce, Ernest W. Burgess, Albert J. Harno, and John Landesco, "The Workings of the Indeterminate-Sentence Law and the Parole System in Illinois" (1928), pp. 205–11. Cf. pp. 240–43, where additional personal testimony is given under the head "The Courts and Parole in the Eyes of the Discharged Prisoner." This has been claimed to be the first published device for parole prediction success. James T. Carey says everyone he interviewed for his inquiry "agreed on the critical role played by Ernest Burgess as broker between sociologists and local reformers," *Sociology and Public Affairs*, p. 148, n. 9. As early as 1894, two of the first three members of the Chicago sociology department (Small and Vincent) wrote: "There is little likelihood that men who personally observe actual social conditions, according to the method we propose, instead of speculating about them in the study, will want to fold their hands and let social evil work out its own salvation" (quoted in ibid., p. 101).

17. Edward Shils, "Tradition," p. 793.

18. Robert E. L. Faris, *Chicago Sociology*, p. 37.

19. See Frances A. Yates, *Art of Memory*.

20. Park, Burgess, and McKenzie, *City*, p. 25.

21. Ibid., pp. 45–46; cf. Plato, *Republic* 368D–E.

22. Ernest W. Burgess, "The Study of the Delinquent as a Person," *American Journal of Sociology* 28, no. 6 (May 1923); reprinted in Burgess, *On Community*.

23. Ernest W. Burgess, "Study of the Delinquent as a Person," p. 663.

24. Ibid., p. 675.

25. Ibid., p. 679.

26. Ibid., p. 680. For a statement that life histories are "the most significant document for personality study," see American Psychiatric Association, *Proceedings: Second Colloquium on Personality Investigation*, pp. 11 ff.

27. Thrasher later organized a Department of Sociological Education at New York University. See Dan W. Dodson, "Frederic Milton Thrasher (1892–1962)."

28. Cf. *Gang* (1927), p. 385.

29. Faris, *Chicago Sociology,* p. 73.

30. *Gang* (1927), p. 36.

31. Ibid., p. 22. According to Sophia M. Robison, writing in 1936, *"Interstitialness,* which is only a new term for slum, needs to be further studied and analyzed" (*Can Delinquency Be Measured?* pp. 172–73). But it never was analyzed much in itself, only applied—to slums.

32. *Gang* (1927), p. 3.

33. Ibid., p. 41.

34. *Gang* (1963), pp. xv–xvi.

35. Ibid., p. liii.

36. Ibid., pp. xviii ff. Thrasher was much more revealing in a later article on "How to Study the Boys' Gang in the Open," a charming essay on how he established rapport with a group of small boys, took them for rides in his car, got home late for dinner, and so forth. From the point of view of later participant observation methods, an equally superficial statement was given by Kimball Young in "Frederic M. Thrasher's Study of Gangs." In his article "Social Attitudes," Thrasher says he taught the boys how to use a dictating machine (pp. 240–41), but that was on a subsequent project.

37. James T. Carey, *Sociology and Public Affairs,* p. 186, n. 2.

38. Henry McKay once told me that Burgess had reprimanded Thrasher on at least one occasion for using inauthentic documents.

39. Thrasher, "Social Attitudes," pp. 253, 263.

40. *Gang* (1927), p. 129.

41. *Gang* (1963), p. xlix.

42. *Gang* (1927), p. xiii.

43. Thrasher, "Social Attitudes," p. 263.

44. *Gang* (1927), p. 25.

45. Ibid., p. 3.

46. Thrasher, introduction to James T. Farrell, *Studs Lonigan,* p. x. Carey quotes Farrell's *Reflections at Fifty and Other Essays* (p. 184): "University of Chicago sociologists were among the pioneers in shifting the course of American sociology from the plane of theory to that of empiricism. They embarked on a search for facts, and they sought these in many social areas, most of them marginal" (James T. Carey, *Sociology and Public Affairs,* p. 180). Carey points out that Farrell "seemed to recognize the distinctions between literature and sociology that his friend Frederic Thrasher blurred in his introduction to *Young Lonigan*" (ibid., p. 190). Bibliographies of sociology courses at the University of Chicago in the 1920s and 1930s included novels: "The purpose of asking the student to read novels and autobiographies was to acquaint him with a particular social world. They seem to have been used in the same way that life history data were" (ibid., p. 178). Nevertheless, life histories were distinguished from "the slice-of-life or stream-of-consciousness emphasis of some of the literary naturalists, because the sociologists made no pretense that these were photographic reproductions of reality presented without selection, organization, or judgment" (ibid., p. 182).

47. *Gang* (1927), pp. 119–21.

48. Shaw apparently never wrote a life history, though Snodgrass quotes a brief autobiographical statement written in application to the University of Chicago in 1919. Snodgrass's article, "Clifford R. Shaw and Henry D. McKay: Chicago Criminologists," is the best readily available source of information about Shaw's life. Other sources are the Stuart Rice article and a brief statement on a vita that formed part of a grant application. Most of Shaw's remaining papers are at the Chicago Historical Society.

49. Rice makes an intriguing reference to Shaw's "two years of medicine" (p. 551), which engendered in him a habit of seeking control groups. Rice interviewed Shaw for this article about 1930, but the medical experience may have been the pharmacy position Snodgrass refers to.

50. Stuart A. Rice, "Hypotheses and Verifications in Clifford R. Shaw's Studies of Juvenile Delinquency," pp. 549–50.

51. This and the following quotation come from a grant application.

52. Snodgrass, "Clifford R. Shaw and Henry D. McKay," p. 4.

53. Stuart A. Rice, "Hypotheses and Verifications," pp. 552–53.

54. Clifford Shaw et al., *Delinquency Areas*, p. ix.

55. Finestone, *Victims of Change*, p. 79.

56. Behavior Research Fund, "Final Report of the Board of Trustees to the Members of the Behavior Research Fund and the Friends of the Institute for Juvenile Research," p. 25.

57. The Behavior Research Fund, like the early institute, was initially funded for five years but remained officially in existence until 1933. Since research projects had not been completed at that time, its final report was not made until 1948. A total of $390,597.45 had been collected, mostly in 1926–31, almost none of it from foundations, and had been spent mostly on salaries and for subsidizing publications. All the works of Shaw and McKay were funded in this manner, including the 1942 publication of *Juvenile Delinquency and Urban Areas*.

58. Two documents by Henry McKay are in the Burgess collection in the Special Collections Department of Regenstein Library, University of Chicago, in box 139, folder 5: a one-page autobiography entitled "A First Delinquency" (in cahoots with a neighborhood boy, McKay and his brother destroy some sparrows' nests), and a term paper for Burgess's course in social pathology, winter quarter 1927, which is a presentation and analysis of a life history of a criminal; the document was "secured through the cooperation of Clifford Shaw, with whom I've been working." Snodgrass's article also contains more biographical material on McKay than is available elsewhere.

59. Snodgrass, "Clifford R. Shaw and Henry D. McKay," p. 3. James F. Short, Jr., has written: "Shaw was, above all, a man of action, and his mission in life became the Area Project. McKay was and is the contemplative scholar, the confirmed skeptic, persistent and unrelenting in his pursuit and analysis of data relevant to a point. The combination worked well" (Clifford R. Shaw et al., *Juvenile Delinquency and Urban Areas* [1969], p. xlv).

60. From a promotional statement about the book, in Shaw's papers.

61. p. xi. Elsewhere Burgess wrote: "Clifford R. Shaw, research sociologist at the Institute of Juvenile Research has, so far as I know, more consciously developed the method of first-person reporting and carried it further than anyone else in the country" ("What Social Case Records Should Contain to Be Useful for

Sociological Interpretation," p. 529). In *Jack-Roller* (p. 2) Shaw refers to Drucker and Hexter's *Children Astray* as a pioneering use of life history, but Richard Cabot points out in his introduction to the book (p. xiv) that these are quotations about episodes, not life histories.

62. Herbert Blumer, *Appraisal*, p. 130. Shaw also took courses in 1920–23 from George Herbert Mead; see J. David Lewis and Richard L. Smith, *American Sociology and Pragmatism*, pp. 280–81; cf. p. 258.

63. Thomas, "Life History," p. 249.

64. Terence Morris, *Criminal Area*, p. 71. Also recall the articles by Levin and Lindesmith that pointed out nineteenth-century antecedents to Shaw's work. Yale Levin was a community organizer with Shaw during the 1930s.

65. Clifford R. Shaw et al., *Delinquency Areas*, p. ix.

66. Burgess and Bogue, *Urban Sociology*, p. 293.

67. William Healy, "Devil's Workshop," p. 129, quoted in Snodgrass, *American Criminological Tradition*, p. 154.

68. Clifford R. Shaw et al., *Delinquency Areas*, p. 10. See also Shaw, "Juvenile Delinquent," p. 256; Shaw et al., *Social Factors*, p. 23; Shaw et al., *Juvenile Delinquency and Urban Areas* (1942), p. ix; and Shaw, "Correlation of Rates of Juvenile Delinquency," pp. 174–77.

69. Robert E. Park, "Concept of Position," p. 7. Cf. Roderick D. McKenzie, *On Human Ecology*.

70. Robert E. Park, "Concept of Position," p. 9. For a thorough contemporary critique of social ecology, see Milla Aïssa Alihan, *Social Ecology: A Critical Analysis,* and, more recently, John Baldwin, "Ecological and Areal Studies." Frederick Engels, like Mayhew, had an appreciation if not a theory for this: see Steven Marcus, *Engels, Manchester, and the Working Class*, pp. 172–73.

71. Clifford R. Shaw et al., *Delinquency Areas*, p. 14.

72. Ibid., pp. 7–8.

73. *Polish Peasant*, 2:1128.

74. Shaw et al., *Delinquency Areas*, pp. 204–5.

75. Ibid., p. 205.

76. Park, Burgess, and McKenzie, *City*, p. 151.

77. Henry D. McKay, "Neighborhood and Child Conduct," pp. 32–33. Park had said: "In a great city, the children are the real neighbors; their habitat is the local community; and when they are allowed to prowl and explore they learn to know the neighborhood as no older person who was not himself born and reared in the neighborhood is ever likely to know it" (Park, Burgess, and McKenzie, *City,* p. 112). Thrasher wrote: "To the narrow outlook and inexperience of the adolescent gang boy, unforeseen dangers lurk in these outside regions. Many of the groups of smaller boys never stray beyond their own neighborhood, although as they get older their horizon gradually expands. In enemy territory the authorities and the police are more formidable; these regions, moreover, are often in possession of other races, nationalities, or social strata, they are decidedly unsafe, particularly if a boy is alone" (*Gang* [1927], p. 127).

78. Park, Burgess, and McKenzie, *City*, p. 148.

79. Janowitz, introduction to Park and Burgess, *Introduction to the Science of Sociology,* p. xvi.

80. Snodgrass, "Clifford R. Shaw and Henry D. McKay," p. 10. This essay is an excellent example of someone with one set of assumptions viewing someone else who does not share those assumptions, which are not themselves supported. Snodgrass nowhere proves that the forces he mentions could account for delinquency, but he uses mere reference to them to criticize Shaw.

81. Harold Finestone, "Theory of Delinquent Gangs," p. 60. (This is a review of *Delinquency and Opportunity*, by Cloward and Ohlin.)

82. Ian Taylor, Paul Walton, and Jock Young, *New Criminology*, p. 125, quoting Downes's *Delinquent Solution*, p. 71.

83. James T. Carey, *Sociology and Public Affairs*, p. 112.

84. "The notion of disorganization is quite often merely the absence of that *type* of organization associated with the stuff of primary-group communities having Christian and Jeffersonian legitimations" (C. Wright Mills, "Professional Ideology," p. 542).

85. Preface to Shaw et al., *Juvenile Delinquency and Urban Areas* (1942), p. xi.

86. Ibid.

87. See *Juvenile Delinquency and Urban Areas* (1969), pp. 321 ff.

88. Marion K. Sanders, *Professional Radical*, p. 30.

89. Snodgrass, "Clifford R. Shaw and Henry D. McKay," pp. 12–13, for a statement on this. Roy Lubove points to the same model as the Chicago Area Project in the nineteenth-century charity organizations: "The charity organization ideal was to reestablish the patterns of social interaction of the small town or village, where the primary group exercised powerful social controls. The charity society was an 'artifice,' designed to restore the 'natural relations' which the city had destroyed" (*Professional Altruist*, p. 14). (See also Steven L. Schlossman, *Love and the American Delinquent*, p. 190, for a similar notion among the progressives.) In addition, the volunteer or friendly visitor in the charity organizations had had control over the paid staff, but as professionalization set in about 1900, the role of the volunteer began to diminish (ibid., p. 51): the same fate of volunteers has taken place in the Chicago Area Project, though less radically because there has been less growth of professional identity among the staff.

90. Shaw et al., *Delinquency Areas*, pp. 11, 9.

91. Robert E. Park, "Reflections on Communication and Culture," in Park, *Crowd and the Public*, p. 115. See also Daniel Glaser, "Marginal Workers."

92. Finestone, *Victims of Change*, p. 129.

93. Ibid., pp. 132, 149.

94. Lowell Juilliard Carr, *Delinquency Control*, p. 224. This was another "anti-institution institution"; see Schlossman, *Love and the American Delinquent*, pp. 222, 65.

95. Solomon Kobrin, "Chicago Area Project," p. 28.

96. Janowitz on the same point again: "The area project was no more than an administrative formulation of the sociological interests and intellectual ferment created by W. I. Thomas. Just as Thomas neglected political process, so did the Chicago area project. And it remained for the civil rights movement to close the gap between political process and the analysis of social organization at the community level" (W. I. Thomas, *On Social Organization*, p. lvii).

97. Quoted in James T. Carey, *Sociology and Public Affairs*, p. 91.

98. Ibid., p. 154.

99. Ibid., pp. 100–101.

100. H. Finestone, "Chicago Area Project in Theory and Practice," p. 156.

101. Shaw et al., *Juvenile Delinquency and Urban Areas* (1969), p. xlix. Compare this with what Snodgrass says: "Rather than founding a spiritual movement, as he might have done in an earlier age, he abandoned Christianity, borrowed many of its principles and values, and attempted methodically to create a community reform movement ostensibly based on science. One early worker has remarked that in the enthusiasm of the early days, many felt as acolytes, zealously hoping to kindle a popular return to hamlets and ethical humanism within the confines of the city. Shaw was an apostle of community organization as a way of saving the American city from its inherently great capacity for generating physical deterioration and social disorganization" ("Clifford R. Shaw and Henry D. McKay," p. 8).

102. Finestone, *Victims of Change,* p. 116.

103. Snodgrass, "Clifford R. Shaw and Henry D. McKay," pp. 8–9.

104. Finestone, *Victims of Change,* p. 60.

105. McKay letter to Snodgrass, 3 March 1971; quoted in part in Snodgrass, "Clifford R. Shaw and Henry D. McKay," p. 8. A few lists of speeches given by Shaw and others do exist; these are in Shaw's papers at the Chicago Historical Society. For example, from 1 July 1938 to 30 June 1939 Shaw gave at least twenty-two speeches: seven to university classes, three to women's clubs, two each to church groups, teachers' colleges, social workers, and school committees, and one each to a citizens' group and a Kiwanis Club; two more are unidentified in the lists. McKay gave five speeches during this period, and Saul Alinsky gave fourteen, the last on 8 May 1939. Kobrin has written about Shaw's strategy in these presentations: "In his public and private statements to lay groups as well as to the professional in the field he exerted great influence in creating an image of the offender as a person endowed with human traits and capacities" (Solomon Kobrin, "Clifford Shaw," p. 89).

106. Finestone, *Victims of Change,* p. 116.

107. John Bartlow Martin, "New Attack on Delinquency."

108. Finestone, *Victims of Change,* p. 132.

109. Richard Sennett, *Fall of Public Man,* p. 298.

110. Ibid., p. 223.

Chapter Eight

1. Clifford R. Shaw et al., *Delinquency Areas,* pp. 37–42. See also Shaw et al., *Social Factors,* pp. 250–51; Shaw, *Jack-Roller,* pp. 6–7; and Shaw, "Case Study Method," p. 5.

2. In the Wickersham Report (*Social Factors,* p. 137, n. 10), Shaw said that *Brothers in Crime* would be published shortly, but the book did not appear until 1938. Collecting life histories and supporting documentation from five brothers while initiating a major reform organization must have caused the delay.

Following is a brief history of publication of Shaw's three life history books: *The Jack-Roller* was published on 6 June 1930 and went out of print 30 June 1936;

it was reissued on 16 November 1938 and went out of print on 30 June 1949. It had sold 2,606 copies, and 733 were "frees." Its best year was its first, when 699 copies were sold; thereafter the typical sales figure was about 150 a year, though after 1939 it dropped to about 75. Since it was reissued as a paperback in 1966, it has sold about 23,000 copies, as of February 1981. *The Natural History of a Delinquent Career* was first published on 2 October 1930, went out of print 30 June 1935, and was reissued in November 1938. From 1930 to 1948 it sold 1,425 copies, and 586 were distributed free. It was issued again in November 1966 and sold 2,165 copies before it went out of print in 1976. A paperback published in 1976 had sold 102 copies up to 30 June 1978. *Brothers in Crime* was published 28 October 1938 and sold 1,461 copies (132 frees) by 1949. Its second publication, in 1969, had had a sale of 2,083 copies up to 30 June 1978. Compared with these, *Juvenile Delinquency and Urban Areas* has had a much more limited distribution: 1,093 copies from 1942 to 1949 and 2,485 copies from 1969 to 1978.

3. For a description of Shaw's procedures in acquiring life histories, see the Appendix.

4. Clifford R. Shaw et al., *Delinquency Areas*, pp. 144–52. Two family interviews appear in *Social Factors*, pp. 15–19 and pp. 293–315, 318–41. The former also appears in Shaw's "Case Study Method," his first publication of personal document material, in which the family is Greek. In *Social Factors* the family has become "European." Burgess wrote: "C. R. Shaw in his study of delinquency has not only secured individual documents from the members of the family but has developed the technique of the family interview in which a verbatim record is made of interaction of the members of the family in the frank and free discussion of their problems" ("Souces and Methods of Family Study," p. 451). Cf.: "Often a *family interview* is of value, as stressed by Mr. Shaw, for its revelation of the difference in attitudes, and even conduct, of the individual as a member of a group and as an independent person" (Burgess, "What Social Case Records Should Contain," p. 529). Perhaps no more dramatic illustration exists than these interviews of Thomas's notion of culture conflict between Old World parents and New World children.

5. Ernst Theodore Krueger, "Autobiographical Documents," p. 46.

6. Harold Finestone, *Victims of Change*, p. 112.

7. W. I. Thomas and D. S. Thomas, *Child in America*, p. 571.

8. Quoted in Lowell Juilliard Carr, *Delinquency Control*, p. 124.

9. Arthur L. Beeley's review of *Jack Roller, Social Service Review* (June 1931), p. 328.

10. The autobiographies did not, as Snodgrass says they do, illustrate an individual case ("Clifford R. Shaw and Henry D. McKay," p. 1). Cf. the use of "case history summaries" by the Gluecks in their *500 Criminal Careers*, chapter 4, "A Sheaf of Lives": "let us now make the acquaintance of a number of human beings who have passed through the institution. This should give us the proper orientation toward the more impersonal statistical treatment of our problem which is to follow" (p. 52). In the Gluecks' *Five Hundred Delinquent Women*, chapter 2, "A Gallery of Women," gives "a more intimate picture of the clientele of the Reformatory than can be painted by the broad brush-strokes of mere statistics" (p. 28). Both these books were published by Alfred A. Knopf, but their *One*

Thousand Juvenile Delinquents, published by Harvard University Press, merely contains some brief illustrative cases in chapter 12, which tend toward the appendix approach rather than the use of histories of individuals to open up an area to be covered by a book aimed at a more or less general public market.

11. John Dollard, "Community Studies," p. 725. (Cf. Anne Humpherys on Mayhew's inability to gain perspective on a horde of microscopic details: *Travels into the Poor Man's Country,* chap. 5.)

12. Edwin H. Sutherland, *Principles of Criminology,* p. 94.

13. Harold Finestone, *Victims of Change,* p. 94.

14. *Christian Century* 47 (June 1930): 818.

15. Walter C. Reckless, *Six Boys in Trouble,* p. ii.

16. Gordon Allport, *Use of Personal Documents,* pp. 26, 29.

17. Ibid., p. 24.

18. William Healy, "Relationship of Psychiatry to Sociology and Criminology," pp. 230–32.

19. Arthur L. Beeley, review of *Jack-Roller,* p. 328.

20. H. D. J. White, review of *Jack-Roller.*

21. Jon Snodgrass, "American Criminological Tradition," p. 185.

22. Ernst T. Krueger, *Autobiographical Documents,* p. 258.

23. Snodgrass, "American Criminological Tradition," p. 141.

24. Gordon Allport, *Use of Personal Documents,* p. 77.

25. Ibid., p. 179.

26. Richard R. Korn, ed., *Juvenile Delinquency,* p. 3. Cf. Marion White. McPherson, "Some Values and Limitations of Oral Histories," p. 35. Marvin Wolfgang has written: "Working with criminal offenders or having one's daily work principally connected with criminals is not a sufficient criterion for designation as a criminologist; else we would be at the *reductio ad absurdum* of claiming that a criminal himself should bear the label of criminologist" ("Criminology and the Criminologist," p. 162). For the oral history temperament, however, this is not absurd.

27. Jon Snodgrass, "Criminologist and His Criminal," p. 1.

28. In the late 1970s Jon Snodgrass located Stanley, the original Jack-Roller, and encouraged him to write a follow-up autobiography after almost fifty years. The manuscript that resulted, "The Jack-Roller at Seventy," had not found a publisher in January 1981. The main thrust of Snodgrass's commentary is a criticism of Shaw's psychological insight and treatment of the boy, but these are not new observations. What is new, information about the further life of Stanley, does not support Snodgrass's conclusion that Shaw failed to rehabilitate Stanley, since Stanley did not continue the criminal career he had followed as a youth.

29. Christen T. Jonassen points out that the inconsistency is even more marked in the books that are not life histories: "While the possible effect of personal and individual factors is recognized, these factors are, in the two works analyzed [*JD* and *SF*], de-emphasized and neglected by the data selected; they seem left on the periphery of Shaw's main theoretical propositions, unintegrated attenuations forced on a rather closed system by the realities of case history data. It is significant that in other works where the data are primarily case study materials, personal and family factors receive greater prominence than in his theoretical conclusions" ("Re-evaluation," p. 614).

30. Robert Angell, "A Critical Review," p. 195. One of Angell's other remarks is of interest in relation to the way delinquency studies developed after Shaw: "This is another way of saying that interest will have to shift from the historical problem of understanding particular delinquent children, or even the whole class of them, to the analytic problem of developing adequate theoretical systems." According to Angell this would require abandoning studies of the whole person, to be replaced by studies of "only those aspects of him that are relevant to the particular conceptual schemes worked out."

31. Shaw, "Case Study Method," pp. 149–50. Terence Morris says: "Without Shaw's refinement of 'situational analysis' it would be quite impossible to explain why not every child in a delinquency area is delinquent, and why even children from upper middle-class districts occasionally come into direct conflict with the law" (Morris, *Criminal Area,* pp. 72–73). But Shaw's own situational analyses are not nearly so refined.

32. Shaw et al., "Housing," p. 17.

33. Dollard, *Criteria,* p. 200.

34. Allport, *Use of Personal Documents,* p. 40. Cf. Edwin H. Sutherland: "The fundamental modification necessary for better conditions [in jails] is publicity. This is the only way to break down the isolation of the public. The public must be made acquainted with the situation, if not by direct experiences in the jails, at least by descriptions and analyses of effects" (*Principles of Criminology,* p. 238). However, criminologists generally have been more interested in building a science than in devising an appropriate rhetoric.

35. Something like the following could occur, however: "One store owner, a woman, sat down with the girls [shoplifters the CAP's Southside Community Committee was trying to reach] and told the story of her own life, describing her early poverty and hardships and eventual rise to ownership of a business in which she had been employed, many years earlier, in a most menial capacity" (Southside Community Committee, *Bright Shadows in Bronzetown,* p. 101). In the film *Scared Straight,* prison inmates try to deter young people from crime by confronting them with the realities of prison. Unfortunately, some such programs have been counterproductive.

36. Stuart A. Rice, "Hypotheses," p. 564.

37. Jonassen, "Re-evaluation," p. 615. In a letter to an editor at the University of Chicago Press in 1953, Shaw wrote: "One impetus for the completion of this study was the fact that higher rates of delinquents among Negroes or children of foreign parentage was continuously being used as evidence of the inferiority of these groups. And there was no basis for refuting this apparently incontrovertible conclusion until we uncovered data which indicated that this evidence was spurious—that the observed higher rates of delinquents among these groups were products largely of the concentration of these groups in areas of high rates. Our feeling is that this study explodes completely the support for the inferiority myth. And by so doing it helps to destroy a bit of circular reasoning which so often goes unchallenged in the field, namely: the high rate of delinquents among Negroes is the proof of their inferiority, and the inferiority is the cause of the higher rate of delinquents. Additional proof of the fact that the issues of this study are not dead is to be found in the current immigration law. The quotas in the law favoring certain groups over others furnish rather vivid proof that at least among Senators

the straw man has life. It suggests further that some factual materials might be useful in the formulation of public policy on questions such as immigration. Lombroso's theories, long since disproved, never seem to die. They were revived vividly by Hooten in the late thirties, by Sheldon in the late forties, and there is a possibility that some supporter will appear in the fifties. The reason is that imputations of inadequacy—physical, mental, or moral—represent the standard devices used by superordinate groups to keep subordinate groups 'in their place.' As Tannenbaum says, 'The outstanding characteristic of all criminological discussion has been the assumption that there was a qualitative difference between the nature of the criminal and that of the non-criminal.' '' It is clear that Shaw believed he still had to oppose naturalist theories of delinquency and racial inferiority. In conversations during the mid-1970s, Henry McKay also emphasized this as their chief accomplishment. But this battle is never absolutely won: witness William Shockley.

38. According to a memo, this includes the memberships of the American Sociological Society, Orthopsychiatric Association, American Association of Social Workers, American Psychological Association, American Prison Congress, National Conference of Juvenile Agencies, National Probation Association, Chicago Women's Club, Women's City Club, and the Illinois Congress of Parents and Teachers. The journals mentioned are *American Journal of Criminal Law and Criminology, American Journal of Psychiatry, International Journal of Ethics,* and *Survey Graphic.* Some of the publications that reviewed *The Jack-Roller* are as follows: *Social Science* (October 1931, pp. 449–50), *American Journal of Sociology* (November 1930, pp. 474–76), *Social Service Review* (June 1931, pp. 326–28), *Howard Journal* (1932), *Christian Advocate* (3 August 1934, p. 978), *Chicago Daily News* (18 July 1931), *Christian Century* (June 1930, pp. 817–18), *Welfare Bulletin* (1930, p. 5), *Revue Internationale de Sociologie* (March–April 1931, pp. 184–85), and *Annals of the American Academy of Political Science* (September 1930, pp. 285–86).

39. Burgess and Bogue, *Urban Sociology,* p. 596.

40. Carey, *Public Affairs,* p. 144. "The jack-roller, Stanley, ended his saga with the story of his escape from the ghetto—an ending that could not fail to clutch a social worker's heart" (Korn, *Juvenile Delinquency,* p. 194). Social workers were more the opposition than psychologists because the former were closer to the sociological position.

41. Bruno, "Some Case Work," p. 532.

42. Ibid., p. 533.

43. Robert E. L. Faris, *Chicago Sociology,* p. 83. For the broader context of public interest in "documentary expression," see Stott's book and Burnham's "The New Psychology."

44. See Norman Kiell, *Universal Experience of Adolescence.*

45. Howard Vincent O'Brien, "Footnotes," *Chicago Daily News,* 18 July 1931.

46. Joseph D. Lohman, "A Sociologist-Sheriff Speaks out about Juvenile Delinquency."

47. John Landesco, *Organized Crime,* p. 280.

48. James T. Carey, *Sociology and Public Affairs,* pp. 144–45.

49. Ibid., pp. 143–44.

50. Ibid., p. 144.

51. Lecture on James Joyce delivered at the University of Chicago, November 1959, broadcast on radio station WFMT, Chicago, 24 May 1973.

52. Harold Finestone, *Victims of Change,* p. 117. Cf. Kobrin, "Clifford Shaw," p. 89: "[Shaw] made unceasing efforts in his discussions with institutional work-ers...to communicate to them the importance of keeping in focus the human needs of the young offender rather than the career needs of institutional person-nel."

53. H. D. J. White, review of *Jack-Roller, Howard Journal* (1932).

54. William F. Whyte had wanted to be a writer but obtained a fellowship that allowed him to do work in sociology and social anthropology, areas about which he was "woefully ignorant." He was thus professionally marginal. He was in-fluenced by *The Autobiography of Lincoln Steffens,* and he says: "It was a long time before I realized that I could explain Cornerville better through telling the stories of those individuals and groups than I could in any other way" (*Street Corner Society,* p. 357).

Another case in which the use of an oral history is associated with a call for penal reform and programs of community corrections is Austin L. Porterfield's *Youth in Trouble;* see pp. 71–88 and chapter 6, where Porterfield invokes the concept of social disorganization.

55. Miriam Van Waters, *Youth in Conflict.* One might ponder the rhetoric of the titles of these books.

56. Jon Snodgrass, "American Criminological Tradition," p. 198.

Chapter Nine

1. Patrick T. Murphy, *Our Kindly Parent,* p. 14.

2. *Playboy* interview, p. 62.

3. Unless otherwise noted, information and quotations about Alinsky's life come from Marion K. Sanders, *Professional Radical.* I am indebted to Michael Connolly for assistance in studying Alinsky.

4. These life histories are now at the Chicago Historical Society.

5. In the extant documents written by these boys Alinsky is always remembered fondly. For example: "Bennie came out of jail and he came to see me in the hospital [his leg had been shot in a heist]. His brother Felix came too and brought me a box of candy and a few life savers and some gum and cigarettes. Even Alinsky came. He bought me a 'sponge' cake and told me to eat it slow and when he saw me eat it, he taught I didn't eat for a year. I completely swallowed it. He said he wouldn't give me any more and I don't remember what I said he was."

6. Saul D. Alinsky, "Sociological Technique in Clinical Criminology," p. 178.

7. Ibid., pp. 172–73.

8. Ibid., p. 176.

9. Cf. what Studs Terkel has said about his motive: "I think it's curiosity. I suppose my essential impulse is curiosity about what Mark Twain would call 'the damned human race,' and each one unique, as he is, each one is an individual" (Denis Brian, *Murderers and Other Friendly People,* p. 294).

10. Studs Terkel, *Hard Times,* p. 351.

11. Cf. Short in the 1969 edition of *Juvenile Delinquency and Urban Areas*, p. xlviii: "In the current lexicon, Shaw was concerned with the problem of alienation, and he attributed alienation in large part to powerlessness." However, I have never come across a statement by Shaw that explicitly used the category of *power*.

12. Alinsky, "A Departure in Community Organization," p. 38. "Departure" was ambiguous: this article appeared in the same month when Alinsky was himself departing from Shaw's institute. On transcendence, cf. Finestone: "Like Thomas, [Robert E.] Park started with the impingement of a larger world upon the smaller more personal world. It was this broadening of the sphere of required participation that was connected with the emergence of the problem of juvenile delinquency. It was difficult for the young person to identify with the goals of the larger community since they were impersonal and transcended his own personal interests" (*Victims of Change*, pp. 71–72).

The need for analytical linkage between the microcosm and the macrocosm was noted from time to time even by more conventional sociologists, such as Joseph Lohman, who nevertheless was something of a maverick and like Alinsky had a falling out with Shaw. On the need for "systemic" sociological analysis, see Lohman's "Participant Observer in Community Studies."

13. Shaw's statement appears in Snodgrass, "American Criminological Tradition," pp. 137–38.

14. John Hall Fish, *Black Power/White Control*, p. 111. Alinsky himself is reported to have said: "We are fine at demonstrations and protesting.... But we don't yet have the organizations to compel the power structure to follow through on the concessions they make. It's as though a labor union won a contract, then decided to disband and expected the employer to live up to the contract" (*New York Times*, 19 May 1969, p. 64).

15. Both Becker and Studs Terkel wrote their first major work on jazz: Terkel's was *Giants of Jazz*, and Becker's master's thesis was "The Professional Dance Musician in Chicago" (1949). Chicago was a pioneer place for jazz, in which personal improvisation may be similar to the expression in a life history. Terkel edits his material into continuities that resemble jazz themes and variations.

16. Eighty-four interviews with drug users were conducted. The typescripts of these are still on file at the Institute for Juvenile Research. Many of the interviewees came from the same areas of the city as the earlier delinquents who wrote their life histories. Almost none of this material was ever published, though some of it was used by Harold Finestone in "Cats, Kicks, and Color," which reveals that more than fifty of the interviewees were black; and in "Drug Addiction among Young Persons in Chicago," by Solomon Kobrin and Harold Finestone, which appears in *Gang Delinquency and Delinquent Subcultures*, ed. James F. Short, Jr. On the drug study, see also Burgess and Bogue, *Urban Sociology*, 1st ed., p. 615.

17. See Alfred Lindesmith, *Opiate Addiction*. Some of Becker's experience went into *Outsiders* (see p. viii; Becker must mean chapters 3 and 4, not 5 and 6.) Becker says he conducted fifty interviews with marijuana users, though not all of these were through IJR. Sol Kobrin and Harold Finestone made available to Becker some additional interviews (*Outsiders*, pp. 45–46).

18. Personal communication (19 September 1974). I am indebted to Howard Becker, Helen Hughes, Everett Hughes, and Solomon Kobrin for assistance in writing this section.

19. *Fantastic Lodge,* p. ix. This information in the preface was supplied by Becker to the authors of the preface, Helen and Everett Hughes.

20. Ibid., p. viii.

21. In 1964 Monarch Books brought the book out in paperback. Fawcett-Premier brought it out in paperback in 1971 with a selection of Janet's poems. In 1963 it was put out as a hardback book in London by Arthur Barker and as a paperback by Digit Books (Brown Watson). It came out in Paris in 1972 as *La confrérie fantastique: Autobiographie d'une droguée* (Editions Denoël Gonthier).

22. Janowitz, introduction to W. I. Thomas, *On Social Organization,* p. liv. According to Faris, no students were closer to Park than Helen and Everett Hughes (*Chicago Sociology,* p. 109).

23. McKay has remarked: "Shaw was a great organizer. He kept a research department alive throughout a long depression, and a great war, which is no mean achievement" (quoted in Snodgrass, "Clifford R. Shaw and Henry D. McKay," p. 6). At least Shaw's apprehension over the public impact of a personal document supports the claim that he was aware of the rhetorical dimension of such material.

24. David Ebin, ed., *Drug Experience,* p. 215.

25. "The distribution of drug use as a social problem . . . [in Chicago] can be pinpointed with great accuracy as having its incidence preponderantly among the young male colored persons in a comparatively few local community areas" (Harold Finestone, "Cats, Kicks, and Color," p. 14).

26. In a letter to me of 22 October 1975, Solomon Kobrin wrote: "in those days the public panic over the drug use epidemic among ghetto youngsters rendered IJR realistically vulnerable to attack. At the time we were completing the interviewing of heroin addicts from the Black community and from the nearby Italian neighborhood. We were using Federal research funds to pay the respondents, many of whom were in various stages of euphoria, somnolence, or withdrawal pains. All were in desperate need of money and were more than eager to talk about their experiences with drugs, their personal histories, or any other topic we might suggest in exchange for the five dollars fee, paid in cash. Some took to using IJR johns to shoot up, a matter we had difficulty controlling. On a number of occasions typewriters and calculating machines were stolen by several of the more desperate junkies who were also skilled thieves. Our relationships with them were such that we were able to persuade them to give us the tickets needed to redeem these items of State property from pawn shops. I paid for these recoveries out of my own pocket. From time to time we were visited by detectives from the Chicago Police Department Narcotics Squad, who apparently suspected that IJR had become something of a junkie hangout. As we had taken the precaution to give each respondent a pseudonym at the first interview by which he was to be known henceforth, we were able honestly to claim no knowledge of persons named by the gendarmes. To understand the jeopardy all this represented we must remember that in the early 1950s hard drug use was seen as a critical enforcement problem, with the media more than ready to sensationalize any event related to the drug use issue. Both Shaw and McKay were fully aware of the problems Hal [Finestone] and I were having keeping our operation in hand. That they were willing to tolerate the risk in behalf of a commitment to the value of the research hardly fits the picture of a couple of timid, conventional establishment type people. At the same time, however, if they were to sustain the Sociology Department in the

always tenuous framework of the IJR, some caution had to be exercised. As things worked out, all of the anxieties occasioned by the drug addict study came to be focused around the matter of publishing *The Fantastic Lodge*. As in all such anxiety states, it is possible that the dangers of suits, etc., were exaggerated."

27. *Fantastic Lodge*, pp. 214–15.

28. Ibid., pp. 200–205.

29. "Men who had been disposed to challenge the intellectual order began in time to reject new styles" (Morris Janowitz, introduction to Robert E. L. Faris, *Chicago Sociology*, p. x).

30. Howard S. Becker, *Outsiders*, p. 46.

31. Personal communication (3 November 1975).

32. Becker, *Outsiders*, p. 84.

33. Becker explored one moral dimension of sociologists' work in an article eloquently entitled "Whose Side Are We On?" and claimed that sociologists cannot avoid being on one side or the other in the social issues they study, though that does not excuse deception: "We take sides as our personal and political commitments dictate, use our theoretical and technical resources to avoid the distortions that might introduce into our work, limit our conclusions carefully, recognize the hierarchy of credibility for what it is, and field as best we can the accusations and doubts that will surely be our fate" (p. 247).

34. *Confrérie fantastique*, p. 262.

35. James, *Varieties of Religious Experience*, p. 486.

36. Allport says of *A Mind That Found Itself*, which contains no interpretative editorial writing: "From the point of view of controls, few documents are worse, and yet from the pragmatic point of view we are warned that scientific safeguards will not in themselves save a poor document from the dust pile, nor prevent a good one from contributing somehow to the course of scientific progress" (*Use of Personal Documents*, pp. 11–12).

37. *Fantastic Lodge*, p. 51.

38. Ibid., pp. 184–85. "But a person who is thus labeled an outsider may have a different view of the matter. He may not accept the rule by which he is being judged and may not regard those who judge him as either competent or legitimately entitled to do so. Hence, a second meaning of the term emerges: the rule-breaker may feel his judges are *outsiders*" (Howard S. Becker, *Outsiders*, pp. 1–2).

39. Introduction to Clifford R. Shaw, *Jack-Roller* (1966), p. xvii.

40. Ibid., p. xvi. Daniel Bertaux, in a draft for the introduction to *Biography and Society* that I read before the book's publication, claims that a major revival of life histories is now under way in sociology. If so, life histories could be brought in and used to do precisely what they did earlier in this century: reorient thought from empty abstractions to concrete phenomena. However, it is too early to tell whether this is a renaissance or merely the wish for one and in fact an extension of subordinate functions that never disappeared: it is one thing to theorize about life histories, another to acquire them, and yet another to publish them to some point. This book does not cover delinquency explicitly, but it does seem to call into question three of my hypotheses: (1) that oral histories cannot grasp the macro level, (2) that oral histories and their accompanying interpretation tend to be untheoretical, and (3) that this is an Anglo-American tradition not found else-

where. Perhaps what I have asserted as characteristics of a form of expression will have to be limited to certain past instances of it, but I doubt it. See also: *Cahiers Internationaux de sociologie* 69.

41. C. Wright Mills, "Professional Ideology," pp. 532, 534.

42. See *Jack-Roller,* p. 103. In Shaw's *Natural History,* which begins with a chapter entitled "Labeled a 'Moron,'" Burgess says: "Gabriel Tarde has stated with his discerning insight that the criminal is created first by his act and second by the way society treats that act" (p. 244).

43. Harold Finestone, *Victims of Change,* p. 14.

44. Robert Angell, "Critical Review," p. 184.

45. Richard P. Rettig et al., *Manny,* p. 1. In *Box Man,* by Harry King, Bill Chambliss refers to this audience as "professors who write books about thieves, students who study them (and thereby stay a little longer from the already overly populated labor market)" (p. 172).

46. Richard P. Rettig et al., *Manny,* p. 8.

47. Ibid., p. 9.

48. Duane Denfeld, *Street-Wise Criminology,* p. 6.

49. Harry King, *Box Man,* pp. 168–69.

50. Thomas J. Cottle, *Children in Jail,* p. 174.

51. Thomas J. Cottle, *Private Lives and Public Accounts,* pp. xii, 23. Nevertheless, Cottle exhibits many features of an oral history practitioner, re-stating several commonplaces, such as that members of the middle class are not normally interested in the lives of poor people (p. 8), the marginality of his project in the tradition of humanistic sociology (p.xi), his goal "to understand human behavior and to enhance human life" (p. 22), and hence the union of research and therapeutic interests. Chapter 2 of this book is the best autobiographical account I have found of the discovery of the importance of the subjective by someone who uses personal documents extensively, but the prominence of Cottle himself in this account carries over into the rest of his writing. Perhaps the reason the purer oral historian does not write about his own experiences is to avoid any interference in another person's "life," or rather in the message of that life. For additional self-reflection on "subjective inquiry," see Cottle's "Life Study."

52. Bruce Jackson, *Thief's Primer,* p. 10.

53. Annabel Faraday and Kenneth Plummer, "Doing Life Histories."

Chapter Ten

1. Louis Cazamian, *Roman social en angleterre, 1830–1850,* p. 3. See also Steven Marcus, *The Other Victorians,* pp. 282–83.

2. Terence Morris, *Criminal Area,* p. 67.

3. Cf. de Tocqueville: "Nothing, in my opinion, is more deserving of our atten-tion than the intellectual and moral associations of America. The political and industrial associations of that country strike us forcibly; but the others elude our observation, or if we discover them, we understand them imperfectly, because we have hardly ever seen anything of the kind. It must, however, be acknowledged that they are as necessary to the American people as the former, and perhaps more so" (*Democracy in America,* p. 118; cf. p. 117, where a similar point is made about the British).

4. Gordon W. Allport, *Use of Personal Documents*, p. 127.

5. Howard S. Becker, "Whose Side Are We On?" p. 242.

6. Philip Rieff, *Freud: The Mind of the Moralist*, p. 23.

7. Robert E. Park, introduction to Stonequist, *Marginal Man*, p. xviii.

8. Anne Humpherys, *Travels into the Poor Man's Country*, p. 155.

9. See McKeon's unpublished paper "Philosophic Semantics and Philosophic Inquiry."

10. The only representation of the juvenile court I have found in a book is a transcript in Lois Forer's *"No One Will Lissen,"* pp. 87–92. It has been remarked "how limited are the demands for accountability on juvenile courts and how few effective monitoring mechanisms exist.... It is a system in which the voices of those it claims to serve are least likely to be heard" (Rosemary Sarri and Yeheskel Hansenfeld, eds., *Brought to Justice?* [Ann Arbor: National Assessment of Juvenile Corrections, 1976], p. 215; quoted in Anthony M. Platt, *Child Savers*, 1977 ed., p. 191).

11. Richard Sennett, *Fall of Public Man*. For a related contradiction between public and private in the "new history," see *The Past before Us*, ed. Michael Kammen. Even if the social scientist wanted to bring systemic order out of the oral history phenomena, could he? In a review of Oscar Lewis's *Four Men*, Lisa R. Peattie wrote: "In the earlier books, Oscar Lewis clearly wanted to display for us the nature of the capitalist system, via its human consequences. 'The culture of poverty,' he said in the introduction to *La Vida,* 'is both an adaptation and a reaction of the poor to their marginal position in a class-stratified, highly individuated capitalist society.' But I get the impression that the books were generally read another way: not for their light on capitalism as a system but for their revelations about the poor and the depressing yet fascinating disorder of lives at the bottom" (*New York Times Book Review,* 12 June 1977, p. 13). Peattie speculates on why Lewis was ejected from Cuba: "There were probably many reasons for this. Lewis was a notoriously difficult man. But there is no reason to doubt Mrs. Lewis's interpretation that a substantial problem was the dissonance with the revolutionary image produced by research that looked at the system in all its human imperfection" (ibid.).

12. Norman K. Denzin, *Research Act*.

13. An often-cited example of this is Lemert's discovery that check forgers work alone, an exception to Sutherland's theory of criminal subcultures. Edwin Lemert, "Behavior of the Systematic Check Forger." Another example of "exceptional data" is in Paul Lazarsfeld's introduction to Mirra Komarovsky's *Unemployed Man and His Family*, p. xii.

14. Howard S. Becker, introduction to *Jack-Roller*, pp. x–xi.

15. Ibid., p. xi.

16. Robert Angell, "Critical Review," p. 181. Stott says of some incidents portrayed in 1930s life histories: "The particular event seems not only the warrant but also the source of the generalization" (*Documentary Expression*, p. 161). It seems this way because only the particular event is shown in the book, but the source of the generalization is much broader, in the researcher's whole experience. John Dollard wrote: "From a methodological standpoint, the intensive life history may be a valuable way of making an exploratory study. Too often the

exploratory phase is missed in sociological researches, and the researcher relies on his own intuition in discerning the variables to be studied and measured" ("Life History in Community Studies," p. 724). However, neither Dollard nor anyone else has explained concretely and in detail how life histories function in exploration except to make reference to the sociologist's intuition.

17. Gordon W. Allport, *Use of Personal Documents,* p. 138.

18. Howard S. Becker, introduction to *Jack-Roller,* p. xii.

19. Robert Angell, "Critical Review," p. 180.

20. John Dollard, *Criteria for the Life History,* p. 270.

21. Allport, *Use of Personal Documents,* p. 35.

22. Cf. Richard Sennett on the nineteenth century: "When belief was governed by the principle of immanence, there broke down distinctions between perceiver and perceived, inside and outside, subject and object. If everything counts potentially, how am I to draw a line between what relates to my personal needs and what is impersonal, unrelated to the immediate realm of my experience? It may all matter, nothing may matter, but how am I to know? I must therefore draw no distinction between categories of objects and of sensations, because in distinguishing them I may be creating a false barrier. The celebration of objectivity and hardheaded commitment to fact so prominent a century ago, all in the name of Science, was in reality an unwitting preparation for the present era of radical subjectivity" (*Fall of Public Man,* p. 22).

23. Michel Foucault, *Discipline and Punish,* p. 251.

24. Alan Gewirth, *Reason and Morality.*

25. Here are a few typical statements: In a letter to Howard S. Becker commenting on his introduction to the new edition of *The Jack-Roller,* Henry McKay wrote: "I like especially your emphasis on the human document as a means of communication between classes. Often I tell people who are disturbed about whether or not a life history is pure science that the human document is most successful as an educative device. Stanley has been more successful than anyone else, as far as I know, in demonstrating that what goes on in a training school corresponds little with what the public assumes is going on." Mennel wrote in *Thorns and Thistles* (p. 200): "In many respects, the ultimate authorities on juvenile delinquency have always been the delinquent children themselves. Better than their keepers, they judged the efficacy of reform school programs. For the most part, their judgment has been unfavorable. From the anonymous children who confided to Elijah Devoe, to the accounts of Josiah Flint Willard and Stanley the jack-roller, the tale has been one of drudgery and debasement. Institutions and juvenile courts smothered decent instincts and encouraged further crime and deviance."

Robert J. Minton, Jr., wrote in *Inside: Prison American Style* (p. xvii): "The hope is that, once these men have been able to tell their stories—stories that are often covered up or lied about by the administrators whose job it is to maintain the status quo—the status quo will change." Reform of prisons is also an aim of *Hustler! The Autobiography of a Thief,* by Henry Williamson. In a concluding statement, Paul Bohannan wrote: "Despite undeniable improvements in the mid-twentieth century, we are nowhere near a sensible solution to the age-old question of punishment and reform. Until real innovative genius gets to work on the problem, the prisons will remain what they are because they are self-perpetuating" (pp. 218–19). The Community Research Forum at the University of Illinois at Urbana estimated that in 1978 there were 479,908 admissions of juveniles to adult jails and lockups in the United States.

26. Discussions of Shaw's work that put his life histories to one side overlook the fact that the histories contain principles that are at least as important to the understanding of the Chicago Area Project as Shaw's life and his theory are.

27. Hermann Mannheim, *Comparative Criminology*, 1:160.

28. Michel Foucault, *Discipline and Punish*, p. 305.

29. Herbert Goldhammer, "Recent Developments in Personality Studies," p. 565. In 1975 Robert Bogdan and Steven J. Taylor wrote: "Over the past decade, there has been growing interest in the subjective, in meaning, and in common-sense understandings" (*Introduction to Qualitative Research Methods*, p. ix). See also *Mining and Social Change*, ed. Martin Bulmer, Appendix C. One probably could find alternations of fashions of more subjective or objective methods, each lasting for perhaps a decade. But there seems no hope of encouraging qualitative methods by trying to quantify or standardize them: Charles E. Frazier has written: "In the field of criminology, where it [the life history method] has been used most often, the evolution of a growing number of competing theories seems an appropriate place for reviving the life-history method. The task of standardizing techniques of collecting, analyzing, and reporting life-history data still remain. Full recognition as a scientifically suitable method will probably not come until such standards are established" ("Use of Life Histories in Testing Theories of Criminal Behavior," p. 139). Then it will never come, unless sociologists come to grips with the rhetorical qualities of life histories. As George A. Lundberg has asserted, the "case study method" is only a first step toward a scientific method, not a scientific method itself ("Case Work and the Statistical Method," p. 61). Moves toward making life history into a scientific method end with something quite different. Of course, the future of criminology depends partly on its past evolution, the stages of which correspond to the levels in Plato's ladder of loves in the *Symposium*.

30. Leon Radzinowitz, *Ideology and Crime*, p. 95.

31. Jo Manton, *Mary Carpenter and the Children of the Street*, p. 5.

32. See *Soviet Life* magazine, September 1978, p. 24.

33. Clifford R. Shaw, *Natural History of a Delinquent Career*, p. 65.

34. Three instances are: Albert K. Cohen, *Delinquent Boys*, p. 9; Howard S. Becker, *Jack-Roller* (1966), p. xviii; and Anthony M. Platt, *The Child-Savers*, p. 9.

Appendix

1. *Morning Chronicle*, 22 April 1850, p. 6. Cf. Edward W. Said on a speech by Arthur Balfour in the House of Commons: "It does not occur to Balfour to let the Egyptian speak for himself" (*Orientalism*, p. 33).

2. *Morning Chronicle*, 25 April 1850, p. 6.

3. *London Labour* (1851), vol. 1, no. 5, Answers to Correspondents.

4. Ibid., vol. 2, no. 42.

5. *Morning Chronicle*, 22 January 1850, p. 6.

6. E. P. Thompson, "Political Education of Henry Mayhew," p. 57.

7. Thucydides, *Peloponnesian War*, 1. 22.

8. H. Sutherland Edwards, quoted in Eileen Yeo, "Mayhew as a Social Investigator," p. 60.

9. Anne Humpherys, *Travels into the Poor Man's Country,* p. 189.

10. Studs Terkel, *Working,* p. xix. According to Humpherys, the earlier interviews were predominantly short questions and answers about quantitative matters, but eventually "the questions about the causes of low wages lead to more rambling conversations and extensive probing on how the worker can live on such wages. Consequently, the interviews become much more interesting human documents" (*Voices of the Poor,* pp. x–xi). A further stage was reached with a change of subject, from tradespeople to street people: "The kind of information he wanted about the street folk was different; he hoped to elucidate their minds and hearts as well as the details of their incomes" (Humpherys, *Travels,* p. 154).

11. Cf. Studs Terkel: "I pay everybody. W. Clement Stone a buck, a domestic $100. What they get paid is absolutely nominal compared with what they give me, which is their life, which is invaluable" (interview with Tom Snyder on the "Tomorrow" show, NBC–TV, 9 May 1974).

12. *London Labour* (1851), vol. 1, no. 22, Answers to Correspondents.

13. "Dickens cast some of his acquaintances from *Punch* in the amateur productions that he directed, managed, and acted in, and Henry Mayhew played in the first of these, as old Knowell in Jonson's *Every Man in His Humour,* on September 20, 1845" (Harland S. Nelson, "Dickens' *Our Mutual Friend* and Henry Mayhew's *London Labour and the London Poor,*" p. 211). After reading Mayhew, Auden says he concluded that Dickens is a more realistic novelist than he had thought. Cf. Steven Marcus, *The Other Victorians,* pp. 100, 288.

14. W. H. Auden, "A Very Inquisitive Old Party," pp. 131–33. Thomas Cottle has written: "If there is a rule about this form of research, it might be reduced to something as simple as pay attention" ("Life Study," p. 351).

15. "[Terkel] is like some sort of magician or genie, bringing an incredible abundance of marvelous beings before our eyes, yet as soon as we reach out and grasp at any one, he whisks it away from us and replaces it with another and another, in dizzying and exhausting succession . . . . What this book needs is a more active intelligence; giving some sort of structure and coherence to the marvelous material" (Marshall Berman, review of *Working, New York Times Book Review,* 24 March 1974). John Lofland makes the same observation about the "protocol style" from the perspective of the "generic style" ("Styles of Reporting Qualitative Field Research," p. 104). According to Alan Cedric Thomas, the "surround" of Mayhew's oral histories strengthened their credibility: "That Mayhew chose to surround the statements of his subjects with 'official' material, often irrelevant or manufactured and even, sometimes, erroneous, suggests the powerful compulsion he felt to create the appearance of Blue Book literature." "Blue books" were government publications. Use of other modes of presentation, according to Thomas, "would have brought his work into association, in the public mind, with a less serious journalism, or with fictional writing" ("Henry Mayhew's Rhetoric," p. 188).

16. *Morning Chronicle,* 15 January 1850, supplement, p. 29.

17. Studs Terkel, interviewed by Herman Kogan, radio station WFMT, Chicago, 31 March 1974. (I am indebted to Lois Baum for a recording of this

interview.) The transitional device between oral histories might be called a "bird swing": the word is used in the glass industry to refer to a filament extending from one wall of a bottle to another.

18. *Morning Chronicle,* 25 April 1850, p. 5.

19. Ibid., 29 January 1850, p. 5.

20. Ibid., 15 January 1850, p. 6.

21. *London Labour* (1851), vol. 3, no. 47, Answers to Correspondents.

22. William Healy and Augusta F. Bronner, *Judge Baker Foundation Case Studies,* p. 29a.

23. Healy Oral History, pp. 267–68.

24. William Healy, *Individual Delinquent,* p. 44.

25. Ibid., p. 35.

26. Healy Oral History, p. 87.

27. Healy, *Individual Delinquent,* p. 39.

28. Healy Oral History, p. 93.

29. The first six psychologists at the Juvenile Psychopathic Institute were women.

30. Healy Oral History, p. 341.

31. Healy, *Individual Delinquent,* p. 39.

32. Ibid., p. 35.

33. Ibid.

34. Jon Snodgrass, "American Criminological Tradition," chap. 3.

35. Jacob Panken, *Child Speaks,* p. 241.

36. Healy, *Individual Delinquent,* p. 12. Lowell S. Selling advises that ages ten to fourteen are best ("Autobiography as a Psychiatric Technique," p. 168). But Gordon Allport says: "The autobiographies of children have little value. Until the age of 13 or after, the child records events wholly in external terms . . . . Subjective life grows important as adulthood approaches, and after puberty there is less dependence upon surrounding influences than in childhood" (*Use of Personal Documents,* p. 80). Thus different positions require different ages for their best speakers, age-graded from simple to complex.

37. Healy, *Individual Delinquent,* p. 40.

38. Ibid.

39. Ibid., p. 48.

40. Ibid., p. 44.

41. Healy Oral History, p. 268.

42. Ibid., p. 191.

43. Ibid., pp. 308–9.

44. Floyd N. House, "Social Forces," p. 505. Cf. Selling's three methods: Lowell S. Selling, "Autobiography as a Psychiatric Technique," pp. 163–64.

45. Healy Oral History, p. 309.

46. Ibid., p. 256.

47. Ibid., p. 85.

48. Ernest W. Burgess and Donald J. Bogue, *Urban Sociology,* p. 600. Two articles during the earlier period that covered interviewing techniques, unfortunately with what can only appear to us as truisms, are Ruth Shonle Cavan, "Interviewing for Life History Material," and Ernest Theodore Krueger, "Tech-

nique of Securing Life History Documents." A more recent treatment is in Robert Bogdan and Steven J. Taylor's *Introduction to Qualitative Research Methods.* For a recent use of a collection of old life histories, see Herman R. Lantz, "Family and Kin as Revealed in the Narratives of Ex-Slaves."

49. See the original relatively brief essay by the Jack-Roller, in appendix 2 of that book. In the case of the five brothers of *Brothers in Crime,* none was aware of what the others wrote, and none was given access to official records (*BC* 143).

50. Krueger, "Autobiographical Documents and Personality," p. 244. Kimball Young, in "Measurement of Personal and Social Traits" (p. 100), made reference to "Krueger, in his forthcoming book," but this study of life histories was never published.

51. "Self-consciousness itself does not arise from mere self-contemplation but only through our struggles with the world—i.e., in the course of the process in which we first become aware of ourselves" (Paul Delany, *British Autobiography in the 17th Century,* p. 19, quoting an unidentified "modern sociologist").

52. A letter dated 1941 in the IJR files reads as follows: "Friend McKay, I wish to take this means to express my deep appreciation of the help, financial and otherwise, that has been extended to me by Mr. Shaw, Ted, yourself and others in the near past. I thank you all from the bottom of my heart and only hope that I may be able to repay it at some future date. None of my prospects have materialized . . . ." So further aid was requested.

53. These workers included Saul Alinsky, Jerome Sampson, William Mac-Donald, Maurice Moore, Ed Conover, and Yale Levin. I am grateful to Yale Levin for information about this enterprise (interview of 1 October 1973).

54. Nathan F. Leopold, *Life Plus 99 Years,* pp. 191 ff. In a letter to Yale Levin, Leopold says that while reading Shaw and McKay's part of the Wickersham Report he came across one of the documents he had obtained, though he does not say which one it was.

According to Henry McKay, prison authorities did not object to criticism of prison life expressed in the life histories but were very disturbed when a sociologist promised an inmate more than he could deliver, such as helping someone escape, an event that McKay claims one of Shaw's sociologists did on one occasion. McKay was then asked to give the escapee, whom he did not know to be such, a ride downtown. McKay says he wondered why the man was slouching down in his overcoat with the collar turned up—in the middle of summer.

55. Jon Snodgrass, "Clifford R. Shaw and Henry D. McKay," p. 8. Cf. a remark by Kluckhohn: "There is some real conflict between the type of temperament and training required for doing ethnography successfully and that which a superior worker in personal documents ought to possess. For example, the gentle techniques which promote a free flow of spontaneous reminiscence are often incompatible with getting the specific details and the cross-checking of data required in good ethnographic work" ("Personal Document in Anthropological Science," p. 110). Kimball Young noted: "Some people are too rigid, too compulsive, and too impatient for such investigations" ("Frederic M. Thrasher's Study of Gangs," p. 521).

56. Ernest Theodore Krueger, "Autobiographical Documents," p. 252. "He often receives the most surprising revelations and confidences, at times rem-

iniscent of a confessional, about matters which are kept carefully hidden from everybody with whom one is close" (Georg Simmel, *On Individuality*, p. 145).

57. Ibid., p. 143. Cf. Donald A. Levine, "Simmel at a Distance." By considering a series of misunderstandings of Simmel's concept of the stranger, Levine derives a series of distinct types of stranger: guest, sojourner, newcomer, intruder, inner enemy, and marginal man. Anyone attempting to move the theme of marginality into a hypothesis should consult this article.

58. Allport set forth thirteen possible motivations: special pleading, exhibitionism, desire for order, literary delight, securing personal perspective, relieving tension, monetary gain, performing an assignment, assisting in therapy, redemption and social reincorporation, scientific interest, public service and example, and the desire for immortality (*Use of Personal Documents*, pp. 69 ff.). Kluckhohn gives six: to get money or a service, to attract an audience ("deviants or those who are somehow maladjusted in their group . . . someone who needs an audience"), pride ("a person who conceives his life to have been full of unusual adventures and accomplishments, who is proud of his history—he also is often ready to talk"), personal attachment of the informant to the interviewer, to state the truth and correct lies, and, finally, immortality ("Personal Document," p. 117). Krueger discriminated the confessional type of document and motive, the egotistical type (introspective, such as Rousseau; conventional, such as success stories; and the emancipated, "at variance but not at war with the social order"), as well as scientific and naive (conventional) documents ("Autobiographical Documents," p. 57). Krueger was mainly concerned with the confessional type, of which Shaw's published histories do not appear to be examples. Allport refers to Nicolaysen's claim "that the essential conditions for autoanalytic writing are that the subject must experience dissatisfactions with his present behavior and a desire for self-improvement and for self-understanding; and that he be willing to face reality and have confidence in his ability to carry the project through to successful completion" (*Use of Personal Documents*, p. 42). Krueger's dissertation is full of helpful hints about how to motivate the confessional type: " 'Writing on both sides of the paper' tends to prolong the probable length of time a person in mental catharsis will write without fatigue and lassitude. The total amount written will appear less than it actually is" ("Autobiographical Documents," p. 250). "W. I. Thomas suggests a tactful expression of doubt that the person will relate the full details of experiences as a way of committing the person, if he decides to write, to a complete narrative without reservations. This has the effect of a dare" (ibid., p. 255, n. 1).

59. Cf. B. Karpman's very different opinion: "Very few are the patients who can present an account in clear, unambiguous, and at the same time grammatically correct English; in the main we are dealing here with individuals who although often intelligent, are not freely able to express themselves in grammatically correct and contextually clear language. It was therefore necessary to transcribe all of this material into language that would be true to the meaning of the text and at the same time not offend the reader's ear" (B. Karpman, *Case Studies in the Psychopathology of Crime*, 1:viii).

60. Louis Gottschalk, "Historian and the Historical Document."

61. Edwin Sutherland, review of *Natural History of a Delinquent Career*, p. 135.

62. Clifford R. Shaw and Henry D. McKay, "Broken Homes," p. 524: "It was found that the difference between rates in the delinquent and the control group furnished a very inadequate basis for the conclusion that the broken home is an important factor in delinquency. This should not be interpreted to mean that family situations are not important influences in cases of delinquency among boys; the foregoing data suggest that we must look for these influences in the more subtle aspects of family relationships rather than in the formal break in the family organization."

63. Allport called for a "Guide to Rationalizations and Projections" (*Use of Personal Documents*, p. 132) and added to the collection of nostrums: "the presence of superlative and absolute statements, as well as excessive repetition, may indicate that the autobiographer is fooling himself" (ibid., p. 31). These warnings may help "in training readers and analysts to become suspicious in the right places" (ibid.). Matza's discussion of "neutralization" devices is relevant here.

64. Allport, *Use of Personal Documents*, p. 84.

65. Clyde Kluckhohn, "Personal Document," pp. 139, 97.

66. Edwin H. Sutherland, review of *Natural History of a Delinquent Career*, p. 136.

Bibliography

Addams, Jane. *My Friend, Julia Lathrop*. New York: Macmillan, 1935.
———. *The Second Twenty Years at Hull House*. New York: Macmillan, 1930.
———. *Twenty Years at Hull House*. New York: New American Library, 1960.
Aichhorn, August. *Delinquency and Child Guidance: Selected Papers*. New York: International Universities Press, 1964.
———. *Wayward Youth*. New York: Viking Press, 1925, 1965.
Alihan, Milla Aïssa. *Social Ecology: A Critical Analysis*. New York: Columbia University Press, 1938.
Alinsky, Saul D. "A Departure in Community Organization." *Proceedings of the National Conference of Juvenile Agencies* (January 1949), pp. 36–48.
———. *John L. Lewis: An Unauthorized Biography*. New York: Putnam, 1949.
———. "Playboy Interview" (by Eric Norden). *Playboy Magazine,* March 1972.
———. *Reveille for Radicals*. Chicago: University of Chicago Press, 1945.
———. *Rules for Radicals*. New York: Vintage Books, 1972.
———. "A Sociological Technique in Clinical Criminology." *Proceedings of the Sixty-fourth Annual Congress of the American Prison Association* (1934), pp. 167–78.
Allport, Gordon W. *Personality in Formation and Action*. New York: Norton, 1938.
———. *The Use of Personal Documents in Psychological Science*. New York: Social Science Research Council, 1942.
American Psychiatric Association (Committee on Relations with the Social Sciences). *Proceedings: Second Colloquium on Personality Investigation*. Baltimore: Lord Baltimore Press, 1930.
Andrews, Alexander. *The History of British Journalism*. 2 vols. London: Rich and Bentley, 1859.
Angell, Robert. "A Critical Review of the Development of the Personal Document Method in Sociology, 1920–1940." In *The Use of Personal Documents in History, Anthropology and Sociology,* ed. Louis Gottschalk et al. New York: Social Science Research Council, 1945.
Auden, W. H. "A Very Inquisitive Old Party." *New Yorker,* 24 February 1968, pp. 121–34.
Baker, Paul J. "The Life Histories of W. I. Thomas and Robert E. Park." *American Journal of Sociology* 79, no. 2 (September 1974): 243–60.
Baldwin, John. "Ecological and Areal Studies." In *Crime and Justice: An Annual Review of Research,* ed. Norval Morris and Michael Tonry, vol. 1. Chicago: University of Chicago Press, 1979.
Barnes, Harry Elmer. "William Isaac Thomas: The Fusion of Psychological and Cultural Sociology." In *An Introduction to the History of Sociology,* ed. Harry Elmer Barnes. Chicago: University of Chicago Press, 1948.

Becker, Howard S. Introduction to Clifford Shaw, *The Jack-Roller*. Chicago: University of Chicago Press, 1966.
———. "Labelling Theory Reconsidered." Paper presented at the British Sociological Association meetings, April 1971.
———. *The Other Side: Perspectives on Deviance*. New York: Free Press of Glencoe, 1964.
———. *Outsiders: Studies in the Sociology of Deviance*. New York: Free Press, 1963.
———. "Whose Side Are We On?" *Social Problems* 14 (winter 1967): 239–47.
Beeley, Arthur L. Review of *The Jack-Roller*. *Social Service Review* 5, no. 2 (June 1931): 326–28.
Beers, Clifford Whittingham. *A Mind That Found Itself*. London: Longmans, Green, 1908.
Behavior Research Fund. "The Final Report of the Board of Trustees to the Members of the Behavior Research Fund and the Friends of the Institute for Juvenile Research." Chicago, 1948.
Bertaux, Daniel, ed. *Biography and Society: The Life History Approach in the Social Sciences*. Beverly Hills, Calif.: Sage Publications, 1981.
Bierstedt, Robert. Introduction to *On Humanistic Sociology*, by Florian Znaniecki. Chicago: University of Chicago Press, 1969.
"A Biographical Sketch of Benjamin Barr Lindsey." New York: James T. White, 1913.
Blasing, Motlu Konuk. *The Art of Life: Studies in American Autobiographical Literature*. Austin: University of Texas Press, 1977.
Blumer, Herbert. *An Appraisal of Thomas and Znaniecki's "The Polish Peasant in Europe and America."* New York: Social Science Research Council, 1939.
———. *Symbolic Interactionism: Perspective and Method*. Englewood Cliffs, N.J.: Prentice-Hall, 1969.
Bogardus, Emory S. "Personal Experiences and Social Research." *Journal of Applied Sociology* 8 (May–June 1924): 294–303.
Bogdan, Robert, and Taylor, Steven J. *Introduction to Qualitative Research Methods*. New York: John Wiley, 1975.
Boorstin, Daniel. *The Americans: The Democratic Experience*. New York: Random House, 1973.
Boston, City of. *Report of the Standing Committee of the Common Council on the Subject of the House of Reformation for Juvenile Offenders*. Boston: J. H. Eastburn, 1832.
Brace, Charles Loring. *The Dangerous Classes of New York, and Twenty Years Working among Them*. New York: Wynkoop and Hallenbeck, 1872.
Brace, Emma, ed. *The Life of Charles Loring Brace*. New York: Charles Scribner's Sons, 1894.
Bradley, John L., ed. *Selections from London Labour and the London Poor*. London: Oxford University Press, 1965.
Breckinridge, Sophonisba, and Abbott, Edith. *The Delinquent Child and the Home*. New York: Russell Sage Foundation, 1912.
Bressler, Marvin. "Selected Family Patterns in W. I. Thomas' Unfinished Study of the *Bintl Brief*." *American Sociological Review* 17 (October 1952): 563–71.
Brian, Denis. *Murderers and Other Friendly People: The Public and Private Worlds of Interviewers*. New York: McGraw-Hill, 1973.
Brown, Claude. *Manchild in the Promised Land*. New York: Macmillan, 1965.
Bruce, Andrew A.; Burgess, Ernest W.; Harno, Albert J.; and Landesco, John.

The Workings of the Indeterminate-Sentence Law and the Parole System in Illinois. n.p.: State of Illinois, 1928.

Bruno, Frank J. "Some Case Work Recording Limitations of Verbatim Reporting." *Social Forces* 6 (1928): 532–34.

Buckland, Gail. *Reality Recorded: Early Documentary Photography.* Greenwich, Conn.: New York Graphic Society, 1974.

Bulmer, Martin, ed. *Mining and Social Change.* London: Croom Helm, 1977.

Burgess, Ernest W. *On Community, Family and Delinquency.* Edited by Leonard S. Cottrell, Jr., Albert Hunter, and James F. Short, Jr. Chicago: University of Chicago Press, 1973.

———. "The Sources and Methods of Family Study." In *The Fields and Methods of Sociology,* ed. L. L. Bernard. New York: Ray Long and Richard R. Smith, 1934.

———. "The Study of the Delinquent as a Person." *American Journal of Sociology* 28, no. 6 (May 1923): 657–79. Reprinted in Burgess, *On Community.*

———. "W. I. Thomas as a Teacher." *Sociology and Social Research* 32 (March–April 1948): 760–64.

———. "What Social Case Records Should Contain to Be Useful for Sociological Interpretation." *Social Forces* 6 (1928): 524–32.

Burgess, Ernest W., and Bogue, Donald J., eds. *Urban Sociology.* Chicago: University of Chicago Press, 1967.

Burnham, John C. "The New Psychology: From Narcissism to Social Control." In *Change and Continuity in Modern America in the 1920's,* ed. John Braeman, Robert Bremmer, and David Brodz. Columbus: Ohio State University Press, 1968.

———. "The Struggle between Physicians and Paramedical Personnel in American Psychiatry, 1917–41." *Journal of the History of Medicine and Allied Sciences* 29, no. 1 (January 1974): 93–106.

Burt, Cyril. *The Young Delinquent.* London: University of London Press, 1925.

Carey, James T. *Sociology and Public Affairs: The Chicago School.* Beverly Hills, Calif.: Sage Publications, 1975.

Carpenter, J. Estlin. *The Life and Work of Mary Carpenter.* London: Macmillan, 1879.

Carpenter, Mary. *Juvenile Delinquents, Their Condition and Treatment.* London: W. and F. G. Cash, 1853.

———. *Our Convicts.* 2 vols. London: Longman, Green, Longman, Roberts and Green, 1864.

———. *Reformatory Schools for the Children of the Perishing and Dangerous Classes and for Juvenile Offenders.* London: C. Gilpin, 1851.

Carr, Lowell Juilliard. *Delinquency Control.* New York: Harper, 1940.

Cartwright, Dorwin, and French, John R. P., Jr. "The Reliability of Life-History Studies." *Character and Personality* 8 (1939): 110–19.

Cavan, Ruth Shonle. "Interviewing for Life History Material." *American Journal of Sociology* 35 (1929–30): 100–115.

Cazamian, Louis. *Le roman social en Angleterre, 1830–1850.* Paris: Société Nouvelle de Librairie et d'Edition, 1903.

Chesney, Kellow. *The Victorian Underworld.* London: Temple Smith, 1970.

Chicago Vice Commission. *The Social Evil in Chicago.* Chicago: City of Chicago, 1911.

Clark, Janet. *La confrérie fantastique: Autobiographie d'une droguée.* Paris: Denoël Gonthier, 1972.

Clay, John. *Chaplain's Report on the Preston House of Correction*. Preston, 1841, 1848, 1849, 1852.
Clay, Walter Lowe. *The Prison Chaplain: A Memoir of the Rev. John Clay, B.D.* Cambridge: Macmillan, 1861.
Cohen, Albert K. *Delinquent Boys: The Culture of the Gang*. Glencoe, Ill.: Free Press, 1955.
Collins, Philip. *Dickens and Crime*. Bloomington: Indiana University Press, 1968.
———. *Dickens and Education*. London: Macmillan, 1963.
Connolly, Michael P. "An Historical Study of Change in Saul D. Alinsky's Community Organization Practice and Theory, 1939–1972." Ph.D. diss., University of Minnesota, 1976.
Conwell, Chic. *The Professional Thief*, ed. Edwin H. Sutherland. Chicago: University of Chicago Press, 1937, 1972.
Cottle, Thomas J. *Children in Jail: Seven Lessons in American Justice*. Boston: Beacon Press, 1977.
———. "The Life Study: On Mutual Recognition and the Subjective Inquiry." *Urban Life and Culture* 2, no. 3 (October 1973): 344–60.
———. *Private Lives and Public Accounts*. New York: Franklin Watts, 1978.
———. *The Voices of School: Educational Issues through Personal Accounts*. Boston: Little, Brown, 1973.
Cruz, Nicky. *Run Baby Run*. Plainfield, N.J.: Logos Books, 1968.
Davis, Fred. "Stories and Sociology" *Urban Life and Culture* 3, no. 3 (October 1974): 310–16.
Dawley, David. *A Nation of Lords: The Autobiography of the Vice Lords*. New York: Anchor Books, 1973.
Delany, Paul. *British Autobiography in the 17th Century*. New York: Columbia University Press, 1969.
Denfeld, Duane. *Street-Wise Criminology*. Cambridge, Mass.: Schenkman, 1974.
Denver Juvenile Court. *The Problem of the Children and How the State of Colorado Cares for Them*. Denver: Juvenile Court, 1904.
Denzin, Norman K. *The Research Act: A Theoretical Introduction to Sociological Methods*. Chicago: Aldine, 1970.
Diner, Steven J. *A City and Its Universities: Public Policy in Chicago, 1892–1919*. Chapel Hill: University of North Carolina Press, 1980.
Dodson, Dan W. "Frederic Milton Thrasher (1892–1962)." *American Sociological Review* 27 (August 1962): 580–81.
Dollard, John. *Criteria for the Life History*. New York: Yale University Press, 1935.
———. "The Life History in Community Studies." *American Sociological Review* 3 (1938): 724–37.
Dressler, David, ed. *Readings in Criminology and Penology*. New York: Columbia University Press, 1964.
Drucker, Saul, and Hexter, Maurice Beck. *Children Astray*. Cambridge: Harvard University Press, 1923.
Duffey, Bernard. *The Chicago Renaissance in American Letters*. n.p.: Michigan University Press, 1956.
Dummer, Ethel S. "Life in Relation to Time." In *Orthopsychiatry 1923–1948: Retrospect and Prospect*, ed. Lawson G. Lowrey. n.p.: American Orthopsychiatric Association, 1948.
———. *Why I Think So: An Autobiography of an Hypothesis*. Chicago: Clarke-McElroy, n.d.
Duncan, Hugh Dalziel. *Culture and Democracy: The Struggle for Form in Society*

and Architecture in Chicago and the Middle West during the Life and Times of Louis H. Sullivan. Totowa, N.J.: Bedminster Press, 1965.

Durkheim, Emile. *The Rules of Sociological Method.* New York: Free Press, 1964.

Earle, William. *The Autobiographical Consciousness.* Chicago: Quadrangle Books, 1972.

Earlix, Davida Arlene. "Life-History in Social Gerontology: Its Validity and Use." Ph.D. diss., University of Southern California, 1977.

Ebin, David, ed. *The Drug Experience: First-Person Accounts of Addicts, Writers, Scientists and Others.* New York: Orion Press, 1961.

Engels, Frederick. *The Condition of the Working Class in England.* London: Granada, 1969.

Erikson, Erik H. *Life History and the Historical Moment.* New York: W. W. Norton, 1975.

Escott, T. H. S. *Masters of English Journalism.* London: T. Fisher Unwin, 1911.

Faraday, Annabel, and Plummer, Kenneth. "Doing Life Histories." *Sociological Review* 27, no. 4, n.s. (November 1979): 773–98.

Faris, Ellsworth. "W. I. Thomas (1863–1947)." *Sociology and Social Research* 32 (March–April 1948): 755–59.

Faris, Robert E. L. *Chicago Sociology, 1920–1932.* Chicago: University of Chicago Press, 1970.

Ferrero, Gina Lombroso. *Criminal Man According to the Classification of Cesare Lombroso.* New York: G. P. Putnam Sons, 1911.

Fine, Benjamin. *1,000,000 Delinquents.* Cleveland: World, 1955.

Finestone, Harold. "Cats, Kicks, and Color." *Social Problems* 5, no. 1 (July 1957): 3–13.

———. "The Chicago Area Project in Theory and Practice." In *Community Organization: Studies in Constraint,* ed. Irving A. Spergel. Beverly Hills, Calif.: Sage Publications, 1972.

———. "The Delinquent and Society: The Shaw and McKay Tradition." In *Delinquency, Crime and Society,* ed. James F. Short, Jr. Chicago: University of Chicago Press, 1976.

———. "A Theory of Delinquent Gangs." *Federal Probation* 25, no. 2 (June 1961): 61.

———. *Victims of Change: Juvenile Delinquents in American Society.* Westport, Conn.: Greenwood Press, 1976.

Fish, John Hall. *Black Power/White Control.* Princeton: Princeton University Press, 1973.

Forer, Lois. *"No One Will Lissen."* New York: John Day, 1970.

Foucault, Michel. *Discipline and Punish: The Birth of the Prison.* New York: Pantheon Books, 1977.

———. *The History of Sexuality.* 1. *An Introduction.* Translated by Robert Hurley. New York: Vintage, 1978.

———. *I, Pierre Rivière, Having Slaughtered My Mother, My Sister and My Brother...A Case of Parricide in the 19th Century.* Translated by F. Jellinek. New York: Pantheon, 1975.

Fox Bourne, H. R. *English Newspapers.* 2 vols. London: Chatto and Windus, 1887.

Frazier, Charles E. "The Use of Life-Histories in Testing Theories of Criminal Behavior: Toward Reviving a Method." *Qualitative Sociology* 1 (May 1978): 122–42.

Gardner, George E. "William Healy, 1869–1963." *Journal of the American*

Academy of Child Psychiatry 11, no. 1 (1972): 1–29.

Gass, William. *On Being Blue: A Philosophical Inquiry.* Boston: David P. Godine, 1975.

Gaylin, Willard; Glasser, Ira; Marcus, Steven; and Rothman, David. *Doing Good: The Limits of Benevolence.* New York: Pantheon Books, 1978.

George, William R. *The Adult Minor.* New York: D. Appleton-Century, 1937.

Gewirth, Alan. *Reason and Morality.* Chicago: University of Chicago Press, 1978.

Gitlin, Todd, and Hollander, Nanci. *Uptown: Poor Whites in Chicago.* New York: Harper and Row, 1971.

Glaser, Daniel. "Marginal Workers: Some Antecedents and Implications of an Idea from Shaw and McKay." In *Delinquency, Crime, Society,* ed. James F. Short, Jr. Chicago: University of Chicago Press, 1976.

Glueck, Sheldon, and Glueck, Eleanor T. *500 Criminal Careers.* New York: Alfred A. Knopf, 1930.

———. *Five Hundred Delinquent Women.* New York: Alfred A. Knopf, 1934.

———. *One Thousand Juvenile Delinquents.* Cambridge: Harvard University Press, 1934.

Goldhammer, Herbert. "Recent Developments in Personality Studies." *American Sociological Review* 13, no. 5 (1948): 555–65.

Gottschalk, Louis. "The Historian and the Historical Document." In *The Use of Personal Documents in History, Anthropology and Sociology,* ed. Louis Gottschalk et al. New York: Social Science Research Council, 1945.

Gottschalk, Louis; Kluckhohn, Clyde; and Angell, Robert. *The Use of Personal Documents in History, Anthropology and Sociology.* New York: Social Science Research Council, 1945.

Gusfield, Joseph R. *The Culture of Public Problems: Drinking-Driving and the Symbolic Order.* Chicago: University of Chicago Press, 1980.

———. "The Literary Rhetoric of Science: Comedy and Pathos in Drinking Driver Research." *American Sociological Review* 41 (February 1976): 16–34.

Guthrie, W. K. C. *The Sophists.* Cambridge: Cambridge University Press, 1971.

Gwaltney, John Langston. *Drylongso: A Self Portrait of Black America.* New York: Random House, 1980.

Hall, G. Stanley. *Adolescence.* New York: D. Appleton, 1908 (1st ed. 1904).

Hawes, Joseph M. *Children in Urban Society: Juvenile Delinquency in Nineteenth-Century America.* New York: Oxford University Press, 1971.

Healy, William. *Case Studies of Mentally and Morally Abnormal Types.* Cambridge: Harvard Summer School, 1912.

———. "The Devil's Workshop." *Century* 120 (winter 1930): 122–32.

———. "Dr. Healy Speaks." *Welfare Bulletin.* Springfield, Ill.: Illinois Department of Public Welfare (November–December 1952).

———. *The Individual Delinquent: A Text-Book of Diagnosis and Prognosis for All Concerned in Understanding Offenders.* Boston: Little, Brown, 1927 (1st ed. 1915).

———. *Mental Conflicts and Misconduct.* Boston: Little, Brown, 1936 (1st ed. 1917).

———. *New Light on Delinquency and Its Treatment.* New Haven: Yale University Press, 1936.

———. Oral history interview conducted by John Burnham, 1960.

———. "The Psychology of the Situation in Delinquency and Crime." In *The Child, the Clinic and the Court.* New York: New Republic, 1927.

———. "The Relationship of Psychiatry to Sociology and Criminology." In *Psy-*

chiatry and the War, ed. Frank J. Salder. Springfield, Ill.: Charles C. Thomas, 1942.

――――. *The Structure and Meaning of Psychoanalysis*. New York: Alfred A. Knopf, 1930.

――――. *Twenty-five Years of Child Guidance*. Springfield, Ill.: Department of Public Welfare, 1934.

Healy, William, and Bronner, Augusta F. "The Child Guidance Clinic: Birth and Growth of an Idea." In *Orthopsychiatry 1923–48: Retrospect and Prospect*, ed. Lawson G. Lowrey. American Orthopsychiatric Association, 1948.

――――. *Judge Baker Foundation Case Studies*, ser. 1. Boston, 1922.

Healy, William; Bronner, Augusta; and Shimberg, Myra. "The Close of Another Chapter in Criminology." *Mental Hygiene* 19 (April 1935): 208–22.

Healy, William, and Healy, Mary Tenney. *Pathological Lying, Accusation, and Swindling*. Boston: Little, Brown, 1915.

Hegel, G. W. F. *The Phenomenology of Mind*. Translated by J. B. Baillie. New York: Harper and Row, 1967.

"Henry Mayhew." *Bulletin of the Society for the Study of Labour History* 16 (spring 1968): 10–12.

Himmelfarb, Gertrude. "Mayhew's Poor: A Problem of Identity." *Victorian Studies* 14 (March 1971): 307–20.

Holl, Jack M. *Juvenile Reform in the Progressive Era: William R. George and the Junior Republic Movement*. Ithaca: Cornell University Press, 1971.

Horowitz, I. L. *Professing Sociology: Studies in the Life Cycle of a Social Science*. Chicago: Aldine, 1968.

House, Floyd N. "Social Forces in Personal-Behavior Sequences Studied by the Judge Baker Foundation." In *Methods in Social Science: A Case Book*, ed. Stuart A. Rice. Chicago: University of Chicago Press, 1931.

Howard, John. *An Account of the Principal Lazarettos in Europe*. London: J. Johnson, 1791.

――――. *The State of the Prisons* [1777]. London and Toronto: J. M. Dent, 1929.

Hoyles, J. Arthur. *Religion in Prison*. London: Epworth Press, 1955.

Hughes, Everett Cherrington. "Social Change and Status Protest: An Essay on the Marginal Man." In *Where Peoples Meet: Racial and Ethnic Frontiers*, ed. Everett Cherrington and Helen MacGill Hughes. Glencoe, Ill.: Free Press, 1952.

Hughes, Helen MacGill, ed. *The Fantastic Lodge: The Autobiography of a Girl Drug Addict*. Boston: Houghton Mifflin, 1961.

――――. "From Politics to Human Interest." In *The Social Fabric of the Metropolis*, ed. James F. Short, Jr. Chicago: University of Chicago Press, 1971.

――――. *News and the Human Interest Story*. Chicago: University of Chicago Press, 1940.

Humpherys, Anne. *Travels into the Poor Man's Country: The Work of Henry Mayhew*. Athens: University of Georgia Press, 1977.

――――, ed. *Voices of the Poor*. London: Frank Cass, 1971.

Jackson, Bruce. *A Thief's Primer*. London: Macmillan, 1969.

James, Howard. *Children in Trouble*. New York: David McKay, 1970.

James, William. *The Varieties of Religious Experience*. London: Longmans, Green, 1906.

Janowitz, Morris. Introduction to W. I. Thomas, *On Social Organization and Social Personality*, ed. Morris Janowitz. Chicago: University of Chicago Press, 1966.

———. "Professionalization of Sociology." *American Journal of Sociology* 78 (July 1972): 105–36.

Jonassen, Christen T. "A Re-evaluation and Critique of the Logic and Some Methods of Shaw and McKay." *American Sociological Review* 14, no. 5 (October 1949): 608–17.

Kammen, Michael, ed. *The Past before Us: Contemporary Historical Writing in the United States.* Ithaca, N.Y.: Cornell University Press, 1980.

Kaplan, Louis, comp. *A Bibliography of American Autobiographies.* Madison: University of Wisconsin Press, 1962.

Karpman, B. *Case Studies in the Psychopathology of Crime.* Washington: Mimeoform Press, 1933.

Kiell, Norman. *The Universal Experience of Adolescence.* New York: International Universities Press, 1964.

King, Harry. *Box-Man: A Professional Thief's Journey.* Edited by Bill Chambliss. New York: Harper and Row, 1972.

Klockars, Carl B. "Field Ethics for the Life History." In *Street Ethnography,* ed. R. S. Weppner. Beverly Hills, Calif.: Sage Publications, 1977.

Kluckhohn, Clyde. "The Personal Document in Anthropological Science." In *The Use of Personal Documents in History, Anthropology and Sociology,* ed. Louis Gottschalk et al. New York: Social Sciences Research Council, 1945.

Kobrin, Solomon. "The Chicago Area Project—a 25-Year Assessment." *Annals of the American Academy of Political and Social Science* 322 (March 1959): 19–29.

———. "Clifford Shaw (1895–1957)." *American Sociological Review* 23 (February 1958): 89.

Kobrin, Solomon, and Finestone, Harold. "Drug Addiction among Young Persons in Chicago: A Report on the Prevalence, Incidence, Distribution, and Character of Drug Use and Addiction in Chicago during the Years 1947–53." In *Gang Delinquency and Delinquent Subcultures,* ed. James F. Short, Jr. New York: Harper and Row, 1969.

Komarovsky, Mirra. *The Unemployed Man and His Family.* New York: Dryden Press, 1940.

Korn, Richard R., ed. *Juvenile Delinquency.* New York: Thomas Y. Crowell, 1968.

Krueger, Ernest Theodore. "Autobiographical Documents and Personality." Ph.D. diss., University of Chicago, 1925.

———. "The Technique of Securing Life History Documents." *Journal of Applied Sociology* 9 (1925): 290–98.

———. "The Value of Life History Documents for Social Research." *Journal of Applied Sociology* 9 (1925): 196–201.

Kurella, Hans. *Cesare Lombroso: A Modern Man of Science.* Translated by M. Eden Paul. London: Rebman, 1911.

Landesco, John. "Life History of a Member of the Forty-two Gang." *Journal of Criminal Law and Criminology* 22 (March 1933): 964–98. (Cf. same journal 25 (September 1934): 341–57, and 25 (March 1935): 928–40.)

———. *Organized Crime in Chicago.* Chicago: University of Chicago Press, 1968 (1st ed. 1929). (Contains "The Gangster's Apologia pro Vita Sua.")

Landis, Carney. *Varieties of Psychopathological Experience.* Edited by Fred A. Mettler. New York: Holt, Rinehart and Winston, 1964.

Langness, Lewis L. *The Life History in Anthropological Science.* New York: Holt, Rinehart and Winston, 1965.

Langsam, Miriam Z. *Children West: A History of the Placing-out of the New York Children's Aid Society, 1853–1890.* Madison: Department of History, University of Wisconsin, 1964.

Lantz, Herman R. "Family and Kin as Revealed in the Narratives of Ex-Slaves." *Social Science Quarterly* 60, no. 4 (March 1980): 667–75.

Larner, Jeremy, and Tefferteller, Ralph. *The Addict in the Street.* New York: Grove Press, 1964.

Larsen, Thomas. *The Good Fight: The Life and Times of Ben B. Lindsey.* Chicago: Quadrangle Books, 1972.

Lemert, Edwin. "The Behavior of the Systematic Check Forger." *Social Problems* 6 (fall 1958): 141–48.

Leopold, Nathan F. *Life Plus 99 Years.* Garden City, N.Y.: Doubleday, 1958.

Letkemann, Peter. *Crime as Work.* Englewood Cliffs, N.J.: Prentice-Hall, 1973.

Levin, Yale. "The Treatment of Juvenile Delinquency in England during the Early Nineteenth Century." *Journal of Criminal Law and Criminology* 31, no. 1 (May–June 1940): 38–54.

Levin, Yale, and Lindesmith, Alfred. "English Ecology and Criminology of the Past Century." *Journal of Criminal Law and Criminology* 27, no. 6 (March–April 1937): 801–16.

Levine, Donald N. "Simmel at a Distance: On the History and Systematics of the Sociology of the Stranger." *Sociological Focus* 10, no. 1 (January 1977): 15–29.

Lewis, J. David, and Smith, Richard L. *American Sociology and Pragmatism: Mead, Chicago Sociology, and Symbolic Interaction.* Chicago: University of Chicago Press, 1980.

Lewis, W. David. *From Newgate to Dannemora: The Rise of the Penitentiary in New York, 1796–1848.* Ithaca: Cornell University Press, 1965.

Lindesmith, Alfred. *Opiate Addiction.* Bloomington: Indiana University Press, 1947.

Lindesmith, Alfred, and Levin, Yale. "The Lombrosian Myth in Criminology." *American Journal of Sociology* 42 (March 1937): 653–71. (Comments by Thorsten Sellin in the May 1937 issue, pp. 897–99, with authors' reply.)

Lindsey, Ben B. "The Trial of Criminal Cases and Adult Probation in the Chancery Court." *Annual Report and Proceedings of the National Probation Association,* 1925.

Lindsey, Ben B., and Borough, Rube. *The Dangerous Life.* New York: Horace Liveright, 1931.

Lindsey, Ben B., and Evans, Wainwright. *The Revolt of Modern Youth.* New York: Boni and Liveright, 1925.

———. *The Companionate Marriage.* New York: Boni and Liveright, 1927.

Lindsey, Ben B., and O'Higgins, Harvey J. *The Beast.* Garden City, N.Y.: Doubleday, Page, 1912.

Lofland, John. "Styles of Reporting Qualitative Field Research." *American Sociologist* 9 (August 1974): 101–11.

Lohman, Joseph D. "The Participant Observer in Community Studies." *American Sociological Review* 2 (December 1937): 890–98.

———. "A Sociologist-Sheriff Speaks out about Juvenile Delinquency." *Phi Delta Kappan,* February 1958.

Lombroso, Cesare. *Crime: Its Causes and Remedies.* Translated by Henry P. Horton. Boston: Little, Brown, 1911.

———. *L'homme criminel: Atlas.* Turin: n.p., 1888.

Lombroso, Cesare, and Laschi, R. *Le crime politique et les révolutions*. Translated by A. Bouchard: Paris, 1892.

Lubove, Roy. *The Professional Altruist: The Emergence of Social Work as a Career: 1880–1930*. Cambridge: Harvard: Harvard University Press, 1965.

Luckey, John. *Life in Sing Sing State Prison, as Seen in a Twelve Years' Chaplaincy*. New York: N. Tibbals, 1860.

Lundberg, George A. "Case Work and the Statistical Method." *Social Forces* 5, no. 1 (September 1926): 60–65.

Lynd, Staughton, and Lynd, Alice, eds. *Rank and File: Personal Histories of Working-Class Organizers*. Boston: Beacon Press, 1973.

MacDonald, Arthur. *Criminology*. New York: Funk and Wagnalls, 1893.

McKay, Henry. "The Neighborhood and Child Conduct." *Annals of the American Academy of Political and Social Science* 262 (January 1949): 32–41.

McKenzie, Roderick D. *On Human Ecology*. Edited by Amos H. Hawley. Chicago: University of Chicago Press, 1968.

McPherson, Marion White. "Some Values and Limitations of Oral Histories." *Journal of the History of the Behavioral Sciences* 11, no. 1 (January 1975), 34–36.

Madge, John. *The Origins of Scientific Sociology*. New York: Free Press of Glencoe, 1962.

Managers of the Society. *Reports of the Managers of the Society for the Reformation of Juvenile Delinquents in the City and State of New York*. New York: Mahlon Day, 1835.

Mannheim, Hermann. *Comparative Criminology: A Text Book*. 2 vols. London: Routledge and Kegan Paul, 1965.

Manton, Jo. *Mary Carpenter and the Children of the Streets*. London: Heinemann, 1976.

Marcus, Steven. *Engels, Manchester, and the Working Class*. New York: Random House, 1974.

————. *The Other Victorians: A Study of Sexuality and Pornography in Mid-Nineteenth-Century England*. New York: New American Library, 1977.

Martin, John Bartlow. "A New Attack on Delinquency: How the Chicago Area Project Works." *Harper's Magazine*, May 1944.

May, Margaret. "Innocence and Experience: The Evolution of the Concept of Juvenile Delinquency in the Mid-Nineteenth Century." *Victorian Studies* 17 (September 1973): 7–29.

Mayhew, Henry. "Answers to Correspondents." *London Labour and the London Poor*. Wrappers for weekly numbers (1851–52). [A more complete bibliography for Mayhew may be found in Anne Humpherys, *Travels into the Poor Man's Country*.]

————. *The Boyhood of Martin Luther; or, The Sufferings of the Heroic Little Beggar-Boy Who afterwards Became the Great German Reformer*. London: S. Low, 1863.

————. *German Life and Manners as Seen in Saxony at the Present Day*. 2 vols. London: William Allen, 1864.

————. "The Great World of London." London: D. Bogue, 1856.

————. *The Image of His Father; or, One Boy Is More Trouble Than a Dozen Girls, Being a Tale of a "Young Monkey."* London: H. Hurst, 1846.

————. *London Labour and the London Poor*. 3 vols. London: 1851 (pamphlets with Answers to Correspondents).

————. *London Labour and the London Poor: The Condition and Earnings of*

Those That Will Work, Cannot Work, and Will Not Work. 4 vols., 4th vol. with John Binny et al. London: Charles Griffin, [1864 or 1865?].

———. *London Labour and the London Poor.* 4 vols. New York: Augustus M. Kelley, 1967.

———. *Low Wages, Their Causes, Consequences, and Remedies.* London: n.p., 1851.

———. *The Story of the Peasant-Boy Philosopher; or, "A Child Gathering Pebbles on the Sea-Shore."* 4th ed. London: Routledge, Warne and Routledge, 1860.

———. *The Street Trader's Lot.* Edited by Stanley Rubinstein, introduction by M. Dorothy George. London: Sylvan Press, 1947 (first published 1851).

———. *What to Teach, and How to Teach It: So That the Child May Become a Wise and Good Man.* London: William Smith, 1842.

———. *The Wonders of Science; or, Young Humphrey Davy, the Life of a Wonderful Boy, Written for Boys.* New York: n.p., 1863.

———. *Young Benjamin Franklin; or, The Right Road through Life, a Boy's Book on a Boy's Subject.* New York: Harper, n.d.

Mayhew, Henry, and Binny, John. *The Criminal Prisons of London and Scenes of Prison Life.* London: Charles Griffin, 1862.

Mayhew, Henry, and Cruikshank, George. *1851; or, The Adventures of Mr. and Mrs. Sandboys and Family, Who Came up to London to "Enjoy Themselves," and to See the Great Exhibition.* London: David Bogue, 1851.

Mayhew, Henry, and Mayhew, Augustus, eds. *The Comic Almanac.* London: J. C. Hotten, 1870–72. (Illustrated by George Cruikshank et al.)

———. *The Good Genius, That Turned Everything into Gold; or, The Queen-Bee and the Magic Dress: A Christmas Fairy Tale.* New York: n.p., 1848.

———. *The Greatest Plague in Life; or, The Adventures of a Lady in Search of a Good Servant.* London: n.p., 1847.

———. *The Magic of Kindness; or, The Wondrous Story of the Good Huan.* New York: Harper and Brothers, 1849.

Mennel, Robert M. *Thorns and Thistles: Juvenile Delinquents in the United States 1825–1940.* Hanover, N.H.: University Press of New England, 1973.

Mills, C. Wright. *Power, Politics, and People.* New York: Ballantine, 1961.

———. "The Professional Ideology of the Social Pathologists." In C. Wright Mills, *Power, Politics, and People.* New York: Ballantine, 1961.

———. *The Sociological Imagination.* New York: Oxford University Press, 1959.

———. *Sociology and Pragmatism.* New York: Oxford University Press, 1966.

Minehan, Thomas. *Boy and Girl Tramps of America.* New York: Farrar and Rinehart, 1934 (new ed. 1976).

Minton, Robert J., Jr., ed. *Inside: Prison American Style.* New York: Random House, 1971.

Mitchell, Joseph L. *Joe Gould's Secret.* New York: Viking, 1965.

Momigliano, Arnaldo. *The Development of Greek Biography.* Cambridge: Harvard University Press, 1971.

Morris, Terence. *The Criminal Area: A Study in Social Ecology.* London: Routledge and Kegan Paul, 1957.

Morrissey, Charles T. "Why Call It 'Oral History'? Searching for Early Usage of a Generic Term." In *The Oral History Review 1980.* New York: Oral History Association, 1980.

Murchison, Carl, et al., eds. *A History of Psychology in Autobiography.* Worcester, Mass.: Clark University Press, 1930–.

Murphy, Patrick T. *Our Kindly Parent...The State.* New York: Viking Press, 1974.

Needham, George C. *Street Arabs and Gutter Snipes.* Boston: D. L. Guernsey, 1884.

Nelson, Harland S. "Dickens' *Our Mutual Friend* and Henry Mayhew's *London Labour and the London Poor.*" *Nineteenth-Century Fiction* 20 (1965): 207–22.

O'Connor, Len. *They Talked to a Stranger.* New York: St. Martin's Press, 1959.

Olney, James, ed. *Autobiography: Essays Theoretical and Critical.* Princeton: Princeton University Press, 1980.

———. "*Autos, Bios, Graphein:* The Study of Autobiographical Literature." *South Atlantic Quarterly* 77, no. 91 (winter 1978): 113–23.

O'Malley, Raymond, ed. *London Street Life.* London: Chatto and Windus, 1966. (Selections from Mayhew's *London Labour,* with introduction.)

Panken, Jacob. *The Child Speaks: The Prevention of Delinquency.* New York: Henry Holt, 1941.

Park, Robert E. "The Concept of Position in Sociology." *Proceedings of the Twentieth Annual Meeting of the American Sociological Society,* 20 (1925): 1–14.

———. *The Crowd and the Public, and Other Essays.* Translated by Charlotte Elsner. Chicago: University of Chicago Press, 1972.

———. "Human Migration and the Marginal Man." *American Sociology* 33 (March): 881–93.

———. "Life History." In "The Life Histories of W. I. Thomas and Robert E. Park," ed. Paul J. Baker, *American Journal of Sociology* 79, no. 2:251–60.

———. *Race and Culture.* Glencoe, Ill.: Free Press, 1950.

———. *On Social Control and Collective Behavior.* Edited by Ralph H. Turner. Chicago: University of Chicago Press, 1967.

———. "The Sociological Methods of William Graham Sumner and of William I. Thomas and Florian Znaniecki." In *Methods in Social Science,* ed. Stuart A. Rice. Chicago: University of Chicago Press, 1931.

Park, Robert E., and Burgess, Ernest W. *Introduction to the Science of Sociology.* Rev. ed. Chicago: University of Chicago Press, 1970.

Park, Robert E.; Burgess, Ernest W.; and McKenzie, Roderick D. *The City.* Chicago: University of Chicago Press, 1925, 1967.

Petras, John W. "Changes of Emphasis in the Sociology of W. I. Thomas." *Journal of the History of the Behavioral Sciences* 6 (1970): 70–79.

Pickett, Robert S. *House of Refuge: Origins of Juvenile Justice Reform in New York State 1815–1857.* New York: Syracuse University Press, 1969.

Platt, Anthony M. *The Child Savers: The Invention of Delinquency.* Chicago: University of Chicago Press, 1969, 1977.

Polansky, Norman A. "How Shall a Life-History Be Written?" *Journal of Personality* 9 (1941): 188–207.

Polsky, Ned. *Hustlers, Beats, and Others.* Chicago: Aldine Publishing Company, 1967.

Porterfield, Austin L. *Youth in Trouble: Studies in Delinquency and Despair.* Fort Worth: Leo Potishman Foundation, 1946.

Quennell, Peter. *London's Underworld.* London: William Kimber, 1950. (Selections from vol. 4 of *London Labour,* with introduction.)

———. *Mayhew's Characters.* London: Spring Books, 1967.

———. *Mayhew's London.* London: Pilot Press, 1949. (Selections from *London Labour,* with introduction.)

Radzinowitz, Leon. *Ideology and Crime*. New York: Columbia University Press, 1966.

Radzinowitz, Leon, and King, Joan. *The Growth of Crime: The International Experience*. New York: Basic Books, 1977.

Read, Kenneth E. *The High Valley*. New York: Charles Scribner's Sons, 1965.

Reckless, Walter C. *Six Boys in Trouble*. Ann Arbor: Michigan University Press, 1929.

Reiser, Stanley J. "The 'M' in M.D. Isn't 'Machine.'" *New York Times*, 3 May 1978, Op-Ed page.

Remick, Cecile P. "The House of Refuge of Philadelphia." Ph.D. diss., University of Pennsylvania, 1975.

"Report of Commissioners on the Best Means of Establishing an Effective Constabulary Force in the Counties of England and Wales." *Parliamentary Papers*, vol. 19 (1839).

Rettig, Richard P.; Torres, Manual J.; and Garrett, Gerald R. *Manny: A Criminal Addict's Story*. Boston: Houghton Mifflin, 1977.

Rice, Stuart A. "Hypotheses and Verifications in Clifford R. Shaw's Studies of Juvenile Delinquency." In *Methods in Social Science*, ed Stuart A. Rice. Chicago: University of Chicago Press, 1931.

————, ed. *Methods in Social Science: A Case Book*. Chicago: University of Chicago Press, 1931.

Rieff, Philip. *Freud: The Mind of the Moralist*. Garden City, N.Y.: Doubleday, 1961.

Robison, Sophia M. *Can Delinquency Be Measured?* New York: Columbia University Press, 1936.

Rosenberg, John D., ed. *London Labour and the London Poor*. New York: Dover, 1968.

Rothman, David J. *The Discovery of the Asylum*. Boston: Little, Brown, 1971.

Said, Edward W. *Orientalism*. New York: Vintage, 1979.

Sanders, Marion K. *The Professional Radical: Conversations with Saul Alinsky*. New York: Harper and Row, 1970.

Sanders, Wiley B., ed. *Juvenile Offenders for a Thousand Years*. Chapel Hill: University of North Carolina Press, 1970.

Schlossman, Steven L. *Love and the American Delinquent: The Theory and Practice of "Progressive" Juvenile Justice, 1825–1920*. Chicago: University of Chicago Press, 1977.

————. "Traditionalism and Revisionism in Juvenile Correctional History." *Reviews in American History* 2 (March 1974): 59–65.

Schlossman, Steven L., and Wallach, Stephanie. "The Crime of Precocious Sexuality: Female Juvenile Delinquency in the Progressive Era." *Harvard Educational Review* 48, no. 1 (February 1978): 65–94.

Schur, Edwin M. *Our Criminal Society*. Englewood Cliffs, N.J.: Prentice-Hall, 1960.

Schwartz, Gary, and Merten, Don. *Love and Commitment*. Beverly Hills, Calif.: Sage Publications, 1980.

Schwitzgebel, Ralph. "A New Approach to Understanding Delinquency." *Federal Probation* 24, no. 1 (March 1960): 31–35.

Sellin, Thorsten. "Methods of Etiological Research in Criminology." *Sociology and Social Research* 17 (March–April 1933): 393–95.

————. Note on Shaw's Life Histories. *Sociology and Social Research* 17 (March–April 1933): 394.

Selling, Lowell S. "The Autobiography as a Psychiatric Technique." *American Journal of Orthopsychiatry* 2, no. 2 (April 1932): 162–71.

Sennett, Richard. *The Fall of Public Man.* New York: Vintage Books, 1978.

Shattuck, Roger. *The Forbidden Experiment: The Wild Boy of Aveyron.* New York: Farrar, Straus and Giroux, 1980.

Shaw, Clifford R. "Case Study Method." *Proceedings of the American Sociological Society* 21 (1926): 149–57.

———. "Correlation of Rates of Juvenile Delinquency with Certain Indices of Community Organization and Disorganization." *Proceedings of the American Sociological Society* 22 (1927): 174–79.

———. "Delinquency and the Social Situation." *Religious Education* 24 (1929): 409–17.

———. "The Delinquent and His Neighbors." In *The Delinquent and His Neighbors,* ed. Anthony Sorrentino. Millburn, N.J.: R. F. Publishing, 1975.

———. *The Jack-Roller: A Delinquent Boy's Own Story.* Chicago: University of Chicago Press, 1930, 1966.

———. "Juvenile Delinquency: A Case History." *Bulletin of the State University of Iowa,* 12 August 1933. (Child Welfare Pamphlets no. 23. Reprinted, in part, in Short, *Gang Delinquency and Delinquent Subcultures.*)

———. "The Juvenile Delinquent." In *Organized Crime in Chicago,* ed. John Landesco. (Part 3 of the 1929 Illinois Crime Survey.) Chicago: University of Chicago Press, 1968.

———. "Methods, Accomplishments, and Problems of the Chicago Area Project." Unpublished, dated 20 September 1944.

———. *The Natural History of a Delinquent Career.* Chicago: University of Chicago Press, 1931.

———. "What the Delinquent Boy's Own Story Reveals." *Religious Education* 26 (1931): 163–69.

Shaw, Clifford R., and McKay, Henry D. "Are Broken Homes a Causative Factor in Juvenile Delinquency?" *Social Forces* 10, no. 4 (May 1932): 514–24.

Shaw, Clifford R.; McKay, Henry D.; and McDonald, James F. *Brothers in Crime.* Chicago: University of Chicago Press, 1938.

Shaw, Clifford R., et al. *Delinquency Areas: A Study of the Geographic Distribution of School Truants, Juvenile Delinquents, and Adult Offenders in Chicago.* Chicago: University of Chicago Press, 1929.

———. *Juvenile Delinquency and Urban Areas: A Study of Rates of Delinquency in Relation to Differential Characteristics of Local Communities in American Cities.* Chicago: University of Chicago Press, 1942, 1969.

———. *Social Factors in Juvenile Delinquency: A Study of the Community, the Family, and the Gang in Relation to Delinquent Behavior.* Vol. 2 of *Report on the Causes of Crime.* Washington, D.C.: National Commission on Law Observance and Enforcement, 1931.

Shaw, Clifford R., with Gehlke, Charles Elmer; Glueck, Sheldon; Warren Stearns, A., M.D.; and Sutherland, Edwin H. "Housing and Delinquency." In *Housing and the Community: Home Repair and Remodeling,* ed. John M. Grimes and James Ford. Washington, D.C.: President's Conference on Home Building and Home Ownership, 1932.

Sheldon, William H. *Varieties of Delinquent Youth.* New York: Harper and Brothers, 1949.

Shils, Edward. "Tradition, Ecology, and Institution in the History of Sociology." *Daedalus* 99, no. 4 (fall 1977): 760–825.

Short, James F., Jr., ed. *Gang Delinquency and Delinquent Subcultures*. New York: Harper and Row, 1969.
———. Introduction to Frederic Thrasher, *The Gang*. Rev. ed. Chicago: University of Chicago Press, 1963.
———, ed. *The Social Fabric of the Metropolis: Contributions of the Chicago School of Urban Sociology*. Chicago: University of Chicago Press, 1971.
Simmel, Georg. *On Individuality and Social Forms*. Edited by Donald M. Levine. Chicago: University of Chicago Press, 1971.
Slater, Peter Gregg. "Ben Lindsey and the Denver Juvenile Court: A Progressive Looks at Human Nature." *American Quarterly* 20 (1968): 211–23.
Snodgrass, Jon. "The American Criminological Tradition: Portraits of the Men and Ideology in a Discipline." Ph.D. diss., University of Pennsylvania, 1972.
———. "Clifford R. Shaw and Henry D. McKay: Chicago Criminologists." *British Journal of Criminology* 16, no. 1 (January 1976): 1–19.
———. "The Criminologist and His Criminal: The Case of Edwin H. Sutherland and Broadway Jones." *Issues in Criminology* 8 (spring 1973): 1–17.
Sontag, Susan. *On Photography*. New York: Ferrar, Straus and Giroux, 1977.
Sorrentino, Anthony. "The Chicago Area Project after 25 Years." *Federal Probation* 23, no. 2 (June 1959): 40–45.
———, ed. *The Delinquent and His Neighbors*. Millburn, N.J.: R. F. Publishing, 1975.
———. *Organizing against Crime: Redeveloping the Neighborhood*. New York: Human Sciences Press, 1977.
Sorrentino, Joseph N. *Up from Never*. New York: Bantam, 1978.
Southside Community Committee. *Bright Shadows in Bronzetown: The Story of the Southside Community Committee*. Chicago, 1949.
Stanley, the Jack-Roller. "The Jack-Roller at Seventy: A Fifty Year Follow-up of the Delinquent Boy's Own Story." Edited by Jon Snodgrass. Unpublished manuscript, 1978.
Stonequist, Everett V. *The Marginal Man*. New York: Charles Scribner's Sons, 1937.
Stott, William. *Documentary Expression and Thirties America*. New York: Oxford University Press, 1973.
Sutherland, Arthur E. *The Law at Harvard: A History of Ideas and Men, 1817–1967*. Cambridge: Harvard University Press, 1967.
Sutherland, Edwin H. *Principles of Criminology*. Chicago: Lippincott, 1934.
———. Review of *The Natural History of a Delinquent Career. American Journal of Sociology* 38 (July 1932): 135–36.
Tabor, Margaret E. *Pioneer Women*. London: Sheldon Press, 1927.
Taylor, Ian; Walton, Paul; and Young, Jock. *The New Criminology*. New York: Harper and Row, 1973.
Terkel, Studs. *Hard Times: An Oral History of the Great Depression*. New York: Pantheon Books, 1970.
———. *Working*. New York: Pantheon Books, 1974.
Thomas, Alan Cedric. "Henry Mayhew's Rhetoric: A Study of His Presentation of Social 'Facts.'" Ph.D. diss., University of Toronto, 1971.
Thomas, Evan A. "Herbert Blumer's Critique of *The Polish Peasant*: A Post Mortem on the Life History Approach in Sociology." *Journal of the History of the Behavioral Sciences* 14 (1978): 124–31.
Thomas, W. I. "The Configurations of Personality." In *The Unconscious: A Symposium*, ed. Charles M. Child. New York: Alfred A. Knopf, 1929.

———. "Life History." *American Journal of Sociology* 79, no. 2 (1973): 246–50.
———. *Old World Traits Transplanted.* Edited by Robert E. Park and Herbert A. Miller. New York: Harper and Brothers, 1921.
———. *On Social Organization and Social Personality.* Edited by Morris Janowitz. Chicago: University of Chicago Press, 1966.
———. "Outline of a Program for the Study of Personality and Culture." In *Social Behavior and Personality,* ed. Edmund H. Volkart. New York: Social Science Research Council, 1951.
———. "The Relation of Research to the Social Process." In *Essays on Research in the Social Sciences,* ed. W. F. G. Swann et al. Washington, D.C.: Brookings Institution, 1931. Reprinted in W. I. Thomas, *On Social Organization and Social Personality.*
———. *The Unadjusted Girl.* Boston: Little, Brown, 1928.
Thomas, William I., and Thomas, Dorothy Swaine. *The Child in America: Behavior Problems and Programs.* New York: Alfred A. Knopf, 1928.
Thomas, William I., and Znaniecki, Florian. *The Polish Peasant in Europe and America.* Vols. 1 and 2, Chicago: University of Chicago Press, 1918; vols. 3–5, Boston: Richard G. Badger, 1919–20. New York: Alfred A. Knopf, 1927; reprinted 1958, New York: Dover Publications.
Thompson, E. P. "Mayhew and the *Morning Chronicle.*" In *The Unknown Mayhew,* ed. Eileen Yeo and E. P. Thompson. New York: Pantheon, 1971.
———. "The Political Education of Henry Mayhew." *Victorian Studies* 11, no. 1 (September 1967): 41–62.
Thrasher, Frederic Milton. "A Community Study." *Religious Education* 25 (May 1930): 398–400.
———. *The Gang: A Study of 1,313 Gangs in Chicago.* Chicago: University of Chicago Press, 1927, 1963.
———. "How to Study the Boys' Gang in the Open." *Journal of Educational Sociology* 1 (1928): 244–54.
———. Introduction to James T. Farrell, *Young Lonigan: A Boyhood in Chicago Streets.* New York: Vanguard Press, 1932.
———. "Social Attitudes of Superior Boys in an Interstitial Community." In *Social Attitudes,* ed. Kimball Young. New York: Henry Holt, 1931.
Tobias, J. J. *Crime and Industrial Society in the 19th Century.* New York: Shocken Books, 1967.
Tocqueville, Alexis de. *Democracy in America.* New York, 1840.
Tulchin, Simon H. "A History of the Child Study Movement." Springfield, Ill.: Department of Public Welfare, 1926.
Van Waters, Miriam. *Youth in Conflict.* New York: New Republic, 1932.
Vasoli, Robert H., and Terzola, Dennis A. "Sutherland's Professional Thief." *Criminology* 12, no. 2 (August 1974): 131–54.
Volkart, Edmund H., ed. *Social Behavior and Personality.* New York: Social Science Research Council, 1951. (Edition of W. I. Thomas's papers.)
Weintraub, Karl J. "Autobiography and Historical Consciousness." *Critical Inquiry* 1, no. 4 (June 1975): 821–48.
———. *The Value of the Individual: Self and Circumstance in Autobiography.* Chicago: University of Chicago Press, 1978.
White, H. D. J. Review of *The Jack-Roller. Howard Journal* 3, no. 3 (1932): 103–4.
Whyte, William Foote. *Street Corner Society.* 2d ed. Chicago: University of Chicago Press, 1955.

Williamson, Henry. *Hustler! The Autobiography of a Thief.* Edited by R. Lincoln Keiser. Garden City, N.Y.: Doubleday, 1965.

Winslow, Robert W., and Winslow, Virginia. *Deviant Reality: Alternate World Views.* Boston: Allyn and Bacon, 1974.

Wolfgang, Marvin E. "Criminology and the Criminologist." *Journal of Criminal Law, Criminology and Police Science* 54, no. 2 (June 1963): 155–62.

————. "Pioneers in Criminology: Cesare Lombroso (1835–1909)." *Journal of Criminal Law, Criminology and Police Science* 52, no. 4 (November–December 1961): 361–91.

Woodward, Ernest Llewellyn. *The Age of Reform.* Oxford: Clarendon Press, 1962.

Wright, Richard. Introduction to St. Clair Drake and Horace R. Cayton, *Black Metropolis,* vol. 1. New York: Harper and Row, 1962.

Yates, Frances A. *The Art of Memory.* Chicago: University of Chicago Press, 1966.

Yeo, Eileen. "Mayhew as a Social Investigator." In *The Unknown Mayhew,* ed. Eileen Yeo and E. P. Thompson. New York: Pantheon, 1971.

Yeo, Eileen, and Thompson, E. P., eds. *The Unknown Mayhew.* New York: Pantheon, 1971.

Young, A. F., and Ashton, E. T. *British Social Work in the 19th Century.* London: Routledge and Kegan Paul, 1956.

Young, Kimball. "Contributions of W. I. Thomas to Sociology." *Sociology and Social Research* 47, nos. 1–4 (October 1962–July 1963). (Articles begin on pp. 3, 123, 251, 381.)

————. "Frederic M. Thrasher's Study of Gangs." In *Methods in Social Science,* ed. Stuart A. Rice. Chicago: University of Chicago Press, 1931.

————. "The Measurement of Personal and Social Traits." In *Publications of the American Sociological Society* (1927): 92–105.

————, ed. *Social Attitudes.* New York: Henry Holt, 1931.

Znaniecki, Florian. *On Humanistic Sociology.* Edited by Robert Bierstedt. Chicago: University of Chicago Press, 1969.

————. "W. I. Thomas as a Collaborator." *Sociology and Social Research* 32 (March–April 1948): 765–67.

Index